*Areopagitica*

AND OTHER

Political Writings

OF

John Milton

JOHN MILTON

# *Areopagitica*

## AND OTHER

# Political Writings

## OF

# John Milton

JOHN MILTON
FOREWORD BY JOHN ALVIS

**LIBERTY FUND**
INDIANAPOLIS

This book is published by Liberty Fund, Inc., a foundation established to encourage study of the ideal of a society of free and responsible individuals.

The cuneiform inscription that serves as our logo and as the design motif for our endpapers is the earliest-known written appearance of the word "freedom" (*amagi*), or "liberty." It is taken from a clay document written about 2300 B.C. in the Sumerian city-state of Lagash.

**Library of Congress Cataloging-in-Publication Data**
Milton, John, 1608–1674.
Areopagitica, and other political writings of John Milton / by John Milton; with a foreword by John Alvis.
    p.  cm.
Includes bibliographical references (p.     ) and index.
Contents: Areopagitica—The tenure of kings and magistrates—Defence of the people of England—Second defence of the people of England—The ready and easy way to establish a free commonwealth—John Milton's character of the Long Parliament.
ISBN 0-86597-196-X (hc).—ISBN 0-86597-197-8 (pb)
1. Great Britain—Politics and government—1642–1660—Sources.
2. Freedom of the press—Early works to 1800. 3. Political science—Early works to 1800. I. Alvis, John. II. Title.
DA400.M55      1999
942.06´2—dc21                                97-46853

03  02  01  00  99  C  5  4  3  2  1

03  02  01  00  99  P  5  4  3  2  1

Liberty Fund, Inc.
8335 Allison Pointe Trail, Suite 300
Indianapolis, IN 46250-1684

# CONTENTS

# FOREWORD:
## MILTON'S POLITICAL WRITINGS

---

Throughout his career as poet, political theorist, and embattled publicist, John Milton pursued the one paramount project of discovering ground for his love of liberty in laws of nature and of nature's God. This effort required a delay of his plans for a national epic during a two-decade interval wherein Milton produced a series of prose works defending and seeking to affect the course of the Puritan revolution. Inspired by specific occasions, these writings were responses to antagonists within his party, preemptive strikes against Royalist partisans, or appeals to Parliament. Though Milton professed to deprecate these pamphlets as work of his "left hand," they develop a carefully articulated course of thought and reveal connections between principle and consequence on the order of acuity one looks for in works of more than partisan polemical intent and transitory significance.

Milton concerned himself with a diversity of issues: church government, divorce, freedom of thought, speech, and press, British constitutional history, church-state relations, the characters of regimes, the political implications of Christianity, the nature of representation in Parliament, the interdependence of civil and personal virtue, the progress of Reformation. Diversity of subject answers always, however, to the unifying theme of preparing individuals to understand and cultivate that coordination of freedoms and responsibilities that Milton identified in the phrase "Christian liberty"—that is, the freedom to work out one's salvation won for all mankind by the Savior's intercession, example, and express teachings.

We should not be surprised therefore to discover that religious and political issues are throughout the prose writings inseparably intertwined. Milton's life as religious controversialist parallels his changing affiliations in political controversy. The young man destined, as he thought, for the clergy, first made common cause with Anglicans against papist oppression. "Church-outed" by his refusal to subscribe to oaths of conformity, Milton subsequently joined the Presbyterians in their repudiation of the episcopal form of Protestantism, only to break with John Knox's sect when it became clear that the Presbyterians meant to establish another national church. During the Civil War, Milton initially found his party with the Independents, but eventually he ceased to hold communion with any sect and ended by constituting himself a church of one, professing the unique theology worked out in his posthumously published *The Christian Doctrine*.

Similarly, in politics Milton began by accepting a monarchy prescribed, he acknowledges, by British tradition, then transferred his allegiance to the parliamentary revolution while maintaining that his opposition to Charles I was a matter of resisting not monarchy but tyranny. Appealing to the right of the people to establish such government as they approve, Milton supported the Commonwealth and Oliver Cromwell but thereafter argued the right of a minority to act for the people against a return to royal government. He reposed his allegiance consecutively in the people, then in the Long Parliament, then in the Rump, then in Oliver Cromwell and his army, then, after Cromwell's death, in the restored Rump, then in the reseated full Parliament, and, at last, on the eve of the Restoration, in General Monk.

Against tyrant—as Milton judged Charles to be—and bishops Milton used the sword of a Presbyterian Parliament; against the Presbyters' usurpation of conscience he invoked a purged Parliament representing, he was aware, a minority. Against the Parliament remnant he appealed to the troops of a military dictator whom Milton considered a justifiable monarch. Against the return of king and bishops, Milton reverted to a lesser evil in his first weapon, a Presbyterian Parliament. Up through Cromwell's Protectorate Milton was bargaining for better terms, an ever-widening scope for the independent conscience. After Cromwell's death he sought to salvage the one indispensable thing—a Protestant republic—by yielding on almost everything else: on tithing, on an established church, on a Parliament expanded to include his inveterate Presbyterian opponents. When he appealed to Monk in the letter that presented his eleventh-hour scheme for sustaining a republic, Milton was willing to impose liberty by force on a recalcitrant majority of the population. Presumably he did not know that General Monk was already compounding with Charles II for a Stuart restoration. At the end of his twenty years of pamphleteering, with most of his confederates dead or on the way to prison or execution, a Milton now blind and forced into hiding found himself without a church and without a party.

His enemies charged both blindness and isolation to a bad cause or inconsistency in a dubious one. The alternative lies in supposing that a prudent consistency of principle required Milton to change affiliations by adjusting to altered circumstances and by distancing himself from associates less firm in their adherence to the main point. That can be determined, if determined it can be, only by considering the force of the argument that recorded the transitions, the most substantial portions of which are represented in this collection of the political writings. Milton's career may be viewed as a continuing argument and self-examination, the chief stations of which the following synopsis will touch upon.

*Areopagitica* attests Milton's hopes for the reformers who would come to constitute the Long Parliament. The pamphlet is dedicated to that body, and its famous peroration on the nation's rousing from its long sleep under monks and prelates envisions all the good to be expected from continued reformation. Even under Tudor and Stuart monarchs censorship had been somewhat porous, and Milton himself had been able to publish half a dozen tracts without passing them before the eyes of a licenser. Parliament proposed no greater restrictions than authors had previously evaded. Nonetheless, Milton expects better from those who have stood out against Charles and his prelates.

Unlike his previously published divorce tracts (*Doctrine and Discipline of Divorce* in 1643, *The Judgement of Martin Bucer* in 1644) that had subjected Milton to some notoriety, the argument for a free press provoked little response. An unconvinced Parliament went forward with its restraints upon what it deemed offensive publication. The interest of Milton's essay lies not in its effects—evidently it had none—but in its intrinsic merits of reasoning upon the scope and limits of political speech.

*The Tenure of Kings and Magistrates* (February 1648), arguing circumstantially from Charles's bad faith dealing with Cromwell's Parliament in the final months of the Civil War, attempts to convert, or at any rate to neutralize, a Presbyterian faction, which, after first opposing the Royalists, thereafter broke with an Independent-dominated House of Commons over the question of what to do with the defeated king. Against the Presbyterians-turned-Royalist Milton argues chiefly the pusillanimity of their having become thus belatedly squeamish after years of armed conflict during which they tried their best to kill Charles in combat. Why do they now pull back from an execution decreed after due judicial process? The more universal significance of the pamphlet derives from Milton's effort to discover theoretical grounds in reason and revelation for setting limits to the authority of monarchs and for punishing kings who overstep those boundaries.

Of the four works written to justify the parliamentary cause in the Civil War—*Tenure of Kings and Magistrates, Eikonoklastes, A Defence of the English People,* and *The Second Defence*—the first *Defence* is the lengthiest and most circumstantial. Milton wrote in response to an indictment of the Independents published in late 1649 by the famed continental scholar Salmasius (Claude de Saumaise). Milton's opponent's Latin work had been titled *Defensio Regia* (*A Defence of the King*) and had been addressed to the Stuart heir, Charles II. Milton's reply, written upon commission of Parliament, appeared in February 1651 bearing the title *Joannis Miltoni Angli Pro Populo Anglicano Defensio contra Claudii Anonymi, alias Salmasii, Defensionem Destructivam;* Milton had it reprinted in 1658 with fairly extensive additions. The text presented in this collection is the later, expanded version referred to subsequently by one of its variant abbreviations *Def.* 1.

A reader today will likely direct his interest toward the key ideas that associate *Def.* 1 with Milton's other political writings. In line with *Tenure of Kings and Magistrates,* Milton proposes in *Def.* 1 that one distinguish between kings proper—who by their devotion to the common good deserve allegiance—and tyrants who, ruling for their own interest at the expense of their subjects, ought to be resisted and, if the means are available, deposed or even slain. Milton also invokes Aristotle's *Politics* as he had in *Tenure of Kings and Magistrates* to make a further distinction based on the four kinds of kingship Aristotle says are subordinate to law and the one form, *pambasileia,* which acknowledges no restraint upon the will of the monarch (p. 132). However, there may be a difference from *Tenure of Kings and Magistrates* in the emphasis Milton now gives to church-state relations in *Def.* 1. Quite clearly he makes in the latter a large assertion regarding the source of a tyranny unique to Christendom. This new form of tyranny unanticipated by Aristotle and Cicero perverts Gospel liberty because, from Milton's point of view, secular authority may not justly employ civil coercion to produce doctrinal uniformity in religion. It is within this conception of a Christian liberty necessary for determining from scripture alone what to believe and thereupon freely living pursuant to such beliefs that Milton equates tyranny with the ruler's attempt to enforce orthodoxy of doctrine and uniformity of church discipline and liturgy.

The *Second Defence of the People of England* seeks, as had *Def.* 1, to reply to the partisans of Charles by upholding the right of Parliament to war against Charles and to execute the defeated enemy. This time, however, Milton found himself obliged in view of personal attacks launched by an anonymous author to vindicate not only his cause but also his own character and role in the revolution. Consequently, large portions of the work are personal apologia accompanied with vivid, if not always edifying, counter invective directed against the man Milton supposed to have been the author of *The Cry of the Royal Blood to Heaven Against the English Parricides.*

The other subject of the *Second Defence* is Oliver Cromwell. Milton considers himself called upon to rescue Cromwell from the aspersions cast his way in *The Cry,* but he may also have been impelled by his own awareness that the deeds of the Lord Protector posed a serious problem for such a thinker as Milton prided himself upon being— one for whom consistency of principle was the touchstone guaranteeing self-respect and courage. The difficulty existed because championing Cromwell required speaking on behalf of a powerful figure who in turning out a parliament and ruling through the army seemed to have gathered in his hands fully as much power as Charles, or rather more. Without the title of king, was not Cromwell subject to the same onus against arbitrary power as Charles Stuart?

Cromwell can best keep his claim to the honors due the *"pater patriae"* if, but only if, he can reverse his present inclination to side with that Presbyterian faction bent upon substituting their own version of a state-sponsored clergy for the bishops they have displaced. Milton enjoins Cromwell to "leave the church to itself," by which he means to require of Cromwell a positive effort in the direction of disestablishment of religion, entailing the abolition of laws taxing Englishmen for support of clergymen. Milton makes the principle as plain as he can state it: "I could wish that you should take away all power from the church" (p. 406).

Generally speaking, Cromwell must preside over a government that governs less. Milton would have him institute fewer new laws than he abrogates old ones: "laws have been provided only to restrain malignity; to form and increase virtue, the most excellent thing is liberty" (p. 407). Finally, the failed advocate of removing prior restraints upon publications renews his plea for "freedom of inquiry" (p. 407). Cromwell will forfeit his greatness if he should favor the repressive element of his party over the libertarian.

The more radical contractarian feature of the doctrine first argued in *Tenure of Kings and Magistrates* still obtains: Cromwell's tenure as chief magistrate rests, as had Charles Stuart's tenure of his kingship, upon Cromwell's observance of that natural, if implicit, understanding between rulers and ruled, which lays it down that the ruler forfeits his authority once he begins to govern with a view to self-interest at the expense of the common good of the people. The common good Milton tends to view under the aspect of liberty, and liberty he tends to view, at least in the period from 1640 to 1660, in terms of a salutary but not an inevitable progression from what he terms private to what he terms "civil" freedom. On the political front that progress moves from ecclesiastical liberation (congregational replacing hierarchical organization) to republican government dominated by an aristocracy of Protestant leaders who act in the name of the people even if they cannot count on popular approval. This progress from one recovered liberty to the next constitutes the historic drama; in order to take a part in that drama Milton chose to put aside for a time his poetic ambitions.

One may gather further indications of Milton's reservations regarding Commonwealth achievements and his recognition of notable limitations of Puritan policy from the characterization of the revolution Parliament inserted as a digression into his *History of Britain* (included in the present volume as *Mr. John Miltons Character of the Long Parliament*). These observations were written most probably sometime in 1648 after Milton had had time to assess the illiberal turn given the revolution by Presbyterian ambitions toward establishmentarianism, by Parliament's continuation of the Royalists' restraints upon free speech, and by various repressive measures deemed necessary by the victorious Roundheads that bore down hard on the liberties of local communities and individuals within them. Milton seems to have considered his own personal financial reverses—suffered largely because his wife's family were loyalists—to have been a parcel of the victor's reliance on oppressive, if not downright vindictive, administration of their newly acquired offices. Still, by far the graver offense in Milton's eyes was his party's violation of that particular liberty won by Christ's blood and the birthright de jure, though under neither kings nor Parliament de facto, of every Christian soul. The Puritan cohort had tainted their good cause, Milton maintained, by selling Christian liberty for such emoluments as hireling ministers could snatch from their

Anglican predecessors while committee men for their own gain practiced a similar debauchery upon civil freedom. In the *Character* Milton comes near stating outright the revolution has failed, and he does state clearly enough that his fellow partisans squandered the best chances of England for that full liberty that he had envisioned as his country's reward for assuming world leadership in reform.

*The Readie and Easie Way to Establish a Free Commonwealth* holds interest for us as a record of Milton's final thoughts on the constitutional crisis that had absorbed his energies for two decades and now seemed to threaten his position, certainly, his life not improbably. The treatise has besides an importance out of all proportion to its brevity because it reveals the positive side of an argument Milton had hitherto conducted chiefly from the negative. Here he not only recasts the liabilities of monarchy but also itemizes the advantages of a practical and immediate republican remedy. The impending Parliament must seat members predominately "well-affected," meaning: opposed to monarchy, resolved against any reinstitution of a House of Lords, and sympathetic to the Good Old Cause. This urgent expedient merely gives force to the purpose of fashioning a polity adapted to advancing religious reformation as a confirmed way of life for the British people. That purpose in turn creates the genetic code that will find articulation in every feature of the new body politic.

Perhaps the most remarkable feature of Milton's proposal lies in its scheme for transforming England into a federation of semi-independent counties, "every county . . . made a kind of subordinate commonwealth." He urges a compound government on the supposition that national concerns diverge from local. The national legislative body would confine itself to matters of foreign policy, war, and "rais[ing] and manag[ing] the public revenue"(p. 427). The counties would send representatives to the national legislature and keep in their own hands the administration of civil law, elections of magistrates, and education. Milton seeks to remove some of the odium toward Parliament that had been aroused in the smaller towns and the countryside by Cromwell's "committees" (p. 432). But there are also sufficient reasons of principle for the idea of decentralizing. Milton thinks a citizenry's exercise of its freedoms instills love of independence as well as energy and competency in the conduct of public business. From such a vantage a large, centralized government—even if it be the arm of a commonwealth—appears halfway to the despotism and sloth of a centralized monarchy. Milton acknowledges that the great failing of his party was its inability to put England on a course tending toward decentralization during, or at least after, the Civil War (p. 426). He takes confidence, however, from the example of the Dutch states, which have shown how even an excess of decentralization (individual states may nullify without limit) has produced vigorous industry and resolute Protestantism.

Milton would thus erect his commonwealth on the foundation of a new aristocracy determined by election rather than birth or royal patent. The electorate, one observes, has already been winnowed of the "disaffected," leaving the reins of political power in the hands of men antimonarchical, antiprelatical, and pro-Reformation. Now, at the moment when he perceives England in such peril that he risks nothing further by plain speaking, Milton in this his most openly revolutionary work deals explicitly with a matter that may be discerned in earlier writings by investigation but that never before had been so manifest. Milton's political thinking veers toward democratic or seemingly democratic principles of contract when his object is to contest the prerogatives of monarchs. Yet when it comes to envisioning the terms of an actual workable model of a republic, Milton's distrust of the capacities of the populace comes to make itself felt. He devises institutions that in some sort consult the people so as to be able to claim the sanctions of general consent. At the same time, however, Milton conceives the necessity of so distancing the legislature from the general populace as to insulate policy-making from popular clamors. Accordingly, in the present model he proposes to moderate the democratic feature of nationwide elections with the aristocratic device of a pyramidal electoral scheme. He devises a combination of successively narrowing suffrages with successively refined rosters of candidates. Obviously Milton desires to see an aristocracy arising from a popular base so as to combine the advantages of consent-grounded authority with the less universally distributed virtues of intelligence, stability, and deliberative ability, not to say, dedication to Protestant reform. Milton's aim in this final effort is the same as that which underlines both *Defences*, *The Tenure of Kings and Magistrates*, *Areopagitica*, and *Of Education* as well as the antiprelatical arguments and even the divorce tracts: to seek in a select minority of Protestant anti-Royalists the seedground for a commonwealth devoted to recovery of the civil liberty produced by ancient republics combined with that inner, private liberty to be had only by adding to classical republicanism the purifying zeal of a Christianity intent on perpetual reform.

JOHN ALVIS

# A NOTE ON THE TEXT

For the texts of *Areopagitica, The Tenure of Kings and Magistrates,* the *First* and *Second Defence, The Readie and Easie Way to Establish a Free Commonwealth,* and *Mr. John Milton's Character of the Long Parliament,* I have worked from the Columbia University Press edition of *The Works of John Milton,* 18 vols., ed. Frank Allen Patterson *et al.* (New York, 1931–38). The most definitive edition of the prose is the Yale *Complete Prose Works of John Milton,* 8 vols. (New Haven, 1966), under the general editorship of Don M. Wolfe.

Consistent with the editorial aims established by Liberty Fund, which have in view the needs of the general reader, the annotations have been compiled for the sake of providing only so much information as seems indispensable for making Milton's thought accessible to a nonspecialist, twentieth-century audience. For this purpose I have drawn upon, and in most instances distilled, the more copious annotations to be found in such sources as *John Milton: Complete Poems and Major Prose,* ed. Merrit Y. Hughes (New York: Odyssey Press, 1957); *John Milton: Political Writings,* ed. Martin Dzelzainis (Cambridge: Cambridge University Press, 1991); and the Yale *Complete Prose Works.* The latter two editions are especially exhaustive in their treatment of allusions obscure or subject to scholarly controversy and should be consulted by readers who require a sense of the present state of the scholarship.

*Areopagitica*

AND OTHER

Political Writings

OF

John Milton

# AREOPAGITICA

*By a decree of Charles's Star Chamber July 11, 1637, the licensing of all printed works was deputed to the two archbishops, the chancellors of Oxford and Cambridge, and the Bishop of London, thereby insuring that control would ultimately fall to Archbishop Laud. Although Milton expected prior censorship to be relaxed under the revolutionary regime, on June 14, 1643, Parliament passed an ordinance providing for licensing the press. Milton composed* Areopagitica *as an appeal to Parliament to reconsider its recent decision, arguing that England now deserved a press freed from most of the restraints that the king had imposed. Milton published his pamphlet in 1644 under a title intended to recall the usages of ancient Greece. The Areopagus was a court and senate of oldest Athens composed of about three hundred members elected by the entire body of free Athenian citizens. Its name derives from the site of assembly, a hill within the city dedicated to the god Ares. Although Milton writes the appeal in the form of a public address to the legislative body in the manner of the Greek orator Isocrates, he never intended that it be delivered as an actual speech before Parliament. The argument failed of its practical purpose—Parliament continued to impose constraints of prior licensing upon authors.*

# AREOPAGITICA

A Speech of Mr. John Milton
for the Liberty of Unlicenc'd Printing,
to the Parliament of England

*This is true liberty, when free-born men,*
*Having to advise the public, may speak free,*
*Which he who can, and will deserves high praise;*
*Who neither can, nor will, may hold his peace:*
*What can be juster in a state than this?*

EURIPID. HICETID.

## FOR THE LIBERTY OF UNLICENC'D PRINTING.

They who to States and Governours of the Commonwealth direct their Speech, High Court of Parlament, or wanting such accesse in a private condition, write that which they foresee may advance the publick good; I suppose them as at the beginning of no meane endeavour, not a little alter'd and mov'd inwardly in their mindes: Some with doubt of what will be the successe, others with feare of what will be the censure; some with hope, others with confidence of what they have to speake.[1] And me perhaps each of these dispositions, as the subject was whereon I enter'd, may have at other times variously affected; and likely might in these formost expressions now also disclose which of them sway'd most, but that the very attempt of this addresse thus made, and the thought of whom it hath recourse to, hath got the power within me to a passion, farre more welcome then incidentall to a Preface. Which though I stay not to

1. Milton places himself in the position of a speaker who benefits from the state of liberty praised by Euripides in the passage from *Suppliants,* which Milton takes as his epigraph for *Areopagitica.*

confesse ere any aske, I shall be blamelesse, if it be no other, then the joy and gratulation which it brings to all who wish and promote their Countries liberty; whereof this whole Discourse propos'd will be a certaine testimony, if not a Trophey. For this is not the liberty which wee can hope, that no grievance ever should arise in the Common-wealth, that let no man in this World expect; but when complaints are freely heard, deeply consider'd, and speedily reform'd, then is the utmost bound of civill liberty attain'd, that wise men looke for. To which if I now manifest by the very sound of this which I shall utter, that wee are already in good part arriv'd, and yet from such a steepe disadvantage of tyranny and superstition grounded into our principles as was beyond the manhood of a *Roman* recovery, it will bee attrib-uted first, as is most due, to the strong assistance of God our deliv-erer, next to your faithfull guidance and undaunted Wisdome, Lords and Commons of *England*. Neither is it in Gods esteeme the diminu-tion of his glory, when honourable things are spoken of good men and worthy Magistrates; which if I now first should begin to doe, af-ter so fair a progresse of your laudable deeds, and such a long oblige-ment upon the whole Realme to your indefatigable vertues, I might be justly reckn'd among the tardiest, and the unwillingest of them that praise yee. Neverthelesse there being three principall things, without which all praising is but Courtship and flattery, First, when that only is prais'd which is solidly worth praise: next when greatest likelihoods are brought that such things are truly and really in those persons to whom they are ascrib'd, the other, when he who praises, by shewing that such his actuall perswasion is of whom he writes, can demonstrate that he flatters not; the former two of these I have heretofore endeavour'd, rescuing the employment from him who went about to impaire your merits with a triviall and malignant *En-comium;* the latter as belonging chiefly to mine owne acquittall, that whom I so extoll'd I did not flatter, hath been reserv'd opportunely to this occasion. For he who freely magnifies what hath been nobly done, and fears not to declare as freely what might be done better, gives ye the best cov'nant of his fidelity; and that his loyalest affection and his hope waits on your proceedings. His highest praising is not flattery, and his plainest advice is a kinde of praising; for though I should affirme and hold by argument, that it would fare better with truth, with learning, and the Commonwealth, if one of your publisht Orders which I should name, were call'd in, yet at the same time it could not but much redound to the lustre of your milde and equall Government, when as private persons are hereby animated to thinke ye better pleas'd with publick advice, then other statists have been delighted heretofore with publicke flattery. And men will then see what difference there is between the magnanimity of a trienniall Parlament,[2] and that jealous hautinesse of Prelates and cabin Counsellours that usurpt of late, when as they shall observe yee in the midd'st of your Victories and successes more gently brooking writt'n exceptions against a voted Order, then other Courts, which had produc't nothing worth memory but the weake ostentation of wealth, would have endur'd the least signifi'd dislike at any sudden Proclamation. If I should thus farre presume upon the meek demeanour of your civill and gentle greatnesse, Lords and Commons, as what your publisht Order hath directly said, that to gainsay, I might defend my selfe with ease, if any should accuse me of being new or insolent, did they but know how much better I find ye esteem it to imitate the old and elegant humanity of Greece, then the barbarick pride of a *Hunnish* and *Norwegian* statelines. And out of those ages, to whose polite wisdom and letters we ow that we are not yet *Gothes* and *Jutlanders,* I could name him[3] who from his private house wrote that discourse to the Parlament of *Athens,* that perswades them to change the forme of *Democraty* which was then establisht. Such honour was done in those dayes to men who profest the study of wisdome and eloquence, not only in their own Country, but in other Lands, that Cities and Siniories heard them gladly, and with great respect, if they had ought in publick to admonish the State. Thus did *Dion Prusoeus* a stranger and a privat Orator counsell the *Rhodians* against a former Edict: and I

2.   In February 1641 Parliament passed an act requiring a session to be summoned at least once every three years.

3.   That is, Isocrates; see headnote.

abound with other like examples, which to set heer would be super-fluous. But if from the industry of a life wholly dedicated to studious labours, and those naturall endowments haply not the worst for two and fifty degrees of northern latitude, so much must be derogated, as to count me not equall to any of those who had this priviledge, I would obtain to be thought not so inferior, as your selves are superior to the most of them who receiv'd their counsell: and how farre you excell them, be assur'd, Lords and Commons, there can no greater testimony appear, then when your prudent spirit acknowledges and obeyes the voice of reason from what quarter soever it be heard speaking; and renders ye as willing to repeal any Act of your own setting forth, as any set forth by your Predecessors.

If ye be thus resolv'd, as it were injury to thinke ye were not, I know not what should withhold me from presenting ye with a fit instance wherein to shew both that love of truth which ye eminently professe, and that uprightnesse of your judgement which is not wont to be partiall to your selves; by judging over again that Order which ye have ordain'd *to regulate Printing. That no Book, pamphlet, or paper shall be henceforth Printed, unlesse the same be first approv'd and licenc't by such,* or at least one of such as shall be thereto appointed. For that part which preserves justly every mans Copy[4] to himselfe, or provides for the poor, I touch not, only wish they be not made pretenses to abuse and persecute honest and painfull Men, who offend not in either of these particulars. But that other clause of Licencing Books, which we thought had dy'd with his brother *quadragesimal* and *matrimonial*[5] when the Prelats expir'd, I shall now attend with such a Homily, as shall lay before ye, first the inventors of it to bee those whom ye will be loath to own; next what is to be thought in generall of reading, what ever sort the Books be; and that this Order avails nothing to the suppressing of scandalous, seditious, and libellous Books, which were mainly

4. Copyright.

5. *Quadragesimal* refers to the forty days of the Lenten penitential season. *Matrimonial* refers to the parliamentary provision for the transfer of marriage registration from church to civil authorities.

intended to be supprest. Last, that it will be primely to the discouragement of all learning, and the stop of Truth, not only by disexer-
cising and blunting our abilities in what we know already, but by
hindring and cropping the discovery that might bee yet further made
both in religious and civill Wisdome.

I deny not, but that it is of greatest concernment in the Church
and Commonwealth, to have a vigilant eye how Bookes demeane
themselves as well as men; and thereafter to confine, imprison, and
do sharpest justice on them as malefactors: For Books are not absolutely dead things, but doe contain a potencie of life in them to be as
active as that soule was whose progeny they are; nay they do preserve
as in a violl the purest efficacie and extraction of that living intellect
that bred them. I know they are as lively, and as vigorously produc-
tive, as those fabulous Dragons teeth; and being sown up and down,
may chance to spring up armed men. And yet on the other hand unlesse warinesse be us'd, as good almost kill a Man as kill a good Book;
who kills a Man kills a reasonable creature, Gods Image; but hee who
destroyes a good Booke, kills reason it selfe, kills the Image of God,
as it were in the eye. Many a man lives a burden to the Earth; but a
good Booke is the pretious life-blood of a master spirit, imbalm'd and
treasur'd up on purpose to a life beyond life. 'Tis true, no age can restore a life, whereof perhaps there is no great losse; and revolutions
of ages doe not oft recover the losse of a rejected truth, for the want
of which whole Nations fare the worse. We should be wary therefore
what persecution we raise against the living labours of publick men,
how we spill that season'd life of man preserv'd and stor'd up in Books;
since we see a kinde of homicide may be thus committed, sometimes
a martyrdome, and if it extend to the whole impression, a kinde of
massacre, whereof the execution ends not in the slaying of an ele-
mentall life, but strikes at that ethereall and fift essence,[6] the breath of
reason it selfe, slaies an immortality rather then a life. But lest I should
be condemn'd of introducing licence, while I oppose Licencing, I
refuse not the paines to be so much Historicall, as will serve to shew

6. Quintessence.

what hath been done by ancient and famous Commonwealths, against this disorder, till the very time that this project of licencing crept out of the *Inquisition,* was catcht up by our Prelates, and hath caught some of our Presbyters.

In *Athens* where Books and Wits were ever busier then in any other part of *Greece,* I finde but only two sorts of writings which the Magistrate car'd to take notice of; those either blasphemous and Atheisticall, or Libellous. Thus the Books of *Protagoras* were by the Judges of *Areopagus* commanded to be burnt, and himselfe banisht the territory for a discourse begun with his confessing not to know *whether there were gods, or whether not:* And against defaming, it was decreed that none should be traduc'd by name, as was the manner of *Vetus Comoedia,*[7] whereby we may guesse how they censur'd libelling: And this course was quick enough, as *Cicero* writes, to quell both the desperate wits of other Atheists, and the open way of defaming, as the event shew'd. Of other sects and opinions though tending to voluptuousnesse, and the denying of divine providence they tooke no heed. Therefore we do not read that either *Epicurus,* or that libertine school of *Cyrene,* or what the *Cynick* impudence utter'd, was ever question'd by the Laws. Neither is it recorded that the writings of those old Comedians were supprest, though the acting of them were forbid; and that *Plato* commended the reading of *Aristophanes* the loosest of them all, to his royall scholler *Dionysius,* is commonly known, and may be excus'd, if holy *Chrysostome,* as is reported, nightly studied so much the same Author and had the art to cleanse a scurrilous vehemence into the stile of a rousing Sermon. That other leading City of *Greece, Lacedaemon,* considering that *Lycurgus* their Lawgiver was so addicted to elegant learning, as to have been the first that brought out of *Ionia* the scatter'd workes of *Homer,* and sent the Poet *Thales* from *Creet* to prepare and mollifie the *Spartan* surlinesse with his smooth songs and odes, the better to plant among them law and civility, it is to be wonder'd how muselesse and unbookish they were, minding nought but

7. "Old Comedy"; such as the work of Aristophanes, whose plays yet are filled with such personal references as these Milton supposes were at some time proscribed.

the feats of Warre. There needed no licencing of Books among them for they dislik'd all, but their owne *Laconick Apothegms,* and took a slight occasion to chase *Archilochus* out of their City, perhaps for composing in a higher straine then their owne souldierly ballats and roundels could reach to: Or if it were for his broad verses, they were not therein so cautious, but they were as dissolute in their promiscuous conversing; whence *Euripides* affirmes in *Andromache,* that their women were all unchaste. Thus much may give us light after what sort Bookes were prohibited among the Greeks. The Romans also for many ages train'd up only to a military roughnes, resembling most the *Lacedaemonian* guise, knew of learning little but what their twelve Tables, and the *Pontifick* College[8] with their *Augurs* and *Flamins* taught them in Religion and Law, so unacquainted with other learning, that when *Carneades* and *Critolaus,* with the *Stoick Diogenes* comming Embassadors to *Rome,* tooke thereby occasion to give the City a tast of their Philosophy, they were suspected for seducers by no lesse a man then *Cato* the Censor, who mov'd it in the Senat to dismisse them speedily, and to banish all such *Attick* bablers out of *Italy.* But *Scipio* and others of the noblest Senators withstood him and his old *Sabin* austerity; honour'd and admir'd the men; and the Censor himself at last in his old age fell to the study of that whereof before hee was so scrupulous. And yet at the same time *Naevius* and *Plautus* the first Latine comedians had fill'd the City with all the borrow'd Scenes of *Menander* and *Philemon.* Then began to be consider'd there also what was to be don to libellous books and Authors; for *Naevius* was quickly cast into prison for his unbridl'd pen, and releas'd by the *Tribunes* upon his recantation: We read also that libels were burnt, and the makers punisht by *Augustus.* The like severity no doubt was us'd if ought were impiously writt'n against their esteemed gods. Except in these two points, how the world went in Books, the Magistrat kept no reckning. And therefore *Lucretius* without impeachment versifies his Epicurism to *Memmius,* and had the honour to be set forth the second

8.    Presided over by the Pontifex Maximus, the Pontific College was instituted by the early king and legendary founder of Roman religion, Numa.

time by *Cicero* so great a father of the Commonwealth; although him-selfe disputes against that opinion in his own writings. Nor was the Satyricall sharpnesse, or naked plainnes of *Lucilius,* or *Catullus,* or *Flaccus,* by any order prohibited. And for matters of State, the story of *Titus Livius,* though it extoll'd that part which *Pompey* held, was not therefore supprest by *Octavius Caesar* of the other Faction. But that *Naso*[9] was by him banisht in his old age, for the wanton Poems of his youth, was but a meer covert of State over some secret cause: and besides, the Books were neither banisht nor call'd in. From hence we shall meet with little else but tyranny in the Roman Empire, that we may not marvell, if not so often bad, as good Books were silenc't. I shall therefore deem to have bin large anough in producing what among the ancients was punishable to write, save only which, all other arguments were free to treat on.

By this time the Emperors were become Christians, whose disci-pline in this point I doe not finde to have bin more severe then what was formerly in practice. The Books of those whom they took to be grand Hereticks were examin'd, refuted, and condemn'd in the gen-erall Councels; and not till then were prohibited, or burnt by autor-ity of the Emperor. As for the writings of Heathen authors, unlesse they were plaine invectives against Christianity, as those of *Porphyrius* and *Proclus,* they met with no interdict that can be cited, till about the year 400. in a *Carthaginian* Councel, wherein Bishops themselves were forbid to read the Books of Gentiles, but Heresies they might read: while others long before them on the contrary scrupl'd more the Books of Hereticks, then of Gentiles. And that the primitive Councels and Bishops were wont only to declare what Books were not commendable, passing no furder, but leaving it to each ones con-science to read or to lay by, till after the yeare 800. is observ'd already by *Padre Paolo* the great unmasker of the *Trentine* Councel. After which time the Popes of *Rome* engrossing what they pleas'd of Polit-icall rule into their owne hands, extended their dominion over mens eyes, as they had before over their judgements, burning and prohibit-

9.   Publius Ovidius Naso, Ovid.

ing to be read, what they fansied not; yet sparing in their censures, and the Books not many which they so dealt with: till *Martin* the 5. by his Bull[10] not only prohibited, but was the first that excommunicated the reading of hereticall Books; for about that time *Wicklef* and *Husse* growing terrible, were they who first drove the Papall Court to a stricter policy of prohibiting. Which cours *Leo* the 10, and his successors follow'd, untill the Councell of Trent, and the Spanish Inquisition engendring together brought forth, or perfected those Catalogues, and expurging Indexes that rake through the entralls of many an old good Author, with a violation wors then any could be offer'd to his tomb. Nor did they stay in matters Hereticall, but any subject that was not to their palat, they either condemn'd in a prohibition, or had it strait into the new Purgatory of an Index. To fill up the measure of encroachment, their last invention was to ordain that no Book, pamphlet, or paper should be Printed (as if S. *Peter* had bequeath'd them the keys of the Presse also out of Paradise) unlesse it were approv'd and licenc't under the hands of 2 or 3 glutton Friers. For example:

> Let the Chancellor *Cini* be pleas'd to see if in this present work be contain'd ought that may withstand the Printing,
> > *Vincent Rabatta* Vicar of *Florence.*

> I have seen this present work, and finde nothing athwart the Catholick faith and good manners: In witnesse whereof I have given, &c.
> > *Nicolò Cini* Chancellor of *Florence.*

> Attending the precedent relation, it is allow'd that this present work of *Davanzati* may be Printed,
> > *Vincent Rabatta,* &c.

> It may be Printed, *July* 15.
> > Friar *Simon Mompei d' Amelia*
> > Chancellor of the holy office in *Florence.*

10. Martin V was pope from 1417 to 1431; the title of his Bull of 1418 was *Inter cunctas.*

Sure they have a conceit, if he of the bottomlesse pit had not long since broke prison, that this quadruple exorcism would barre him down. I feare their next designe will be to get into their custody the licencing of that which they say★ *Claudius* intended, but went not through with. Voutsafe to see another of their forms the Roman stamp:

> *Imprimatur,* If it seem good to the reverend Master of the holy Palace,
> *Belcastro* Vicegerent.

> *Imprimatur*
> Friar *Nicolò Rodolphi* Master of the holy Palace.

Sometimes 5 *Imprimaturs* are seen together dialogue-wise in the Piatza of one Title page, complementing and ducking each to other with their shav'n reverences, whether the Author, who stands by in perplexity at the foot of his Epistle, shall to the Presse or to the spunge.[11] These are the prety responsories, these are the deare Antiphonies that so bewitcht of late our Prelats, and their Chaplaines with the goodly Eccho they made; and besotted us to the gay imitation of a lordly *Imprimatur,* one from Lambeth house, another from the West end of *Pauls;* so apishly Romanizing, that the word of command still was set downe in Latine; as if the learned Grammaticall pen that wrote it, would cast no ink without Latine: or perhaps, as they thought, because no vulgar tongue was worthy to expresse the pure conceit of an *Imprimatur;* but rather, as I hope, for that our English, the language of men ever famous, and formost in the atchievements of liberty, will not easily finde servile letters anow to spell such a dictatorie presumption English. And thus ye have the Inventors and the originall of Book-licencing ript up, and drawn as lineally as any pedigree. We have it not, that can be heard of, from any ancient State, or politie, or Church, nor by any Statute left us by our Ancestors elder or later; nor from the moderne custom of any reformed Citty, or Church

★   Quo veniam daret flatum crepitumque ventris in convivio emittendi. Sueton. in Claudio.

11.  *To the spunge:* to be wiped clear by a sponge.

abroad; but from the most Antichristian Councel, and the most tyrannous Inquisition that ever inquir'd. Till then Books were ever as freely admitted into the World as any other birth; the issue of the brain was no more stifl'd then the issue of the womb: no envious *Juno* sate cros-leg'd over the nativity of any mans intellectuall off-spring;[12] but if it prov'd a Monster, who denies, but that it was justly burnt, or sunk into the Sea. But that a Book in wors condition then a peccant soul, should be to stand before a Jury ere it be borne to the World, and undergo yet in darknesse the judgement of *Radamanth* and his Collegues, ere it can passe the ferry backward into light, was never heard before, till that mysterious iniquity provokt and troubl'd at the first entrance of Reformation, sought out new limbo's and new hells wherein they might include our Books also within the number of their damned. And this was the rare morsell so officiously snatcht up, and so ilfavourdly imitated by our inquisiturient Bishops, and the attendant minorites their Chaplains. That ye like not now these most certain Authors of this licencing order, and that all sinister intention was farre distant from your thoughts, when ye were importun'd the passing it, all men who know the integrity of your actions, and how ye honour Truth, will clear yee readily.

But some will say, What though the Inventors were bad, the thing for all that may be good? It may so; yet if that thing be no such deep invention, but obvious, and easie for any man to light on, and yet best and wisest Commonwealths through all ages, and occasions have forborne to use it, and falsest seducers, and oppressors of men were the first who tooke it up, and to no other purpose but to obstruct and hinder the first approach of Reformation; I am of those who beleeve, it will be a harder alchymy then *Lullius*[13] ever knew, to sublimat any good use out of such an invention. Yet this only is what I request to gain from this reason, that it may be held a dangerous and suspicious

12. Juno attempted to prevent Alcmena from giving birth to Hercules by having the goddess of childbirth sit with crossed legs beside her. Milton may have read the story in Ovid's *Metamorphoses*.

13. Raymond Lully, a medieval writer on alchemy who was martyred in North Africa during the early thirteenth century.

fruit, as certainly it deserves, for the tree that bore it, untill I can dissect one by one the properties it has. But I have first to finish, as was propounded, what is to be thought in generall of reading Books, what ever sort they be, and whether be more the benefit, or the harm that thence proceeds?

Not to insist upon the examples of *Moses, Daniel & Paul,* who were skilfull in all the learning of the Aegyptians, Caldeans, and Greeks, which could not probably be without reading their Books of all sorts, in *Paul* especially, who thought it no defilement to insert into holy Scripture the sentences of three Greek Poets, and one of them a Tragedian, the question was, notwithstanding sometimes controverted among the Primitive Doctors, but with great odds on that side which affirm'd it both lawfull and profitable, as was then evidently perceiv'd, when *Julian* the Apostat, and suttlest enemy to our faith, made a decree forbidding Christians the study of heathen learning: for, said he, they wound us with our own weapons, and with our owne arts and sciences they overcome us. And indeed the Christians were put so to their shifts by this crafty means, and so much in danger to decline into all ignorance, that the two *Apollinarii*[14] were fain as a man may say, to coin all the seven liberall Sciences out of the Bible, reducing it into divers forms of Orations, Poems, Dialogues, ev'n to the calculating of a new Christian Grammar. But saith the Historian *Socrates,* The providence of God provided better then the industry of *Apollinarius* and his son,[15] by taking away that illiterat law with the life of him who devis'd it. So great an injury they then held it to be depriv'd of *Hellenick* learning; and thought it a persecution more undermining, and secretly decaying the Church, then the open cruelty of *Decius* or *Dioclesian.* And perhaps it was the same politick drift that the Divell whipt St. *Jerom* in a lenten dream, for reading *Cicero;* or else it was a fantasm bred by the feaver which had then

14. According to the fifth-century ecclesiastical historian Socrates Scholasticus, Apollinarius wrote a verse version of the Pentateuch, and Apollinarius's son Julian produced dialogues based on the writings of the Apostles.

15. Julian the Apostate.

seis'd him. For had an Angel bin his discipliner, unlesse it were for dwelling too much upon Ciceronianisms, & had chastiz'd the reading, not the vanity, it had bin plainly partiall; first to correct him for grave *Cicero,* and not for scurrill *Plautus* whom he confesses to have bin reading not long before; next to correct him only, and let so many more ancient Fathers wax old in those pleasant and florid studies without the lash of such a tutoring apparition; insomuch that *Basil* teaches how some good use may be made of *Margites* a sportfull Poem, not now extant, writ by *Homer;* and why not then of *Morgante*[16] an Italian Romanze much to the same purpose. But if it be agreed we shall be try'd by visions, there is a vision recorded by *Eusebius* far ancienter then this tale of *Jerom* to the Nun *Eustochium,* and besides has nothing of a feavor in it. *Dionysius Alexandrinus* was about the year 240, a person of great name in the Church for piety and learning, who had wont to avail himself much against hereticks by being conversant in their Books; untill a certain Presbyter laid it scrupulously to his conscience, how he durst venture himselfe among those defiling volumes. The worthy man loath to give offence fell into a new debate with himselfe what was to be thought; when suddenly a vision sent from God, it is his own Epistle that so averrs it, confirm'd him in these words: Read any books what ever come to thy hands, for thou art sufficient both to judge aright, and to examine each matter. To this revelation he assented the sooner, as he confesses, because it was answerable to that of the Apostle to the Thessalonians, Prove all things, hold fast that which is good. And he might have added another remarkable saying of the same Author; To the pure all things are pure,[17] not only meats and drinks, but all kinde of knowledge whether of good or evill; the knowledge cannot defile, nor consequently the books, if the will and conscience be not defil'd. For books are as meats and viands are; some of good, some of evill substance; and yet God in that unapocryphall vision, said without ex-

16. A mock-heroic verse romance by Luigi Pulci (1431–87) published in 1488.
17. Titus 1:15.

ception, Rise *Peter,* kill and eat,[18] leaving the choice to each mans discretion. Wholesome meats to a vitiated stomack differ little or nothing from unwholesome; and best books to a naughty mind are not unappliable to occasions of evill. Bad meats will scarce breed good nourishment in the healthiest concoction; but herein the difference is of bad books, that they to a discreet and judicious Reader serve in many respects to discover, to confute, to forewarn, and to illustrate. Wherof what better witnes can ye expect I should produce, then one of your own now sitting in Parlament, the chief of learned men reputed in this Land, Mr. *Selden,* whose volume of naturall & national laws proves, not only by great autorities brought together, but by exquisite reasons and theorems almost mathematically demonstrative, that all opinions, yea errors, known, read, and collated, are of main service & assistance toward the speedy attainment of what is truest.[19] I conceive therefore, that when God did enlarge the universall diet of mans body, saving ever the rules of temperance, he then also, as before, left arbitrary the dyeting and repasting of our minds; as wherein every mature man might have to exercise his owne leading capacity. How great a vertue is temperance, how much of moment through the whole life of man? yet God committs the managing so great a trust, without particular Law or prescription, wholly to the demeanour of every grown man. And therefore when he himself tabl'd the Jews from heaven, that Omer which was every mans daily portion of Manna, is computed to have bin more then might have well suffic'd the heartiest feeder thrice as many meals. For those actions which enter into a man, rather then issue out of him, and therefore defile not, God uses not to captivat under a perpetuall childhood of prescription, but trusts him with the gift of reason to be his own chooser; there were but little work left for preaching, if law and compulsion should grow so fast upon those things which hertofore were govern'd only by exhortation. *Salomon* informs us that much reading is a wearines

18. Acts 11:5.

19. Milton quotes John Selden (1584–1654), *De Jure Naturali et Gentium Iuxta Disciplinam Hebraecorum* (1640).

to the flesh;[20] but neither he, nor other inspir'd author tells us that such, or such reading is unlawfull: yet certainly had God thought good to limit us herein, it had bin much more expedient to have told us what was unlawfull, then what was wearisome. As for the burning of those Ephesian books by St. *Pauls* converts, tis reply'd the books were magick, the Syriack so renders them. It was a privat act, a voluntary act, and leaves us to a voluntary imitation: the men in remorse burnt those books which were their own; the Magistrat by this example is not appointed: these men practiz'd the books, another might perhaps have read them in some sort usefully. Good and evill we know in the field of this World grow up together almost inseparably; and the knowledge of good is so involv'd and interwoven with the knowledge of evill, and in so many cunning resemblances hardly to be discern'd, that those confused seeds which were impos'd on *Psyche* as an incessant labour to cull out, and sort asunder, were not more intermixt.[21] It was from out the rinde of one apple tasted, that the knowledge of good and evill as two twins cleaving together leapt forth into the World. And perhaps this is that doom which *Adam* fell into of knowing good and evill, that is to say of knowing good by evill. As therefore the state of man now is; what wisdome can there be to choose, what continence to forbeare without the knowledge of evill? He that can apprehend and consider vice with all her baits and seeming pleasures, and yet abstain, and yet distinguish, and yet prefer that which is truly better, he is the true wayfaring Christian. I cannot praise a fugitive and cloister'd vertue, unexercis'd & unbreath'd, that never sallies out and sees her adversary, but slinks out of the race, where that immortall garland is to be run for, not without dust and heat. Assuredly we bring not innocence into the world, we bring impurity much rather: that which purifies us is triall, and triall is by what is contrary. That vertue therefore which is but a youngling in the contemplation of evill, and knows not the utmost that vice

20. Eccles. 12:12.

21. In Apuleius's *The Golden Ass,* Venus punishes Psyche by ordering her to separate many kinds of grain from a huge, mixed pile.

promises to her followers, and rejects it, is but a blank vertue, not a pure; her whitenesse is but an excrementall whitenesse; Which was the reason why our sage and serious Poet *Spencer,* whom I dare be known to think a better teacher then *Scotus* or *Aquinas,* describing true temperance under the person of *Guion,*[22] brings him in with his palmer through the cave of Mammon, and the bowr of earthly blisse that he might see and know, and yet abstain. Since therefore the knowledge and survay of vice is in this world so necessary to the con-stituting of human vertue, and the scanning of error to the confirma-tion of truth, how can we more safely, and with lesse danger scout into the regions of sin and falsity then by reading all manner of trac-tats, and hearing all manner of reason? And this is the benefit which may be had of books promiscuously read. But of the harm that may result hence three kinds are usually reckn'd. First, is fear'd the infec-tion that may spread; but then all human learning and controversie in religious points must remove out of the world, yea the Bible it selfe; for that oftimes relates blasphemy not nicely, it describes the carnall sense of wicked men not unelegantly, it brings in holiest men pas-sionately murmuring against providence through all the arguments of *Epicurus:* in other great disputes it answers dubiously and darkly to the common reader: And ask a Talmudist what ails the modesty of his marginall Keri, that *Moses* and all the Prophets cannot perswade him to pronounce the textuall Chetiv.[23] For these causes we all know the Bible it selfe put by the Papist into the first rank of prohibited books. The ancientest Fathers must be next remov'd, as *Clement* of *Alexan-dria,* and that *Eusebian* book of Evangelick preparation, transmitting our ears through a hoard of heathenish obscenities to receive the Gospel. Who finds not that *Irenaeus, Epiphanius, Jerom,* and others dis-cover more heresies then they well confute, and that oft for heresie which is the truer opinion. Nor boots it to say for these, and all the heathen Writers of greatest infection, if it must be thought so, with

22. The knight representative of temperance in *The Faerie Queene.* The episodes to which Milton refers occur in bk. 2, cantos 7 and 12.

23. *Keri,* meaning "what is read," as distinct from *Chetiv,* meaning "what is writ-ten;" (i.e., the keri were euphemisms marginally inserted by Talmudists).

whom is bound up the life of human learning, that they writ in an unknown tongue, so long as we are sure those languages are known as well to the worst of men, who are both most able, and most diligent to instill the poison they suck, first into the Courts of Princes, acquainting them with the choicest delights, and criticisms of sin. As perhaps did that *Petronius* whom *Nero* call'd his *Arbiter,* the Master of his revels; and that notorious ribald of *Arezzo,*[24] dreaded, and yet dear to the Italian Courtiers. I name not him for posterities sake, whom *Harry* the 8. nam'd in merriment his Vicar of hell.[25] By which compendious way all the contagion that foreine books can infuse, will finde a passage to the people farre easier and shorter then an Indian voyage, though it could be sail'd either by the North of *Cataio* Eastward, or of *Canada* Westward, while our Spanish licencing gags the English Presse never so severely. But on the other side that infection which is from books of controversie in Religion, is more doubtfull and dangerous to the learned, then to the ignorant; and yet those books must be permitted untoucht by the licencer. It will be hard to instance where any ignorant man hath bin ever seduc't by Papisticall book in English, unlesse it were commended and expounded to him by some of that Clergy: and indeed all such tractats whether false or true are as the Prophesie of *Isaiah* was to the *Eunuch,* not to be *understood without a guide.*[26] But of our Priests and Doctors how many have bin corrupted by studying the comments of Jesuits and *Sorbonists,* and how fast they could transfuse that corruption into the people, our experience is both late and sad. It is not forgot, since the acute and distinct *Arminius* was perverted meerly by the perusing of a namelesse discours writt'n at *Delf,* which at first he took in hand to confute.[27] Seeing therefore that those books, & those in great abundance which are likeliest to taint both life and doctrine, cannot be

24. Pietro Aretino (1492–1557).

25. Said to be Sir Francis Brian.

26. Acts 8:23–35.

27. Arminius (1560–1609) was supposedly swayed from his adherence to Calvin's strict view of predestination as the result of taking up some voluntarist writings that he had meant to confute.

supprest without the fall of learning, and of all ability in disputation, and that these books of either sort are most and soonest catching to the learned, from whom to the common people what ever is hereticall or dissolute may quickly be convey'd, and that evill manners are as perfectly learnt without books a thousand other ways which cannot be stopt, and evill doctrine not with books can propagate, except a teacher guide, which he might also doe without writing, and so beyond prohibiting, I am not able to unfold, how this cautelous enterprise of licencing can be exempted from the number of vain and impossible attempts. And he who were pleasantly dispos'd, could not well avoid to lik'n it to the exploit of that gallant man who thought to pound up the crows by shutting his Parkgate. Besides another inconvenience, if learned men be the first receivers out of books, & dispredders both of vice and error, how shall the licencers themselves be confided in, unlesse we can conferr upon them, or they assume to themselves above all others in the Land, the grace of infallibility, and uncorruptednesse? And again, if it be true, that a wise man like a good refiner can gather gold out of the drossiest volume, and that a fool will be a fool with the best book, yea or without book, there is no reason that we should deprive a wise man of any advantage to his wisdome, while we seek to restrain from a fool, that which being restrain'd will be no hindrance to his folly. For if there should be so much exactnesse always us'd to keep that from him which is unfit for his reading, we should in the judgement of *Aristotle* not only, but of *Salomon,* and of our Saviour, not voutsafe him good precepts, and by consequence not willingly admit him to good books; as being certain that a wise man will make better use of an idle pamphlet, then a fool will do of sacred Scripture. 'Tis next alleg'd we must not expose our selves to temptations without necessity, and next to that, not imploy our time in vain things. To both these objections one answer will serve, out of the grounds already laid, that to all men such books are not temptations, nor vanities; but usefull drugs and materialls wherewith to temper and compose effective and strong med'cins, which mans life cannot want. The rest, as children and childish men, who have not the art to qualifie and prepare these working mineralls, well may be exhorted to forbear, but hinder'd forcibly they cannot be by all the licencing that Sainted Inquisition could ever yet contrive; which is what I promis'd to deliver next, That this order of licencing conduces nothing to the end for which it was fram'd; and hath almost prevented me by being clear already while thus much hath bin explaining. See the ingenuity of Truth, who when she gets a free and willing hand, opens her self faster, then the pace of method and discours can overtake her. It was the task which I began with, To shew that no Nation, or well instituted State, if they valu'd books at all, did ever use this way of licencing; and it might be answer'd, that this is a piece of prudence lately discover'd. To which I return, that as it was a thing slight and obvious to think on, so if it had bin difficult to finde out, there wanted not among them long since, who suggested such a cours; which they not following, leave us a pattern of their judgement, that it was not the not knowing, but the not approving, which was the cause of their not using it. *Plato,* a man of high autority indeed, but least of all for his Commonwealth, in the book of his laws, which no City ever yet receiv'd, fed his fancie with making many edicts to his ayrie Burgomasters, which they who otherwise admire him, wish had bin rather buried and excus'd in the *genial* cups of an *Academick* night-sitting. By which laws he seems to tolerat no kind of learning, but by unalterable decree, consisting most of practicall traditions, to the attainment whereof a Library of smaller bulk then his own dialogues would be abundant. And there also enacts that no Poet should so much as read to any privat man, what he had writt'n, untill the judges and Law-keepers had seen it, and allow'd it: [28] But that *Plato* meant this Law peculiarly to that Commonwealth which he had imagin'd, and to no other, is evident. Why was he not else a Law-giver to himself, but a transgressor, and to be expell'd by his own Magistrats; both for the wanton epigrams and dialogues which he made, and his perpetuall reading of *Sophron Mimus,* and *Aristophanes,*

28. Milton is probably referring to a provision for prior censorship in bk. 7 of Plato's *Laws.*

books of grossest infamy, and also for commending the latter of them though he were the malicious libeller of his chief friends, to be read by the Tyrant *Dionysius,* who had little need of such trash to spend his time on? But that he knew this licencing of Poems had reference and dependence to many other proviso's there set down in his fancied republic, which in this world could have no place: and so neither he himself, nor any Magistrat, or City ever imitated that cours, which tak'n apart from those other collaterall injunctions must needs be vain and fruitlesse. For if they fell upon one kind of strictnesse, unlesse their care were equall to regulat all other things of like aptnes to corrupt the mind, that single endeavour they knew would be but a fond labour; to shut and fortifie one gate against corruption, and be necessitated to leave others round about wide open. If we think to regulat Printing, thereby to rectifie manners, we must regulat all recreations and pastimes, all that is delightfull to man. No musick must be heard, no song be set or sung, but what is grave and *Dorick.* There must be licencing dancers, that no gesture, motion, or deportment be taught our youth but what by their allowance shall be thought honest; for such *Plato* was provided of; It will ask more then the work of twenty licencers to examin all the lutes, the violins, and the ghittarrs in every house; they must not be suffer'd to prattle as they doe, but must be licenc'd what they may say. And who shall silence all the airs and madrigalls, that whisper softnes in chambers? The Windows also, and the *Balcone's* must be thought on, there are shrewd books, with dangerous Frontispices set to sale; who shall prohibit them, shall twenty licencers? The villages also must have their visitors to enquire what lectures the bagpipe and the rebbeck reads ev'n to the ballatry, and the gammuth of every *municipal* fidler, for these are the Countrymans *Arcadia's* and his *Monte Mayors.*[29] Next, what more Nationall corruption, for which England hears ill abroad, then houshold gluttony; who shall be the rectors of our daily rioting? and what shall be done to inhibit the multitudes that frequent those houses where

29. Sir Philip Sidney's *Arcadia* and the Portuguese pastoral *Diana Enamorada,* by Jorge de Montemayor.

drunk'nes is sold and harbour'd? Our garments also should be referr'd
to the licencing of some more sober work-masters to see them cut
into a lesse wanton garb. Who shall regulat all the mixt conversation of our youth, male and female together, as is the fashion of this
Country, who shall still appoint what shall be discours'd, what pre-
sum'd, and no furder? Lastly, who shall forbid and separat all idle resort, all evill company? These things will be, and must be; but how
they shall be lest hurtfull, how lest enticing, herein consists the grave
and governing wisdom of a State. To sequester out of the world into
*Atlantick* and *Eutopian* polities, which never can be drawn into use,
will not mend our condition; but to ordain wisely as in this world of
evill, in the midd'st whereof God hath plac't us unavoidably. Nor is
it *Plato's* licencing of books will doe this, which necessarily pulls
along with it so many other kinds of licencing, as will make us all
both ridiculous and weary, and yet frustrat; but those unwritt'n, or at
least unconstraining laws of vertuous education, religious and civill
nurture, which *Plato* there mentions, as the bonds and ligaments of
the Commonwealth, the pillars and the sustainers of every writt'n
Statute; these they be which will bear chief sway in such matters as
these, when all licencing will be easily eluded. Impunity and remisse-
nes, for certain are the bane of a Commonwealth, but here the great
art lyes to discern in what the law is to bid restraint and punishment,
and in what things perswasion only is to work. If every action which
is good, or evill in man at ripe years, were to be under pittance, and
prescription, and compulsion, what were vertue but a name, what
praise could be then due to well-doing, what grammercy to be sober,
just or continent? many there be that complain of divin Providence
for suffering *Adam* to transgresse, foolish tongues! when God gave
him reason, he gave him freedom to choose, for reason is but choosing; he had bin else a meer artificiall *Adam,* such an *Adam* as he is in
the motions. We our selves esteem not of that obedience, or love, or
gift, which is of force: God therefore left him free, set before him a
provoking object, ever almost in his eyes; herein consisted his merit,
herein the right of his reward, the praise of his abstinence. Where-

fore did he creat passions within us, pleasures round about us, but that these rightly temper'd are the very ingredients of vertu? They are not skilfull considerers of human things, who imagin to remove sin by removing the matter of sin; for, besides that it is a huge heap increasing under the very act of diminishing, though some part of it may for a time be withdrawn from some persons, it cannot from all, in such a universall thing as books are; and when this is done, yet the sin remains entire. Though ye take from a covetous man all his treasure, he has yet one jewell left, ye cannot bereave him of his covetousnesse. Banish all objects of lust, shut up all youth into the severest discipline that can be exercis'd in any hermitage, ye cannot make them chaste, that came not thither so: such great care and wisdom is requir'd to the right managing of this point. Suppose we could expell sin by this means; look how much we thus expell of sin, so much we expell of vertue: for the matter of them both is the same; remove that, and ye remove them both alike. This justifies the high providence of God, who though he command us temperance, justice, continence, yet powrs out before us ev'n to a profusenes all desirable things, and gives us minds that can wander beyond all limit and satiety. Why should we then affect a rigor contrary to the manner of God and of nature, by abridging or scanting those means, which books freely permitted are, both to the triall of vertue, and the exercise of truth. It would be better done to learn that the law must needs be frivolous which goes to restrain things, uncertainly and yet equally working to good, and to evill. And were I the chooser, a dram of well-doing should be preferr'd before many times as much the forcible hindrance of evill-doing. For God sure esteems the growth and compleating of one vertuous person, more then the restraint of ten vitious. And albeit what ever thing we hear or see, sitting, walking, travelling, or conversing may be fitly call'd our book, and is of the same effect that writings are, yet grant the thing to be prohibited were only books, it appears that this order hitherto is far insufficient to the end which it intends. Do we not see, not once or oftner, but weekly that continu'd Court-libell against the Parlament and City, Printed, as the wet sheets can

witnes, and dispers't among us, for all that licencing can doe? yet this
is the prime service a man would think, wherein this order should
give proof of it self. If it were executed, you'l say. But certain, if execution be remisse or blindfold now, and in this particular, what will
it be hereafter, and in other books. If then the order shall not be vain
and frustrat, behold a new labour, Lords and Commons, ye must repeal and proscribe all scandalous and unlicenc't books already printed
and divulg'd; after ye have drawn them up into a list, that all may
know which are condemn'd, and which not; and ordain that no
forrein books be deliver'd out of custody, till they have bin read over.
This office will require the whole time of not a few overseers, and
those no vulgar men. There be also books which are partly usefull
and excellent, partly culpable and pernicious; this work will ask as
many more officials, to make expurgations, and expunctions, that the
Commonwealth of learning be not damnify'd. In fine, when the
multitude of books encrease upon their hands, ye must be fain to
catalogue all those Printers who are found frequently offending, and
forbidd the importation of their whole suspected *typography*. In a
word, that this your order may be exact, and not deficient, ye must
reform it perfectly according to the model of *Trent* and *Sevil*, which
I know ye abhorre to doe. Yet though ye should condiscend to this,
which God forbid, the order still would be but fruitlesse and defec-
tive to that end whereto ye meant it. If to prevent sects and schisms,
who is so unread or so uncatechis'd in story, that hath not heard of
many sects refusing books as a hindrance, and preserving their doctrine
unmixt for many ages, only by unwritt'n traditions. The Christian
faith, for that was once a schism, is not unknown to have spread all
over *Asia*, ere any Gospel or Epistle was seen in writing. If the amendment of manners be aym'd at, look into Italy and Spain, whether those
places be one scruple the better, the honester, the wiser, the chaster,
since all the inquisitionall rigor that hath bin executed upon books.

Another reason, whereby to make it plain that this order will
misse the end it seeks, consider by the quality which ought to be in
every licencer. It cannot be deny'd but that he who is made judge to

sit upon the birth, or death of books whether they may be wafted into this world, or not, had need to be a man above the common measure, both studious, learned, and judicious; there may be else no mean mistakes in the censure of what is passable or not; which is also no mean injury. If he be of such worth as behoovs him, there cannot be a more tedious and unpleasing journey-work, a greater losse of time levied upon his head, then to be made the perpetuall reader of unchosen books and pamphlets, oftimes huge volumes. There is no book that is acceptable unlesse at certain seasons; but to be enjoyn'd the reading of that at all times, and in a hand scars legible, whereof three pages would not down at any time in the fairest Print, is an imposition which I cannot beleeve how he that values time, and his own studies, or is but of a sensible nostrill should be able to endure. In this one thing I crave leave of the present licencers to be pardon'd for so thinking: who doubtlesse took this office up, looking on it through their obedience to the Parlament, whose command perhaps made all things seem easie and unlaborious to them; but that this short triall hath wearied them out already, their own expressions and excuses to them who make so many journeys to sollicit their licence, are testimony anough. Seeing therefore those who now possesse the imployment, by all evident signs wish themselves well ridd of it, and that no man of worth, none that is not a plain unthrift of his own hours is ever likely to succeed them, except he mean to put himself to the salary of a Presse-corrector, we may easily foresee what kind of licencers we are to expect hereafter, either ignorant, imperious, and remisse, or basely pecuniary. This is what I had to shew wherein this order cannot conduce to that end, whereof it bears the intention.

I lastly proceed from the no good it can do, to the manifest hurt it causes, in being first the greatest discouragement and affront, that can be offer'd to learning and to learned men. It was the complaint and lamentation of Prelats, upon every least breath of a motion to remove pluralities, and distribute more equally Church revennu's, that then all learning would be for ever dasht and discourag'd. But as for that opinion, I never found cause to think that the tenth part of learning stood or fell with the Clergy: nor could I ever but hold it for a sordid and unworthy speech of any Churchman who had a competency left him. If therefore ye be loath to dishearten utterly and discontent, not the mercenary crew of false pretenders to learning, but the free and ingenuous sort of such as evidently were born to study, and love lerning for it self, not for lucre, or any other end, but the service of God and of truth, and perhaps that lasting fame and perpetuity of praise which God and good men have consented shall be the reward of those whose publisht labours advance the good of mankind, then know, that so far to distrust the judgement & the honesty of one who hath but a common repute in learning, and never yet offended, as not to count him fit to print his mind without a tutor and examiner, lest he should drop a scism, or something of corruption, is the greatest displeasure and indignity to a free and knowing spirit that can be put upon him. What advantage is it to be a man over it is to be a boy at school, if we have only scapt the ferular, to come under the fescu of an *Imprimatur?* if serious and elaborat writings, as if they were no more then the theam of a Grammar lad under his Pedagogue must not be utter'd without the cursory eyes of a temporizing and extemporizing licencer. He who is not trusted with his own actions, his drift not being known to be evill, and standing to the hazard of law and penalty, has no great argument to think himself reputed in the Commonwealth wherin he was born, for other then a fool or a foreiner. When a man writes to the world, he summons up all his reason and deliberation to assist him; he searches, meditats, is industrious, and likely consults and conferrs with his judicious friends; after all which done he takes himself to be inform'd in what he writes, as well as any that writ before him; if in this the most consummat act of his fidelity and ripenesse, no years, no industry, no former proof of his abilities can bring him to that state of maturity, as not to be still mistrusted and suspected, unlesse he carry all his considerat diligence, all his midnight watchings, and expence of *Palladian* oyl, to the hasty view of an unleasur'd licencer, perhaps much his younger, perhaps far his inferiour in judgement, perhaps one who never knew the labour of book-writing, and if he be not repulst, or slighted, must appear in Print like a punie with his guardian, and his censors hand on the back of his title to be his bayl and surety, that he is no idiot, or seducer, it cannot be but a dishonor and derogation to the author, to the book, to the priviledge and dignity of Learning. And what if the author shall be one so copious of fancie, as to have many things well worth the adding, come into his mind after licencing, while the book is yet under the Presse, which not seldom happ'ns to the best and diligentest writers; and that perhaps a dozen times in one book. The Printer dares not go beyond his licenc't copy; so often then must the author trudge to his leav-giver, that those his new insertions may be viewd; and many a jaunt will be made, ere that licencer, for it must be the same man, can either be found, or found at leisure; mean while either the Presse must stand still, which is no small damage, or the author loose his accuratest thoughts, & send the book forth wors then he had made it, which to a diligent writer is the greatest melancholy and vexation that can befall. And how can a man teach with autority, which is the life of teaching, how can he be a Doctor in his book as he ought to be, or else had better be silent, whenas all he teaches, all he delivers, is but under the tuition, under the correction of his patriarchal licencer to blot or alter what precisely accords not with the hidebound humor which he calls his judgement. When every acute reader upon the first sight of a pedantick licence, will be ready with these like words to ding the book a coits distance from him, I hate a pupil teacher, I endure not an instructer that comes to me under the wardship of an overseeing fist. I know nothing of the licencer, but that I have his own hand here for his arrogance; who shall warrant me his judgement? The State Sir, replies the Stationer, but has a quick return, The State shall be my governours, but not my criticks; they may be mistak'n in the choice of a licencer, as easily as this licencer may be mistak'n in an author: This is some common stuffe; and he might adde from Sir *Francis Bacon,* That *such authoriz'd books are but the language of the times.*[30] For though a licencer should happ'n to be judicious more then ordnary, which will be a great jeopardy of the next succession, yet his very office, and his commission enjoyns him to let passe nothing but what is vulgarly receiv'd already. Nay, which is more lamentable, if the work of any deceased author, though never so famous in his life time, and even to this day, come to their hands for licence to be Printed, or Reprinted, if there be found in his book one sentence of a ventrous edge, utter'd in the height of zeal, and who knows whether it might not be the dictat of a divine Spirit, yet not suiting with every low decrepit humor of their own, though it were *Knox*[31] himself, the Reformer of a Kingdom that spake it, they will not pardon him their dash: the sense of that great man shall to all posterity be lost, for the fearfulnesse, or the presumptuous rashnesse of a perfunctory licencer. And to what an author this violence hath bin lately done, and in what book of greatest consequence to be faithfully publisht, I could now instance, but shall forbear till a more convenient season. Yet if these things be not resented seriously and timely by them who have the remedy in their power, but that such iron moulds as these shall have autority to knaw out the choisest periods of exquisitest books, and to commit such a treacherous fraud against the orphan remainders of worthiest men after death, the more sorrow will belong to that haples race of men, whose misfortune it is to have understanding. Henceforth let no man care to learn, or care to be more then worldly wise; for certainly in higher matters to be ignorant and slothfull, to be a common stedfast dunce will be the only pleasant life, and only in request.

And as it is a particular disesteem of every knowing person alive, and most injurious to the writt'n labours and monuments of the dead, so to me it seems an undervaluing and vilifying of the whole Nation. I cannot set so light by all the invention, the art, the wit, the grave

---

30. From Bacon's *An Advertisement Touching the Controversies of the Church of England.*

31. John Knox, the founder of Scottish Presbyterianism.

and solid judgement which is in England, as that it can be comprehended in any twenty capacities how good soever, much lesse that it
should not passe except their superintendence be over it, except it be
sifted and strain'd with their strainers, that it should be uncurrant
without their manuall stamp. Truth and understanding are not such
wares as to be monopoliz'd and traded in by tickets and statutes, and
standards. We must not think to make a staple commodity of all the
knowledge in the Land, to mark and licence it like our broad cloath,
and our wooll packs. What is it but a servitude like that impos'd by
the Philistims, not to be allow'd the sharpning of our own axes and
coulters, but we must repair from all quarters to twenty licencing
forges.[32] Had any one writt'n and divulg'd erroneous things & scandalous to honest life, misusing and forfeiting the esteem had of his
reason among men, if after conviction this only censure were adjudg'd
him, that he should never henceforth write, but what were first examin'd by an appointed officer, whose hand should be annext to passe
his credit for him, that now he might be safely read, it could not be
apprehended lesse then a disgracefull punishment. Whence to include
the whole Nation, and those that never yet thus offended, under such
a diffident and suspectfull prohibition, may plainly be understood
what a disparagement it is. So much the more, when as dettors and
delinquents may walk abroad without a keeper, but unoffensive books
must not stirre forth without a visible jaylor in thir title. Nor is it
to the common people lesse then a reproach; for if we be so jealous
over them, as that we dare not trust them with an English pamphlet,
what doe we but censure them for a giddy, vitious, and ungrounded
people; in such a sick and weak estate of faith and discretion, as to be
able to take nothing down but through the pipe[33] of a licencer. That
this is care or love of them, we cannot pretend, whenas in those
Popish places where the Laity are most hated and dispis'd the same

32. 1 Sam. 13:20.
33. Tube through which medicine was ingested.

strictnes is us'd over them. Wisdom we cannot call it, because it stops but one breach of licence, nor that neither; whenas those corruptions which it seeks to prevent, break in faster at other dores which cannot be shut.

And in conclusion it reflects to the disrepute of our Ministers also, of whose labours we should hope better, and of the proficiencie which thir flock reaps by them, then that after all this light of the Gospel which is, and is to be, and all this continuall preaching, they should be still frequented with such an unprincipl'd, unedify'd, and laick [34] rabble, as that the whiffe of every new pamphlet should stagger them out of thir catechism, and Christian walking. This may have much reason to discourage the Ministers when such a low conceit is had of all their exhortations, and the benefiting of their hearers, as that they are not thought fit to be turn'd loose to three sheets of paper without a licencer, that all the Sermons, all the Lectures preacht, printed, vented in such numbers, and such volumes, as have now well-nigh made all other books unsalable, should not be armor anough against one single *enchiridion*, [35] without the castle St. *Angelo* of an *Imprimatur*.

And lest som should perswade ye, Lords and Commons, that these arguments of lerned mens discouragement at this your order, are meer flourishes, and not reall, I could recount what I have seen and heard in other Countries, where this kind of inquisition tyrannizes; when I have sat among their lerned men, for that honor I had, and bin counted happy to be born in such a place of *Philosophic* freedom, as they suppos'd England was, while themselvs did nothing but bemoan the servil condition into which lerning amongst them was brought; that this was it which had dampt the glory of Italian wits; that nothing had bin there writt'n now these many years but flattery and fustian. [36] There it was that I found and visited the famous *Galileo* grown old, a prisner to the Inquisition, for thinking in Astronomy

34. Pertaining to the laity.
35. A handbook.
36. Milton here refers to his youthful journey through Italy in 1638–39.

otherwise then the Franciscan and Dominican licencers thought. And though I knew that England then was groaning loudest under the Prelaticall yoak, neverthelesse I took it as a pledge of future happines, that other Nations were so perswaded of her liberty. Yet was it beyond my hope that those Worthies were then breathing in her air, who should be her leaders to such a deliverance, as shall never be forgott'n by any revolution of time that this world hath to finish. When that was once begun, it was as little in my fear, that what words of complaint I heard among lerned men of other parts utter'd against the Inquisition, the same I should hear by as lerned men at home utterd in time of Parlament against an order of licencing; and that so generally, that when I had disclos'd my self a companion of their discontent, I might say, if without envy, that he whom an honest *quaestorship* had indear'd to the *Sicilians,*[37] was not more by them importun'd against *Verres,* then the favourable opinion which I had among many who honour ye, and are known and respected by ye, loaded me with entreaties and perswasions, that I would not despair to lay together that which just reason should bring into my mind, toward the removal of an undeserved thraldom upon lerning. That this is not therefore the disburdning of a particular fancie, but the common grievance of all those who had prepar'd their minds and studies above the vulgar pitch to advance truth in others, and from others to entertain it, thus much may satisfie. And in their name I shall for neither friend nor foe conceal what the generall murmur is; that if it come to inquisitioning again, and licencing, and that we are so timorous of our selvs, and so suspicious of all men, as to fear each book, and the shaking of every leaf, before we know what the contents are, if some who but of late were little better then silenc't from preaching, shall come now to silence us from reading, except what they please, it cannot be guest what is intended by som but a second tyranny over learning: and will soon put it out of controversie that Bishops and Presbyters are the same

---

37. Cicero served as quaestor in Sicily in 75 B.C.

---

to us both name and thing. That those evills of Prelaty which before
from five or six and twenty Sees were distributivly charg'd upon the
whole people, will now light wholly upon learning, is not obscure to
us: whenas now the Pastor of a small unlearned Parish, on the sudden
shall be exalted Archbishop over a large dioces of books, and yet not
remove, but keep his other cure too, a mysticall pluralist. He who but
of late cry'd down the sole ordination of every novice Batchelor of
Art, and deny'd sole jurisdiction over the simplest Parishioner, shall
now at home in his privat chair assume both these over worthiest and
excellentest books and ablest authors that write them. This is not, Yee
Covnants and Protestations that we have made, this is not to put down
Prelaty, this is but to chop an Episcopacy, this is but to translate the
Palace *Metropolitan*[38] from one kind of dominion into another, this is
but an old canonicall slight of *commuting* our penance. To startle thus
betimes at a meer unlicenc't pamphlet will after a while be afraid of
every conventicle,[39] and a while after will make a conventicle of every
Christian meeting. But I am certain that a State govern'd by the rules
of justice and fortitude, or a Church built and founded upon the
rock of faith and true knowledge, cannot be so pusillanimous. While
things are yet not constituted in Religion, that freedom of writing
should be restrain'd by a discipline imitated from the Prelats, and
learnt by them from the Inquisition to shut us up all again into the
brest of a licencer, must needs give cause of doubt and discouragement to all learned and religious men. Who cannot but discern the
finenes of this politic drift, and who are the contrivers; that while
Bishops were to be baited down,[40] then all Presses might be open;
it was the peoples birthright and priviledge in time of Parlament, it
was the breaking forth of light. But now the Bishops abrogated and
voided out of the Church, as if our Reformation sought no more,

38. An archbishop.
39. A meeting of a dissident religious sect that was forbidden by law.
40. *Baited down* refers to bear baiting.

but to make room for others into their seats under another name, the Episcopall arts begin to bud again, the cruse of truth must run no more oyle, liberty of Printing must be enthrall'd again under a Prelaticall commission of twenty, the privilege of the people nullify'd, and which is wors, the freedom of learning must groan again, and to her old fetters; all this the Parlament yet sitting. Although their own late arguments and defences against the Prelats might remember them that this obstructing violence meets for the most part with an event utterly opposite to the end which it drives at: instead of suppressing sects and schisms, it raises them and invests them with a reputation: *The punishing of wits enhaunces their autority*, saith the Vicount St. *Albans, and a forbidd'n writing is thought to be a certain spark of truth that flies up in the faces of them who seeke to tread it out.*[41] This order therefore may prove a nursing mother to sects, but I shall easily shew how it will be a stepdame to Truth: and first by disinabling us to the maintenance of what is known already.

Well knows he who uses to consider, that our faith and knowledge thrives by exercise, as well as our limbs and complexion. Truth is compar'd in Scripture to a streaming fountain;[42] if her waters flow not in a perpetuall progression, they sick'n into a muddy pool of conformity and tradition. A man may be a heretick in the truth; and if he beleeve things only because his Pastor sayes so, or the Assembly so determins, without knowing other reason, though his belief be true, yet the very truth he holds, becomes his heresie. There is not any burden that som would gladlier post off to another, then the charge and care of their Religion. There be, who knows not that there be of Protestants and professors who live and dye in as arrant an implicit faith, as any lay Papist of Loretto. A wealthy man addicted to his pleasure and to his profits, finds Religion to be a traffick so entangl'd, and of so many piddling accounts, that of all mysteries he cannot skill to

41. Milton is citing again Bacon's *An Advertisement.* . . .
42. Ps. 85:11.

keep a stock going upon that trade. What should he doe? fain he would have the name to be religious, fain he would bear up with his neighbours in that. What does he therefore, but resolvs to give over toyling, and to find himself out som factor, to whose care and credit he may commit the whole managing of his religious affairs; som Divine of note and estimation that must be. To him he adheres, resigns the whole warehouse of his religion, with all the locks and keyes into his custody; and indeed makes the very person of that man his religion; esteems his associating with him a sufficient evidence and commendatory of his own piety. So that a man may say his religion is now no more within himself, but is becom a dividuall movable, and goes and comes neer him, according as that good man frequents the house. He entertains him, gives him gifts, feasts him, lodges him; his religion comes home at night, praies, is liberally supt, and sumptuously laid to sleep, rises, is saluted, and after the malmsey, or some well spic't bruage, and better breakfasted then he whose morning appetite would have gladly fed on green figs between *Bethany* and *Ierusalem,*[43] his Religion walks abroad at eight, and leavs his kind entertainer in the shop trading all day without his religion.

Another sort there be who when they hear that all things shall be order'd, all things regulated and setl'd; nothing writt'n but what passes through the custom-house of certain Publicans that have the tunaging and the poundaging[44] of all free spok'n truth, will strait give themselvs up into your hands, mak'em & cut'em out what religion ye please; there be delights, there be recreations and jolly pastimes that will fetch the day about from sun to sun, and rock the tedious year as in a delightfull dream. What need they torture their heads with that which others have tak'n so strictly, and so unalterably into their own pourveying. These are the fruits which a dull ease and cessation of our knowledge will bring forth among the people. How

43. Milton refers to Jesus in Mark 11:12–13.
44. "[T]he tunaging and the poundaging," or excise taxes.

goodly, and how to be wisht were such an obedient unanimity as this, what a fine conformity would it starch us all into? doubtles a stanch and solid peece of frame-work, as any January could freeze together.

Nor much better will be the consequence ev'n among the Clergy themselvs; it is no new thing never heard of before, for a *parochiall* Minister, who has his reward, and is at his *Hercules* pillars in a warm benefice, to be easily inclinable, if he have nothing else that may rouse up his studies, to finish his circuit in an English concordance and a *topic folio,* the gatherings and savings of a sober graduatship, a *Harmony* and a *Catena,*[45] treading the constant round of certain common doctrinall heads, attended with their uses, motives, marks and means, out of which as out of an alphabet or sol-fa by forming and transforming, joyning and dis-joyning variously a little book-craft, and two hours meditation might furnish him unspeakably to the performance of more then a weekly charge of sermoning: not to reck'n up the infinit helps of interlinearies, breviaries, *synopses,* and other loitering gear. But as for the multitude of Sermons ready printed and pil'd up, on every text that is not difficult, our London trading St. *Thomas* in his vestry, and adde to boot St. *Martin,* and St. *Hugh,* have not within their hallow'd limits more vendible ware of all sorts ready made: so that penury he never need fear of Pulpit provision, having where so plenteously to refresh his magazin. But if his rear and flanks be not impal'd, if his back dore be not secur'd by the rigid licencer, but that a bold book may now and then issue forth, and give the assault to some of his old collections in their trenches, it will concern him then to keep waking, to stand in watch, to set good guards and sentinells about his receiv'd opinions, to walk the round and counter-round with his fellow inspectors, fearing lest any of his flock be seduc't, who also then would be better instructed, better exercis'd and disciplin'd. And God send that the fear of this diligence which

45. *Harmony:* a work devoted to bringing together diverse scriptural texts; *Catena:* a chain, or a work of systematic theology sequentially developed.

must then be us'd, doe not make us affect the lazines of a licencing Church.

For if we be sure we are in the right, and doe not hold the truth guiltily, which becomes not, if we our selves condemn not our own weak and frivolous teaching, and the people for an untaught and irreligious gadding rout, what can be more fair, then when a man judicious, learned, and of a conscience, for ought we know, as good as theirs that taught us what we know, shall not privily from house to house, which is more dangerous, but openly by writing publish to the world what his opinion is, what his reasons, and wherefore that which is now thought cannot be sound. Christ urg'd it as wherewith to justifie himself, that he preacht in publick; yet writing is more publick then preaching; and more easie to refutation, if need be, there being so many whose businesse and profession meerly it is, to be the champions of Truth; which if they neglect, what can be imputed but their sloth, or unability?

Thus much we are hinder'd and dis-inur'd by this cours of licencing toward the true knowledge of what we seem to know. For how much it hurts and hinders the licencers themselves in the calling of their Ministery, more then any secular employment, if they will discharge that office as they ought, so that of necessity they must neglect either the one duty or the other, I insist not, because it is a particular, but leave it to their own conscience, how they will decide it there.

There is yet behind of what I purpos'd to lay open, the incredible losse, and detriment that this plot of licencing puts us to, more then if som enemy at sea should stop up all our hav'ns and ports, and creeks, it hinders and retards the importation of our richest Marchandize, Truth: nay it was first establisht and put in practice by Antichristian malice and mystery on set purpose to extinguish, if it were possible, the light of Reformation, and to settle falshood; little differing from that policie wherewith the Turk upholds his *Alcoran,* by the prohibition of Printing. 'Tis not deny'd, but gladly confest, we are to send our thanks and vows to heav'n, louder then most of Nations, for that great measure of truth which we enjoy, especially in those main points between us and the Pope, with his appertinences the Prelats: but he who thinks we are to pitch our tent here, and have attain'd the utmost prospect of reformation, that the mortall glasse wherein we contemplate, can shew us, till we come to *beatific* vision, that man by this very opinion declares, that he is yet farre short of Truth.

Truth indeed came once into the world with her divine Master, and was a perfect shape most glorious to look on: but when he ascended, and his Apostles after him were laid asleep, then strait arose a wicked race of deceivers, who as that story goes of the *Aegyptian Typhon* with his conspirators, how they dealt with the good *Osiris,* took the virgin Truth, hewd her lovely form into a thousand peeces, and scatter'd them to the four winds. From that time ever since, the sad friends of Truth, such as durst appear, imitating the carefull search that *Isis* made for the mangl'd body of *Osiris,* went up and down gathering up limb by limb still as they could find them. We have not yet found them all, Lords and Commons, nor ever shall doe, till her Masters second comming; he shall bring together every joynt and member, and shall mould them into an immortall feature of lovelines and perfection. Suffer not these licencing prohibitions to stand at every place of opportunity forbidding and disturbing them that continue seeking, that continue to do our obsequies to the torn body of our martyr'd Saint. We boast our light; but if we look not wisely on the Sun it self, it smites us into darknes. Who can discern those planets that are oft *Combust,*[46] and those stars of brightest magnitude that rise and set with the Sun, untill the opposite motion of their orbs bring them to such a place in the firmament, where they may be seen evning or morning. The light which we have gain'd, was giv'n us, not to be ever staring on, but by it to discover onward things more remote from our knowledge. It is not the unfrocking of a Priest, the unmitring of a Bishop, and the removing him from off the *Presbyter-*

---

46. Technical astronomical term for a planet orbiting near the sun.

*ian* shoulders that will make us a happy Nation, no, if other things as great in the Church, and in the rule of life both economicall and po- liticall be not lookt into and reform'd, we have lookt so long upon the blaze that *Zuinglius* and *Calvin* hath beacon'd up to us, that we are stark blind. There be who perpetually complain of schisms and sects, and make it such a calamity that any man dissents from their maxims. 'Tis their own pride and ignorance which causes the disturbing, who neither will hear with meeknes, nor can convince, yet all must be sup- prest which is not found in their *Syntagma*.[47] They are the troublers, they are the dividers of unity, who neglect and permit not others to unite those dissever'd peeces which are yet wanting to the body of Truth. To be still searching what we know not, by what we know, still closing up truth to truth as we find it (for all her body is *homo- geneal,* and proportionall) this is the golden rule in *Theology* as well as in Arithmetick, and makes up the best harmony in a Church; not the forc't and outward union of cold, and neutrall, and inwardly di- vided minds.

Lords and Commons of England, consider what Nation it is wherof ye are, and wherof ye are the governours: a Nation not slow and dull, but of a quick, ingenious, and piercing spirit, acute to in- vent, suttle and sinewy to discours, not beneath the reach of any point the highest that human capacity can soar to. Therefore the studies of learning in her deepest Sciences have bin so ancient, and so eminent among us, that Writers of good antiquity, and ablest judgement have bin perswaded that ev'n the school of *Pythagoras,* and the *Persian* wis- dom took beginning from the old Philosophy of this Iland. And that wise and civill Roman, *Julius Agricola,*[48] who govern'd once here for *Caesar,* preferr'd the naturall wits of Britain, before the labour'd stud- ies of the French. Nor is it for nothing that the grave and frugal *Tran- silvanian* sends out yearly from as farre as the mountanous borders of

47. Systematic treatise.
48. Julius Agricola was proconsul in Britain from A.D. 78 to 85.

*Russia,* and beyond the *Hercynian* wildernes, not their youth, but their stay'd men, to learn our language, and our *theologic* arts. Yet that which is above all this, the favour and the love of heav'n we have great argument to think in a peculiar manner propitious and propending towards us. Why else was this Nation chos'n before any other, that out of her as out of *Sion* should be proclam'd and sounded forth the first tidings and trumpet of Reformation to all *Europ.* And had it not bin the obstinat perversnes of our Prelats against the divine and admirable spirit of *Wicklef,* to suppresse him as a schismatic and *innovator,* perhaps neither the *Bohemian Husse* and *Jerom,*[49] no nor the name of *Luther,* or of *Calvin* had bin ever known: the glory of reforming all our neighbours had bin compleatly ours. But now, as our obdurat Clergy have with violence demean'd the matter, we are become hitherto the latest and the backwardest Schollers, of whom God offer'd to have made us the teachers. Now once again by all concurrence of signs, and by the generall instinct of holy and devout men, as they daily and solemnly express their thoughts, God is decreeing to begin some new and great period in his Church, ev'n to the reforming of Reformation it self: what does he then but reveal Himself to his servants, and as his manner is, first to his English-men; I say as his manner is, first to us, though we mark not the method of his counsels, and are unworthy. Behold now this vast City; a City of refuge, the mansion house of liberty, encompast and surrounded with his protection; the shop of warre hath not there more anvils and hammers waking, to fashion out the plates and instruments of armed Justice in defence of beleaguer'd Truth, then there be pens and heads there, sitting by their studious lamps, musing, searching, revolving new notions and idea's wherewith to present, as with their homage and their fealty the approaching Reformation: others as fast reading, trying all things, assenting to the force of reason and convincement. What could a man require more from a Nation so pliant and so prone

49. Jerome of Prague was a supporter of the proto-Protestant Huss and a student of the writings of Wycliff. He was burned at the stake in 1416.

to seek after knowledge. What wants there to such a towardly and pregnant soile, but wise and faithfull labourers, to make a knowing people, a Nation of Prophets, of Sages, and of Worthies. We reck'n more then five months yet to harvest; there need not be five weeks, had we but eyes to lift up, the fields are white already. Where there is much desire to learn, there of necessity will be much arguing, much writing, many opinions; for opinion in good men is but knowledge in the making. Under these fantastic terrors of sect and schism, we wrong the earnest and zealous thirst after knowledge and under-standing which God hath stirr'd up in this City. What some lament of, we rather should rejoyce at, should rather praise this pious for-wardnes among men, to reassume the ill deputed care of their Reli-gion into their own hands again. A little generous prudence, a little forbearance of one another, and som grain of charity might win all these diligences to joyn, and unite into one generall and brotherly search after Truth; could we but forgoe this Prelaticall tradition of crowding free consciences and Christian liberties into canons and precepts of men. I doubt not, if some great and worthy stranger should come among us, wise to discern the mould and temper of a people, and how to govern it, observing the high hopes and aims, the diligent alacrity of our extended thoughts and reasonings in the pursuance of truth and freedom, but that he would cry out as *Pirrhus*[50] did, ad-miring the Roman docility and courage, if such were my *Epirots,* I would not despair the greatest design that could be attempted to make a Church or Kingdom happy. Yet these are the men cry'd out against for schismaticks and sectaries; as if, while the Temple of the Lord was building, some cutting, some squaring the marble, others hewing the cedars, there should be a sort of irrationall men who could not consider there must be many schisms and many dissections made in the quarry and in the timber, ere the house of God can be built. And when every stone is laid artfully together, it cannot be united into a continuity, it can but be contiguous in this world; nei-

50. Pyrrhus, king of Epirus (318–272 B.C.).

ther can every peece of the building be of one form; nay rather the perfection consists in this, that out of many moderat varieties and brotherly dissimilitudes that are not vastly disproportionall arises the goodly and the gracefull symmetry that commends the whole pile and structure. Let us therefore be more considerat builders, more wise in spirituall architecture, when great reformation is expected. For now the time seems come, wherein *Moses* the great Prophet may sit in heav'n rejoycing to see that memorable and glorious wish of his fulfill'd, when not only our sev'nty Elders, but all the Lords people are become Prophets.[51] No marvell then though some men, and some good men too perhaps, but young in goodnesse, as *Joshua* then was, envy them. They fret, and out of their own weaknes are in agony, lest these divisions and subdivisions will undoe us. The adversarie again applauds, and waits the hour, when they have brancht themselves out, saith he, small anough into parties and partitions, then will be our time. Fool! he sees not the firm root, out of which we all grow, though into branches: nor will beware untill he see our small divided maniples cutting through at every angle of his ill united and unweildy brigade. And that we are to hope better of all these supposed sects and schisms, and that we shall not need that solicitude honest perhaps though over timorous of them that vex in this behalf, but shall laugh in the end, at those malicious applauders of our differences, I have these reasons to perswade me.

First, when a City shall be as it were besieg'd and blockt about, her navigable river infested, inrodes and incursions round, defiance and battell oft rumor'd to be marching up ev'n to her walls, and suburb trenches, that then the people, or the greater part, more then at other times, wholly tak'n up with the study of highest and most important matters to be reform'd, should be disputing, reasoning, reading, inventing, discoursing, ev'n to a rarity, and admiration, things not before discourst or writt'n of, argues first a singular good will,

51. Num. 11:29.

contentednesse and confidence in your prudent foresight, and safe government, Lords and Commons; and from thence derives it self to a gallant bravery and well grounded contempt of their enemies, as if there were no small number of as great spirits among us, as his was, who when Rome was nigh besieg'd by *Hanibal,* being in the City, bought that peece of ground at no cheap rate, whereon *Hanibal* himself encampt his own regiment.[52] Next it is a lively and cherfull presage of our happy successe and victory. For as in a body, when the blood is fresh, the spirits pure and vigorous, not only to vital, but to rationall faculties, and those in the acutest, and the pertest operations of wit and suttlety, it argues in what good plight and constitution the body is, so when the cherfulnesse of the people is so sprightly up, as that it has, not only wherewith to guard well its own freedom and safety, but to spare, and to bestow upon the solidest and sublimest points of controversie, and new invention, it betok'ns us not degenerated, nor drooping to a fatall decay, but casting off the old and wrincl'd skin of corruption to outlive these pangs and wax young again, entring the glorious waies of Truth and prosperous vertue destin'd to become great and honourable in these latter ages. Methinks I see in my mind a noble and puissant Nation rousing herself like a strong man after sleep, and shaking her invincible locks: Methinks I see her as an Eagle muing her mighty youth, and kindling her undazl'd eyes at the full midday beam; purging and unscaling her long abused sight at the fountain itself of heav'nly radiance; while the whole noise of timorous and flocking birds, with those also that love the twilight, flutter about, amaz'd at what she means, and in their envious gabble would prognosticat a year of sects and schisms.

What should ye doe then, should ye suppresse all this flowry crop of knowledge and new light sprung up and yet springing daily in this City, should ye set an *Oligarchy* of twenty ingrossers over it, to bring a famin upon our minds again, when we shall know nothing but what

52. This story of Hannibal is told in Livy's *Roman History.*

is measur'd to us by their bushel? Beleeve it, Lords and Commons, they who counsell ye to such a suppressing, doe as good as bid ye suppresse your selves; and I will soon shew how. If it be desir'd to know the immediat cause of all this free writing and free speaking, there cannot be assign'd a truer then your own mild, and free, and human government; it is the liberty, Lords and Commons, which your own valorous and happy counsels have purchast us, liberty which is the nurse of all great wits; this is that which hath rarify'd and enlightn'd our spirits like the influence of heav'n; this is that which hath enfranchis'd, enlarg'd and lifted up our apprehensions degrees above themselves. Ye cannot make us now lesse capable, lesse knowing, lesse eagarly pursuing of the truth, unlesse ye first make your selves, that made us so, lesse the lovers, lesse the founders of our true liberty. We can grow ignorant again, brutish, formall, and slavish, as ye found us; but you then must first become that which ye cannot be, oppressive, arbitrary, and tyrannous, as they were from whom ye have free'd us. That our hearts are now more capacious, our thoughts more erected to the search and expectation of greatest and exactest things, is the issue of your owne vertu propagated in us; ye cannot suppresse that unlesse ye reinforce an abrogated and mercilesse law, that fathers may dispatch at will their own children. And who shall then stick closest to ye, and excite others? not he who takes up armes for cote and conduct, and his four nobles of Danegelt.[53] Although I dispraise not the defence of just immunities, yet love my peace better, if that were all. Give me the liberty to know, to utter, and to argue freely according to conscience, above all liberties.

What would be best advis'd then, if it be found so hurtfull and so unequall to suppresse opinions for the newnes, or the unsutablenes to a customary acceptance, will not be my task to say; I only shall repeat what I have learnt from one of your own honourable number, a right noble and pious Lord, who had he not sacrific'd his life and fortunes

53. Originally a tax used to buy off Danish invaders and was later under the Norman kings a land tax.

to the Church and Commonwealth, we had not now mist and be-wayl'd a worthy and undoubted patron of this argument. Ye know him I am sure; yet I for honours sake, and may it be eternall to him, shall name him, the Lord *Brook*.[54] He writing of Episcopacy, and by the way treating of sects and schisms, left Ye his vote, or rather now the last words of his dying charge, which I know will ever be of dear and honour'd regard with Ye, so full of meeknes and breathing char-ity, that next to his last testament, who bequeath'd love and peace to his Disciples, I cannot call to mind where I have read or heard words more mild and peacefull. He there exhorts us to hear with patience and humility those, however they be miscall'd, that desire to live purely, in such a use of Gods Ordinances, as the best guidance of their conscience gives them, and to tolerat them, though in some discon-formity to our selves. The book it self will tell us more at large being publisht to the world, and dedicated to the Parlament by him who both for his life and for his death deserves, that what advice he left be not laid by without perusall.

And now the time in speciall is, by priviledge to write and speak what may help to the furder discussing of matters in agitation. The Temple of *Janus* with his two *controversal* faces might now not un-significantly be set open. And though all the windes of doctrin were let loose to play upon the earth, so Truth be in the field, we do inju-riously by licencing and prohibiting to misdoubt her strength. Let her and Falshood grapple; who ever knew Truth put to the wors, in a free and open encounter. Her confuting is the best and surest sup-pressing. He who hears what praying there is for light and clearer knowledge to be sent down among us, would think of other matters to be constituted beyond the discipline of *Geneva*, fram'd and fabric't already to our hands. Yet when the new light which we beg for shines in upon us, there be who envy, and oppose, if it come not first in at their casements. What a collusion is this, whenas we are exhorted by

54. Lord Brook was the author of *A Discourse on the Nature of that Episcopacie Which is Exercised in England* (1641).

the wise man to use diligence, *to seek for wisdom as for hidd'n treasures*[55] early and late, that another order shall enjoyn us to know nothing but by statute. When a man hath bin labouring the hardest labour in the deep mines of knowledge, hath furnisht out his findings in all their equipage, drawn forth his reasons as it were a battell raung'd, scatter'd and defeated all objections in his way, calls out his adversary into the plain, offers him the advantage of wind and sun, if he please; only that he may try the matter by dint of argument, for his opponents then to sculk, to lay ambushments, to keep a narrow bridge of licencing where the challenger should passe, though it be valour anough in shouldier-ship, is but weaknes and cowardise in the wars of Truth. For who knows not that Truth is strong next to the Almighty; she needs no policies, nor stratagems, nor licencings to make her victorious, those are the shifts and the defences that error uses against her power: give her but room, & do not bind her when she sleeps, for then she speaks not true, as the old *Proteus* did, who spake oracles only when he was caught & bound, but then rather she turns herself into all shapes, ex-cept her own, and perhaps tunes her voice according to the time, as *Micaiah* did before *Ahab*,[56] untill she be adjur'd into her own likenes. Yet is it not impossible that she may have more shapes then one. What else is all that rank of things indifferent, wherein Truth may be on this side, or on the other, without being unlike her self. What but a vain shadow else is the abolition of *those ordinances, that hand writing nayl'd to the crosse,* what great purchase is this Christian liberty which *Paul* so often boasts of.[57] His doctrine is, that he who eats or eats not, re-gards a day, or regards it not, may doe either to the Lord. How many other things might be tolerated in peace, and left to conscience, had we but charity, and were it not the chief strong hold of our hypocrisie to be ever judging one another. I fear yet this iron yoke of outward

55. This quotation is similar to Prov. 8:11.

56. In 1 Kings 22:23 the prophet Micaiah for a time joins in the lies of Ahab's court seers before exposing them.

57. Allusions to Col. 2:14; Gal. 5:1; followed by a paraphrase of Rom. 14:6, which begins at "Truth may be on this side. . . ."

conformity hath left a slavish print upon our necks; the ghost of a lin-
nen decency yet haunts us. We stumble and are impatient at the least
dividing of one visible congregation from another, though it be not
in fundamentalls; and through our forwardnes to suppresse, and our
backwardnes to recover any enthrall'd peece of truth out of the gripe
of custom, we care not to keep truth separated from truth, which is
the fiercest rent and disunion of all. We doe not see that while we still
affect by all means a rigid externall formality, we may as soon fall again
into a grosse conforming stupidity, a stark and dead congealment of
*wood and hay and stubble*[58] forc't and frozen together, which is more
to the sudden degenerating of a Church then many *subdichotomies* of
petty schisms. Not that I can think well of every light separation, or
that all in a Church is to be expected *gold and silver and pretious stones:*
it is not possible for man to sever the wheat from the tares,[59] the good
fish from the other frie; that must be the Angels Ministery at the end
of mortall things. Yet if all cannot be of one mind, as who looks they
should be? this doubtles is more wholsome, more prudent, and more
Christian that many be tolerated, rather then all compell'd. I mean
not tolerated Popery, and open superstition, which as it extirpats all
religions and civill supremacies, so it self should be extirpat, provided
first that all charitable and compassionat means be us'd to win and regain the weak and the misled: that also which is impious or evil absolutely either against faith or maners no law can possibly permit, that
intends not to unlaw it self: but those neighboring differences, or
rather indifferences, are what I speak of, whether in some point of
doctrine or of discipline, which though they may be many, yet need
not interrupt *the unity of Spirit,* if we could but find among us *the bond
of peace.*[60] In the mean while if any one would write, and bring his
helpfull hand to the slow-moving Reformation which we labour under, if Truth have spok'n to him before others, or but seem'd at least

58. I Cor. 3:12.
59. Matt. 13:24–30.
60. Eph. 4:3.

to speak, who hath so bejesuited us that we should trouble that man with asking licence to doe so worthy a deed? and not consider this, that if it come to prohibiting, there is not ought more likely to be prohibited then truth it self; whose first appearance to our eyes blear'd and dimm'd with prejudice and custom, is more unsightly and unplausible then many errors, ev'n as the person is of many a great man slight and contemptible to see to. And what doe they tell us vainly of new opinions, when this very opinion of theirs, that none must be heard, but whom they like, is the worst and newest opinion of all others; and is the chief cause why sects and schisms doe so much abound, and true knowledge is kept at distance from us; besides yet a greater danger which is in it. For when God shakes a Kingdome with strong and healthfull commotions to a generall reforming, 'tis not untrue that many sectaries and false teachers are then busiest in seducing; but yet more true it is, that God then raises to his own work men of rare abilities, and more then common industry not only to look back and revise what hath bin taught heretofore, but to gain furder and goe on, some new enlightn'd steps in the discovery of truth. For such is the order of Gods enlightning his Church, to dispense and deal out by degrees his beam, so as our earthly eyes may best sustain it. Neither is God appointed and confin'd, where and out of what place these his chosen shall be first heard to speak; for he sees not as man sees, chooses not as man chooses, lest we should devote our selves again to set places, and assemblies, and outward callings of men; planting our faith one while in the old Convocation house, and another while in the Chappell at Westminster; when all the faith and religion that shall be there canoniz'd, is not sufficient without plain convincement, and the charity of patient instruction to supple the least bruise of conscience, to edifie the meanest Christian, who desires to walk in the Spirit, and not in the letter of human trust, for all the number of voices that can be there made; no though *Harry* the 7. himself there, with all his leige tombs about him, should lend them voices from the dead, to swell their number. And if the men be erroneous who appear to be the leading schismaticks, what witholds us but our sloth, our self-will, and distrust in the right cause, that we doe not give them gentle meetings and gentle dismissions, that we debate not and examin the matter throughly with liberall and frequent audience; if not for their sakes, yet for our own? seeing no man who hath tasted learning, but will confesse the many waies of profiting by those who not contented with stale receits are able to manage, and set forth new positions to the world. And were they but as the dust and cinders of our feet, so long as in that notion they may yet serve to polish and brighten the armoury of Truth, ev'n for that respect they were not utterly to be cast away. But if they be of those whom God hath fitted for the speciall use of these times with eminent and ample gifts, and those perhaps neither among the Priests, nor among the Pharisees, and we in the hast of a precipitant zeal shall make no distinction, but resolve to stop their mouths, because we fear they come with new and dangerous opinions, as we commonly forejudge them ere we understand them, no lesse then woe to us, while thinking thus to defend the Gospel, we are found the persecutors.

There have bin not a few since the beginning of this Parlament, both of the Presbytery and others who by their unlicenc't books to the contempt of an *Imprimatur* first broke that triple ice clung about our hearts, and taught the people to see day: I hope that none of those were the perswaders to renew upon us this bondage which they themselves have wrought so much good by contemning. But if neither the check that *Moses* gave to young *Joshua,* nor the countermand which our Saviour gave to young *John,*[61] who was so ready to prohibit those whom he thought unlicenc't, be not anough to admonish our Elders how unacceptable to God their testy mood of prohibiting is, if neither their own remembrance what evill hath abounded in the Church by this lett of licencing, and what good they themselves have begun by transgressing it, be not anough, but that they will perswade, and execute the most *Dominican* part of the Inquisition over us, and are already with one foot in the stirrup so active at suppressing, it would

61. Num. 11:29 and Luke 9:50.

be no unequall distribution in the first place to suppresse the suppressors themselves; whom the change of their condition hath puft up, more then their late experience of harder times hath made wise.

And as for regulating the Presse, let no man think to have the honour of advising ye better then your selves have done in that Order publisht next before this, that no book be Printed, unlesse the Printers and the Authors name, or at least the Printers be register'd. Those which otherwise come forth, if they be found mischievous and libellous, the fire and the executioner will be the timeliest and the most effectuall remedy, that mans prevention can use. For this *authentic* Spanish policy of licencing books, if I have said ought, will prove the most unlicenc't book it self within a short while; and was the immediat image of a Star-chamber decree to that purpose made in those very times when that Court did the rest of those her pious works, for which she is now fall'n from the Starres with *Lucifer*. Whereby ye may guesse what kinde of State prudence, what love of the people, what care of Religion, or good manners there was at the contriving, although with singular hypocrisie it pretended to bind books to their good behaviour. And how it got the upper hand of your precedent Order so well constituted before, if we may beleeve those men whose profession gives them cause to enquire most, it may be doubted there was in it the fraud of some old *patentees* and *monopolizers* in the trade of book-selling; who under pretence of the poor in their Company not to be defrauded, and the just retaining of each man his severall copy, which God forbid should be gainsaid, brought divers glosing colours to the House, which were indeed but colours, and serving to no end except it be to exercise a superiority over their neighbours, men who doe not therefore labour in an honest profession to which learning is indetted, that they should be made other mens vassals. Another end is thought was aym'd at by some of them in procuring by petition this Order, that having power in their hands, malignant books might the easier scape abroad, as the event shews. But of these *Sophisms* and *Elenchs*[62] of marchandize I skill not: This I know, that

---

62. *Elench* is a term of art in logic for a refutation.

errors in a good government and in a bad are equally almost incident; for what Magistrate may not be mis-inform'd, and much the sooner, if liberty of Printing be reduc't into the power of a few; but to re-dresse willingly and speedily what hath bin err'd, and in highest autority to esteem a plain advertisement more then others have done a sumptuous bribe, is a vertue (honour'd Lords and Commons) answerable to Your highest actions, and whereof none can participat but greatest and wisest men.

*The End.*

# THE TENURE OF KINGS
# AND MAGISTRATES

*The first edition of* The Tenure of Kings and Magistrates *was published in February 1648, a second in February 1649. From the argument itself one can perceive easily enough the political stimulus that impelled Milton to write the tract. Milton envisions two opponents: on the one hand, those who would blame the parliamentary forces for having taken up arms against their legitimate king; on the other hand, those (generally Presbyterians) who, having stood against Charles initially, experienced misgivings subsequently and drew back from executing the defeated monarch. Against the first, Milton, employing a very broad survey of authors who defended the justice of opposing and of killing bad rulers, draws upon classical authorities and Christian writers. Against the rebels who turned back at the point of regicide Milton conducts a much more circumstantial argument that turns upon several contested issues attached to particular events during the Civil War. The chief of these events were the negotiations conducted between Charles and the Presbyterian faction in Parliament that resulted in the king's subscribing to the Presbyterian concept of church government embodied in their "covenant." The resultant softening of Presbyterian opposition to Charles, Milton along with other Independents interpreted as a bid on the part of Presbyterians to make a separate peace for the benefit of their sect and for the purpose of combating the rising influence of Independents who found their strength in the army.*

# THE TENURE OF KINGS AND MAGISTRATES:

Proving, That It Is Lawfull, and Hath Been Held
So Through All Ages, for Any, Who Have the Power,
to Call to Account a Tyrant, or Wicked King, and After
Due Conviction, to Depose, and Put Him to Death;
If the Ordinary Magistrate Have Neglected,
or Deny'd to Doe It

If men within themselves would be govern'd by reason, and not
generally give up thir understanding to a double tyrannie, of Custom from without, and blind affections within, they would dis-
cerne better, what it is to favour and uphold the Tyrant of a Nation.
But being slaves within doors, no wonder that they strive so much to
have the public State conformably govern'd to the inward vitious rule,
by which they govern themselves. For indeed none can love freedom
heartilie, but good men; the rest love not freedom, but licence; which
never hath more scope or more indulgence then under Tyrants. Hence
is it that Tyrants are not oft offended, nor stand much in doubt of bad
men, as being all naturally servile; but in whom vertue and true worth
most is eminent, them they feare in earnest, as by right thir Maisters,
against them lies all thir hatred and suspicion. Consequentlie neither
doe bad men hate Tyrants, but have been alwayes readiest with the
falsifi'd names of *Loyalty,* and *Obedience,* to colour over thir base com-
pliances. And although somtimes for shame, and when it comes to
thir owne grievances, of purse especially, they would seeme good
Patriots, and side with the better cause, yet when others for the deliverance of thir Countrie, endu'd with fortitude and Heroick vertue
to feare nothing but the curse writt'n against those *That doe the worke*

*of the Lord negligently,*[1] would goe on to remove, not only the calamities and thraldoms of a People, but the roots and causes whence they spring, streight these men,[2] and sure helpers at need, as if they hated only the miseries but not the mischiefs, after they have juggl'd and palter'd with the world, bandied and born armes against thir King, devested him, disannointed him, nay curs'd him all over in thir Pulpits and thir Pamphlets, to the ingaging of sincere and real men, beyond what is possible or honest to retreat from, not only turne revolters from those principles, which only could at first move them, but lay the staine of disloyaltie, and worse, on those proceedings, which are the necessary consequences of thir own former actions; nor dislik'd by themselves, were they manag'd to the intire advantages of thir own Faction;[3] not considering the while that he toward whom they boasted thir new fidelitie, counted them accessory; and by those Statutes and Lawes which they so impotently brandish against others, would have doom'd them to a Traytors death, for what they have don alreadie. 'T is true, that most men are apt anough to civill Wars and commotions as a noveltie, and for a flash hot and active; but through sloth or inconstancie, and weakness of spirit either fainting, ere thir own pretences, though never so just, be half attain'd, or through an inbred falshood and wickednes, betray oft times to destruction with themselves, men of noblest temper joyn'd with them for causes, whereof they in their rash undertakings were not capable.

If God and a good cause give them Victory, the prosecution whereof for the most part, inevitably draws after it the alteration of Lawes, change of Goverment, downfal of Princes with thir families; then comes the task to those Worthies which are the soule of that enterprize, to be swett and labour'd out amidst the throng and noises of Vulgar and irrational men. Some contesting for privileges, cus-

---

1. Jer. 48:10.

2. With the phrase "streight these men," Milton refers to the Presbyterian faction.

3. The Presbyterians sought to win over Charles I to favor their sect against the Independents. Once they had gained the king's assent, the Presbyterians began to urge leniency for the defeated monarch.

---

toms, forms, and that old entanglement of Iniquity, thir gibrish Lawes, though the badge of thir ancient slavery. Others who have beene fiercest against thir Prince, under the notion of a Tryant, and no mean incendiaries of the Warr against him, when God out of his providence and high disposal hath deliver'd him into the hand of thir brethren, on a suddain and in a new garbe of Allegiance, which thir doings have long since cancell'd; they plead for him, pity him, extoll him, protest against those that talk of bringing him to the tryal of Justice, which is the Sword of God, superior to all mortal things, in whose hand soever by apparent signes his testified will is to put it. But certainly if we consider who and what they are, on a suddain grown so pitifull, wee may conclude, thir pitty can be no true, and Christian commiseration, but either levitie and shallowness of minde, or else a carnal admiring of that worldly pomp and greatness, from whence they see him fall'n; or rather lastly a dissembl'd and seditious pity, fain'd of industry to begett new discord. As for mercy, if it be to a Tyrant, under which Name they themselves have cited him so oft in the hearing of God, of Angels, and the holy Church assembl'd, and there charg'd him with the spilling of more innocent blood by farr, then ever *Nero* did, undoubtedly the mercy which they pretend, is the mercy of wicked men; and their mercies, wee read are cruelties; hazarding the welfare of a whole Nation, to have sav'd one, whom so oft they have tearm'd *Agag,*[4] and vilifying the blood of many *Jonathans,* that have sav'd *Israel;* insisting with much niceness on the unnecessariest clause of thir Covnant wrested, wherein the feare of change, and the absurd contradiction of a flattering hostilitie had hamperd them, but not scrupling to give away for complements, to an implacable revenge, the heads of many thousand Christians more.

Another sort there is, who comming in the cours of these affaires, to have thir share in great actions, above the form of Law or Custom, at least to give thir voice and approbation, begin to swerve, and almost shiver at the Majesty and grandeur of som noble deed, as if they

4.   1 Sam. 15:33. At the command of God, Samuel hacked to death Agag, the Amalekite king, when the disobedient Saul hesitated to slay the leader himself.

were newly enter'd into a great sin; disputing presidents, forms, and circumstances, when the Commonwealth nigh perishes for want of deeds in substance, don with just and faithfull expedition. To these I wish better instruction, and vertue equal to thir calling; the former of which, that is to say Instruction, I shall indeavour, as my dutie is, to bestow on them; and exhort them not to startle from the just and pious resolution of adhering with all thir strength & assistance to the present Parlament & Army, in the glorious way wherein Justice and Victory hath set them; the only warrants through all ages, next under immediat Revelation, to exercise supream power, in those proceedings which hitherto appeare equal to what hath been don in any age or Nation heretofore, justly or magnanimouslie. Nor let them be discourag'd or deterr'd by any new Apostate Scarcrowes, who under show of giving counsel, send out their barking monitories and *memento's,* empty of ought else but the spleene of a frustrated Faction. For how can that pretended counsel bee either sound or faithfull, when they that give it, see not for madness and vexation of thir ends lost, that those Statutes and Scriptures which both falsly and scandalously, they wrest against thir Friends and Associates, would by sentence of the common adversarie, fall first and heaviest upon thir own heads. Neither let milde and tender dispositions be foolishly softn'd from thir duty and perseverance, with the unmaskuline Rhetorick of any puling Priest or Chaplain, sent as a friendly Letter of advice, for fashion sake in privat, and forthwith publisht by the Sender himself, that wee may know how much of friend there was in it, to cast an odious envie upon them, to whom it was pretended to be sent in charitie. Nor let any man be deluded by either the ignorance or the notorious hypocrisie and self-repugnance of our dancing Divines, who have the conscience and the boldness, to come with Scripture in thir mouthes, gloss'd and fitted for thir turnes with a double contradictory sense, transforming the sacred verity of God, to an Idol with two Faces, looking at once two several ways; and with the same quotations to charge others, which in the same case they made serve to justifie themselves. For while the hope to bee made Classic and

Provincial Lords[5] led them on, while pluralities greas'd them thick and deep, to the shame and scandal of Religion, more then all the Sects and Heresies they exclaim against, then to fight against the Kings person, and no less a Party of his Lords and Commons, or to put force upon both the Houses, was good, was lawfull, was no resisting of Superior powers; they onely were powers not to be resisted, who countenanc'd the good, and punish't the evil. But now that thir censorious domineering is not suffer'd to be universal, truth and conscience to be freed, Tithes and Pluralities to be no more, though competent allowance provided, and the warme experience of large gifts, and they so good at taking them; yet now to exclude & seize upon impeach't Members, to bring Delinquents without exemption to a faire Tribunal by the common National Law against murder, is now to be no less then *Corah, Dathan,* and *Abiram.*[6] He who but erewhile in the Pulpits was a cursed Tyrant, an enemie to God and Saints, lad'n with all the innocent blood spilt in three Kingdoms, and so to be fought against, is now, though nothing penitent or alter'd from his first principles, a lawful Magistrate, a Sovran Lord, the Lords anointed, not to be touch'd, though by themselves imprison'd. As if this onely were obedience, to preserve the meere useless bulke of his person, and that onely in prison, not in the field, and to disobey his commands, deny him his dignity and office, every where to resist his power but where they thinke it onely surviving in thir own faction.

But who in particular is a Tyrant cannot be determin'd in a general discours, otherwise then by supposition; his particular charge, and the sufficient proof of it must determin that: which I leave to Magistrates, at least to the uprighter sort of them, and of the people, though in number less by many, in whom faction least hath prevaild above the Law of nature and right reason, to judge as they find cause. But this I dare owne as part of my faith, that if such a one there be,

5. Milton here refers to a provision of the Presbyterian-dominated Westminster Assembly that would have divided England into provinces and subdivided these into "classical assemblies," or "classes."

6. Three rebel Levites who suffered divine punishment for having defied Moses.

by whose Commission, whole massachers have been committed on his faithfull Subjects, his Provinces offered to pawn or alienation, as the hire of those whom he had sollicited to come in and destroy whole Citties and Countries; be he King, or Tyrant, or Emperour, the Sword of Justice is above him; in whose hand soever is found sufficient power to avenge the effusion, and so great a deluge of innocent blood. For if all human power to execute, not accidentally but intendedly, the wrath of God upon evil doers without exception, be of God; then that power, whether ordinary, or if that faile, extraordinary so executing that intent of God, is lawfull, and not to be resisted. But to unfold more at large this whole Question, though with all expedient brevity, I shall here set downe from first beginning, the original of Kings; how and wherfore exalted to that dignitie above thir Brethren; and from thence shall prove, that turning to Tyranny they may bee as lawfully depos'd and punish'd, as they were at first elected: This I shall doe by autorities and reasons, not learnt in corners among Scisms and Heresies, as our doubling Divines are ready to calumniat, but fetch't out of the midst of choicest and most authentic learning, and no prohibited Authors, nor many Heathen, but Mosaical,[7] Christian, Orthodoxal, and which must needs be more convincing to our Adversaries, Presbyterial.

No man who knows ought, can be so stupid to deny that all men naturally were borne free, being the image and resemblance of God himself, and were by privilege above all the creatures, born to command[8] and not to obey: and that they liv'd so. Till from the root of *Adams* transgression, falling among themselves to doe wrong and violence, and foreseeing that such courses must needs tend to the destruction of them all, they agreed by common league to bind each other from mutual injury, and joyntly to defend themselves against any that gave disturbance or opposition to such agreement. Hence came Citties, Townes and Common-wealths. And because no faith in

7. The books of the Bible attributed to Moses (i.e., the books from Genesis through Deuteronomy).

8. Gen. 1:26.

all was found sufficiently binding, they saw it needfull to ordaine som authoritie, that might restrain by force and punishment what was violated against peace and common right. This autoritie and power of self-defence and preservation being originally and naturally in every one of them, and unitedly in them all, for ease, for order, and least each man should be his own partial Judge, they communicated and deriv'd either to one, whom for the eminence of his wisdom and integritie they chose above the rest, or to more then one whom they thought of equal deserving: the first was call'd a King; the other Magistrates. Not to be thir Lords and Maisters (though afterward those names in som places were giv'n voluntarily to such as had been Authors of inestimable good to the people) but, to be thir Deputies and Commissioners, to execute, by vertue of thir intrusted power, that justice which else every man by the bond of nature and of Cov'nant must have executed for himself, and for one another. And to him that shall consider well why among free Persons, one man by civil right should beare autority and jurisdiction over another, no other end or reason can be imaginable. These for a while govern'd well, and with much equity decided all things at thir own arbitrement: till the temptation of such a power left absolute in thir hands, perverted them at length to injustice and partialitie. Then did they who now by tryal had found the danger and inconveniences of committing arbitrary power to any, invent Laws either fram'd, or consented to by all, that should confine and limit the autority of whom they chose to govern them: that so man, of whose failing they had proof, might no more rule over them, but law and reason abstracted as much as might be from personal errors and frailties. While as the Magistrate was set above the people, so the Law was set above the Magistrate. When this would not serve, but that the Law was either not executed, or misapply'd, they were constrain'd from that time, the onely remedy left them, to put conditions and take Oaths from all Kings and Magistrates at thir first instalment to doe impartial justice by Law: who upon those termes and no other, receav'd Allegeance from the people, that is to say, bond or Covnant to obey them in execution of those Lawes which they the people had themselves made, or assented to. And this ofttimes with express warning, that if the King or Magistrate prov'd unfaithfull to his trust, the people would be disingag'd. They added also Counselors and Parlaments, nor to be onely at his beck, but with him or without him, at set times, or at all times, when any danger threatn'd to have care of the public safety. Therefore saith *Claudius Sesell* a French Statesman, *The Parliament was set as a bridle to the King;*[9] which I instance rather, not because our English Lawyers have not said the same long before, but because that French Monarchy is granted by all to be a farr more absolute then ours. That this and the rest of what hath hitherto been spok'n is most true, might be copiously made appeare throughout all Stories Heathen and Christian; ev'n of those Nations where Kings and Emperours have sought meanes to abolish all ancient memory of the Peoples right by thir encroachments and usurpations. But I spare long insertions, appealing to the known constitutions of both the latest Christian Empires in Europe, the Greek and German, besides the French, Italian, Arragonian, English, and not least the Scottish Histories: not forgetting this onely by the way, that *William* the Norman though a Conqueror, and not unsworn at his Coronation, was compell'd the second time to take oath at S. *Albanes,* ere the people would be brought to yeild obedience.

It being thus manifest that the power of Kings and Magistrates is nothing else, but what is only derivative, transferr'd and committed to them in trust from the People, to the Common good of them all, in whom the power yet remaines fundamentally, and cannot be tak'n from them, without a violation of thir natural birthright, and seeing that from hence *Aristotle* and the best of Political writers have defin'd a King, him who governs to the good and profit of his People, and not for his own ends, it follows from necessary causes, that the Titles of Sov'ran Lord, natural Lord, and the like, are either arrogancies, or flatteries, not admitted by Emperours and Kings of best note, and dislikt by the Church both of Jews, *Isai.* 26. 13. and ancient Christians,

9.   Claude de Seyssel, *La grant monarchie de France composée par missire Claude de Seyssel* (1519).

as appears by *Tertullian*[10] and others. Although generally the people of Asia, and with them the Jews also, especially since the time they chose a King against the advice and counsel of God, are noted by wise Authors much inclinable to slavery.

Secondly, that to say, as is usual, the King hath as good right to his Crown and dignitie, as any man to his inheritance, is to make the Subject no better then the Kings slave, his chattell, or his possession that may be bought and sould. And doubtless if hereditary title were sufficiently inquir'd, the best foundation of it would be found either but in courtesie or convenience. But suppose it to be of right hereditarie, what can be more just and legal, if a subject for certain crimes be to forfet by Law from himself, and posterity, all his inheritance to the King, then that a King for crimes proportional, should forfet all his title and inheritance to the people: unless the people must be thought created all for him, he not for them, and they all in one body inferior to him single, which were a kinde of treason against the dignitie of mankind to affirm.

Thirdly it follows, that to say Kings are accountable to none but God, is the overturning of all Law and government. For if they may refuse to give account, then all cov'nants made with them at Coronation; all Oathes are in vaine, and meer mockeries, all Lawes which they sweare to keep, made to no purpose; for if the King feare not God, as how many of them doe not? we hold then our lives and estates, by the tenure of his meer grace and mercy, as from a God, not a mortal Magistrate, a position that none but Court Parasites or men besotted would maintain. *Aristotle* therefore, whom we commonly allow for one of the best interpreters of nature and morality, writes in the fourth of his politics chap. 10. that Monarchy unaccountable, is the worst sort of Tyranny; and least of all to be endur'd by free born men. And surely no Christian Prince, not drunk with high mind, and prouder then those Pagan *Caesars* that deifi'd themselves, would arrogate so unreasonably above human condition, or derogate so basely

10. Tertullian was a third-century theologian who wrote a treatise on the vanity of earthly glories, including the pride of kings.

from a whole Nation of men his Brethren, as if for him only subsisting, and to serve his glory; valuing them in comparison of his owne brute will and pleasure, no more then so many beasts, or vermin under his Feet, not to be reasond with, but to be trod on; among whom there might be found so many thousand Men for wisdom, vertue, nobleness of mind, and all other respects, but the fortune of his dignity, farr above him. Yet some would perswade us, that this absurd opinion was King *Davids;* because in the 51 *Psalm* he cries out to God, *Against thee onely have I sinn'd;* as if *David* had imagin'd that to murder *Uriah* and adulterate his Wife, had bin no sinn against his Neighbour, when as that Law of *Moses* was to the King expresly, *Deut.* 17. not to think so highly of himself above his Brethren. *David* therfore by those words could mean no other, then either that the depth of his guiltiness was known to God onely, or to so few as had not the will or power to question him, or that the sin against God was greater beyond compare then against *Uriah.* Whatever his meaning were, any wise man will see that the pathetical words of a Psalme can be no certaine decision to a poynt that hath abundantly more certain rules to goe by. How much more rationally spake the Heathen King *Demophoon* in a Tragedy of *Euripides*[11] then these Interpreters would put upon King *David, I rule not my people by Tyranny, as if they were Barbarians, but am my self liable, if I doe unjustly, to suffer justly.* Not unlike was the speech of *Trajan* the worthy Emperor, to one whom he made General of his Praetorian Forces. Take this drawn sword, saith he, to use for me, if I reigne well, if not, to use against me. Thus *Dion*[12] relates. And not *Trajan* onely, but *Theodosius* the yonger, a Christian Emperor and one of the best, causd it to be enacted as a rule undenyable and fit to be acknowledg'd by all Kings and Emperors, that a Prince is bound to the Laws; that on the autority of Law the autority of a Prince depends, and to the Laws ought submitt. Which Edict of his remains yet in the *Code* of *Justinian. l.* 1. *tit.* 24. as a sacred constitution to all the succeeding Emperors. How then can any King

11. Euripides *Heraclidae* 418–21.
12. Dio Cassius *History of Rome* 68.16.

in Europe maintain and write himself accountable to none but God, when Emperors in thir own imperial Statutes have writt'n and decreed themselves accountable to Law. And indeed where such account is not fear'd, he that bids a man reigne over him above Law, may bid as well a savage Beast.

It follows lastly, that since the King or Magistrate holds his autoritie of the people, both originaly and naturally for their good in the first place, and not his own, then may the people as oft as they shall judge it for the best, either choose him or reject him, retaine him or depose him though no Tyrant, meerly by the liberty and right of free born Men, to be govern'd as seems to them best. This, though it cannot but stand with plain reason, shall be made good also by Scripture. *Deut.* 17. 14. *When thou art come into the Land which the Lord thy God giveth thee, and shalt say I will set a King over mee, like as all the Nations about mee.* These words confirme us that the right of choosing, yea of changing thir own Goverment is by the grant of God himself in the People. And therfore when they desir'd a King, though then under another form of goverment, and though thir changing displeas'd him, yet he that was himself thir King, and rejected by them, would not be a hindrance to what they intended, furder then by perswasion, but that they might doe therein as they saw good, 1 *Sam.* 8. onely he reserv'd to himself the nomination of who should reigne over them. Neither did that exempt the King, as if he were to God onely accountable, though by his especial command anointed. Therfore *David first made a Covnant with the Elders of Israel, and so was by them anointed King, 2 Sam. 5. 3. 1 Chron. 11.* And *Jehoiada* the Priest making *Jehoash* King, made a Cov'nant between him and the People, 2 *Kings* 11. 17. Therfore when *Roboam* at his comming to the Crown, rejected those conditions which the Israelites brought him, heare what they answer him, *What portion have we in David, or Inheritance in the son of Jesse? See to thine own House David.* And for the like conditions not perform'd, all Israel before that time depos'd *Samuel;* not for his own default, but for the misgoverment of his Sons. But som will say to both these examples, it was evilly don. I answer, that not the latter, because it was expressly allow'd them in the Law to set up a King if they pleas'd; and God himself joyn'd with them in the work; though in som sort it was at that time displeasing to him, in respect of old *Samuel* who had govern'd them uprightly. As *Livy* praises the Romans who took occasion from *Tarquinius* a wicked Prince to gaine thir libertie, which to have extorted, saith hee, from *Numa,* or any of the good Kings before, had not bin seasonable.[13] Nor was it in the former example don unlawfully; for when *Roboam* had prepar'd a huge Army to reduce the Israelites, he was forbidd'n by the Prophet,[14] 1 *Kings* 12. 24. *Thus saith the Lord yee shall not goe up, nor fight against your brethren, for this thing is from me.* He calls them thir Brethren, not Rebels, and forbidds to be proceeded against them, owning the thing himself, not by single providence, but by approbation, and that not onely of the act, as in the former example, but of the fit season also; he had not otherwise forbidd to molest them. And those grave and wise Counselors whom *Rehoboam* first advis'd with, spake no such thing, as our old gray headed Flatterers now are wont, stand upon your birth-right, scorn to capitulate, you hold of God, not of them; for they knew no such matter, unless conditionally, but gave him politic counsel, as in a civil transaction. Therfore Kingdom and Magistracy, whether supreme or subordinat, is without difference, call'd *a human ordinance,* 1 *Pet.* 2. 13. &c. which we are there taught is the will of God wee should alike submitt to, so farr as for the punishment of evil doers, and the encouragement of them that doe well. *Submitt* saith he, *as free men.* But to any civil power unaccountable, unquestionable, and not to be resisted, no not in wickedness, and violent actions, how can we submit as free men? *There is no power but of God,* saith *Paul, Rom.* 13. as much as to say, God put it into mans heart to find out that way at first for common peace and preservation, approving the exercise therof; els it contradicts *Peter* who calls the same autority an Ordinance of man. It must be also understood of lawfull and just power, els we read of great power in the affaires and Kingdoms of the

13. Livy *Roman History* bk. 2.
14. The prophet was Shemiah.

World permitted to the Devil: for saith he to Christ, *Luke 4. 6. All this power will I give thee and the glory of them, for it is deliver'd to me, & to whomsoever I will, I give it:* neither did he ly, or Christ gainsay what he affirm'd; for in the thirteenth of the *Revelation* wee read how the Dragon gave to the beast *his power, his seate, and great autority:* which beast so autoriz'd most expound to be the tyrannical powers and Kingdoms of the earth.[15] Therfore Saint *Paul* in the forecited Chapter tells us that such Magistrates he meanes, as are, not a terror to the good but to the evil; such as beare not the sword in vaine, but to punish offenders, and to encourage the good. If such onely be mentiond here as powers to be obeyd, and our submission to them onely requir'd, then doubtless those powers that doe the contrary, are no powers ordain'd of God, and by consequence no obligation laid upon us to obey or not to resist them. And it may bee well observd that both these Apostles, whenever they give this precept, express it in termes not *concrete* but *abstract,* as Logicians are wont to speake, that is, they mention the ordinance, the power, the autoritie before the persons that execute it; and what that power is, least we should be deceav'd, they describe exactly. So that if the power be not such, or the person execute not such power, neither the one nor the other is of God, but of the Devil, and by consequence to bee resisted. From this exposition *Chrysostome*[16] also on the same place dissents not; explaining that these words were not writt'n in behalf of a tyrant. And this is verify'd by *David,* himself a King, and likeliest to bee Author of the *Psalm 94. 20.* which saith *Shall the throne of iniquity have fellowship with thee?* And it were worth the knowing, since Kings in these dayes, and that by Scripture, boast the justness of thir title, by holding it immediately of God, yet cannot show the time when God ever set on the throne them or thir forefathers, but onely when the people chose them, why by the same reason, since God ascribes as oft to himself the casting down of Princes from the throne, it should not be thought as lawful, and as much from God, when none are seen to do it but the people,

15. Rev. 13:1–4.

16. Milton cites a homily of St. John Chrysostom.

and that for just causes. For if it needs must be a sin in them to depose, it may as likely be a sin to have elected. And contrary if the peoples act in election be pleaded by a King, as the act of God, and the most just title to enthrone him, why may not the peoples act of rejection, bee as well pleaded by the people as the act of God, and the most just reason to depose him? So that we see the title and just right of raigning or deposing, in reference to God, is found in Scripture to be all one; visible onely in the people, and depending meerly upon justice and demerit. Thus farr hath bin considerd briefly the power of Kings and Magistrates; how it was and is originally the peoples, and by them conferr'd in trust onely to bee imployed to the common peace and benefit; with liberty therfore and right remaining in them to reassume it to themselves, if by Kings or Magistrates it be abus'd; or to dispose of it by any alteration, as they shall judge most conducing to the public good.

Wee may from hence with more ease, and force of argument determin what a Tyrant is, and what the people may doe against him. A Tyrant whether by wrong or by right comming to the Crown, is he who regarding neither Law nor the common good, reigns onely for himself and his faction: Thus St. *Basil*[17] among others defines him. And because his power is great, his will boundless and exorbitant, the fulfilling whereof is for the most part accompanied with innumerable wrongs and oppressions of the people, murders, massachers, rapes, adulteries, desolation, and subversion of Citties and whole Provinces, look how great a good and happiness a just King is, so great a mischeife is a Tyrant; as hee the public father of his Countrie, so this the common enemie. Against whom what the people lawfully may doe, as against a common pest, and destroyer of mankinde, I suppose no man of cleare judgement need goe furder to be guided then by the very principles of nature in him. But because it is the vulgar folly of men to desert thir own reason, and shutting thir eyes to think they see best with other mens, I shall show by such examples as ought to have most waight with us, what hath bin don in this case heretofore.

17. St. Basil the Great, fourth-century bishop and theologian.

The *Greeks* and *Romans,* as thir prime Authors witness, held it not onely lawfull, but a glorious and Heroic deed, rewarded publicly with Statues and Garlands, to kill an infamous Tyrant at any time without tryal: and but reason, that he who trod down all Law, should not be voutsaf'd the benefit of Law. Insomuch that *Seneca* the Tragedian brings in *Hercules* the grand suppressor of Tryants, thus speaking,

> ——Victima haud ulla amplior
> Potest, magisque opima mactari Jovi
> Quam Rex iniquus——
> ——There can be slaine
> No sacrifice to God more acceptable
> Then an unjust and wicked King——

But of these I name no more, lest it bee objected they were Heathen; and come to produce another sort of men that had the knowledge of true Religion. Among the Jews this custom of tyrant-killing was not unusual. First *Ehud,* a man whom God had raysd to deliver Israel from *Eglon* King of *Moab,*[18] who had conquerd and rul'd over them eighteene years, being sent to him as an Ambassador with a present, slew him in his own house. But hee was a forren Prince, an enemie, and *Ehud* besides had special warrant from God. To the first I answer, it imports not whether forren or native: For no Prince so native but professes to hold by Law; which when he himself overturns, breaking all the Covnants and Oaths that gave him title to his dignity, and were the bond and alliance between him and his people, what differs he from an outlandish King, or from an enemie? For look how much right the King of *Spaine* hath to govern us at all, so much right hath the King of *England* to govern us tyrannically. If he, though not bound to us by any League, comming from *Spaine* in person to subdue us or to destroy us, might lawfully by the people of *England* either bee slaine in fight, or put to death in captivity, what hath a native King to plead, bound by so many Covnants, benefits and honours to

18. Judg. 3:14–16.

the welfare of his people, why he through the contempt of all Laws and Parlaments, the onely tie of our obedience to him, for his own wills sake, and a boasted prerogative unaccountable, after sev'n years warring and destroying of his best Subjects, overcom, and yeilded prisoner, should think to scape unquestionable, as a thing divine, in respect of whom so many thousand Christians destroy'd, should lie unaccounted for, polluting with their slaughterd carcasses all the Land over, and crying for vengeance against the living that should have righted them. Who knows not that there is a mutual bond of amity and brother-hood between man and man over all the World, neither is it the English Sea that can sever us from that duty and relation: a straiter bond yet there is between fellow-subjects, neighbours, and friends; But when any of these doe one to another so as hostility could doe no worse, what doth the Law decree less against them, then op'n enemies and invaders? or if the Law be not present, or too weake, what doth it warrant us to less then single defence, or civil warr? and from that time forward the Law of civil defensive warr differs nothing from the Law of forren hostility. Nor is it distance of place that makes enmitie, but enmity that makes distance. He therfore that keeps peace with me, neer or remote, of whatsoever Nation, is to mee as farr as all civil and human offices an Englishman and a neighbour: but if an Englishman forgetting all Laws, human, civil and religious, offend against life and liberty, to him offended and to the Law in his behalf, though born in the same womb, he is no better then a Turk, a Sarasin, a Heathen. This is Gospel, and this was ever Law among equals; how much rather then in force against any King whatever, who in respect of the people is confessed inferior and not equal: to distinguish therfore of a Tyrant by outlandish, or domestic is a weak evasion. To the second that he was an enemie, I answer, what Tyrant is not? yet *Eglon* by the Jewes had bin acknowledged as thir Sovran; they had serv'd him eighteen yeares, as long almost as we our *William* the Conqueror, in all which time he could not be so unwise a Statesman but to have tak'n of them Oaths of Fealty and Allegeance, by which they made themselves his proper Subjects, as thir homage and present sent by *Ehud* testify'd. To the third, that he had special warrant to kill *Eglon* in that manner, it cannot bee granted, because not expressd; tis plain that he was raysd by God to be a Deliverer, and went on just principles, such as were then and ever held allowable, to deale so by a Tyrant that could no otherwise be dealt with. Neither did *Samuel* though a Profet, with his own hand abstain from *Agag;* a forren enemie no doubt; but mark the reason. *As thy Sword hath made women childless;*[19] a cause that by the sentence of Law it self nullifies all relations. And as the Law is between Brother and Brother, Father and Son, Maister and Servant, wherfore not between King or rather Tyrant and People? And whereas *Jehu* had special command to slay *Jehoram*[20] a successive and hereditarie Tyrant, it seems not the less imitable for that; for where a thing grounded so much on natural reason hath the addition of a command from God, what does it but establish the lawfulness of such an act. Nor is it likely that God who had so many wayes of punishing the house of *Ahab* would have sent a subject against his Prince, if the fact in it self, as don to a Tyrant, had bin of bad example. And if *David* refus'd to lift his hand against the Lords anointed,[21] the matter between them was not tyranny, but privat enmity, and *David* as a privat person had bin his own revenger, not so much the peoples. But when any tyrant at this day can shew to be the Lords anointed, the onely mention'd reason why *David* withheld his hand, he may then but not till then presume on the same privilege.

Wee may pass therfore hence to Christian times. And first our Saviour himself, how much he favour'd Tyrants, and how much intended they should be found or honourd among Christians, declares his mind not obscurely; accounting thir absolute autority no better then Gentilism, yea though they flourish'd it over with the splendid name of Benefactors; charging those that would be his Disciples to usurp no such dominion; but that they who were to bee of most autoritie among them, should esteem themselves Ministers and Servants

19. 1 Sam. 15:33.
20. 2 Kings 9:7 and 9:24.
21. 1 Sam. 24:10.

to the public. *Matt.* 20. 25. *The Princes of the Gentiles excercise Lordship over them,* and *Mark* 10. 42. *They that seem to rule,* saith he, either slighting or accounting them no lawful rulers, *but yee shall not be so, but the greatest among you shall be your Servant.* And although hee himself were the meekest, and came on earth to be so, yet to a Tyrant we hear him not voutsafe an humble word: but *Tell that Fox, Luc.* 13. So farr we ought to be from thinking that Christ and his Gospel should be made a Sanctuary for Tyrants from justice, to whom his Law before never gave such protection. And wherfore did his Mother the Virgin *Mary* give such praise to God in her profetic song, that he had now by the comming of Christ *Cutt down Dynasta's or proud Monarchs from the throne,*[22] if the Church, when God manifests his power in them to doe so, should rather choose all miserie and vassalage to serve them, and let them stil sit on thir potent seats to bee ador'd for doing mischief. Surely it is not for nothing that tyrants by a kind of natural instinct both hate and feare none more then the true Church and Saints of God, as the most dangerous enemies and subverters of Monarchy, though indeed of tyranny; hath not this bin the perpetual cry of Courtiers, and Court Prelats? whereof no likelier cause can be alleg'd, but that they well discern'd the mind and principles of most devout and zealous men, and indeed the very discipline of Church, tending to the dissolution of all tyranny. No marvel then if since the faith of Christ receav'd, in purer or impurer times, to depose a King and put him to death for Tyranny, hath bin accounted so just and requisite, that neighbour Kings have both upheld and tak'n part with subjects in the action. And *Ludovicus Pius,* himself an Emperor, and Son of *Charles* the great, being made Judge, *Du Haillan*[23] is my author, between *Milegast* King of the *Vultzes* and his Subjects who had depos'd him, gave his verdit for the Subjects, and for him whom they had chos'n in his room. Note here that the right of electing whom they please is by the impartial testimony of an Emperor in the people. For, said he, *A just Prince ought to be prefer'd before an unjust, and the end*

22. Luke 1:51–52.
23. *Histoire de France,* bk. 13.

*of goverment before the prerogative.* And *Constantinus Leo,* another Emperor, in the *Byzantine* Laws saith, *that the end of a King is for the general good, which he not performing is but the counterfet of a King.* And to prove that som of our own Monarchs have acknowledg'd that thir high office exempted them not from punishment, they had the Sword of St. *Edward* born before them by an officer who was call'd Earle of the Palace, eev'n at the times of thir highest pomp and solemnities,[24] to mind them, saith *Matthew Paris,* the best of our Historians, that if they errd, the Sword had power to restraine them. And what restraint the Sword comes to at length, having both edge and point, if any *Sceptic* will doubt, let him feel. It is also affirm'd from diligent search made in our ancient books of Law,[25] that the Peers and Barons of England had a legal right to judge the King: which was the cause most likely, for it could be no slight cause, that they were call'd his Peers, or equals. This however may stand immovable, so long as man hath to deale with no better then man; that if our Law judge all men to the lowest by thir Peers, it should in all equity ascend also, and judge the highest. And so much I find both in our own and forren Storie, that Dukes, Earles, and Marqueses were at first not hereditary, not empty and vain titles, but names of trust and office, and with the office ceasing, as induces me to be of opinion, that every worthy man in Parlament, for the word Baron imports no more, might for the public good be thought a fit Peer and judge of the King; without regard had to petty caveats, and circumstances, the chief impediment in high affaires, and ever stood upon most by circumstantial men. Whence doubtless our Ancestors who were not ignorant with what rights either Nature or ancient Constitution had endowd them, when Oaths both at Coronation, and renewd in Parlament would not serve, thought it no way illegal to depose and put to death thir tyrannous Kings. Insomuch that the Parlament drew up a charge against *Richard the second,* and the Commons requested to have judgement decree'd against him, that

24. Milton refers to the wedding of Henry III.

25. Probably the seventeenth-century translation of Andrew Horne's *The Booke Called The Mirror of Justices* (1642).

the realme might not bee endangerd. And *Peter Martyr*[26] a Divine of formost rank, on the third of *Judges* approves thir doings. Sir *Thomas Smith* also a Protestant and a Statesman, in his Commonwelth of *England,*[27] putting the question whether it be lawfull to rise against a Tyrant, answers that the vulgar judge of it according to the event, and the lerned according to the purpose of them that do it. But far before these days, *Gildas*[28] the most ancient of all our Historians, speaking of those times wherein the Roman Empire decaying quitted and relinquishd what right they had by Conquest to this Iland, and resign'd it all into the peoples hands, testifies that the people thus re-invested with thir own original right, about the year 446, both elected them Kings, whom they thought best (the first Christian Brittish Kings that ever raign'd heer since the Romans) and by the same right, when they apprehended cause, usually depos'd and put them to death. This is the most fundamental and ancient tenure that any King of *England* can produce or pretend to; in comparison of which, all other titles and pleas are but of yesterday. If any object that *Gildas* condemns the Britans for so doing, the answer is as ready; that he condemns them no more for so doing, then hee did before for choosing such, for saith he, *They anointed them Kings, not for God, but such as were more bloody then the rest.* Next hee condemns them not at all for deposing or putting them to death, but for doing it over hastily, without tryal or well examining the cause, and for electing others wors in thir room. Thus we have heer both domestic and most ancient examples that the people of Britain have depos'd and put to death thir Kings in those primitive Christian times. And to couple reason with example, if the Church in all ages, Primitive, Romish, or Protestant, held it ever no less thir duty then the power of thir Keyes, though without express warrant of Scripture, to bring indifferently both King and Peasant under the utmost rigor of thir Canons and Censures Ecclesiastical, eev'n to the smiting him with a final excommunion, if he persist impenitent,

26. A reformer who lived from 1500 to 1562.

27. Sir Thomas Smith, *The Commonwealth of England* (1583).

28. *The Fall of Britain,* by Gildas (493−570).

what hinders but that the temporal Law both may and ought, though without a special Text or precedent, extend with like indifference the civil Sword, to the cutting off without exemption him that capitally offends. Seeing that justice and Religion are from the same God, and works of justice ofttimes more acceptable. Yet because that some lately, with the tongues and arguments of Malignant backsliders, have writt'n that the proceedings now in Parlament against the King, are without precedent from any Protestant State or Kingdom, the examples which follow shall be all Protestant and chiefly Presbyterian.

In the yeare 1546. The *Duke of Saxonie, Lantgrave of Hessen,* and the whole Protestant league raysd op'n Warr against *Charles the fifth* thir Emperor, sent him a defiance, renounc'd all faith and allegeance towards him, and debated long in Councel whither they should give him so much as the title of *Caesar. Sleidan. l.* 17.[29] Let all men judge what this wanted of deposing or of killing, but the power to doe it.

In the yeare 1559. The Scotch Protestants claiming promise of thir Queen Regent for libertie of conscience, she answering that promises were not to be claim'd of Princes beyond what was commodious for them to grant, told her to her face in the Parlament then at *Sterling,* that if it were so, they renounc'd thir obedience; and soon after betook them to Armes. *Buchanan Hist. l.* 16.[30] certainly when allegeance is renounc'd, that very hour the King or Queen is in effect depos'd.

In the yeare 1564. *John Knox* a most famous Divine and the reformer of *Scotland* to the Presbyterian discipline, at a general Assembly maintained op'nly in a dispute against *Lethington* the Secretary of State, that Subjects might & ought execute Gods judgements upon thir King; that the fact of *Jehu* and others against thir King having the ground of Gods ordinary command to put such and such offenders to death was not extraordinary, but to bee imitated of all that preferr'd the honour of God to the affection of flesh and wicked Princes; that Kings, if they offend, have no privilege to be exempted from the

29. Sleidan's proper name was Johann Philippson (1506–56); the book to which Milton refers is *The State of Religion and Public Affairs* (1555).

30. George Buchanan's *History of Scotland* (1582).

punishments of Law more then any other subject; so that if the King be a Murderer, Adulterer, or Idolater, he should suffer, not as a King, but as an offender; and this position he repeates again and again before them. Answerable was the opinion of *John Craig*[31] another learned Divine, and that Lawes made by the tyranny of Princes, or the negligence of people, thir posterity might abrogate, and reform all things according to the original institution of Common-welths. And *Knox* being commanded by the Nobilitie to write to *Calvin* and other lerned men for thir judgement in that question, refus'd; alleging that both himself was fully resolv'd in conscience, and had heard thir judgements, and had the same opinion under handwriting of many the most godly and most lerned that he knew in Europe; that if he should move the question to them againe, what should he doe but shew his own forgetfulness or inconstancy. All this is farr more largely in the Ecclesiastic History of *Scotland l.* 4.[32] with many other passages to this effect all the Book over; set out with diligence by Scotchmen of best repute among them at the beginning of these troubles, as if they labourd to inform us what wee were to doe, and what they intended upon the like occasion.

And to let the world know that the whole Church and Protestant State of *Scotland* in those purest times of reformation were of the same beleif, three years after, they met in the feild *Mary* thir lawful and hereditary Queen, took her prisoner yeilding before fight, kept her in prison, and the same yeare depos'd her. *Buchan. Hist. l.* 18.

And four years after that, the Scots in justification of thir deposing Queen *Mary,* sent Ambassadors to Queen *Elizabeth,* and in a writt'n Declaration alleg'd that they had us'd toward her more lenity then shee deserv'd, that thir Ancestors had heretofore punish'd thir Kings by death or banishment; that the Scots were a free Nation, made King whom they freely chose, and with the same freedom unkingd him if they saw cause, by right of ancient laws and Ceremonies yet remain-

31. John Craig was a Calvinist who maintained that every monarchy should be a commonwealth though not vice versa.

32. Knox's *The History of the Reformation in Scotland* (1644).

ing, and old customs yet among the High-landers in choosing the head of thir Clanns, or Families; all which with many other arguments bore witness that regal power was nothing else but a mutual Covnant or stipulation between King and people. *Buch. Hist. l.* 20. These were Scotchmen and Presbyterians; but what measure then have they lately offerd, to think such liberty less beseeming us then themselves, presuming to put him upon us for a Maister whom thir law scarce allows to be thir own equal? If now then we heare them in another strain then heretofore in the purest times of thir Church, we may be confident it is the voice of Faction speaking in them, not of truth and Reformation. Which no less in *England* then in *Scotland,* by the mouthes of those faithful witnesses commonly call'd Puritans, and Nonconformists, spake as clearly for the putting down, yea the utmost punishing of Kings, as in thir several Treatises may be read; eev'n from the first raigne of *Elizabeth* to these times. Insomuch that one of them, whose name was *Gibson,* foretold K. *James,* he should be rooted out, and conclude his race, if he persisted to uphold Bishops. And that very inscription stampt upon the first Coines at his Coronation, a naked Sword in a hand with these words, *Si mereor in me, Against me, if I deserve,* not only manifested the judgement of that State, but seem'd also to presage the sentence of Divine justice in this event upon his Son.

In the yeare 1581. the States of *Holland* in a general Assembly at the *Hague,* abjur'd all obedience and subjection to *Philip* King of *Spaine;* and in a Declaration justifie thir so doing; for that by his tyrannous goverment against faith so many times giv'n & brok'n he had lost his right to all the Belgic Provinces; that therfore they depos'd him and declar'd it lawful to choose another in his stead. *Thuan. l.* 74.[33] From that time, to this, no State or Kingdom in the world hath equally prosperd: But let them remember not to look with an evil and prejudicial eye upon thir Neighbours walking by the same rule.

But what need these examples to Presbyterians, I mean to those who now of late would seem so much to abhorr deposing, when as

33. From *History of His Own Times* (1620) by the French historian Jacques-Auguste de Thou (1553–1617).

they to all Christendom have giv'n the latest and the liveliest example of doing it themselves. I question not the lawfulness of raising Warr against a Tyrant in defence of Religion, or civil libertie; for no Protestant Church from the first *Waldenses* of *Lyons,* and *Languedoc* to this day but have don it round, and maintain'd it lawful. But this I doubt not to affirme, that the Presbyterians, who now so much condemn deposing, were the men themselves that deposd the King, and cannot with all thir shifting and relapsing, wash off the guiltiness from thir own hands. For they themselves, by these thir late doings have made it guiltiness, and turn'd thir own warrantable actions into Rebellion.

There is nothing that so actually makes a King of *England,* as rightful possession and Supremacy *in all causes both civil and Ecclesiastical:* and nothing that so actually makes a Subject of *England,* as those two Oaths of Allegeance and Supremacy[34] observ'd *without equivocating, or any mental reservation.* Out of doubt then when the King shall command things already constituted in Church, or State, obedience is the true essence of a subject, either to doe, if it be lawful, or if he hold the thing unlawful, to submitt to that penaltie which the Law imposes, so long as he intends to remaine a Subject. Therfore when the people or any part of them shall rise against the King and his autority executing the Law in any thing establish'd civil or Ecclesiastical, I doe not say it is rebellion, if the thing commanded though establish'd be unlawful, and that they sought first all due means of redress (and no man is furder bound to Law) but I say it is an absolute renouncing both of Supremacy and Allegeance, which in one word is an actual and total deposing of the King, and the setting up of another supreme autority over them. And whether the Presbyterians have not don all this and much more, they will not put mee, I suppose, to reck'n up a seven years story fresh in the memory of all men. Have they not utterly broke the Oath of Allegeance, rejecting the Kings command and autority sent them from any part of the Kingdom whether in things lawful or unlawful? Have they not abjur'd the Oath

34. The oaths acknowledging the king to be head of the English church.

of Supremacy by setting up the Parlament without the King, supreme to all thir obedience, and though thir Vow and Covnant bound them in general to the Parlament, yet somtimes adhering to the lesser part of Lords and Commons that remaind faithful, as they terme it, and eev'n of them, one while to the Commons without the Lords, another while to the Lords without the Commons? Have they not still declar'd thir meaning, whatever thir Oath were, to hold them onely for supreme whom they found at any time most yeilding to what they petition'd? Both these Oaths which were the straitest bond of an English subject in reference to the King, being thus broke & made voide, it follows undenyably that the King from that time was by them in fact absolutely depos'd, and they no longer in reality to be thought his subjects, notwithstanding thir fine clause in the Covnant to preserve his person, Crown, and dignity, set there by som dodging Casuist with more craft then sincerity to mitigate the matter in case of ill success and not tak'n I suppose by any honest man, but as a condition subordinat to every the least particle that might more concerne Religion, liberty, or the public peace. To prove it yet more plainly that they are the men who have depos'd the King, I thus argue. We know that King and Subject are relatives, and relatives have no longer being then in the relation; the relation between King and Subject can be no other then regal autority and subjection. Hence I inferr past their defending, that if the Subject who is one relative, take away the relation, of force he takes away also the other relative; but the Presbyterians who were one relative, that is to say Subjects, have for this sev'n years tak'n away the relation, that is to say the Kings autority, and thir subjection to it, therfore the Presbyterians for these sev'n years have remov'd and extinguishd the other relative, that is to say the King, or to speak more in brief have depos'd him; not onely by depriving him the execution of his autoritie, but by conferring it upon others. If then thir Oaths of subjection brok'n, new Supremacy obey'd, new Oaths and Covnants tak'n, notwithstanding frivolous evasions, have in plaine termes unking'd the King, much more then hath thir sev'n years Warr; not depos'd him onely but outlaw'd him, and defi'd him as an alien, a rebell to Law, and enemie to the State. It must needs be clear to any man not avers from reason, that hostilitie and subjection are two direct and positive contraries; and can no more in one subject stand together in respect of the same King, then one person at the same time can be in two remote places. Against whom therfore the Subject is in act of hostility we may be confident that to him he is in no subjection: and in whom hostility takes place of subjection, for they can by no meanes consist together, to him the King can be not onely no King, but an enemie. So that from hence we shall not need dispute whether they have depos'd him, or what they have defaulted towards him as no King, but shew manifestly how much they have don toward the killing him. Have they not levied all these Warrs against him whether offensive or defensive (for defence in Warr equally offends, and most prudently before hand) and giv'n Commission to slay where they knew his person could not be exempt from danger? And if chance or flight had not sav'd him, how oft'n had they killd him, directing thir Artillery without blame or prohibition to the very place where they saw him stand? Have they not Sequester'd him[35] judg'd or unjudgd, and converted his revenew to other uses, detaining from him as a grand Delinquent,[36] all meanes of livelyhood, so that for them long since he might have perisht, or have starv'd? Have they not hunted and pursu'd him round about the Kingdom with sword and fire? Have they not formerly deny'd to Treat with him, and thir now recanting Ministers preach'd against him, as a reprobate incurable, an enemy to God and his Church markt for destruction, and therfore not to be treated with? Have they not beseig'd him, & to thir power forbidd him Water and Fire, save what they shot against him to the hazard of his life? Yet while they thus assaulted and endangerd it with hostile deeds, they swore in words to defend it with his Crown and dignity; not in order, as it seems now, to a firm and lasting peace, or to his repentance after all this blood;

35. Sequestering was the appropriation of income in order to settle claims against Royalist property.

36. One found to be a serious resister of Parliament.

but simply, without regard, without remorse, or any comparable value of all the miseries and calamities sufferd by the poore people, or to suffer hereafter through his obstinacy or impenitence. No understanding man can bee ignorant that Covnants are ever made according to the present state of persons and of things; and have ever the more general laws of nature and of reason included in them, though not express'd. If I make a voluntary Covnant as with a man, to doe him good, and he prove afterward a monster to me, I should conceave a disobligement. If I covnant, not to hurt an enemie, in favour of him & forbearance, & hope of his amendment, & he, after that, shall doe me tenfould injury and mischief, to what he had don when I so Covnanted, and stil be plotting what may tend to my destruction, I question not but that his after actions release me; nor know I Covnant so sacred that withholds me from demanding justice on him. Howbeit, had not thir distrust in a good cause, and the fast and loos of our prevaricating Divines oversway'd, it had bin doubtless better not to have inserted in a Covnant unnecessary obligations, and words not works of a supererogating Allegeance to thir enemy; no way advantageous to themselves, had the King prevail'd, as to thir cost many would have felt; but full of snare and distraction to our friends, usefull onely, as we now find, to our adversaries, who under such a latitude and shelter of ambiguous interpretation have ever since been plotting and contriving new opportunities to trouble all again. How much better had it bin, and more becomming an undaunted vertue, to have declar'd op'nly and boldly whom and what power the people were to hold Supreme; as on the like occasion Protestants have don before, and many conscientious men now in these times have more then once besought the Parlament to doe, that they might goe on upon a sure foundation, and not with a ridling Covnant in thir mouths, seeming to sweare counter almost in the same breath Allegeance and no Allegeance; which doubtless had drawn off all the minds of sincere men from siding with them, had they not discern'd thir actions farr more deposing him then thir words upholding him; which words made now the subject of cavillous interpretations, stood

ever in the Covnant, by judgement of the more discerning sort, an
evidence of thir feare, not of thir fidelity. What should I return to
speak on, of those attempts for which the King himself hath oft'n
charg'd the Presbyterians of seeking his life, when as in the due estimation of things, they might without a fallacy be sayd to have don
the deed outright. Who knows not that the King is a name of dignity
and office, not of person: Who therfore kills a King, must kill him
while he is a King. Then they certainly who by deposing him have
long since tak'n from him the life of a King, his office and his dignity, they in the truest sence may be said to have killd the King: nor
onely by thir deposing and waging Warr against him, which besides
the danger to his personal life, sett him in the fardest opposite point
from any vital function of a King, but by thir holding him in prison,
vanquishd and yeilded into thir absolute and *despotic* power, which
brought him to the lowest degradement and incapacity of the regal
name. I say not by whose matchless valour next under God, lest the
story of thir ingratitude thereupon carry me from the purpose in
hand, which is to convince them that they, which I repeat againe,
were the men who in the truest sense killd the King, not onely as is
prov'd before, but by depressing him thir King farr below the rank of
a subject to the condition of a Captive, without intention to restore
him, as the Chancellour of *Scotland* in a speech told him plainly at
*Newcastle,*[37] unless hee granted fully all thir demands, which they
knew he never meant. Nor did they Treat or think of Treating with
him, till thir hatred to the Army that deliverd them, not thir love or
duty to the King, joyn'd them secretly with men sentenc'd so oft for
Reprobats in thir own mouthes, by whose suttle inspiring they grew
madd upon a most tardy and improper Treaty. Whereas if the whole
bent of thir actions had not bin against the King himself, but only
against his evil counselers, as they faind, & publishd, wherfore did
they not restore him all that while to the true life of a King, his office,
Crown, and Dignity, when he was in thir power, & they themselves his

37. John Campbell, "the Chancellour of *Scotland,*" who negotiated with Charles
at Newcastle in 1646.

neerest Counselers. The truth therfore is, both that they would not, and that indeed they could not without thir own certain destruction; having reduc'd him to such a final pass, as was the very death and burial of all in him that was regal, and from whence never King of *England* yet reviv'd, but by the new re-inforcement of his own party, which was a kind of resurrection to him. Thus having quite extinguisht all that could be in him of a King, and from a total privation clad him over, like another specifical thing, with formes and habitudes destructive to the former, they left in his person, dead as to Law, and all the civil right either of King or Subject, the life onely of a Prisner, a Captive and a Malefactor. Whom the equal and impartial hand of justice finding, was no more to spare then another ordnary man; not onely made obnoxious to the doom of Law by a charge more then once drawn up against him, and his own confession to the first Article at *Newport*,[38] but summond and arraign'd in the sight of God and his people, curst & devoted to perdition worse then any Ahab, or Antiochus,[39] with exhortation to curse all those in the name of God that made not Warr against him, as bitterly as *Meroz* [40] was to be curs'd, that went not out against a Canaanitish King, almost in all the Sermons, Prayers, and Fulminations that have bin utterd this sev'n yeares by those clov'n tongues of falshood and dissention; who now, to the stirring up of new discord, acquitt him; and against thir own disciplin, which they boast to be the throne and scepter of Christ, absolve him, unconfound him, though unconverted, unrepentant, unsensible of all thir pretious Saints and Martyrs whose blood they have so oft laid upon his head: and now againe with a new sovran anointment can wash it all off, as if it were as vile, and no more to be reckn'd

38. At Newport in the autumn of 1648 Charles was presented with a list of propositions by a parliamentary commission to which he responded in such conciliatory fashion as to permit Milton to maintain that the king had confessed violations of traditional rights.

39. Antiochus was overthrown by Judas Maccabeus, who restored the worship of Jehovah in Jerusalem.

40. In Judg. 5:23 Deborah curses the men of Meroz for failing to support Barak in his struggle against the Canaanite king.

for, then the blood of so many Dogs in a time of Pestilence: giving the most opprobrious lye to all the acted zeale that for these many yeares hath filld thir bellies, and fed them fatt upon the foolish people. Ministers of sedition, not of the Gospel, who while they saw it manifestly tend to civil Warr and blood shed, never ceasd exasperating the people against him; and now that they see it likely to breed new commotion, cease not to incite others against the people that have sav'd them from him, as if sedition were thir onely aime, whether against him or for him. But God, as we have cause to trust, will put other thoughts into the people, and turn them from giving eare or heed to these Mercenary noisemakers, of whose fury, and fals prophecies we have anough experience; and from the murmurs of new discord will incline them to heark'n rather with erected minds to the voice of our Supreme Magistracy, calling us to liberty and the flourishing deeds of a reformed Common-wealth; with this hope that as God was heretofore angry with the Jews who rejected him and his forme of Goverment to choose a King, so that he will bless us, and be propitious to us who reject a King to make him onely our leader and supreme governour in the conformity as neer as may be of his own ancient goverment; if we have at least but so much worth in us to entertaine the sense of our future happiness, and the courage to receave what God voutsafes us: wherein we have the honour to precede other Nations who are now labouring to be our followers. For as to this question in hand what the people by thir just right may doe in change of goverment, or of governour, we see it cleerd sufficiently; besides other ample autority eev'n from the mouths of Princes themselves. And surely they that shall boast, as we doe, to be a free Nation, and not have in themselves the power to remove, or to abolish any governour supreme, or subordinat, with the goverment it self upon urgent causes, may please thir fancy with a ridiculous and painted freedom, fit to coz'n babies; but are indeed under tyranny and servitude; as wanting that power, which is the root and sourse of all liberty, to dispose and *oeconomize*[41] in the Land which God hath giv'n them, as

41. To set up household or civil government.

Maisters of Family in thir own house and free inheritance. Without which natural and essential power of a free Nation, though bearing high thir heads, they can in due esteem be thought no better then slaves and vassals born, in the tenure and occupation of another inheriting Lord. Whose goverment, though not illegal, or intolerable, hangs over them as a Lordly scourge, not as a free goverment; and therfore to be abrogated. How much more justly then may they fling off tyranny, or tyrants; who being once depos'd can be no more then privat men, as subject to the reach of Justice and arraignment as any other transgressors. And certainly if men, not to speak of Heathen, both wise and Religious have don justice upon Tyrants what way they could soonest, how much more milde & human then is it, to give them faire and op'n tryal? To teach lawless Kings, and all who so much adore them, that not mortal man, or his imperious will, but Justice is the onely true sovran and supreme Majesty upon earth. Let men cease therfore out of faction & hypocrisie to make out-cries and horrid things of things so just and honorable. Though perhaps till now no protestant State or kingdom can be alleg'd to have op'nly put to death thir King, which lately some have writt'n, and imputed to thir great glory; much mistaking the matter.[42] It is not, neither ought to be the glory of a Protestant State, never to have put thir King to death; It is the glory of a Protestant King never to have deserv'd death. And if the Parlament and Military Councel doe what they doe without precedent, if it appeare thir duty, it argues the more wisdom, vertue, and magnanimity, that they know themselves able to be a precedent to others. Who perhaps in future ages, if they prove not too degenerat, will look up with honour, and aspire toward these exemplary, and matchless deeds of thir Ancestors, as to the highest top of thir civil glory and emulation. Which heretofore, in the persuance of fame and forren dominion, spent it self vaingloriously abroad; but henceforth may learn a better fortitude, to dare execute highest Justice on them that shall by force of Armes endeavour the oppressing

42. Milton has in mind recent Presbyterian pamphlet writers who compared the parliamentary judges with Jesuits.

and bereaving of Religion and thir liberty at home: that no unbridl'd Potentate or Tyrant, but to his sorrow for the future, may presume such high and irresponsible licence over mankinde, to havock and turn upside-down whole Kingdoms of men, as though they were no more in respect of his perverse will then a Nation of Pismires. As for the party calld Presbyterian, of whom I believe very many to be good and faithfull Christians, though misledd by som of turbulent spirit, I wish them earnestly and calmly not to fall off from thir first principles; nor to affect rigor and superiority over men not under them; not to compell unforcible things, in Religion especially, which if not voluntary, becomes a sin; nor to assist the clamor and malicious drifts of men whom they themselves have judg'd to be the worst of men, the obdurat enemies of God and his Church: nor to dart against the actions of thir brethren, for want of other argument, those wrested Lawes and Scriptures thrown by Prelats and Malignants against thir own sides, which though they hurt not otherwise, yet tak'n up by them to the condemnation of thir own doings, give scandal to all men, and discover in themselves either extreame passion, or apostacy. Let them not oppose thir best friends and associats, who molest them not at all, infringe not the least of thir liberties; unless they call it thir liberty to bind other mens consciences, but are still seeking to live at peace with them and brotherly accord. Let them beware an old and perfet enemy, who though he hope by sowing discord to make them his instruments, yet cannot forbeare a minute the op'n threatning of his destind revenge upon them, when they have servd his purposes. Let them, feare therfore if they be wise, rather what they have don already, then what remaines to doe, and be warn'd in time they put no confidence in Princes whom they have provok'd, lest they be added to the examples of those that miserably have tasted the event. Stories can informe them how *Christiern* the second, King of *Denmark* not much above a hundred yeares past, driv'n out by his Subjects, and receav'd againe upon new Oaths and conditions, broke through them all to his most bloody revenge; slaying his chief opposers when he saw his time, both them and thir children invited to a feast for that purpose. How *Maximilian*[43] dealt with those of *Bruges,* though by mediation of the *German* Princes reconcil'd to them by solem and public writings drawn and seald. How the massacre at *Paris* was the effect of that credulous peace which the French Protestants made with *Charles* the ninth thir King: and that the main visible cause which to this day hath sav'd the *Netherlands* from utter ruin, was thir final not beleiving the perfidious cruelty which, as a constant maxim of State, hath bin us'd by the Spanish Kings on thir Subjects that have tak'n Armes and after trusted them; as no later age but can testifie, heretofore in *Belgia* it self, and this very yeare in *Naples.*[44] And to conclude with one past exception, though farr more ancient, *David,* whose sanctify'd prudence might be alone sufficient, not to warrant us only, but to instruct us, when once he had tak'n Armes, never after that trusted *Saul,* though with tears and much relenting he twise promis'd not to hurt him. These instances, few of many, might admonish them both English and Scotch not to let thir own ends, and the driving on of a faction betray them blindly into the snare of those enemies whose revenge looks on them as the men who first begun, fomented and carri'd on, beyond the cure of any sound or safe accommodation, all the evil which hath since unavoidably befall'n them and thir King.

I have somthing also to the Divines, though brief to what were needfull; not to be disturbers of the civil affairs, being in hands better able and more belonging to manage them; but to study harder, and to attend the office of good Pastors, knowing that he whose flock is least among them hath a dreadfull charge, not performd by mounting twise into the chair with a formal preachment huddl'd up at the odd hours of a whole lazy week, but by incessant pains and watching *in season and out of season, from house to house*[45] over the soules of whom they have to feed. Which if they ever well considerd, how little leasure would they find to be the most pragmatical Sidesmen[46] of every

43. Maximilian I punished rebels who sought reforms in 1490.
44. Milton refers to Spanish repression of a revolt in Naples in 1648.
45. 2 Tim. 4:2.
46. Greedy partisans.

popular tumult and Sedition? And all this while are to learn what the true end and reason is of the Gospel which they teach; and what a world it differs from the censorious and supercilious lording over conscience. It would be good also they liv'd so as might perswade the people they hated covetousness, which worse then heresie, is idolatry; hated pluralities[47] and all kind of Simony; left rambling from Benefice to Benefice, like rav'nous Wolves seeking where they may devour the biggest. Of which if som, well and warmely seated from the beginning, be not guilty, twere good they held not conversation with such as are: let them be sorry that being call'd to assemble about reforming the Church, they fell to progging[48] and solliciting the Parlament, though they had renounc'd the name of Priests, for a new setling of thir Tithes and Oblations;[49] and double lin'd themselves with spiritual places of commoditie beyond the possible discharge of thir duty. Let them assemble in Consistory with thir Elders and Deacons, according to ancient Ecclesiastical rule, to the preserving of Church-discipline, each in his several charge, and not a pack of Clergiemen by themselves to belly-cheare in thir presumptuous Sion, or to promote designes, abuse and gull the simple Laity, and stirr up tumult, as the Prelats did, for the maintenance of thir pride and avarice. These things if they observe, and waite with patience, no doubt but all things will goe well without their importunities or exclamations: and the Printed letters which they send subscrib'd with the ostentation of great Characters and little moment, would be more considerable then now they are. But if they be the Ministers of Mammon in stead of Christ, and scandalize his Church with the filthy love of gaine, aspiring also to sit the closest & the heaviest of all Tyrants, upon the conscience, and fall notoriously into the same sinns, wherof so lately and so loud they accus'd the Prelates, as God rooted out those wicked ones immediatly before, so will he root out them thir imitators: and

47. Multiple benefices.
48. Nagging.
49. Consecrated gifts.

to vindicate his own glory and Religion, will uncover thir hypocrisie to the op'n world; and visit upon thir own heads that *curse ye Meroz*, the very *Motto* of thir Pulpits, wherwith so frequently, not as *Meroz*, but more like Atheists they have blasphem'd the vengeance of God, and traduc'd the zeale of his people. And that they be not what they goe for, true Ministers of the Protestant doctrine, taught by those abroad, famous and religious men, who first reformed the Church, or by those no less zealous, who withstood corruption and the Bishops heer at home, branded with the name of Puritans and Nonconformists, wee shall abound with testimonies to make appeare: that men may yet more fully know the difference between Protestant Divines, and these Pulpit-firebrands.

Luther.

*Lib. contra Rusticos apud Sleidan. l. 5.*

Is est hodie rerum status, &c. *Such is the state of things at this day, that men neither can, nor will, nor indeed ought to endure longer the domination of you Princes.*

Neque vero Caesarem, &c. *Neither is Caesar to make Warr as head of Christ'ndom, Protector of the Church, Defender of the Faith; these Titles being fals and Windie, and most Kings being the greatest Enemies to Religion. Lib: De bello contra Turcas. apud Sleid. l. 14.* What hinders then, but that we may depose or punish them?

These also are recited by *Cochlaeus*[50] in his *Miscellanies* to be the words of *Luther,* or some other eminent Divine, then in *Germany,* when the Protestants there entred into solemn Covnant at *Smalcaldia.* Ut ora ijs obturem &c. *That I may stop thir mouthes, the Pope and Emperor are not born but elected, and may also be depos'd as hath bin oft'n don.* If *Luther,* or whoever els thought so, he could not stay there; for the right of birth or succession can be no privilege in nature to let a Tyrant sit irremoveable over a Nation free born, without transforming that Nation from the nature and condition of men born free, into natural,

---

50. Cochlaeus is Johannes Dobeneck (1479–1552), a secretary to one of Luther's principal opponents, Duke George of Saxony.

hereditary, and successive slaves. Therfore he saith furder; *To displace and throw down this Exactor, this Phalaris, this Nero, is a work well pleasing to God;* Namely, for being such a one: which is a moral reason. Shall then so slight a consideration as his happ to be not elective simply, but by birth, which was a meer accident, overthrow that which is moral, and make unpleasing to God that which otherwise had so well pleasd him? certainly not: for if the matter be rightly argu'd, Election much rather then chance, bindes a man to content himself with what he suffers by his own bad Election. Though indeed neither the one nor other bindes any man, much less any people to a necessary sufferance of those wrongs and evils, which they have abilitie and strength anough giv'n them to remove.

*Zwinglius.*[51] *tom.* 1. *articul.* 42.

Quando vero perfidè, &c. *When Kings raigne perfidiously, and against the rule of Christ, they may according to the word of God be depos'd.*

Mihi ergo compertum non est, &c. *I know not how it comes to pass that Kings raigne by succession, unless it be with consent of the whole people.* ibid.

Quum vero consensu, &c.: *But when by suffrage and consent of the whole people, or the better part of them, a Tyrant is depos'd or put to death, God is the chief leader in that action.* ibid.

Nunc cum tam tepidi sumus, &c. *Now that we are so luke warm in upholding public justice, we indure the vices of Tyrants to raigne now a dayes with impunity; justly therfore by them we are trod and underfoot, and shall at length with them be punisht. Yet ways are not wanting by which Tyrants may be remoov'd, but there wants public justice.* ibid.

Cavete vobis ô tyranni. *Beware yee Tyrants for now the Gospell of Jesus Christ spreading farr and wide, will renew the lives of many to love innocence and justice; which if yee also shall doe, yee shall be honourd. But if yee shall goe on to rage and doe violence, yee shall be trampl'd on by all men.* ibid.

51. Milton cites from *Opus Articularum sive Conclusium Huldrichi Zuingli,* a 1545 compilation of a work Zwingli composed in German.

Romanum imperium imò quodq; &c. *When the Roman Empire or any other shall begin to oppress Religion, and wee negligently suffer it, wee are as much guilty of Religion so violated, as the Oppressors themselvs.* Idem Epist. ad Conrad. Somium.

*Calvin on Daniel.*[52] *c. 4. v. 25.*

Hodie Monarchae semper in suis titulis, &c. *Now adays Monarchs pretend alwayes in thir Titles, to be Kings by the grace of God: but how many of them to this end onely pretend it, that they may raigne without controule; for to what purpose is the grace of God mentiond in the Title of Kings, but that they may acknowledge no Superiour? In the meane while God, whose name they use, to support themselves, they willingly would tread under thir feet. It is therfore a meer cheat when they boast to raigne by the grace of God.*

Abdicant se terreni principes, &c. *Earthly Princes depose themselves while they rise against God, yea they are unworthy to be numbered among men: rather it behooves us to spitt upon thir heads then to obey them.* On *Dan: c. 6. v. 22.*

*Bucer on Matth.*[53] *c. 5.*

Si princeps superior, &c. *If a Sovran-Prince endeavour by armes to defend transgressors, to subvert those things which are taught in the word of God, they who are in autority under him, ought first to disswade him; if they prevaile not, and that he now beares himself not as a Prince, but as an enemie, and seekes to violate privileges and rights granted to inferior Magistrates or commonalities, it is the part of pious Magistrates, imploring first the assistance of God, rather to try all ways and means, then to betray the flock of Christ, to such an enemie of God: for they also are to this end ordain'd, that they may defend the people of God, and maintain those things which are good and just. For to have supreme power less'ns not the evil committed by that power, but makes it the less tolerable, by how much the more generally hurtful.* Then certainly the less tolerable, the more unpardonably to be punish'd.

52. Milton is quoting from Calvin's *Praelectiones in librum prophetiarum Danielis* (1561).

53. This quotation is taken from Martin Bucer's *Sacra quattuor Evangelia* (1555).

Of *Peter Martyr* we have spoke before.

*Paraeus in Rom.* 13.[54]

Quorum est constituere Magistratus, &c. *They whose part it is to set up Magistrates, may restrain them also from outragious deeds, or pull them down; but all Magistrates are set up either by Parlament, or by Electors, or by other Magistrates; They therfore who exalted them, may lawfully degrade and punish them.*

Of the Scotch Divines I need not mention others then the famousest among them, *Knox,* & and his fellow Labourers in the reformation of *Scotland;* whose large Treatises on this subject, defend the same Opinion. To cite them sufficiently, were to insert thir whole Books, writt'n purposely on this argument. *Knox Appeal;*[55] and to the Reader; where he promises in a Postscript that the Book which he intended to set forth, call'd, The second blast of the Trumpet, should maintain more at large, that the same men most justly may depose, and punish him whom unadvisedly they have elected, notwithstanding birth, succession, or any Oath of Allegeance. Among our own Divines, *Cartwright* and *Fenner,*[56] two of the Lernedest, may in reason satisfy us what was held by the rest. *Fenner* in his Book of *Theologie* maintaining, That *they who have power, that is to say a Parlament, may either by faire meanes or by force depose a Tyrant,* whom he defines to be him, that wilfully breakes all, or the principal conditions made between him and the Common-wealth. *Fen. Sac: Theolog. c.* 13. and *Cartwright* in a prefix'd Epistle testifies his approbation of the whole Book.

Gilby de obientiâ.[57] p. 25. & 105.

*Kings have thir autoritie of the people, who may upon occasion reassume it to themselves.*

54. David Paraeus, *Theological Works* (1647).

55. Milton refers to *The Appellation of John Knox etc.*, published in 1558 along with *John Knox to the Reader.*

56. Thomas Cartwright was one of the leading lights of Presbyterianism in the late sixteenth century; Dudley Fenner was Cartwright's associate.

57. In fact a quotation from John Poynet's *A Short Treatise of Political Power.*

Englands Complaint against the Canons.
*The people may kill wicked Princes as monsters and cruel beasts.*
Christopher Goodman of Obedience.[58]

When Kings or Rulers become blasphemers of God, oppressors and murderers of thir Subjects, they ought no more to be accounted Kings or lawfull Magistrates, but as privat men to be examind, accus'd, condemn'd and punisht by the Law of God, and being convicted and punisht by that law, it is not mans but Gods doing, *C.* 10. *p.* 139.

By the civil laws a foole or Idiot born, and so prov'd shall loose the lands and inheritance wherto he is born, because he is not able to use them aright. And especially ought in no case be sufferd to have the goverment of a whole Nation; But there is no such evil can come to the Commonwealth by fooles and idiots as doth by the rage and fury of ungodly Rulers; Such therfore being without God ought to have no autority over Gods people, who by his Word requireth the contrary. *C.* 11. *p.* 143, 144.

No person is exempt by any Law of God from this punishment, be he King, Queene, or Emperor, he must dy the death, for God hath not plac'd them above others, to transgress his laws as they list, but to be subject to them as well as others, and if they be subject to his laws, then to the punishment also, so much the more as thir example is more dangerous. *C.* 13. *p.* 184.

When Magistrates cease to doe thir Duty, the people are as it were without Magistrates, yea worse, and then God giveth the sword into the peoples hand, and he himself is become immediatly thir head. *p.* 185.

If Princes doe right and keep promise with you, then doe you owe to them all humble obedience: if not, yee are discharg'd, and your study ought to be in this case how ye may depose and punish according to the Law such Rebels against God and oppressors of thir Country. *p.* 190.

This *Goodman* was a Minister of the *English* Church at *Geneva,* as

58. Goodman was co-pastor with Knox in Geneva.

*Dudley Fenner* was at *Middleburrough,* or some other place in that Country. These were the Pastors of those Saints and Confessors who flying from the bloudy persecution of Queen *Mary,* gather'd up at length thir scatterd members into many Congregations; wherof som in upper, some in lower *Germany,* part of them settl'd at *Geneva;* where this Author having preachd on this subject to the great liking of certain lerned and godly men who heard him, was by them sundry times & with much instance requir'd to write more fully on that point. Who therupon took it in hand, and conferring with the best lerned in those parts (among whom *Calvin* was then living in the same City) with their special approbation he publisht this treatise, aiming principally, as is testify'd by *Whittingham* in the Preface, that his Brethren of *England,* the Protestants, might be perswaded in the truth of that Doctrine concerning obedience to Magistrates. *Whittingham in Prefat.*[59]

These were the true Protestant Divines of *England,* our fathers in the faith we hold; this was their sense, who for so many yeares labouring under Prelacy, through all stormes and persecutions kept Religion from extinguishing; and delivered it pure to us, till there arose a covetous and ambitious generation of Divines (for Divines they call themselves) who feining on a sudden to be new converts and proselytes from Episcopacy, under which they had long temporiz'd, op'nd thir mouthes at length, in shew against Pluralities and Prelacy, but with intent to swallow them down both; gorging themselves like Harpy's on those simonious places and preferments of thir outed predecessors, as the quarry for which they hunted, not to pluralitie onely but to multiplicitie: for possessing which they had accusd them thir Brethren, and aspiring under another title to the same authoritie and usurpation over the consciences of all men.

Of this faction diverse reverend and lerned Divines, as they are stil'd in the Phylactery[60] of thir own Title page, pleading the lawfulnes of defensive Armes against this King, in a Treatise call'd *Scrip-*

59. William Whittingham (1524–79), a collaborator in drafting the *Genevan Service Book.*

60. Transcriptions of Mosaic law worn by Jews on their foreheads.

*ture and Reason,* seem in words to disclaime utterly the deposing of a King; but both the Scripture and the reasons which they use, draw consequences after them, which without their bidding, conclude it lawfull. For if by Scripture, and by that especially to the *Romans,* which they most insist upon, Kings, doing that which is contrary to Saint *Pauls* definition of a Magistrat, may be resisted, they may altogether with as much force of consequence be depos'd or punishd. And if by reason the unjust autority of Kings *may be forfeted in part, and his power be reassum'd in part, either by the Parlament or People, for the case in hazard and the present necessitie,* as they affirm *p.* 34, there can no Scripture be alleg'd, no imaginable reason giv'n, that necessity continuing, as it may alwayes, and they in all prudence and thir duty may take upon them to foresee it, why in such a case they may not finally amerce him with the loss of his Kingdom, of whose amendment they have no hope. And if one wicked action persisted in against Religion, Laws, and liberties may warrant us to thus much in part, why may not forty times as many tyrannies, by him committed, warrant us to proceed on restraining him, till the restraint become total. For the ways of justice are exactest proportion; if for one trespass of a King it require so much remedie or satisfaction, then for twenty more as hainous crimes, it requires of him twentyfold; and so proportionably, till it com to what is utmost among men. If in these proceedings against thir King they may not finish by the usual cours of justice what they have begun, they could not lawfully begin at all. For this golden rule of justice and moralitie, as well as of Arithmetic, out of three termes which they admitt, will as certainly and unavoydably bring out the fourth, as any Probleme that ever *Euclid,* or *Apollonius* made good by demonstration.

And if the Parlament, being undeposable but by themselves, as is affirm'd, *p.* 37, 38, might for his whole life, if they saw cause, take all power, authority, and the sword out of his hand, which in effect is to unmagistrate him, why might they not, being then themselves the sole Magistrates in force, proceed to punish him who being lawfully depriv'd of all things that define a Magistrate, can be now no Magistrate to be degraded lower, but an offender to be punisht. Lastly, whom they may defie, and meet in battell, why may they not as well prosecute by justice? For lawfull warr is but the execution of justice against them who refuse Law. Among whom if it be lawfull (as they deny not, *p.* 19, 20.) to slay the King himself comming in front at his own peril, wherfore may not justice doe that intendedly, which the chance of a defensive warr might without blame have don casually, nay purposely, if there it finde him among the rest. They aske *p.* 19. *By what rule of Conscience or God, a State is bound to sacrifice Religion, Laws and liberties, rather then a Prince defending such as subvert them, should com in hazard of his life.* And I ask by what conscience, or divinity, or Law, or reason, a State is bound to leave all these sacred concernments under a perpetual hazard and extremity of danger, rather then cutt off a wicked Prince, who sitts plotting day and night to subvert them: They tell us that the Law of nature justifies any man to defend himself, eev'n against the King in Person: let them shew us then why the same Law, may not justifie much more a State or whole people, to doe justice upon him, against whom each privat man may lawfully defend himself; seing all kind of justice don, is a defence to good men, as well as a punishment to bad; and justice don upon a Tyrant is no more but the necessary self-defence of a whole Common wealth. To Warr upon a King, that his instruments may be brought to condigne punishment, and therafter to punish them the instruments, and not to spare onely, but to defend and honour him the Author, is the strangest peece of justice to be call'd Christian, and the strangest peece of reason to be call'd human, that by men of reverence and learning, as thir stile imports them, ever yet was vented. They maintain in the third and fourth Section, that a Judge or inferior Magistrate, is anointed of God, is his Minister, hath the Sword in his hand, is to be obey'd by St. *Peters* rule,[61] as well as the Supreme, and without difference any where exprest: and yet will have us fight against the Supreme till he remove and punish the inferior Magistrate

---

61. 1 Pet. 2:13–14.

(for such were greatest Delinquents) when as by Scripture, and by reason, there can no more autority be shown to resist the one then the other; and altogether as much, to punish or depose the Supreme himself, as to make Warr upon him, till he punish or deliver up his inferior Magistrates, whom in the same terms we are commanded to obey, and not to resist. Thus while they, in a cautious line or two here and there stuft in, are onely verbal against the pulling down or punishing of Tyrants, all the Scripture and the reason which they bring, is in every leafe direct and rational to inferr it altogether as lawful, as to resist them. And yet in all thir Sermons, as hath by others bin well noted, they went much furder. For Divines, if ye observe them, have thir postures, and thir motions no less expertly, and with no less variety then they that practice feats in the Artillery-ground. Sometimes they seem furiously to march on, and presently march counter; by and by they stand, and then retreat; or if need be can face about, or wheele in a whole body, with that cunning and dexterity as is almost unperceavable; to winde themselves by shifting ground into places of more advantage. And Providence onely must be the drumm, Providence the word of command, that calls them from above, but always to som larger Benefice, or acts them into such or such figures, and promotions. At thir turnes and doublings no men readier; to the right, or to the left; for it is thir turnes which they serve cheifly; heerin only singular; that with them there is no certain hand right or left; but as thir own commodity thinks best to call it. But if there come a truth to be defended, which to them, and thir interest of this world seemes not so profitable, strait these nimble motionists can finde no eev'n leggs to stand upon: and are no more of use to reformation throughly performd, and not superficially, or to the advancement of Truth (which among mortal men is alwaies in her progress) then if on a sudden they were strook maime, and crippl'd. Which the better to conceale, or the more to countnance by a general conformity to thir own limping, they would have *Scripture,* they would have *reason* also made to halt with them for company; and would putt us off with impotent conclusions, lame and shorter then the premises. In this posture they seem to stand with great zeale and confidence on the wall of *Sion;* but like *Jebusites,*[62] not like *Israelites,* or *Levites;*[63] blinde also as well as lame, they discern not *David* from *Adonibezec:*[64] but cry him up for the Lords anointed, whose thumbs and great toes not long before they had cut off upon thir Pulpit cushions. Therfore he who is our only King, the root of *David,* and whose Kingdom is eternal righteousness, with all those that Warr under him, whose happiness and final hopes are laid up in that only just & rightful kingdom (which we pray incessantly may com soon, and in so praying wish hasty ruin and destruction to all Tyrants) eev'n he our immortal King, and all that love him, must of necessity have in abomination these blind and lame Defenders of *Jerusalem;* as the soule of *David* hated them, and forbid them entrance into Gods House, and his own. But as to those before them, which I cited first (and with an easie search, for many more might be added) as they there stand, without more in number, being the best and chief of Protestant Divines, we may follow them for faithful Guides, and without doubting may receive them, as Witnesses abundant of what wee heer affirme concerning Tyrants. And indeed I find it generally the cleere and positive determination of them all, (not prelatical, or of this late faction subprelatical) who have writt'n on this argument; that to doe justice on a lawless King, is to a privat man unlawful, to an inferior Magistrate lawfull: or if they were divided in opinion, yet greater then these here alleg'd, or of more autority in the Church, there can be none produc'd. If any one shall goe about by bringing other testimonies to disable these, or by bringing these against themselves in other cited passages of thir Books, he will not only faile to make good that fals and impudent assertion of those mutinous Ministers, that the deposing and punishing of a King or Tyrant, *is against the constant Judgement of all Protestant Divines,* it being quite the contrary, but will prove rather, what perhaps he intended

62. The Jebusites unsuccessfully held out in Jerusalem against David.

63. The Levites were a Jewish priestly tribe.

64. Adonibezek, although a heathen king, acknowledged his responsibility to God; see Judg. 1:5-6.

not, that the judgement of Divines, if it be so various and inconstant to it self, is not considerable, or to be esteem'd at all. Ere which be yeilded, as I hope it never will, these ignorant assertors in thir own art will have prov'd themselves more and more, not to be Protestant Divines, whose constant judgement in this point they have so audaciously bely'd, but rather to be a pack of hungrie Churchwolves, who in the steps of *Simon Magus* [65] thir Father, following the hot sent of double Livings and Pluralities, advousons, donatives, inductions, and augmentations, [66] though uncall'd to the Flock of Christ, but by the meer suggestion of their Bellies, like those Priests of *Bel,* [67] whose pranks *Daniel* found out; have got possession, or rather seis'd upon the Pulpit, as the strong hold and fortress of thir sedition and rebellion against the civil Magistrate. Whose friendly and victorious hand having rescu'd them from the Bishops thir insulting Lords, fed them plenteously, both in public and in privat, rais'd them to be high and rich of poore and base; onely suffer'd not thir covetousness & fierce ambition, which as the pitt that sent out thir fellow locusts, hath bin ever bottomless and boundless, to interpose in all things, and over all persons, thir impetuous ignorance and importunity.

## The End

65. In Acts 8:9–25 Simon sought to buy from Peter and John the spiritual gifts of grace.

66. The preceding four terms are defined as follows: *advowson,* the right to an ecclesiastical benefice; *donative,* a benefice that may be inherited; *induction,* the formal occupation of a parish post by a clergyman; *augmentation,* an increase of clerical stipend.

67. The apocryphal Book of Bel records a stratagem whereby corrupt priests got access to the offerings intended for the god.

# DEFENCE OF THE PEOPLE OF ENGLAND

*In the reaction to Parliament's execution of Charles I probably no single writing posed such a threat to Milton's party as the indictment of their deed by Claude Salmasius (1588–1653) in a lengthy Latin tract entitled* Defensio Regia pro Carlo Primo. *Salmasius enjoyed a distinguished reputation as the successor to the chair of the famous humanist J. C. Scaliger at Leyden, and after the publication of his attack on the English regicides he was received at the court of Queen Christina of Sweden. Salmasius's* Defence *argued monarchist fundamentals as well as making an extended case against the parliamentary rebels for having broken their oaths of fealty to Charles, for having incited the realm to revolt, and for having executed the king without just cause or due process of law. Salmasius drew upon philosophical sources, scriptural interpretation, and the legal customs of England as he understood these.*

*In February 1651 Milton brought out his reply,* Defensio pro Populo Anglicano *in Latin, at the behest of Parliament acting in his capacity of Secretary of Foreign Tongues, a post to which he had been appointed in March 1649. Milton responds to Salmasius in kind following his opponent's argument chapter by chapter and offering his own view of the philosophical tradition, scripture, and the British constitution as well as quite a different understanding of the events leading to the trial and execution of the king. Milton also follows Salmasius in a vituperative, satirical invective that argues the man as frequently as the principle. Thus Milton will ridicule his adversary for having changed sides in controversy, for meddling in the affairs of a nation foreign to him, and for having written in the pay of the son of the king he champions. Milton's* Defence *is called the* First *to distinguish the work from another included in this volume in which he replies to a renewed attack mounted by an anonymous follower of Salmasius the year after the* First Defence *was published. Salmasius also wrote his own reply, which was published posthumously in 1660.*

John Milton an Englishman His

# DEFENCE OF THE PEOPLE OF ENGLAND

Against
Claudius Anonymous, Alias Salmasius
his Defence of the King

**PREFACE.**

If I be as copious of words and empty of matter in my Defence of the People of England as most men think Salmasius has been in his Defence of the King, I fear that I shall apparently have deserved to be called a defender at once wordy and silly. Yet no man thinks he must make such haste, even in handling any ordinary subject, as not to employ an opening worthy of its importance. In handling well-nigh the greatest of all subjects, then, if I neither omit an introduction, nor overdo it, I am in hopes of attaining two things, both of which I earnestly desire: the one, that I be nowise wanting, as far as in me lies, to this cause, most renowned and most worth the remembrance of all the generations of men; the other, that I myself be yet deemed to have avoided the silliness and verbosity which I blame in my antagonist.

For I shall relate no common things, or mean; but how a most puissant king, when he had trampled upon the laws, and stricken down religion, and was ruling at his own lust and wantonness, was at last subdued in the field by his own people, who had served a long term of slavery; how he was thereupon put under guard, and when he gave no ground whatever, by either word or action, to hope better things of him, was finally by the highest council of the realm condemned to die, and beheaded before his very palace gate. I shall likewise relate (which will much conduce to the easing men's minds of a great superstition) under what system of laws, especially what laws of England, this judgment was rendered and executed; and shall easily defend my valiant and worthy countrymen, who have extremely well deserved of all subjects and nations in the world, from the most wicked calumnies of both domestic and foreign railers, and chiefly from the reproaches of this utterly empty sophister, who sets up to be captain and ringleader of all the rest. For what king's majesty high enthroned ever shone so bright as did the people's majesty of England, when, shaking off that age-old superstition which had long prevailed, they overwhelmed with judgment their very king (or rather him who from their king had become their enemy), ensnared in his own laws him who alone among men claimed by divine right to go unpunished, and feared not to inflict upon this very culprit the same capital punishment which he would have inflicted upon any other.

Yet why do I proclaim as done by the people these actions, which themselves almost utter a voice, and witness everywhere the presence of God? Who, as often as it hath seemed good to his infinite wisdom, useth to cast down proud unbridled kings, puffed up above the measure of mankind, and often uprooteth them with their whole house. As for us, it was by His clear command we were on a sudden resolved upon the safety and liberty that we had almost lost; it was He we followed as our Leader, and revered His divine footsteps imprinted everywhere; and thus we entered upon a path not dark but bright, and by His guidance shown and opened to us. I should be much in error if I hoped that by my diligence alone, such as it is, I might set forth all these matters as worthily as they deserve, and might make such records of them as, haply, all nations and all ages would read. For what eloquence can be august and magnificent enough, what man has parts sufficient, to undertake so great a task? Yea, since in so many ages as are gone over the world there has been but here and there a man found able to recount worthily the actions of great heroes and potent states, can any man have so good an opinion of himself as to think that by any style or language of his own he can compass these glorious and wonderful works—not of men, but, evidently, of almighty God?

Yet such is the office which the most eminent men of our commonwealth have by their influence prevailed upon me to undertake, and have wished this next best task assigned to me of defending their deeds from envy and calumny, against which steel and the furniture of war avail not—of defending, I say, with far other arms and other weapons, the works which under God's guidance they had gloriously wrought. Their decision, certainly, I count a great honor to myself—that they voted me, before all others,[1] the one to render this never-to-be-regretted assistance to the valiant liberators of my country; and indeed from my youth upward I had been fired with a zeal which kept urging me, if not to do great deeds myself, at least to celebrate them. Yet, mistrusting these advantages, I have recourse to the divine assistance, and pray the great and holy God, dispenser of all gifts: Even as successfully and piously as those our glorious guides to freedom crushed in battle the royal insolence and tyranny uncontrolled, and then at last by a memorable punishment utterly ended them; even as easily as I, singlehanded, lately refuted and set aside the king himself when he, as it were, rose from the grave, and in that book published after his death tried to cry himself up before the people with new verbal sleights and harlotries; so, I pray, may I now as auspiciously and as truly refute and demolish this outlandish rhetorician's wanton lies.

Foreign born as he is, and (though he deny it a thousand times) a mere grammarian, yet, not satisfied with the grammarian's dole, he has chosen to mind everybody's business, and has presumed to mix in an affair of state, a foreign state at that, though he brings to the task neither moderation nor understanding nor anything else that so grand

1. The Council of State officially authorized Milton to make reply to Salmasius's *Defensio Regia* on January 8, 1650.

a judge would surely need, save his presumption and his grammar. Indeed if he had published here, and in English, the same things as he now has writ in Latin (such as it is) I think scarce any man would have thought it worth while to return an answer to them, but would partly despise them as common, and exploded over and over already, and partly (even one who sided with the king) abhor them as foul despotic maxims, hardly to be endured by the most worthless of slaves. But as he undertakes to puff his portentous sheet among outsiders, who are quite ignorant of our affairs, they, who thus get an utterly false notion of them, certainly ought to be fully informed; and he, who is so very forward to speak ill of others, should be treated in his own kind.

If haply anyone wonder why, then, we all have suffered him so long to strut unharmed, swollen in triumph at our silence, I know not what others may say, but for myself I can boldly declare that I had neither words nor arguments long to seek for the defence of so good a cause, had I but found leisure, and such health as could bear the toil of writing. Yet as I still possess but slender strength, I am forced to write by piece-meal, and break off almost every hour, though the subject be such as requires unremitted study and attention. If for this reason it be not given me to clarion with right heraldry, befitting their praises, those glorious fellow-citizens of mine, their country's saviors, whose deathless deeds already ring round the world, yet I hope it will not be difficult for me to defend, at least, and justify them, against the impertinence of this bore of a pedant, and the squallings of his professorial tongue. Nature and laws would be in ill case if slavery were eloquent, and liberty mute; if tyrants should find defenders, and they that are potent to master and vanquish tyrants should find none. And it were deplorable indeed, if the reason mankind is endued withal, which is God's gift, should not furnish more arguments for men's preservation, for their deliverance, and, as much as the nature of the thing will bear, for their equality, than for their oppression and utter ruin under one man's dominion. Let me therefore enter upon this noble cause with cheerfulness grounded upon the assurance that on the other side are cheating, and trickery, and ignorance and outlandishness, and on my side the light of truth and reason, and the practice and theory of the best historic ages.

So much by way of introduction. And now, since our affair is with critics, let us consider first the title of this choice volume. What does it say? "A Royal Defence for Charles the First, to Charles the Second." You undertake a wonderful piece of work, whoever you are—to plead the father's cause before his own son: a hundred to one but you carry it! But, Salmasius, though you hide from legal process as you formerly did under an assumed name, and do now under no name at all—I yet summon you to appear before another tribunal and before other judges, where perhaps you shall not get those "Bravo's" and "Hear Hear's" which you are wont to hanker after so desperately in your classroom. But why this royal defence dedicated to the king's own son? We need not put him to the torture; he confesses: "At the king's expense,"[2] says he. Mercenary and costly advocate! so you would not write a defence for Charles the father, whom you pretend to have been the best of kings, to Charles the son, the most indigent of kings, but it must be at the king's own expense? You old rogue, in calling it the "*King's* Defence" you certainly contrived not to have yourself laughed at; for, as you have sold it, 'tis no longer yours, but lawfully the *King's* indeed,—yea, bought for one hundred Jacobuses,[3] a great sum to get from a needy King. I speak not of things unknown: I know who took those gold-pieces to your house in that beaded purse; I know who saw you reach out your greedy hands under pretence of embracing the king's chaplain who brought the gift, but in fact to hug the gift itself, and by taking this single fee almost to empty the king's treasury.

But here comes the man himself; the door creaks; enter the actor.

In silence now and with attention wait,
That ye may learn what th' Eunuch has to prate.[4]

2. Throughout Milton will tax Salmasius with his admission that he accepted payment from Charles's son for writing *Defensio Regia*.

3. Coins first minted by James I, hence the Latin name.

4. From the prologue of Terence's *Eunuchus*.

For whatever's the matter with him, he struts on with heroics more than usual stilted. "A horrible message has lately struck our ears, but our minds more, with a heinous wound concerning a parricide committed in England in the person of a king, by an execrable conspiracy of sacrilegious men." Surely that horrible message must either have had a much longer sword than the one that Peter drew,[5] or those ears must have been exceeding long-eared ears, that it could wound at such a distance; for it could not so much as in the least offend any ears but dull ones. What harm is it to you foreigners—are any of you hurt by it—if we amongst ourselves put our own enemies, our own traitors, to death, be they commoners, noblemen, or kings? Salmasius, you had better mind your own business; for *I* have "a horrible message" to send about *you,* and I shall be surprised if it strike not with a more heinous wound all grammarians' and critics' ears, so these be but refined and learned: "Of a parricide committed in Holland in the person of Aristarchus[6] by the abominable barbarism of Salmasius": to wit, that you, a great critic, hired forsooth, at a king's expense to write a king's defence, did with a sickening exordium, most like the trumpery doleful wailings of hired mourner-women, not only fail to move with pity the mind of any but a fool, but by the end of your first sentence instantly provoke, in those who had scarce read it, laughter at your manifold barbarisms. For, pray what is "parricidium in persona regis admittere"? What is "in persona regis"?[7] What Latinity ever used such diction?—as it were a murder committed in the mask or disguise of a king! Unless maybe you are telling us of some sham Philip[8]—some Perkin Warbeck[9]—who by *impersonating* a king did in a way perpetrate parricide in England. This word, methinks, you have spoken better than you knew. For a tyrant is no real king;

5.  Milton refers to Peter's actions at the arrest of Jesus, Matt. 26:51.
6.  Alexandrian literary scholar who wrote in the second century before Christ.
7.  *Persona* in Latin can mean "mask" or "character" as well as "individual."
8.  Andiscus pretended to be Philip, son of King Perseus of Macedon.
9.  A Flemish impostor and pretender to the English throne who was murdered in 1499.

he is but a player-king, the mere mask and spectre of a king. At all events, for such Frenchified Latin blunders as this, with which you abound, you shall be punished not by me, for I have no time, but by your own fellow-grammarians; to them I turn you over to be laughed and flogged out of court—and much good may it do them.

Far more heinous is it, that what was decreed by our supreme magistracy to be done to the king should be said by you to have been done "by an execrable conspiracy of sacrilegious men." Rogue, is it thus you name the acts and decrees of our late most potent realm and present yet more potent commonwealth, concerning whose deeds no king, even, could hitherto be brought to utter or publish aught more abusive?

Rightly, then, have the High and Mighty States of Holland, true offspring of the ancient liberators of their country, by their edict damned to darkness this defence of tyranny, most noxious to the liberty of all peoples. As for the author, him every free state ought to keep out of its bounds, or cast out; especially the state which supports and subsidizes so ungrateful and so foul an enemy of the republic. That republic's foundations and causes he attacks precisely as he attacks ours; by one and the same effort, in fact, he strives to undermine them both, and make them totter to their fall; and under our names foully maligns the most eminent champions of liberty there. Consider with yourselves, most illustrious States General of the United Netherlands, and bethink you who it was that moved this assertor of kingly power to write; who it was that lately began to king it among you; what counsels were taken, what attempts made, what tumults at length ensued throughout Holland; to what pass things might have been brought by this time—how slavery and a new master were made ready for you, and that liberty of yours, vindicated by so many years' war and toil—how near spent it had now been among you, had it not recovered breath again of late by the exceeding timely death of a rash young man.[10]

10.  William II, Stadtholder of Orange, who died November 6, 1650.

But that fellow of ours goes on with his bombast, play-acting strange tragedies: "Whomsoever this dreadful news reached"—the news, doubtless, of Salmasius's parricidal barbarism—"suddenly, as if they had been scorched by lightning's flash, 'Up on end stood their hair in horror, and voice in their throat stuck.'" Something hitherto unheard of for natural philosophers to learn—that to be struck by lightning makes hair stand on end! But who knows not that base and coward minds do get thunderstruck even at the mere noise of any great deed soever, and then most unmistakably show themselves for the blockheads they have been all along? Some, he says, "could not but weep"—some *petites femmes,* I suppose, and *cortegiane,* or others yet more sentimental,—among whom, indeed, Salmasius himself has by a modern metamorphosis turned into Salmacis, and in this his counterfeit fountain of night-lucubrated tears, attempts to emasculate manly courages. I give warning therefore, and bid beware

> Lest ill-reputed Salmacis with wave
> Of evil power some victim shall unman;
> Who, though a man he came, yet thence shall go
> Hermaphrodite, and at the water's touch
> Swift grow effeminate.[11]

"In fact, the more bravely couraged," he says (for I suppose he cannot even name the brave and courageous without nauseous affectation), "burned with such a flame of indignation that they could hardly control themselves." For such madmen we care not a rush, but have a way of driving off your blustering bullies, and routing them with that true courage which does control itself.

"Surely not one but invoked curses upon the authors of so horrible a villainy." Yet, you were just saying, their voice in their throat stuck. And as far as our exiles are concerned—if you mean them—

11. Ovid *Metamorphoses* 4.285–86, 4.385–86.

would that it had stuck there even unto this day; for we have learned to a certainty that nothing is oftener upon their lips than curses and imprecations, to be by all good men abhorred certainly, yet not feared. For the rest, it can scarce be believed that when news of the king's execution arrived, there was found, especially among a free people, anyone so much a slave by nature as to calumniate us or count our deed a crime; but rather that all righteous men said all was righteous—nay even thanked God for having published so high and shining an example of justice for so wholesome a lesson to the rest of the kings.

And so, to those "savage, sternly steeled and stony-hearted" persons who (he says) bewail the "miserable and amazing marvellous murder" (whose, pray?), to them and their jingling spokesman, the dullest, surely, "since ever in the world the kingly name was native and known," I say: "Let them wail again! Let them wail again!" But meanwhile what boy just out of school, or what dear brotherkin from any friary you like, could not have made a rhetorical exercise out of this royal fall more eloquently—yea, more Latinly—than this royal speechmaker?

It would surely be uncalled for were I carefully to follow up the man's babblings and ravings on the present scale throughout his volume; yet I would do it willingly (for he swells, they say, with measureless pride and conceit) did he not shield himself behind the enormous ill-composed disordered bulk of his book, like Terence's soldier skulking behind the front ranks;[12]—and a clever plan too—that even the most energetic might weary of marking all the details, and die of boredom before he could refute them. Yet I did wish to give at least a sample by way, so to speak, of the present curtain-raiser, and offer on the spot to let my thoughtful readers taste the man at the beginning, that by trying these *hors d'oeuvres* and *anti-pasti* from a single page we may learn how splendidly he will entertain us with the rest of his gorgeous dishes: how many silly puerilities he will prove to have

12. Terence *Eunuchus*.

heaped together in his whole work, who has put them so thick—where least seemly—at its very head and front.

Thenceforward I gladly disregard his much-twaddling harangues, predestined as they are to wrap up mackerels; moreover, as far as concerns our affairs, we doubt not that what has been published and proclaimed by authority of Parliament shall have more weight with all right-minded and judicious foreigners than the lies and slanders of one brazen *petit-monsieur* who has been hired at a price by our exiles, their country's enemies, and has unhesitatingly scraped together and written down utter lies, whenever anyone to whom he has leased his pen spreads a bit of malicious gossip, and gives him his orders.

That all may see clearly how it matters nothing to his conscience what he writes—true or false, holy or unholy,—I shall have to call no other witness than Salmasius himself. In his *Apparatus contra Primatum Papae* he writes: "The reasons why the church ought to return from Episcopacy to the Apostolic institution" of Elders "are very strong: in Episcopacy there was brought into the church an evil much greater than those schisms which used to be feared before: the plague which came out of it into the church struck down the whole body of the church beneath a vile despotism: nay, put even kings and princes under the yoke: the church would profit more by the abolition of the whole hierarchy than by the abolition of its head only, the Pope (p. 196). That episcopacy and papacy together might be removed with the greatest benefit to the church: that, episcopacy once removed, papacy itself, as founded thereon, would fall (p. 171). He considers that there are special reasons why it should be done away in those kingdoms which have already renounced papacy, and sees no reason why it should be retained there. That a reformation this part of which has been left unaccomplished seems incomplete: that no jot of reason or probable cause can be adduced why, when Papal supremacy is got rid of, episcopacy ought to be kept, or can be" (p. 197).

But though he wrote all this and much more four years ago, yet now he is so false and so shameless that he dares in this passage violently to reproach the Parliament of England for voting that Episcopacy was to be "not only turned out of the House of Lords, but cast off utterly." [13] Yea, he even recommends and defends episcopacy itself by means of the same reasons and proofs which in that earlier volume of his he had forcibly confuted—namely that "the bishops are necessary" forsooth, "and by all means to be kept, lest a thousand plaguy sects and heresies should burgeon out in England." Sly turncoat, are you not ashamed even in matters of religion to play fast and loose, and—I had almost said—to betray the church, whose most holy ordinances you seem to have defended with so much noise for the very purpose of ridiculing and overturning them with all the deeper ignominy whenever you thought convenient?

Everybody knows that when the Houses of Parliament, ardently desiring to reform our church after the pattern of the rest of the churches, had resolved to abolish episcopacy, first the King vetoed the measure, and next, chiefly for that reason, made war upon us—which at last proved his own undoing. Go now and brag that you defend a king, you, who, to do it to the hilt, now openly betray and attack what you were the very one to support—the cause of the church—and should undergo her heaviest reprimand.

To come back, however, to the constitution of the English Commonwealth. Forasmuch as you, a tuppenny-thrippenny outlandish pedant, neglect those desks and portfolios of yours, stuffed as they are with trumpery that you would do better to put in order,—since you, I say, choose instead to play the hateful busybody in the public affairs of a nation not your own,—I give you, then, or, preferably some wiser man than you, this short answer. Our constitution is what the dissensions of our time will permit: not such as were to be desired, but such as the persistent strife of wicked citizens will suffer it to be. But any state soever which in the throes of partisan strife takes up arms for safety, surely does full justice if it maintains relations with its sound and uncontaminated part alone, and expels or removes the rest, whether populace or patrician,—even though, taught by its own sufferings, it thenceforth utterly refuses a King and a House of Lords.

How absurd of you to rail at our "Supreme Council" and even at

13. Charles I had in fact given his assent to the exclusion of bishops on February 13, 1642, and for abolishing on October 9, 1646.

a supposed "President of the Council"! For that Council—figment of your dreams—is not supreme, but appointed by authority of Parliament, for a definite time only, of about forty of its members, anysoever of whom may by vote of the rest be president.[14] It has always been, moreover, a well-established practice for Parliament, which is our Senate, to fix a comparatively small number of its members, choose and appoint them, and delegate to them authority to meet anywhere, and to hold, as it were, a kind of smaller Senate. To these, often, weightiest matters were turned over and entrusted, to be despatched the more quickly and quietly: the management or administration of the navy, the army, the treasury,—in fine, any and all business of peace or war. This body, call it "council" or anything else, may be new in name, but is ancient in substance; without it no commonwealth can be managed properly.

Moreover—about the king's execution and about our revolution,—stop your howling, stop that celebrated act of vomiting up the venom of your bitterness, till I fight you hand to hand, and despite your struggles show, chapter by chapter, "in accordance with what law, under what system of right, in virtue of what judgment" (as you put it) these things were done. If you yet insist upon your "What right? What law?"—under that law, I say, which God himself and nature hath appointed, that all things for the safety of the commonwealth should be deemed lawful and righteous.[15] Thus did wise men aforetime answer such as you.

You charge us with "having abolished laws that had been settled so many years," but you do not say whether they were good or bad; nor, if you did, would you be entitled to a hearing; for our laws—Olus,[16] what business are they of yours? Would that they had abolished more of the laws as well as more of the pettifogging lawyers:

14. Milton is describing procedure for forming the Council of State, the executive arm of the revolutionary Parliament in 1649.

15. As Cicero stated in his *On the Laws,* "the well-being of the people is the supreme law."

16. Olus is a buffoonish character in Martial's *Epigrams* (7.10).

they would have had more regard for the people, and for the cause of Christianity. You gnash your teeth because "the Manii, sons of the soil, persons scarce of the nobility at home, scarce known to their own countrymen, should have believed themselves entitled to do such things." You should have remembered what not only Scripture but even the Lyrist teaches you:

> God can highest with lowest interchange—
>   Such is his might;
> Degradeth men of mark,
> But hidden fortunes dark
>   Bringeth to light.[17]

Take this, too: of those whom you call "scarce noble," some are second to none of your land or kind in nobility; others, being as it were their own ancestors, tread the path to true nobility by way of industry and personal worth, and are comparable with any the noblest soever. They had rather be called "sons of the soil," too (it being their *own* soil!), and to work hard at home, than be, like you, a landless homeless worthless straw-stuffed scarecrow-knight, selling smoke to stave off starvation in a strange land at the beck and call, and in the pay, of masters. Take my word for it, you would soon be sent packing from your foreign tour back to your own kith and kin, but for your one accomplishment: you do know how to blab out trumpery pamphlets among strangers—and what price to get for them.

You blame our magistrates because they "admit the offscourings of all the sects." Why should they not admit them? It is for the church to expel them from the company of the faithful, not for the magistrates to banish them the country, provided they break no civil law. To live safe and free, without suffering violence or wrong, to this end it was that men first entered into a polity; to live piously and religiously, into a church; the former has its laws, the latter its doctrine

17. Horace's *First Ode.*

and discipline, quite distinct; and it is because the Magistracy and the Church confuse their jurisdictions that for so many years war has sown a harvest of more war throughout all Christendom. This, too, is why we cannot endure Popery; for we perceive it to be not so much a religion as a pontifical despotism decked out, under pretence of religion, with the spoils of civil power, which it has seized unto itself contrary to Christ's own precept.

As for "Independents," none such as are assumed by you (and you alone) have ever been seen among us; except in so far as they recognize no assemblies or synods above each individual congregation, and feel, with you, that such should be uprooted as branches of the Hierarchy, or in fact its very trunk. From this the name of Independents has got popular currency.

Your course is such, I see, as would in the future stir up against us, on the part of all kings and monarchs, not hatred merely, but cruelest war. King Mithridates of old tried to rouse all kings against the Romans[18]—for a different reason, to be sure, but by using almost the same slanders: that the Romans were planning to overturn all thrones; that they would allow nothing human or divine to stand in their way; that from the beginning they had never got anything but by violence; that they were a gang of robbers, enemies above all to royal authority. So wrote King Mithridates to King Arsaces. But you, mouthing your unspeakable baby-rhetoric there in your classroom, what overweening self-assurance carried *your* mind to the point of supposing that you could rouse a king (even one still a boy) to war by your urging, and (though you like not to be caught at it) by your "trumpeting the signal to join battle"?—especially with so foul a scrannel mouth that Homer's mice,[19] had you been their bugler, would never, I do believe, have made war upon tadpoles!

Just as far am I from fearing any war or danger to us which you, arrant coward, can blow up among foreign kings with your windy

18. Recounted by Sallust in his *Histories*.

19. Mice were pitted against frogs in a mock-epic, the *Batrachomyomachia*, once thought to be authored by Homer.

rush of raving yet insipid language. You tell tales of us—you must be joking—that we "toss kings' heads like balls, play hoop with crowns, and make no more of imperial sceptres than of fools' bauble-sticks with heads atop." You, most foolish head, are yourself most fit to top a fool's bauble, when you fancy that kings and princes can by such childish reasonings be persuaded to war. Then you cry aloud to all nations, but they, I know full well, will never heed what you say. Even those depraved and barbarous offscourings of Irish you call to the aid of the King's party; and this one thing may be taken as a measure of your wickedness and folly—how you surpass almost all men in irreligion, impudence, and madness; for you scruple not to beg the loyalty and aid of a nation accursed and set apart for destruction, from whose godless fellowship, stained with the blood of so many harmless citizens, even the King himself always shrank in horror—or pretended to shrink. That treachery he did all he could to cover up, and strove with all his might to clear his skirts of that cruelty, which you, most worthless of two-legged creatures, have not respect enough for God or man to keep you from wilfully and publicly adopting. Come on, then, gird up your loins to defend the King—with your Irish for claque and for company!

At the beginning you take care (by Jove, a necessary caution!) not to be suspected of a possible design to snatch away all of Tully's or Demosthenes's oratorical laurels; you say in your preface that you think it "not proper for you to behave like an orator." Bright mind—to perceive that what you cannot do is not proper for you to do! Who indeed that knows you well ever looked to see you fill the rôle of orator?—you who never do, and never can, produce anything rightly developed, anything clean-cut, anything that has gust or savor, but—like a second Crispinus, or Tzetzes that decadent Greek[20]—so you write much, care not how well you write, nor if you care, can do it.

"This cause," you say, "will be tried with the whole world hear-

---

20. Crispinus is subjected to ridicule by Horace in his *First Satire;* Tzetzes was a twelfth-century Byzantine pedant.

ing, and, as it were, sitting in judgment." That is what we like so well that we could wish unto ourselves an adversary not, like you, hot-headed and unskilled, but full of understanding and sagacity. You are quite the tragic hero—quite the Ajax-with-the-Whip,[21] when you perorate: "These men's injustice, impiety, perfidy, cruelty, I will cry out unto heaven and earth; themselves the perpetrators I will turn over to posterity convicted, and transfix the culprits." Ye Little Flowers of Rhetoric! And so, you senseless witless bawling pettifogger, born only to pick good writers to pieces or transcribe them, do you really think yourself capable of writing anything that will live?—you whom posterity—take my word for it—will damn to oblivion with all your scribbled trumpery.—Except perhaps your Royal Defence shall turn out to be something beholden to my answer to it, and after long slumbering unread be once more handled. And this I would petition of the most Illustrious States of Holland, that they would allow it to be straightway dismissed their Treasury—'tis no treasure!—and to wander whither it will. For if I shall have made clear to all what idle talk and ignorance and deceit it is stuffed with, then the more widely it circulates, the more straitly, methinks, it is suppressed. And now let us see how he will "transfix" us "culprits."

## CHAPTER I.

Inflated empty man that you are, Salmasius, you were haply yet more puffed up at the King of Great Britain's being Defender of the Faith, and your being Defender of the King. For my part, I think you deserve your titles both alike; for the king so defended the faith, and you have so defended him, that each of you seems rather to have ruined his case; as I shall make appear throughout the whole ensuing discourse, and particularly in this first chapter. You told us on the twelfth page of your preface that "so good and just a cause needed no rhe-

---

21. Ajax scourged sheep in his madness, thinking them the Atreides in Sophocles' *Ajax*.

torical colouring, for simply to tell the thing as it occurred was to defend the king." Yet in your first chapter, in which you had promised us that your tale would be plain, you neither tell the thing simply as it occurred, nor abstain from adorning it with such rhetorical colors as you can command; so that—to take your own view of it—the king's cause will be neither good nor just.

Nevertheless, be careful not to attribute to yourself (what nobody grants you) the ability to state the facts of a case as a right orator ought; for you can play the part neither of an orator nor of an historian, nor even of a hired partisan advocate. Like some itinerant hawker, instead, touting from fair to fair, you in your preface kept raising great expectations of next day's performance—not that you might at last relate the facts you promised, but that you might peddle out to as many readers as possible those your wretched bottlefuls of rhetoric-paint and fustian dye. For "being now about to give us an account of the matter of fact," you find yourself "encompassed and affrighted with so many monsters of novelty" that you "know not what to say first, what next, and what last." Is this your plain tale? I will tell you what is the matter with you. First of all you find yourself affrighted at your own monstrous lies, and next you find that empty head of yours not only "encompassed" but set awhirl with so many trifles and follies that what was fit to be said first, what next, what last, you not only do not know, but never did know.

"Amid the difficulties of expressing the heinousness of so incredible a piece of impiety, this expression alone offers itself," you say, "which is easily said and must be oft repeated," to wit, "that the sun itself never beheld a more outrageous action." My good schoolmaster, the sun has beheld many things that Bernard[22] never saw. Yet we are content you should bring in the sun over and over, and you shall act wisely so to do, for it will be insistently required—not by our wickedness but by the frigidity of your defence. "The origin of kings," you say, "arose with the new-created sun." May the gods and god-

22. Bernard of Clairvaux (1091–1153), Cistercian contemplative noted for his synoptic intelligence.

desses, Damasippus,[23] bless you with a solstice to warm yourself withal, that cannot warm a foot enough to stir a foot without "the sun."

Perhaps you would avoid the imputation of being called a doctor that lounges in the shade. Alas, your shade is utter darkness! You make no difference betwixt a paternal power and a regal; and, once you have called kings fathers of their country, fancy this metaphor so persuasive that whatever I would admit concerning a father I would at once grant true of a king. A king and a father are very different things. Our fathers begot and made us; our king made not us, but we him. Nature gave the people fathers, but the people itself gave itself a king; so that the people is not for the king, but the king for the people. We bear with a father, as we do with a king, though he be harsh and severe; but we do not bear with even a father, if he be a tyrant. If a father murder his child, he shall suffer capital punishment; and why should not a king likewise be subject to the same most just law if he have destroyed the people his children? Especially as a father can never cease to be such, but a king can easily bring it to pass that he shall be neither father nor king. If this "action" of ours is to be considered "next" according to its "quality," as you call it, I who am an eye-witness and a native, tell you, who are a foreigner and an utter stranger to our affairs, that we "removed from among us" a king neither "good," nor "just," nor "merciful," nor "devout," nor "godly," nor "peaceable," as you style him, but one who was an enemy to us for almost ten years, and no father, but a destroyer of his country.

You confess, for you dare not deny it, that "such things have been practised, but not by Protestants upon a Protestant king." As if he deserved the name of Protestant, who in a letter to the Pope could give him the title of Most Holy Father, and who was always more favorable to the papists than to those of the right faith. And being such, he is not the first, even of his own family, that has been removed "from among us" by Protestants. What! Was not his grandmother Mary deposed and banished and at last beheaded by Protestants, while not

23. Milton refers to a character in Horace's *Second Satire*.

even the Scottish Protestants took it ill? Nay, if I should say they were parties to it, I should not lie. There being so few Protestant kings, no wonder it never happened that one of them was put to death. But that it is lawful to depose a wicked king or a tyrant, and to punish him according to his deserts, nay, that this is the opinion of eminent divines who have been the very leaders in the late reformation, do you deny it if you dare. You admit that great numbers of kings have met a violent death, some "by the sword," some "by poison," some in a filthy "dungeon," some "in a noose"; but for a king to be brought to trial, "to be put to plead for his life, to be condemned, and brought to the block"—this you think a more lamentable instance than all the rest, and make it a prodigious piece of impiety. Tell me, superlative fool, whether it be not more humane, more just, more agreeable to the laws of all civilized states, to bring a criminal, be his offence what it may, before a court of justice, to give him the opportunity of defending himself, and if the law condemn him, then to put him to death as he has deserved, so as he may have time to repent or to compose himself; than presently, as soon as ever he is taken, to butcher him like a sheep, without trial or hearing? Is there a malefactor in the world who if he might have his choice would not choose to be punished that way rather than this? And if that proceeding be accounted the fairer of the two when used by king against subjects, why should it not be so counted when used by subjects against king? Nay, why should we not think that himself liked it better? You would have had him killed in secret, without witnesses, either that all history might lose the advantage of so good an example, or that this glorious action might in supposed guilt seem to have shunned the light, as having no law or even justice on its side.

Next you aggravate the matter by telling us that it was not done in the uproar of party strife amongst our nobles, or in a raging rebellion either of the people or of the army, or through hatred or fear or ambition or blind precipitate rashness, but was long designed and thought upon, and accomplished deliberately. You did well from advocate to turn grammarian! For from the accidents of a case, so to speak, which in themselves sway neither one way nor another, you inveigh against it before you have proved the deed itself either good or bad. See how easily I refute you: if the deed was well and seemly, they that did it deserve the greater praise in that they were prepossessed with no passions, but did that they did for virtue's sake; if it was difficult and grievous, the greater praise for doing it not upon blind impulse but upon deliberation and design. Though for my own part, when I call to mind with how unexpected an importunity and fervency of mind, and with how unanimous a consent, the whole army and a great part of the people from almost every county in the kingdom cried out with one voice for justice against the king as the very author of all their calamities, I cannot but think that these things were brought about rather by a divine impulse. However that may be, whether we consider the magistrates or the body of the people, no men ever undertook with a loftier courage, and, as our adversaries themselves confess, with a more tranquil mind, an action so distinguished, so worthy of heroic ages—an action whereby they ennobled not only law and its enforcement, which thenceforth seem restored to all men equitably, but Justice's very self, and rendered her after so signal a judgment more glorious, more august, than even she had been before.

We have now toiled to the end of the third page of his first chapter, and have not yet the plain tale he promised us. He complains of our doctrine "that a king ruling burdensomely and odiously may lawfully be deposed: according to this," he says, "if they had had a king better in a thousand respects than the one they had, they would not have spared his life." Keen reasoner! I long to have you tell me how this follows, unless you allow that a king a thousand ways better than our king may rule burdensomely and odiously. So now you have brought yourself to a pass where you make out the king that you defend a thousand ways worse than kings whose government is burdensome and odious, that is, the most monstrous perhaps of all tyrants. Kings, I wish you joy of so brisk a defender!

Now his narrative begins. "They put him to several sorts of torments." Give instances. "They removed him from prison to prison";

and so they might lawfully, for from a tyrant he was become a public enemy taken in war. "Often changing his guards,"—lest his guards should change their fidelity. "Sometimes they gave him hopes of liberty—sometimes even of restoring him to his crown upon articles of agreement." It seems then the taking away his life was not done upon so long premeditation as he talked of before, and that we did not so long before lay hold on all "opportunities and means" to renounce our king. Those things that we demanded of him in the beginning of the war, when he had almost brought us under—things the denial of which would cut our people off from all hope of liberty and safety—those very things we petitioned of him when he was our prisoner, petitioned humbly and submissively, not once or twice, but thrice and oftener,[24] and were as often denied. When we had now lost all hopes of the king's complying with us, then was made that noble order of Parliament that from that time forward there should no articles be sent to the king;[25] so that we left off not from the time he began to be a tyrant, but from the time he began to be incurable. Still, afterward some Parliament men set upon a new project, and meeting with a convenient opportunity to put it in practice, passed a vote to send proposals once more to the king. Their wickedness and folly nearest resembles that of the Roman Senate, who, against the opinion of Marcus Tullius and all honest men, voted to send ambassadors to Antony; and the event had been the same, but that it pleased God Almighty to order it otherwise—to deliver *them* into slavery, but to assert our liberty. For though the king did not agree to anything that might conduce to a firm peace and settlement more than he had before, they go and vote themselves satisfied. Then the sounder part of the house, finding themselves and the commonwealth betrayed, implore the aid of the army, valiant and ever faithful to the common-

24. Milton probably means the appeals made at Newcastle in July of 1646, at Hampton Court in August of 1647, and in the official overtures sent Charles when he had fled to the Isle of Wight late in 1647.

25. On January 15, 1648, Parliament passed a resolution that there should be "no further addresses or application to the King."

wealth. Whereon I can observe only this, which yet I am loath to utter: that our soldiers showed better judgment than our senators, and saved the commonwealth by their arms, when the other by their votes had almost ruined it.

Then he tells a long tale of woe in a lamentable strain, but so senselessly that he seems rather begging his readers please to be sorrowful than moving them to sorrow. It grieves him "to think that the king should undergo capital punishment after such a manner as no other king had ever done"—though he had often told us before that there never was a king that underwent capital punishment at all. Fool, are you wont to compare manner with manner when you have not fact to compare with fact? "He suffered death," says he, "as a robber, as a murderer, as a parricide, as a traitor, as a tyrant." Is this defending the king, or is it not rather giving a more severe judgment upon him than the one we gave? Who has so suddenly drawn you round to give sentence with us? He complains "that masked executioners cut off the king's head." What shall we do with this fellow? He complained before of "a murder done in the mask of a king"; now he complains that it was done in the mask of an executioner.

It were to no purpose to take particular notice of every false or silly thing he says. He tells stories of "buffetings and kicks that were given by common soldiers, and how it cost fourpence to see the dead body." These and such-like stories betray the ignorance and small-mindedness of our poor scholar, but are far from making any reader ever a whit the sadder. To bewail his father's misfortunes the younger Charles had done better, in good faith, to have hired one of the mountebanks that chant their doleful ballads to the crowd at a street corner, than this lamentable—shall I call him?—or rather most laughable—orator, so flat and tasteless that his very tears want salt.

Now his narrative is done; and it is hard to say what he does next, his discourse runs so muddy and irregular. Now he rages, then he gapes, and keeps no method in his chatter but to repeat the same things ten times over that could not but be disgusting said but once. Really I know not but that the trumpery stuff of any babbling *impro-*

*visatore,* rhymed extempore while he stands on one foot, were better worth daubing paper withal; so far am I from thinking aught he says worthy of a serious answer.

I pass by his praising as "protector of religion" a king who chose to make war upon the church rather than part with those church tyrants and enemies of religion, the bishops. How is it possible, moreover, for one to "maintain religion in its purity" that was himself a slave to those impure traditions and ceremonies of theirs? And pray tell what errors you ascribe to those our "sects, whose sacrilegious meetings," you say, "have a public license" which even Holland grants not. Meanwhile no one is more sacrilegious than you, who take unto yourself—worst license of all—the license of incessant slander. "They could not wound the commonwealth more dangerously than by taking off its master." You menial slave, learn, while you wait the lash, that unless ye take away the master, ye destroy the commonwealth, for 'tis a private wealth, not a common wealth, that owns a master. "They persecute most unjustly those pastors that abhor this deed of theirs." Lest it be not clear what pastors he means, I shall say briefly: they were those very men who by their writings and sermons justified taking up arms against the king; who cursed without ceasing, as Deborah did Meroz,[26] all such as would not help this war with arms or men or money; who kept preaching to their congregations that they were fighting not against a king but against a greater tyrant than any Saul or Ahab,[27] nay, one that out-Nero'd Nero. As soon as the bishops and the priests, whom they used to rail at with the names of pluralists and absentees, were taken out of their way, instantly they jump, some into two, some into three, of their best benefices; so that everybody knows how foully these herdsmen, so deservedly raised above the common herd, neglect their own. Their wild covetousness brake through all restraints of modesty and religion, till they were branded before the church (ill notoriety!) with the same infamy which

26. Judg. 5:23 records a curse against Meroz for failing to assist Israel against its enemy.

27. For Saul, see 1 Sam. 13:1–31; for Ahab, 1 Kings 16:29–22:40.

they had branded but a little before upon the priests. Their covetousness yet unsated, and their restless ambition grown accustomed to raise tumults and hate peace, they cease not to preach up sedition against the government now established, as they had formerly done against the king. He was a kindly king cruelly murdered, they say—this king upon whom but just now themselves had heaped all their curses, and delivered up as by God's will to the Parliament, to be despoiled of his royalty and pursued with a holy war. They now complain that the sects are not extirpated: a most absurd thing to ask of the magistrates, who never yet by any means or method have been able to extirpate avarice and ambition—the two heresies that are most calamitous to the church—out of the very order and estate of the ministers themselves. For the sects which they inveigh against, there are obscure ones, I know; but their own sects are notorious, and much more dangerous to the church of God: their heresiarchs were Simon Magus and Diotrephes.[28] Yet are we so far from persecuting these men, though they are pestilent enough, that, though we know them to be ill-affected to the government, and plotting change, we allow them but too much liberty.

You, vagabond Frenchman, seem displeased that "the English, more fierce and cruel than their own mastiffs," as your barking eloquence has it, "have no regard to the lawful successor and heir of the crown, and take no care of the king's youngest son, or of the Queen of Bohemia."[29] You, not I, shall answer yourself. "When the frame of a government is changed from a monarchy to any other, the succession is not granted among the new-modellers" (*Apparatus de Primatu Papae*). "The great change throughout three kingdoms," you say, "was brought about by a small minority in one of them." If so, that small minority were worthy to have dominion over the rest, as men over women. "These are they that presumptuously took upon them to change the ancient government of the realm into one held by many

28. See Acts 8:9–24, where Simon's presumption in offering to buy spiritual powers is exposed and 3 John 9, where Diotrephes is characterized as ambitious.
29. Elizabeth, daughter of James I.

tyrants"—and well and auspiciously too! You cannot find fault with them without being a filthy barbarian and solecist, as well in morals as in syntax—you shame of all grammarians. "The English will never be able to wash out this stain." Nay, you, though a blot and stain to all learned men, were never yet able to stain the renown and ever-lasting glory of the English nation, that with so great a resolution as we hardly find the like recorded in any history, struggled with, and overcame, not only their enemies in the field, but the hostile—that is, superstitious—persuasions of the common people, and won for themselves in general amongst all posterity the name of Deliverer: the body of the people having undertook and performed an enterprise which in other nations is thought to proceed only from the magnanimity peculiar to heroes.

What "the Protestants and primitive Christians" did or would do upon such an occasion, I will tell you hereafter, when we come to debate the merits of the cause; not to be guilty of your fault, who outdo in prolixity all the babbling Battuses.[30] You wonder how you shall be able to answer all the Jesuits in our behalf. Mind your own business, renegade, and be ashamed of your own actions, for the church is ashamed of you, who, though but of late you so boastfully and fiercely attacked the Pope's supremacy and the bishops, are now yourself become the bishops' sycophant. You confess that "some Protestants have asserted it lawful to depose a tyrant," and you do not name them; but I will, because you say "they are far worse than the Jesuits." They are no other than Luther, and Zwingli, and Calvin, and Bucer, and Pareus, and many besides. "The question, though, who shall be accounted a tyrant," you say, "they have referred to the judgment of learned men and wise. But what for men were these? Were they wise men, or learned? Were they anywise remarkable for either virtue or nobility?" A people that has felt the yoke of slavery heavy on its neck may well be allowed to be wise and learned and noble enough to know what should be done to its oppressor, though

30. Ovid *Metamorphoses* 2.688. Ovid recounts the story of Battus's having been turned to stone for disclosing Mercury's cattle rustling.

it send not to ask either foreigners or grammarians. But that this man was a tyrant not only the Parliaments of England and Scotland have declared by actions and words the clearest, but almost all the people of both nations assented to it—till by the tricks and artifices of the bishops they were divided into two factions. For the execution of His decrees upon the most potent kings of this world, what if it has pleased God to choose such men as He chooses to be made partakers of the light of the Gospel? "Not many wise or learned, not many mighty, not many noble; that by those that are not He might bring to naught those that are; that no flesh glory in His presence."[31]

And who are you to scold at this? A learned man?—you that even unto your old age seem rather to have turned over phrase-books and lexicons and glossaries than to have perused good authors with judgment or profit; so that you prate of naught but manuscripts and various readings and dislocated passages and scribal errors, but show that you have drunk never the least drop of more substantial learning. A wise man?—you that use to carry on your beggarly disputes about the meanest trifles? You that being altogether ignorant in astronomy and physic, yet are always reviling astronomers and physicians who should be trusted in their own faculties? You that if any one should offer to deprive you of the vain glory of having corrected or supplied the least word or letter in any copy you have criticised, would ban him, if you could, with the ban of fire and water? And yet you snarl in anger because everybody calls you a grammarian! In some trumpery book of yours you call Dr. Hammond, who was lately this king's best beloved chaplain, *knave,* for no other reason than because he had called you grammarian. And you would have been as ready to throw the same reproach upon the king himself, I do believe, and to withdraw this whole Defence, if you had heard that he had approved his chaplain's judgment of you.

Take notice now how much I, a single one of those Englishmen that you have the impudence to call "madmen, unlearned, ignoble, wicked," slight and despise you; that the English nation in general

31. I Cor. 1:26–29.

should take any public notice of such a worm as you would be an infinite undervaluing of themselves. For whichever way you turn and twist you roundabout and upside down and inside out, you are a grammarian and nothing but a grammarian; nay, as if you had made to some god or other a foolisher wish than Midas's,[32] whatever you touch—except when you make blunders—*is* grammar. Whosoever therefore he be, though from among "those dregs of the common people" that you are so hard upon (as for those men of eminency amongst us whose great actions evidence their wisdom and nobility and virtue, I will not disgrace them so much as to compare you with them or them with you),—whosoever, I say, among those dregs of the common people has but made this principle his own, that he was not born for kings, but for God and his country, should be deemed far more learned and honest and wise than you, and every way of greater use in the world. For he is learned without letters, while you are lettered without learning,—you that understand so many languages, turn over so many volumes, write so many screeds, and yet are but a sheep when all is done.

## CHAPTER II.

In winding up his first chapter Salmasius urged as "irrefragable" the argument that "a thing really is as it is believed to be, when all men unanimously agree in thinking it so." This argument, when applied, as he was then applying it, "to matter of fact," is an utter fallacy; nevertheless I, that am now about to discourse matter of law—the right of kings—shall be able to turn it upon himself with full truth. He defines a king (if that may be said to be defined which he makes infinite) to be "a person in whom resides the supreme power of the kingdom; who is answerable to God alone; who is permitted to do whatever he lists; who is loosed from the law." I will undertake to demonstrate, not by my own reasons and authorities alone, but even

32. The mythical king who was granted his wish that all he touched might turn to gold.

by his, that there never was a nation or people of any account (for to ransack all the uncivilized parts of the world were to no purpose) that ever allowed it to be their king's right or power "that he should be loosed from the law, do what he pleased, and judge all, but be judged of none." Nor can I think that, save Salmasius alone, there ever was any one of any nation so slavish in spirit as to assert the outrageous enormities of tyrants to be the rights of kings. Those amongst us that were the greatest royalists always abhorred this base opinion; nay, even Salmasius himself in some earlier writings of his—before he was bribed—was evidently of quite another mind. Insomuch that these doctrines, so slavish in nature and spirit, seem to have been penned not by a free man in a free State, much less in the most excellent Dutch Republic and at its University[33] of most renown, but at some prison-house or auction-block of slaves.

If whatever a king has a mind to do, the right of kings will bear him out in (a lesson that the hideous tyrant Antoninus Caracalla,[34] though his stepmother Julia taught it him through incest with herself, yet could not at once accept) then there neither is nor ever was any-one that deserved the name of tyrant. For though he has broken all the laws of God and man, yet the king shall be innocent none the less by the law of kings. Excellent man—what wrong has he done? He has but used his own right upon his own subjects. No king can per-petrate upon his subjects an outrage so frightfully, so madly cruel, as anyone can remonstrate or complain that it exceeds the king's right.

Dare you assert that this "law of kings arises from the law of na-tions, or rather that of nature," you beast? Why should I call you a man, who to the human race are so unjust, so inhuman?—who en-deavor so to bear down and vilify all mankind (made after the image of God) as to assert and maintain that those fierce merciless masters whom the fanaticism of some, or crime, or cowardly indifference, or even treachery, has inflicted upon nations, are provided and appointed by Nature herself, that mild and gentle mother of us all. By which

33. Leyden.
34. Emperor of Rome from 211 until his assassination in 217.

pestilent doctrine of yours having rendered them far more fierce and fell, you not only incite them to tread down all poor mortals, and to trample the wretches under foot in the bargain, but endeavor with the law of nature, the law of kings, nay the very laws of the people, to arm them against the people: the extreme at once of folly and of wickedness. As Dionysius[35] of old from a tyrant became a school-master, so you from a grammarian deserve to become a tyrant; that you may have—not that royal right to live an evil life, but that other—to die an evil death; whereby, like Tiberius shut up in Capri[36]—yourself the author of your own ruin—you shall feel yourself perish daily.

But let us look a little more narrowly into this right of kings that you talk of. "This," you say, "was the sense of the eastern and of the western part of the world." I shall not answer you with what Aristotle in the *Politics* and Cicero in the oration *De Provinciis* (both as trustworthy authorities as any we have) have writ, viz. that the people of Asia easily submit to slavery, but the Syrians and Jews are actually born to it. I confess there are but few, and those men of great wisdom and courage, that are either desirous of liberty or capable of using it. Far the greatest part of the world prefers just masters—masters, observe, but just ones. As for masters unjust and unbearable, neither was God ever so much an enemy to mankind as to constrain our submission to them, nor was there ever any people so destitute of all sense and sunk into such depth of despair as of its own accord to impose so cruel a law upon itself and its posterity.

You produce first "the words, in Ecclesiastes, of the king[37] illustrious for his wisdom." So we too appeal to God's law; of the king we will consider hereafter, whose opinion we shall thence better understand. Let God Himself be heard, Deut. 17. "When thou art come into the land which the Lord thy God giveth thee, and shalt say, I will

---

35. Tyrant of Syracuse given to literary ambitions.

36. Roman emperor (A.D. 14–37) who took refuge on the island of Capri for his security and perverse amusements.

37. Solomon.

set a king over me, like as all the nations that are about me." [38] Which passage I could wish all men would consider again and again, for here it appears by God's own witness that all nations and peoples have always possessed free choice to erect what form of government they will, and also to change it into what they will. This God affirms expressly concerning the Hebrews, and of other nations denies it not. A commonwealth, moreover, in the opinion of God, was, under human conditions, a more perfect form of government than a monarchy, and more useful for His own people; for He himself set up this government, and could hardly be prevailed withal a great while after, and at their own importunate desire, to let them change it into a monarchy. But were they to insist upon a king, then God, to show that He had left the people their choice to be governed by a single person or by more, so they were justly governed, prescribed laws for the king, though still but in prospect, whereby he was forbidden "to multiply to himself horses and wives, or to heap up riches." This was to make him understand that outside the law no power over others was his, who concerning his very self could take no action outside the law. He was commanded therefore to transcribe with his own hand "all the precepts of the law," and, having writ them out, to "observe and keep them, that his mind might not be lifted up above his brethren." Whence it is evident that as well the prince as the people was bound by those laws.

To this effect writes Josephus, a qualified interpreter of the laws of his nation, excellently versed in the Jewish polity, and preferable to a thousand obscure rabbins, *Antiquities,* Book 4. "An aristocracy is the best form of government; wherefore seek ye not any other; it is enough to have God for your ruler. But if so huge desire of a king have seized you, let him yield to the laws and to God more than to his own wisdom; and let him be restrained if he offer at more power than is proper to your affairs." Thus, in part, Josephus upon this passage in Deuteronomy.

Another solid authority, Josephus's contemporary Philo Judaeus,

38. Deut. 17:14.

one very studious in the law of Moses, upon the whole of which he wrote an extensive commentary, when in his book concerning the creation of the king he interprets this chapter of the law, releases the king from the law no otherwise than as an enemy may be said to be so released. "They," says he, "that acquire great power to the prejudice and destruction of their subjects should be named not kings but enemies, for their actions are those of an irreconcilable enemy. Nay, they that under a show of government commit usurpation are worse than open enemies. The latter we may easily ward off, but the wicked craft of the former is not always easy to discover." [39] Once discovered, then, why should they not be dealt with as enemies? In the second book of the *Allegories of the Law*, "A king," says he, "and a tyrant are contraries." And a little after, "A king not only commands, but also obeys." [40]

"All this is very true," someone will say; "a king ought to observe the laws most exactly, but if he will not, what law is there to punish him?" The same law, I answer, that there is to punish all others; I find no exception. There is no express law to punish the priests or even the least important magistrates, who might all, no matter what their guilt, with equal right and reason claim impunity because there is no positive law for their punishment; and yet none of them ever made the claim, nor would it ever, I suppose, be allowed them on that ground.

Hitherto we have learned from the very law of God that a king ought to obey the laws, and not lift himself up above the rest, who also are his brethren. Let us now consider whether the Preacher teaches any other doctrine, Chapter VIII. v. 1, etc. "I counsel thee to keep the king's commandment, and that in regard of the oath of God. Be not hasty to go out of his sight; stand not in an evil thing; for he doeth whatsoever pleaseth him. Where the word of a king is, there is power; and who may say unto him, What doest thou?" It is well enough known that here the Preacher directs his precepts not to the Sanhedrim or to a parliament, but to private persons. He bids "keep the king's commandment, and that in regard of the oath of God"; but who

39. Philo *De specialibus legibus* 4.185.
40. Ibid., bk. 3.

makes oath to the king unless the king for his part have made oath to the laws of God and his country? So the Reubenites and Gadites promise obedience to Joshua, Josh. I: "According as we hearkened unto Moses in all things, so will we hearken unto thee; so but God be with thee as he was with Moses." Here is an express condition. Hear the Preacher else, Chapter IX: "The quiet words of wise men ought to be heard rather than the shouting of him that ruleth among fools." Next he cautions us, "Stand not in an evil thing; for he doeth whatsoever pleaseth him." He does, certainly, to malefactors that persist in evil; for he is armed with the law's authority, and may proceed with mercy or severity as he will. Naught here sounds tyrannical; naught here that a good man need dread. "Where the word of a king is, there is power; and who may say to him, What doest thou?" And yet we read of one that did say to a king not only "What hast thou done?" but "Thou hast done foolishly." I Sam. 13. But Samuel, you may say, was an extraordinary person. I answer you with your own words, further on, from your forty-ninth page. "What was there extraordinary," say you, "in Saul or David?" And so say I, What was there in Samuel extraordinary? He was a prophet, you will say. So are they today that follow his example, for they act according to the will of God, either as "outspoken," or as "implanted in them"; which yourself grant farther on, in your fiftieth page.

Prudently, then, does the Preacher in this passage advise private persons not to contend with princes; for it is passing dangerous to contend with any rich man even, or powerful man soever. But what then? Shall the nobility, shall all the other magistrates, shall the whole body of the people—when a king chooses to rave, shall they not dare open their mouths? Shall they not oppose a foolish, wicked, raging plotter of all good men's ruin? Shall they not meet halfway his attempt to overthrow all things divine and human—lest with plunderings and burnings and murders he riot through the realm—being so "loosed from the law that what he listeth is lawful to him"? O cavalier from Cappadocian slave-blocks![41] Whom every free people, if

---

41. Martial *Epigrams* 10.

hereafter you shall dare set foot among a people that is free, ought to cast out and transport to the world's end as a monstrosity of dire foreboding, or set aside—fit candidate for slavery—to grind in the mill; solemnly obliging themselves, if ever they let you go, to grind in your stead under some tyrant—and him a fool. For what words could be said or borrowed so expressive of cruelty or folly as may not justly be applied to you?

But go on. "When the Israelites asked God for a king, they said they would fain be governed by him under the same rule as all the other nations which had a monarchy. But the kings of the East had supreme rule and unlimited power, as Virgil testifies:

> Not Egypt and huge Lydia, nor the hordes
> Of Parthians, and Hydaspes, Median stream,
> Do so revere a king."[42]

First, what is it to us, what sort of king the Israelites desired? Especially since God was angry with them not only for desiring a king after the manner of the nations and not of his own law, but for desiring a king at all. Nor is it credible that they should have desired a king unjust or loosed from the law, they who could not bear the government of Samuel's sons, though bound by the law, and only from their covetousness sought refuge in a king. Lastly, what you quote out of Virgil does not prove that the kings of the East reigned "with absolute power"; for those bees in Virgil who more revere their kings, he says, than do the Egyptians or Medes, those bees, even by the witness of the same poet,

> Pass their lives under mighty laws—[43]

—not, then, under kings that are loosed from all law. But now I will let you see how little ill-will I bear you. Though most people think you a knave, I will show that you have only put on the borrowed

42. Virgil *Fourth Georgic* 210–12.
43. Virgil *Fourth Georgic* 154.

mask of a knave. In your *Apparatus ad Primatum Papae* you say that some divines of the Council of Trent[44] made use of the example of the bees to prove the Pope's supremacy. This, with equal wickedness, you have borrowed from them. That very answer, therefore, which you gave them whilst you were an honest man, you shall yourself, now you are grown a knave, give yourself, and with your own hand pull off the knave's mask. "The bees," say you, "have a common-wealth, and so do natural philosophers call it; they have a king, but a harmless one; he is a leader rather than a despot; he beats not, pulls not, kills not his subject bees." No wonder therefore that they revere him so. Faith, 'twas under no lucky star of yours that you made contact with those *Tridentine* bees; three-toothed as they are, they show you up as a toothless drone.

Aristotle, a most exact writer on politics, affirms that the Asiatic monarchy, which yet himself calls barbarous, was κατὰ νόμον, that is, according to law, *Pol. 3.* More: whereas he counts five sorts of monarchies, and four he calls governments according to laws, and with the people's approval, yet he calls them tyrannical, because, though with popular consent, so much power had been lodged in them. But the kingdom of the Lacedemonians, he says, is most properly deemed a kingdom, because there not all power is lodged in the king. The fifth sort he calls παμβασιλείαν; to this alone he attributes what you call the right of all kings, the right to rule as they please; but where in the world, or when in the whole course of time, it ever obtained, he saith not. Nor seems he to have mentioned it for any other purpose than to show that it is unjust, absurd, and in the last degree tyrannical.[45]

You say that when Samuel would deter the people from choosing a king, he propounded "to them the right of kings." But where did he get it—from the written law of God? Nay, that law, as we have seen, has shown a very different right of kings. Was it from God Himself speaking through Samuel? But God disapproved it, blamed

44. A general council of the Roman Church called to reform that church; it met from 1545 to 1563.

45. Aristotle *Politics* 3.14.1285a–b.

it, deemed it a fault; so that the prophet expounded not any divinely appointed law for kings, but a mode of government most corrupt, seized by the pride of kings and lust to rule. He tells not what kings ought to do, but what they were fain to do; for he showed the people the manner of a king, as before he had shown the manner of the priests, the sons of Eli—using the same word (which you in your thirty-third page, by a solecism even in Hebrew, call משפת).[46] Ch. 2. v. 13. "Those priests' manner with the people was this"—surely an impious manner, and a hateful and tyrannical. That manner then was nowise a right but a wrong.

The fathers too have explained this passage in the same way: one will serve me as the measure of many—Sulpitius Severus,[47] a contemporary and friend of St. Jerome, and in St. Augustine's opinion, a man of great wisdom and learning. He tells us in his sacred history that Samuel is exhibiting to the people the monarchical despotism and pride of power. Now despotism and pride, to be sure, are not the right of kings; according to Sallust, however, the lawful power and authority granted to kings for the preservation of liberty and the promotion of the common weal degenerates into pride and despotism.[48] This is the sense of all orthodox divines and of all legists upon the interpretation of this passage, and as you might have learned from Sichardus, that of most of the rabbins as well;[49] not a single rabbin ever asserted that what this passage handled was the king's absolute right. Yourself, farther on, in your fifth chapter, page 106, complain that "not only Clement of Alexandria[50] but all others are in error here," and that you alone have hit the mark. Now what a piece of im-

46. The *solecism* is the substitution of *tav* for the correct *tet* as the final letter of the Hebrew *mishpat*. The substantive point Milton makes is that *mishpat* refers not to a right, as Salmasius incorrectly maintained, but to a custom.

47. Milton cites Sulpitius Severus's *Historia sacra* from an edition published in 1635.

48. Sallust *Jugurtha* 31.26.

49. Wilhelm Schickhard (1592–1635), author of *Jus Reginum Hebraeorum e Tenebris Rabbinicis Erutum*.

50. Clement of Alexandria (c. 150–c. 211–16) wrote on the relation between Christianity and pagan thought.

pudence is this,—or is it folly?—in opposition to all the expositors, especially the orthodox, to turn those very ways of kings which God Himself so much condemns, into the right of kings, and to defend them with a specious pretext of law, though yourself confess that that right is too often exercised in committing robberies, injustices, insults, and outrages.

Was any man ever so much "his own master" that he might lawfully prey upon mankind, drive and bear down all that stood in his way, and overturn all things? Did the Romans ever maintain, as you say they did, that anybody "did so by virtue of some right inherent in himself"? In Sallust, Gaius Memmius, a tribune of the people, inveighing against the pride and unpunished crimes of the nobility, did say: "To do whatever one has a mind to, without fear of punishment, is to be a king."[51] This looked good to you; and instantly you put it to your credit—in vain, surely, had you but kept your eyes open. Did he here assert the right of kings? or did he not rather chide the common people's listlessness in suffering the nobility to lord it over them unpunished, and in submitting again to those kinglike ways which, together with the king himself, their ancestors, in the exercise of a rightful independence, had driven into exile? You ought to have consulted Tully; he would have taught you to expound Sallust more correctly, yea Samuel too. In his oration *Pro C. Rabirio,* "None of us," says he, "is ignorant of the way of kings; these are their lordly dictates: mark my words and obey them." There he quotes from the poets other passages to this effect, which speak not of the right, but of the *"way* of kings"; and he says we ought to read and observe them carefully, not only "for our pleasure, but that we may learn to beware and to escape." You perceive what a dead loss you have made of Sallust, whom, utter enemy of tyrants though he is, you thought you had brought into court to advocate your right of tyrants. Take my word for it, the right of kings seems to be tottering, and even hastening its own downfall, when like a sinking man it snatches at all the straws

51. Sallust *Bellum Catilinae* 6.7.

about, and strives to maintain itself by examples and authorities which, were its ruin otherwise to linger on the way, would even speed it.

"The extreme exercise of a legal right," you say, "is the height of injury; this saying is verified most properly in kings, who, when they go to the utmost of their right, fall into those courses in which Samuel says the right of kings consists." Wretched right, which, now that you are brought to bay, you can defend no further than by confessing that it is the height of injury! This it is that is called the extreme exercise of a legal right: when a man hunts after legal formulas, dwells almost upon the letters of the law, and regards not its justice; or too cunningly and maliciously interprets a statute; wherefrom, says Cicero, the proverb arose.[52] But since it is certain that all right flows from the fountain of justice, it follows inevitably that you are most wicked in affirming that "for a king to be unjust, rapacious, tyrannical, and such as they were who were worst," is the king's right, and that it was this "the prophet intimated to the people." For what right, whether extreme or relaxed, whether written or unwritten, can there be to do wrong? Lest you take it into your head to admit this of other men, yet to keep on denying it of kings, I have one to object to you, a king methinks, who avows that your sort of right of kings is odious both to God and to himself: "Shall the throne of iniquity have fellowship with thee, that frameth mischief by law"? Psalm 94. Put not then so black an insult upon God as to ascribe to him the doctrine that the perversities and impious wickednesses of kings are the right of kings. Nay, God Himself tells us that he abhors all fellowship with wicked princes for the very reason that under pretence of royal right they create misery and vexation for their subjects. Neither bring a false accusation against a prophet of God; for by supposing that in this passage he expounds the right of kings, you bring not before us the right Samuel, but call up an empty shade, as did the witch.[53] Though for my part I verily believe that even that Samuel

52. Cicero *Of Duties* 1.10.33.
53. In 1 Sam. 28:7–25, Saul visits the Witch of Endor.

from Hell would not have been such a liar as not to call your right of kings rather the extravagance of tyranny.

We read of impiety countenanced by law, and you yourself say "it was the less good kings that were wont to make use of the right they got under leave granted." Now I have proved that this right, which you have introduced for the destruction of mankind, proceeds not from God; naught remains but that it comes from the Devil; as will appear more clearly hereafter. "This leave," say you, "grants the power if one will"; and for this you pretend to have Cicero's authority. I am never unwilling to mention your authorities, for it generally happens that you spoil your case by means of your own witnesses. Hear then what Cicero says in his Fourth Philippic: "What reason for war can be more just than the driving off a despotism? For under this, even though the master happen not to be irksome, yet 'tis a wretched thing that he can if he will."[54] Can by force, that is; for if Cicero were speaking of a right, he would contradict himself, and of a just cause of war make an unjust cause. What you describe, then, is not the right of a king, but the wrongfulness of kings, their force and their fury.

From a king's leave and license you turn to a private man's. "A private man," say you, "may lie, may be ungrateful." And so may kings, but what then? Shall they therefore have leave to plunder, murder, ravish, with impunity? How does it affect the seriousness of the wrong done to a people whether it be the king, or a robber, or an enemy from some other quarter, that slays, plunders, and enslaves them? And questionless, being both alike enemies and plagues to human society, the one as well as the other ought by the same law to be driven off and punished—a king indeed with even more justice, because, though raised to that dignity by the honors that his people have conferred upon him, and though under his oath entrusted with the public safety, he yet betrays it.

At last you grant that "Moses prescribes laws according to which the king sometime to be chosen ought to govern, though different

54. Actually Cicero's *Eighth Philippic*.

from that right which Samuel promulgated"—a double contradiction to what you have said before. For whereas you had affirmed that a king is quite unbound by law, you here confess he is bound. And you set up two contrary systems of law or right, one according to Moses, the other according to Samuel; which is absurd.

"But," says the prophet, "ye shall be servants to the king."[55] Suppose I did not deny that they were so; yet it was not by royal right, but maybe by the usurpation and injustice of most of their kings. For the prophet had forewarned them that that importunate petition of theirs would turn to their punishment, not through a royal right, but through their own deserts. Indeed if a king, as unbound by the law, have leave to do what he list, he shall be far more than lord and master, and his people sink down lower than the lowest of slaves. For even a slave foreign-born had the law of God to his defender against a cruel master; and shall a whole people, yea a free nation, find no protector upon earth, no law whither to betake themselves for refuge when hurt and stripped and stricken? Were they set free from their bondage under the Egyptian kings only that they might be delivered to one of their own brethren to be crushed, should he choose, under a bondage yet sterner? All which being agreeable neither to the law of God nor to common sense, nobody can doubt that what the prophet declared to the people is not the right of kings, but their manner, nor yet the manner of all kings, but of most.

Then you come down to the rabbins, and quote two of them, but with the same bad luck as you had before; inasmuch as that chapter about a king, which, as Rabbi Joses repeatedly said, contains the right of kings, clearly is the one in Deuteronomy, not the one in Samuel. For Rabbi Judah has declared very truly, and against you, that that discourse of Samuel's was only to put fear into the people. It is most pernicious that a thing should be named a right, and so inculcated, which in itself is utter wrong—unless perhaps it be called a right ironically. Upon this argument verse 18 is in point: "And ye shall cry out

55. 1 Sam. 8:17.

in that day because of your king which ye shall have chosen you; and the Lord will not hear you in that day." Yea, that punishment awaited them for obstinately persisting to desire a king against God's refusal.

Yet these words forbid them not to try prayers or anything else, for if the people might lawfully cry out to God against the king, without doubt they might use all other honorable means to rid themselves of his tyranny. For who that is hard-pressed by misfortune merely cries out to God, and does naught but fall to his lazy prayers, so as to neglect all else his duty?

But be it how it will, what is all this to the rights of kings or of our English people? We neither asked a king against the will of God, nor had one at his hands, but—neither in obedience to nor against any command of God—exercised the right of nations, and appointed a king by laws of our own. And this being the case, I see not why it should not redound to our virtue and our praise to have deposed our king, since it was reckoned a reproach to the Israelites to have asked for theirs. And this the event has confirmed; for we, when we had a king, prayed to God against him, and were heard, and at last delivered; but the Jews, who having no king kept importunately asking God for one, he bade be slaves, till, after their return from Babylon, they betook themselves to their former government again.

Next you throw open your Talmud School, but this too is an unlucky undertaking. In your desire to prove that kings are not to be judged, you quote from the treatise of the Sanhedrim "that the king neither judges nor is judged." But this runs counter to that people's own petition, who kept begging a king for the very purpose that he might judge them. Fain would you patch this up to fit your purpose (but in vain) by telling us that it is to be understood of those kings that reigned after the Babylonish captivity. For here against you is Maimonides,[56] who "makes this difference betwixt the kings of Israel and those of Judah: that the kings of the posterity of David judge and are judged," but the kings of Israel do neither. You work against yourself; for you contradict yourself or your rabbins, and plead my

56. Jewish scholar of the twelfth century.

cause. This, say you, "applied not to the first kings of Israel," for in the 17th verse it is said "Ye shall be his servants." To be sure—that is to say by his actual practice, not by any right; or if by right, then as a penalty for asking a king: a penalty which they kept on paying under most of their kings, though not perhaps under this king or that. So your point has nothing to do with the case. But you need no antagonist, you are such a perpetual antagonist to yourself. For you tell, as if arguing on my side, how first Aristobulus, and after him Jannaeus, surnamed Alexander, did not receive that kingly right of theirs from the Sanhedrim, guardian and interpreter of rights, but usurped it by degrees against the will of the Senate. To please these usurpers, you say, that pretty story of the principal men of the Sanhedrim being "struck dead by Gabriel" was made up for the occasion. And thus you confess that this magnificent prerogative, upon which you seem mainly to rely, viz., "that a king is not to be judged," was forged out of this rabbinical fable, worse than an old wives' tale.

But that the Hebrew kings "were liable to be judged, and even to be punished with stripes," Sichardus shows at large out of the writings of the rabbins; to which author you are indebted for all this erudition, and yet you blush not to clamor against him. Nay, we read that even Saul thought himself bound by a decree of his own making, and in obedience thereunto cast lots with his son Jonathan which of them two should die. Uzziah likewise, when the priests thrust him out of the temple as a leper, submitted as though he had been a subject, and ceased to be king.[57] Suppose he had refused to go out from the temple, to lay down the government, and to dwell in a several house, and had asserted that royal right unbound by law, think you the Jews and their priests would have suffered the temple to be defiled, the laws violated, and the whole people endangered by infection? Shall laws then be of force against a leprous king, and avail naught against a tyrant? Can any man possibly be so mad and foolish as to fancy that while the law has carefully provided against a diseased king's hurting his people, yet, should a wicked unjust cruel king tear and torture and

57. 2 Kings 15:5.

slay them, and quite overturn the state, no legal relief had been devised against these far greater mischiefs?

"But," say you, "no precedent can be shown of any king that has been arraigned in a court of justice, and condemned to die." Whereto Sichardus answers pat, that 'tis as if one should argue on this manner: The Emperor never has been summoned before an Elector; therefore, if the Elector Palatine should set a day for his appearance, the Emperor were not bound to appear or plead; though from the Golden Bull it is clear that Charles IV submitted himself and his successors to that investigating jurisdiction.[58]

No wonder if kings have been indulged so far when the people are depraved, and when so many private persons with either money or interest escape the law, though guilty of crimes the most heinous. That ἀνυπεύθυνον, that is, "to be wholly independent upon any other, and accountable to none upon earth," which you say is peculiar to royal majesty, Aristotle in his *Politics,* Book 4, Chapter 10, calls most tyrannical, and nowise to be endured by a free people. In proof that a king cannot rightfully be required to give an account of his actions, you cite as authority—proper authority forsooth!—that monstrous tyrant Mark Antony, destroyer of the Roman commonwealth; yet Antony, when marching against the Parthians, summoned Herod before him to answer a charge of murder, and it is thought would have punished even a king, had not the king bribed him with gold. So that your *Royal Defence* and Antony's assertion of the royal prerogative have flowed from one and the same spring.

Not without reason, say you, "for kings hold their authority from no other than God, but are indebted and obliged for it to Him alone." What kings, pray? For I deny that there ever were any such kings. Saul, the first king of Israel, had never reigned but that the people desired a king even against the will of God, and though he was proclaimed king at Mizpah, yet he lived almost a private life, and came after the herd of his father, till he was created king a second time by

58. The Golden Bull was handed down in December 1356 at the Diet of Metz.

the people at Gilgal.[59] And what of David? Though anointed by God, was he not anointed a second time in Hebron by the tribe of Judah, and then by all the Hebrews—yet even so only after a mutual covenant betwixt him and them? 2 Sam. 5; 1 Chron. 11. But a covenant binds kings and restrains them within bounds. Solomon, you say, "sat on the throne of the Lord, and was acceptable to all men," 1 Chron. 29. So that it did use to be something to be well-pleasing in the eyes of the people! Jehoiadah, the priest, made Joash king, but first he made him and the people enter into a covenant to one another, 2 Kings 11. I acknowledge that these kings and the rest of David's posterity were appointed both by God and by the people, but all other kings of what country soever were appointed, I affirm, by the people only. I challenge you to show that they were appointed by God, except in the sense that all things, great and small, are said to be made and appointed by him. The throne of David, then, was in a peculiar manner called "the throne of Jehovah," whereas the thrones of other princes are Jehovah's no otherwise than are all things else; which you should have learnt out of the same chapter, verses 11, 12. "All that is in the heaven and in the earth is thine; thine is the kingdom, O Lord. Both riches and honor come of thee, and power and might." This is so often repeated, not that kings may be puffed up, but to warn them that though they think themselves gods yet there is a God above them to whom they owe all. Thus we easily understand what the poets and the Essenes[60] mean when they tell us that "it is by God that kings reign, and they are from Jove"; for Solomon, himself a king, considers that even lesser officers also, namely judges, are from the same God, Prov. 8. 15, 16; and from the same Jove Homer, in the first Iliad: ". . . judges who at Zeus's hand guard the dooms."[61] Surely all we are of God likewise, and God's offspring. Therefore this universal right of God's

59. 1 Sam. 10:24, 11:15.

60. The Essenes were said by Josephus to be the most ascetic of the three chief Jewish sects (the Pharisees and Sadducees were the others).

61. Homer *Iliad* 1.238–39.

takes not away the people's right; so all other kings not named to their office by God are indebted and obliged for their authority to the people only, and consequently are accountable to them for it.

This, though the common people are apt to flatter their kings, yet kings themselves acknowledge, whether good ones, as Sarpedon in Homer, or bad ones, as those tyrants in the Lyrist.

> Glaucus, wherefore have we twain the chiefest honor
> In Lycia, and all men look on us as gods?[62]

Himself answers himself: "Because we outshine the rest in valor; wherefore let us fight manfully," says he, "lest the Lycians tax us with cowardice." In which words he intimates both that kings derive their royalty from the people, and that for their conduct of war they are accountable to them. Bad kings indeed, to strike terror into their people, declare publicly that God is the author of their royal power, yet in their secret prayers reverence no other divinity but Fortune. The well-known passage in Horace is in point:

> Wild Dacians fear thee, thee nomad Scythians fear,
> > Barbarian tyrants' mothers dread thee,
> > > Scarlet-enrobèd usurpers tremble,
>
> Lest thou with foot irreverent tumble down
> Their stately column, while the mob pouring in
> > To arms arouse the slow to arms and
> > > Instantly shatter the tyrant's power.[63]

If it is by God, therefore, that kings nowadays reign, it is by God too that peoples assert their liberty, since all things are of him and by him. Scripture bears like witness both that by him kings reign and that by him they are cast down from their thrones, though yet we perceive that the one and the other are brought about far oftener by the people than by God. The right of the people then is as much from

62. Homer *Iliad* 12.310 ff.
63. Horace *First Ode* 34, 9–17.

God as is the right of the king—whatever that is. And whenever any people, without some visible designation of God Himself, have appointed a king, they can by the same right put him down. To depose a tyrant certainly is a more godlike action than to set one up; and there appears much more of God in the people whenever they depose an unjust king than in the king that oppresses an innocent people. Nay, the people have a warrant from God to judge wicked kings, for God has conferred this very honor upon his saints, Psalm 149, that while they celebrate the praises of Christ their own king, yet as for the kings of the heathen, (and such, according to the Gospel, are all tyrants), "they shall bind them with chains . . . to execute upon them the judgment written"—even upon them that boast themselves unbound by any laws or judgment written! Let none then be so stupid and wicked as to think that kings, commonly the worst of men, are so high in God's account that the whole world is to hang upon their nod and governance, and that for their sakes and on their account the human race divine, if I may so call it, should be reckoned and treated as abject brute beasts.

After all this, rather than say nothing, you publish your discovery that Marcus Aurelius countenanced tyranny; but you had better have let him alone. I cannot say whether he ever affirmed that God is the sole judge of princes. Xiphilinus, to be sure, whom you quote on an αὐταρχία, says: "Concerning an αὐταρχία God alone has power to judge."[64] But that an αὐταρχία is there synonymous with monarchy I cannot agree; and the less the oftener I read what goes before. Indeed any reader would wonder how that outlandish opinion, abruptly engrafted upon the context, hangs together with it, or what is its own meaning; especially since Marcus Aurelius, best of emperors, conducted himself towards the people, Capitolinus tells us,[65] just as if Rome had still been a free republic. And we all know that when it was so, the supreme power was in the people. The same emperor, in

64. Milton cites an epitome of Dio Cassius's *History of Rome,* compiled by Xiphilinus in the eleventh century.
65. Capitolinus *Historia Augusta* 12.1.

the first book of his autobiography,[66] openly professes that he revered Thraseas, and Helvidius, and Cato, and Dion, and Brutus,[67] who were all tyrant-slayers, or affected that reputation, and that he proposed to himself a form of government under which all men might equally enjoy the benefit of the law, and right and justice be equally administered to all. And in his fourth book he says the law is master, and not he. He acknowledged that all power and property belong to the Senate and the people: we are so far, says he, from having anything of our own, that we live in your house. Thus Xiphilinus. So little did he arrogate aught to himself by virtue of a royal right. When he was dying he offered the Romans his son for his successor, to rule upon condition he should prove worthy. He exhibited not, then, that absolute and imaginary right of sovereignty supposed to be delivered by God's hand,—made, in short, no pretence to that αὐταρχία of yours.

Still you say that "the annals of Greece and Rome are full." But nobody has seen them anywhere. "So are the annals of the Jews." And yet, you add, "the Jews in most respects were unfavorable to royal power." Nay, you have found and you will find that both the Greeks and the Latins were exceedingly unfavorable to tyrants; the Jews too—if that book that Samuel wrote of "the manner of the kingdom," 1 Sam. 10., were extant; which book, the Hebrew doctors tell us, the kings tore in pieces or burnt that they might tyrannize over their subjects with the more impunity.

Now look about and see whether you can catch hold of somewhat or other. Finally you come to wrest David's words in Psalm 17: "Let my sentence come forth from thy presence": therefore, says Barnachmoni, "None but God judges the king." And yet it seems rather likely that David penned these words when he was persecuted by Saul, and when, though already God's anointed, he did not decline being judged even by Jonathan. "If there be iniquity in me, slay me thyself," he says, 1 Sam. 20. Thereupon, like anyone else that is

66. *Meditations* 1.14.

67. Noted republicans and tyrannicides in antiquity. Thrasea Paetus and his son-in-law Helvidius Priscus were republicans in the first century.

falsely accused by men, he appeals to the judgment of God, as appears in the sequel: "Thine eyes behold the thing that is right, for thou has searched mine heart," etc. What has this to do with a judgment passed by a king or a court of law? Certainly they do most to shake and pull down the right of kings who expose how it is built upon and rests upon so treacherous a foundation.

Then you come with that threadbare argument, the prize argument of our courtiers: "Against thee, thee only, have I sinned," Ps. 51. 4. As if King David, when doing penance with tears and grief, when in sackcloth and ashes he lay upon the ground imploring God's mercy, said this with any thought of a king's right, at a moment when he deemed himself scarce worthy the right of a slave! And can we think that he despised all God's people, his own brethren, to that degree, as to believe that he might perpetrate upon them murder, and adultery, and robbery, and yet not be sinning against them? Far be it from so holy a king ever to have been guilty of such pride, or such abominable ignorance of himself and his neighbor! Unquestionably, then, "against thee only have I sinned" means "against thee chiefly." But however this may be, the words and thoughts of the psalmist, rhapsodical and passionate, are nowise fitted to expound law, nor should be dragged into that use.

"But David was never summoned, or made to plead for his life before the Sanhedrim." Of course he was not. How could his sin have been found out, which was committed so secretly that perhaps for some years after (such are secrets at court) not above one or two seem to have been privy to it? 2 Sam. 12. "Thou didst it secretly." Moreover, if the Sanhedrim should neglect to punish private persons, would anyone allege this as proof that these are not punishable? But the reason why David was not proceeded against as a malefactor is not much in the dark. Though he had condemned himself in the fifth verse, "The man that hath done this thing shall surely die," and though the prophet at once replies, "Thou art the man," so that in the prophet's judgment also he deserved death, yet God by his sovereignty and his singular mercy to David absolves him both from the guilt of his sin and from the sentence of death as well which he had pronounced against himself: verse 13, "Thou shalt not die."

Next you rage against some "bloodthirsty" advocate[68] or other, and go at it body and soul to refute his peroration. Let him look to that; I will endeavor to be as short as I can in what I have undertaken to perform. Yet some things I cannot pass by,—first your extraordinary self-contradictions. On your thirtieth page you say: "The Israelites are not begging for an unjust, violent, rapacious king, such as kings are at their worst." And yet, page 42, you rail at the advocate for maintaining that the Israelites asked for a tyrant. "Would they have chosen," say you, "to leap headlong out of the frying pan into the fire, and risk the cruelty of the worst tyrants, rather than suffer the bad judges to whom they were by now grown accustomed?" First you said the Hebrews preferred tyrants to judges; here you say they preferred judges to tyrants, and "a tyrant was the thing they least desired." So that the advocate will answer you out of your own book, for according to your principle every king is by royal right a tyrant.

What you say next is very true: "The supreme power was then in the people, as appears by their rejecting judges and choosing a king." Remember this when I shall ask you for it again! It is not true, you say, that "God in his anger gave the Israelites a king as a tyrant or a punishment, but as a thing good and profitable." But that is easily refuted; for why should they cry to God because of the king that they had chosen, were it not that royal government was an evil—not in itself, but because most commonly, even as the prophet here warns, it does degenerate into pride and tyranny? If you are not yet satisfied, acknowledge your own words, acknowledge your own written bond, and blush. In your *Apparatus ad Primatum,* "God gave them a king in his anger," you say, "being offended at their sin in refusing to have God for their king. So the Church, as if in punishment for its crime of forsaking the pure worship of God, has been delivered up to the more than kingly government of one mortal head." Therefore if your own comparison holds, either God gave the children of Israel a king

68. John Cook (1608–60), author of *King Charles His Case.*

to their loss and as an evil, or he gave the Church a Pope for its profit and as a good. Was there ever anything more lightheaded and mad than this man? Who would trust him in the least thing, that in things of so great concern says and presently unsays without attaching the slightest weight to the matter? You tell us in your twenty-ninth page that "among all nations, kings are loosed from law; this was the judgment both of the Eastern and of the Western world." And yet, page 43, you say "that all the kings of the East were legal and lawful, nay, that the very kings of Egypt in all matters great or small were tied to laws"; though in the beginning of this chapter you had undertaken to demonstrate "that kings are bound by no laws, that they give laws but receive none." For my part I am not angry with you, for either you are mad or you are of our side. Surely this is attacking, not defending, the king; this is making game of him; or if you are in earnest, that phrase of Catullus's fits you squarely,[69] but contrariwise, for by as much as anyone was ever the best of poets, by so much are you the worst of all defenders. Unless that stupidity in which, you complain, the advocate you mention is "sunk," has blinded you instead, you shall now feel that you are yourself "become a very brute." For now you confess that "the kings of all nations too have laws prescribed to them, yet not so as to be held to them by fear of judgment and capital punishment." Which yet you have proved neither from Scripture nor from any authority worthy of credit. Observe then in few: to prescribe civil laws to such as are not bound by them is silly and ridiculous; to punish all others, but leave some one man at liberty to commit all sorts of wickedness without fear of punishment, is most unjust, for law makes no exception. These two things simply do not happen to wise lawgivers, much less to God. But for all to see that you nowise prove out of the writings of the Hebrews what you had undertook in this chapter to prove by them, you confess of your own accord that there are some rabbins "who affirm that a king other than God ought not to have been acknowledged by their forefathers, yet was given them for their punishment." With their opinion I agree.

69. Catullus 49.

He is not fit or worthy to be king that does not far excel all the rest. But where many are equal, as in all governments the majority are, they ought, I think, to have an equal interest in the government, and hold it by turns. But that all men should be slaves to one that is their equal, or, as generally happens, their inferior, and most often a fool, who would not think this a thing most unworthy? Nor does it "recommend royal government," that Christ had kings for ancestors, any more than it recommends some very bad kings, that they had Christ for a descendant. "The Messiah is a king." We acknowledge him, we rejoice, and we pray that he will come as soon as may be; for he is worthy, nor is there any that is like unto him or that can follow him. Meanwhile the royal power, entrusted to unworthy and undeserving persons, as most commonly it is, may well be thought to have done mankind more harm than good. Nor does it follow for all this that all kings are tyrants. But suppose it did; I grant you this lest you think me obstinate; now make the best of it. "These two conclusions follow," you say; "God himself would properly be called king of tyrants, and indeed himself the greatest tyrant." If the first of these is a non-sequitur, at least there does follow the thing that almost always follows from your whole book, viz., that you perpetually contradict not only the Scriptures but your own self. For in the very next sentence above, you have affirmed that "there is one God, the king of all things, having himself created them." Now he created as well tyrants and devils, and consequently by your own reasoning is their king too. The second of your conclusions we detest, and wish that blasphemous mouth of yours stopped, with which you affirm God to be the worst of tyrants, if he is to be called, as you so often say he is, their king and lord.

Nor do you much advantage the royal cause by telling us that Moses "was a king, with supreme power." So mote he be indeed, or any other for that matter, who could, like Moses, "bring the causes unto God," Exod. 18. 19. But even Moses, though, so to speak, God's confidant, was not permitted to do whatever he pleased to God's people. For, what says he? "The people come unto me to inquire of God"—not, then, to receive Moses's own commands. Then Jethro takes up the point: "Be thou for the people to Godward, . . . and thou shalt teach them God's ordinances and laws." And Moses again, Deut. 4.5. "I have taught you statutes and judgments, even as the Lord my God commanded me." Hence it is that he is said to have been "faithful in all God's house," Numb. 12. So that the people's king was then Jehovah, and Moses as it were an interpreter only of Jehovah the king. Impious and sacrilegious you must needs be who without warrant have dared shift this supreme power from God to man—a power which, as held by Moses himself, was not supreme, but only deputed or intermediate under God's present deity. To heap up your wickedness to its summit, you here say Moses was a king with absolute power, yet in your *Apparatus ad Primatum,* page 230, you say: "Together with the seventy elders he ruled the people, and was their foremost, but not their master." If Moses therefore was a king, as certainly he was, and the best of kings, and had, as you say he had, "sovereign royal power," and yet, again as you say, was neither the people's master nor their sole ruler, then it necessarily follows that kings, though endued with the supreme power, yet ought not by virtue of that sovereign royal right of theirs be lords over the people, or sole rulers, much less rulers according to their own will and pleasure.

With what shamelessness you counterfeit a supposed command of God "to set up a king over them as soon as they should be possessed of the Holy Land," Deut. 17! For you craftily leave out the preceding words, "*When thou . . . shalt say,* I will set a king over me." And pray call to mind also what you said before, page 42, and what I shall now ask you to recite, viz. "The people were then possessed of quite unlimited power."

Now once more you shall decide whether you are sacrilegious or crazed. "God," you say, "having so long before appointed a kingly government as best and most proper for that people, what shall we say to the Prophet's opposing it, and God's own dealing with the Prophet as if himself were rather against it? How do these things agree?" He sees himself enmeshed, he sees himself entangled; observe now with how great malice against the Prophet, and impiety against God, he seeks to disentangle himself! "We must consider," says he, "that it was Samuel's own sons who then judged the people, and that the people rejected them because of their corruption; now Samuel was loth his sons should be laid aside, and God, to gratify his prophet, intimated that what the people desired did not much please him." Speak out, wretch, and never mince the matter: you mean, Samuel deceived the people, and God Samuel. It is not that advocate of yours, therefore, but yourself, that are the "frantic" and "raving" one; who, so you may but honor a king, cast off all reverence to God. Does Samuel seem to you one that would have preferred his sons' ambition and covetousness before his people's grace or safety; one that, when the people sought what was right and beneficial, would have imposed upon them with such sly crafty advice, and made them believe things that were not? Does God himself seem to you one that in so disgraceful an affair would stoop to oblige a friend? Would God act a part before the people? So, then, either what Samuel taught the people was not the right of kings, or else that right, by the testimony of God and of the Prophet, was an evil thing, burdensome, injurious, unprofitable, and costly to the commonwealth; or lastly (which, as sacrilege, is inadmissible), both God and the Prophet wished to deceive the people.

God frequently protests that he was extremely displeased with them for asking a king, verse 7: "They have not rejected thee, but they have rejected me, that I should not reign over them. According to all the works which they have done . . . wherewith they have forsaken me, and served other gods."[70] As if it were considered a kind of idolatry to ask for a king, who requires adoration and worship almost divine. Surely, whoever subjects himself to an earthly master that is above all law comes but little short of setting up a strange god, a god that at least is seldom rational, but too often abjectly brutish and beastly. So 1 Sam. 10. 19.: "And ye have this day rejected your God, who himself saved you out of all your adversities and your tribulation,

---

70. Milton's favorite antimonarchical biblical passage, 1 Sam. 8.7.

and ye have said unto him, Nay, but set a king over us"; and chapter 12, verse 12: Ye asked for a king "when the Lord your God was your king"; and verse 17: "See that your wickedness is great, which ye have done in the sight of the Lord, in asking you a king." And Hosea speaks contemptuously of the king, chap. 13. 10 − 11: "Where is thy king? Let him now save thee in thy cities. Where are thy judges? For that thou saidst, give me a king and princes, I gave thee a king in mine anger." Hence it is that heroic Gideon, greater than a king, "I will not rule over you," says he, "neither shall my son rule over you; the Lord shall rule over you," Judges 8; intimating thereby that it belongs not to a man, but to God only, to exercise dominion over men. And hence Josephus in his book against Apion,[71] an Egyptian grammarian and a foulmouthed fellow like you, calls the commonwealth of the Hebrews, in which God was sole ruler, a Theocracy. In Isaiah 26. 13 the people, in their right minds at last, complain that it had been mischievous to them to have had other rulers than God. All which passages go to prove that the king was given the Israelites in God's anger.

Who can forbear laughing at the use you make of the story of the usurper Abimelech?[72] Of whom it is said when he was killed, partly by a woman that hurled a piece of millstone upon him, and partly by the sword of his own armor-bearer, that "God rendered the wickedness of Abimelech." "This history," say you, "proves strongly that God alone is the judge and punisher of kings." Yea, if this argument hold, he is the only judge and punisher of tyrants, rascals, and bastard usurpers. Whoever by hook or crook can seize a throne shall have got a sovereign kingly right over the people, and is out of all danger of punishment; instantly the weapons shall fall from the magistrates' hands, and the people thenceforth not dare to mutter. What if some strong thief had perished in like manner by violence, would any man infer that God alone is the judge and punisher of thieves? Or what if he had been legally convicted, and had died by the executioner's

71. Josephus *Contra Apion* 2.165.
72. Judg. 9:53−54.

hand—would it have been any the less God that rendered his wickedness? You have never read that the judges of the children of Israel were ever proceeded against according to law, and yet you admit of your own accord (p. 47) that "in an aristocracy even the prince may and ought to undergo judgment if he break the law." And in a kingdom why may not a tyrant likewise undergo judgment? Because God rendered the wickedness of Abimelech! So did the woman, and so did his own armor-bearer, over both of whom he pretended to a right of sovereignty. And what if a magistrate had rendered his wickedness? Does not a magistrate bear God's sword for that very purpose, to render the wicked their wickedness?

Having done with this "most powerful" argument from the death of Abimelech, he betakes himself, as is his way, to slanders and calumnies; his discourse does naught but sling "mud and dirt"; but as for those things that he promised to prove, he has proved not one, either from the Scriptures or from the rabbinical writings. Nowise does he show that a king is unbound by law, or why a king, alone of all mortal men, if he commit a crime should not be punished. Nay, he gets entangled in those very authorities that he makes use of, and by his own discourse shows the opinion that he argues against to be the truer. And perceiving that he is like to do but little good with his arguments, he endeavors to bring odium upon us by loading us with abominable accusations, as if we had cruelly put to death the most virtuous innocent prince that ever reigned. "Was Solomon," says he, "a better king than Charles I?" I confess some have ventured to compare his father King James with Solomon, nay, to prefer King James for his illustrious descent. Solomon was David's son, and David used to be Saul's musician; but King James was the son of the Earl of Darnley, who, Buchanan tells us,[73] caught David the musician in his wife the Queen's bedchamber at night with the door bolted, and killed him not long after. So that King James was of more distinguished origin, and was frequently called a second Solomon, though whether he was

73. George Buchanan, *History of Scotland* (1582), bk. 2, 309–10.

the son of David the musician the tale has left uncertain, for readers to guess. But how it could ever come into your head to make a comparison between Charles and Solomon, I cannot see. For that very Charles whom you praise thus to the sky, that very man's obstinacy, and covetousness, and cruelty, his hard mastership to all good and honest men, his wars, and arsons, and plunderings, and slaughters innumerable of his wretched subjects, all this, whilst I am a-writing, does his son Charles himself publicly confess and bewail on the stool of repentance in Scotland, nay, renounces there that kingly right of yours.[74]

Still, if you take such pleasure in Parallels, let us compare King Charles and King Solomon. Solomon "began his reign" with the execution "of his brother," who had justly deserved it. Charles began his with his father's funeral—I do not say his father's *murder,* though all the evidences of poison appeared on the dead body, for that suspicion rested upon Buckingham; whom yet, though murderer of the king and Charles's father, Charles not only cleared of guilt in the highest Council of the realm, but dissolved Parliament to keep the affair by hook or crook from Parliamentary investigation.[75] Solomon "oppressed the people with heavy taxes," but he spent that money upon the temple of God and other public buildings; King Charles spent his in extravagances. Solomon was enticed to idolatry by many wives, Charles by one. Though Solomon were himself seduced, we read not that he seduced others; but Charles, as well by the richest benefices of a corrupt Church seduced and enticed others, as by his edicts and ecclesiastical decrees he compelled them to set up altars, which all Protestants abhor, and to bow down to crucifixes painted over them on the wall. But yet not for all this "was Solomon by his people condemned to die." Nor does it follow because he was not, say I, that therefore he ought not to have been; for perhaps there were many circumstances that made it then inexpedient. But not long af-

---

74. Charles (the future king) had signed on May 16, 1650, an acknowledgment of the failings of his father.

75. The investigation took place in June of 1626.

---

ter, the people by both words and actions made clear what was their right, when ten tribes revolted from Solomon's son;[76] and if he had not made speed to flee, very likely they would have stoned to death even a king who had but threatened them.

### CHAPTER III.

It has now been sufficiently argued and proved that the kings of the Jews were by God's ordinance bound to all the laws even as were the people, and that no exemptions from the law are found in Scripture; so that it is quite unauthorized, quite unreasonable, and quite untrue, to say that kings "may do what they list with impunity," or that "they may not be punished by the people," and accordingly that "God has reserved their punishment to his own tribunal." Let us now consider whether the Gospel recommend what the Law not only did not command but discommended; let us consider whether the Gospel, heavenly proclamation of liberty, give us over in slavery to kings and tyrants, from whose outrageous rule the old law, though it taught slavery of some sort, did set God's people free.

Your first argument you take from the person of Christ. But who does not know that he put himself into the condition not only of a subject, but even of a servant, that we might be free? Nor is this to be understood of inward liberty only, to the exclusion of civil liberty. How out of place are the words that Mary mother of Christ spake in prophecy of his coming—"He hath scattered the proud in the imagination of their hearts; he hath put down the mighty from their seats, and exalted them of low degree"[77]—if his coming rather established tyrants on their thrones, and cast all Christians down beneath their cruel sway! He himself, by being born, and serving, and dying, under tyrants, has purchased all rightful liberty for us. As he has not withheld from us the resignation to submit patiently, if we must, to slav-

76. Rehoboam; see 1 Kings 12:18.
77. The Magnificat of Mary; see Luke 1:52.

ery, so he has not forbidden us to strive nobly for our liberty—nay has granted this in fuller measure. Hence it is that Paul, 1 Cor. 7. 21, has resolved thus, not only of evangelical but also of civil liberty: "Art thou called, being a servant? care not for it; but if thou mayest be made free, use it rather. Ye are bought with a price; be not ye the servants of men." Vainly then do you endeavor to argue us into slavery by the example of Christ, who at the price of servitude for himself established liberty for us, even civil liberty. He took upon him indeed in our stead the shape of a servant, but he never did off the soul and purpose of our deliverer; whereby he taught, as I shall show, a quite other notion of the right of kings than this you teach. For you preach not the right of kings, but the right of tyrants (a novel thing in a commonwealth!) and assert that whatever nation has in fate's lottery drawn a tyrant, whether by inheritance or by conquest or by chance, is enslaved not merely under compulsion, but under religious obligation.

Now, as usual, I will turn your own authorities against you. When certain Galilean collectors of the tribute money demanded tribute of Peter, Christ asked him, Matt. 17, of whom the kings of the earth took custom or tribute, of their own children or of strangers. Peter answers him, Of strangers. Jesus saith unto him: "Then are the children free. Notwithstanding, lest we should offend them, . . . give unto them for me and thee." This passage troubles the commentators, who disagree about whom the tribute was paid to. Some say it was paid to the priests for the use of the sanctuary; others that it was paid to the Emperor; I am of opinion that it was paid to Herod, who converted to his own use the revenue of the sanctuary; for Josephus mentions divers sorts of tribute which Herod and his sons exacted, and which Agrippa finally remitted.[78] Now the tribute in question, though small in itself, yet being accompanied with many more, was a heavy burden; indeed that of which Christ speaks here must needs have been oppressive; under other conditions, even during the commonwealth, poor persons were counted only, not taxed. Hence there-

78. Josephus *Jewish Antiquities* 19.6.

fore Christ took occasion to censure the injustice of Herod, under whose government he then was, in that, whereas the rest of the kings of the earth, if indeed they desire to be called fathers of their country, use not to impose excessively heavy taxes upon their children, that is, their subjects, but upon foreigners, especially when subdued in war; he, quite contrary, oppressed not strangers but his children. However it be, whether you agree that children here is to be understood as the king's own subjects, or as the children of God, that is, the faithful, and, in general, Christians, as Augustine understands, this is certain, that if Peter was a child, and therefore free, then we are so too on Christ's own authority, either as citizens or as Christians, and that it therefore is not the right of kings to exact excessive tribute from their own children and freeborn subjects. Christ himself bears witness that he paid this tribute not because he ought, but in order that as an individual he might not bring trouble upon himself by offending those that demanded it; for he knew in his own mind that he had a far different duty and service to perform—a far other race to run. In denying, then, that it is the right of kings to burden their freeborn subjects with grievous exactions, Christ yet more plainly denies that it is their right to spoil and plunder, to massacre and torture their own citizens, especially Christians. As he seems to have discoursed of the right of kings to this same effect elsewhere too, he began to fall under certain persons' suspicion that he did not consider the license of tyrants to be the right of kings. It was not for nothing that the Pharisees put such questions to him, tempting him, and that when they were about to press their inquiries concerning the right of kings they told him that he cared not for any man and regarded not the person of men; nor was it for nothing that he was angry when such an inquiry was propounded to him, Matt. 22. What if someone should endeavor slily to approach *you,* and entangle you in your talk, and question you (this under a monarchy) upon your own principles concerning the right of kings, in order to draw from you somewhat to your hurt— would *you* be angry at him? Oh, no! Hence then pray observe that *his* opinions upon the right of kings were *not* agreeable to kings.

The same may be gathered very clearly from his answer, by which he seems rather to send away his questioners than to instruct them. He asks to be shown the tribute money. "Whose image is that?" he says. "Caesar's," say they. "Render therefore unto Caesar," says he, "the things which are Caesar's; and unto God the things that are God's." And is there anyone who knows not as well that unto the people should be rendered the things that are the people's? "Render to all men their dues," says Paul, Rom. 13. So that not all things are unto Caesar. Our liberty is not Caesar's, nay but God's own birthday gift to us; and to render unto any Caesar you like this which we got not from him were an action most foul, most unworthy the origin of man. If one should look upon the countenance of a man, and inquire whose image was that, would not any one answer at once that it was God's? Being then God's own, that is, free in very truth, and consequently to be rendered to none but God, surely we cannot without sin and sacrilege the greatest deliver ourselves over in slavery to Caesar, to a man, that is, and, what is more, to an unjust man, a wicked man, a tyrant.

Christ leaves undecided, however, what things are God's, and what Caesar's. If that piece of money was the same as the didrachmum that was customarily paid to God, as it certainly was later, under Vespasian,[79] then Christ, instead of limiting the controversy to its issue, has but entangled it; for it is impossible to give the same thing at the same time to God and to Caesar. But, you say, he intimated to them what things were Caesar's, to wit, that piece of money stamped with Caesar's portrait. But does this profit either you or Caesar more than a pennyworth? Either Christ gave Caesar nothing but that penny, and declared everything else ours, or else, if he assigned to Caesar all money that has Caesar's name upon it, he gives Caesar nearly all our property, and contradicts himself; for when he was paying kings only two didrachma of tribute, he protested that it was more than either Peter or he was bound to do. The argument you

79. Roman emperor from A.D. 69 to 79.

rely on, in fine, is weak, for coin bears the prince's portrait not as a token of its being his property, but of its being good metal, and that none may presume to counterfeit it. If indeed stamping or writing availed so much to establish royal right, kings could instantly turn all our property over to themselves by merely writing their names upon it. Or if all our possessions be already theirs, which is your doctrine, then that piece of money was to be rendered unto Caesar not because it bore his name or image, but because of right it belonged to him before, though unstamped with any image. Whence it is clear that Christ in this passage meant not so much to teach us our duty to kings and kesars—so involved and dubious is its doctrine—as he meant to expose the malice and wickedness of the hypocritical Pharisees. Lo, when the Pharisees upon another occasion told him that Herod laid wait to kill him, did they bear from him an humble submissive answer to render unto the tyrant? "Go ye, and tell that fox,"[80] says he, intimating that when kings plot their subjects' destruction, 'tis by a right not kingly but foxy.

You say "he brought himself to endure death under a tyrant." How could he possibly except under a tyrant? "Under a tyrant he suffered death"—thus, forsooth, authorizing and championing the wickedest consequences of the royal right! You make an excellent moralist. Christ, moreover, though—not to put us under the yoke but to set us free—he underwent servitude, yet so measured his conduct as not to yield to royal right a jot beyond its just and proper due.

Now 'tis time for us to come to his teaching upon this subject. The sons of Zebedee were ambitious of the highest places in the kingdom of Christ, which they imagined would shortly be set up on earth. Christ reproved them so as to let all Christians know at once what manner of law concerning officials and the civil power he desired should be set up among them. "Ye know," says he, "that the princes of the Gentiles exercise dominion over them, and they that are great exercise authority upon them. But it shall not be so among you: but whosoever will be great among you, let him be your minis-

80. Luke 13:32.

ter; and whosoever will be chief among you, let him be your servant."[81] Unless you had been distracted, could you ever have imagined that this passage makes for you, and that by such reasonings you
win us to regard our kings as masters over us and ours? May enemies
like you fall to our lot in war—enemies who, though we know well
enough we can beat them even when they are armed, blunder blindly
unarmed, as you have a way of doing, into our hostile camp instead of
their own; for whatever makes most against you, that very thing you
usually are foolish enough to allege as the strongest support of your
cause. The Israelites kept asking God for a king "like as all the nations
that are about" had; God dissuaded them by many arguments, whereof
Christ here gives an epitome: "Ye know that the princes of the Gentiles exercise dominion over them"; yet, because the Israelites persisted
in asking, God gave them one, though in his wrath. Christ, lest a
Christian people should anywise desire one who would exercise dominion over them as did the kings of the Gentiles, prevents them with
the caution "but it shall not be so among you." What could be said
plainer than this? There shall not be among you that haughty sway of
kings, though by a plausible title they be called Euergetae[82] and benefactors. But he that will fain be great amongst you—and who is
greater than the prince?—"let him be your minister"; and he that will
be "foremost," or "prince" (Luke 22), "let him be your servant." So
that the lawyer[83] you inveigh against was not wrong, but had Christ's
authority if he said that a Christian king is the people's servant, as
every good magistrate certainly is. Insomuch that a king either is no
Christian at all, or is the people's servant: if he would be lord and
master out and out, he cannot at the same time be Christian.

Moses himself, ordainer of a law that to a certain degree legalized
slavery, yet did not lord it haughtily over his people, but himself bore
the burden of the people, and carried them in his bosom, as a nursing

81. Matt. 20:25–27.

82. "Doers of good" or "benefactors"; Hellenistic rulers sometimes employed this
title.

83. John Cook.

father does a sucking child, Numb. 11; moreover a nursing father is a servant. Plato would have the magistrates called not lords, but servants and helpers of the people, nor the people called servants, but maintainers of their magistrates, because even when these are kings, the people give them food and wages.[84] Aristotle called the magistrates the keepers and ministers of the laws;[85] Plato, both ministers and servants. The Apostle, to be sure, calls them ministers of God; but that does not prevent their being ministers of the laws and of the people; for the laws and the magistrates as well are for the people's sake.

Yet this, you keep howling, is merely "the opinion of the raving mastiffs of England." Of course I had not thought the people of England mastiffs, did not you, mongrel, bark at them so currishly. The Lord and Seigneur de St. Loup,[86] God 'ield you, yea the Holy Wolf himself, complains that the mastiffs rave! There was a time when St. Germain, whose colleague was that famous St. Loup of Troyes, deposed our unchaste king Vortigern by his own authority. So St. Loup despise you, the master of no saintly wolf, but of some thievish starveling of a wolf, and more contemptible than that master of vipers of whom Martial makes mention.[87] Yes, and at home you even have a barking Lycisca[88] too, and, though you be Lord of the Wolf, this She-wolf lords it pitifully over you, and loudly rails at your Seigneurie, and unlords your lordship. No wonder, then, that you endeavor to obtrude absolute regal government upon others, who are yourself grown accustomed to bear female rule so slavishly at home. Go on then, be Master of the Wolf; a She-wolf be your mistress; be a Wolf yourself, be a Werewolf: be what you will, you are bound to be the English mastiffs' plaything. But I have no time now to hunt wolves; so having got out of the woods, let us go back to the King's highway.

You that but of late writ against all primacy in the church, now call

84. Plato *Laws* 4.715.
85. Aristotle *Politics* 3.16.1287a.
86. Salmasius owned an estate at St. Loup in France.
87. Martial *Epigrams* 1.41.7.
88. In Virgil's *Eclogues* (3.18), the name of a barking bitch.

"Peter prince of the Apostolic fellowship." Who can trust you, little man, when your own principles are so unstable? What says Peter? "Submit yourselves to every ordinance of man for the Lord's sake: whether it be to the king, as supreme; or unto governors, as unto them that are sent by him for the punishment of evildoers and for the praise of them that do well: for so is the will of God."[89] This epistle Peter wrote to persons who were not only private individuals, but actually strangers scattered astray throughout most of Asia Minor, and who in those places where they sojourned had no other right than what the laws of hospitality entitled them to. Do you think that what befits scattered strangers in a strange land befits likewise inhabitants freeborn and noble, or meetings, assemblies, and parliaments of native citizens in their own country? or that, in their own land, what befits private persons equally befits members of Parliament and officers of state, without whom kings themselves cannot subsist? But suppose the epistle addressed to natural-born subjects, suppose them not private persons but the very Senate of Rome; what then? When a command has some express reason attached to it, nobody, generally speaking, is or can be bound by it beyond the extent of that reason. Now the command is: "Submit," ὑποτάγητε: that is (regarding the essential force of the word) "be subordinate, or *legally* subject"; ἡ γὰρ τάξις νόμος, as Aristotle says:[90] For order is law. "Submit for the Lord's sake." For what *reason*? Because as well the king as the governor is appointed by God *for the punishment of evildoers and the praise of them that do well.* "For so is the will of God," to wit, that we should submit and yield obedience to such as are here writ down; of others there is not a word here. You see how firmly grounded is the reason for this command; and in the 16th verse he adds: "as free,"—therefore not as slaves. What then if princes reverse their office, and rule to the torture and destruction of good men, and the license and praise and reward of evildoers, shall we all still submit forevermore, not private persons only, but our nobility, all our officers of state, our very Parliament

89. 1 Pet. 2:13–15.
90. Aristotle *Politics* 3.14.1287a.

in fine? Is not the ordinance called "of man"? How then? Shall human power avail to appoint what is good and profitable for men, but not avail to rid them of what is mischievous and destructive to them?

But that king, you say, to whom we are bidden to submit, was Nero, in those days tyrant at Rome: therefore we must submit even to tyrants. But I say that it is uncertain whether it was Nero or Claudius[91] that then held sway; moreover they that are bidden to submit were scattered foreign private persons, not consuls or high officers of the law, not the Roman Senate.

Now let us come to Paul (for with the Apostles you allow yourself liberties that you will not allow us to take with princes; now you give Peter the primacy, now you snatch it away). Paul, Romans 13, says: "Let every soul be subject unto the higher powers. For there is no power but of God: the powers that be are ordained of God." This he writes to the Romans, not to strangers dispersed, as Peter did, but rather to private persons and those of the meaner rank; writes it, too, so as to set forth brilliantly the whole reason, origin, and end of government. Whereby also it is clear as day that the true and proper ground of our obedience has no connection whatsoever with slavery. "Let every soul," says he, that is, every man, "be subject." What the Apostle purposes in this chapter Chrysostom has sufficiently explained. "St. Paul writes thus," says he, "to make it plain that Christ introduced his principles with no intent to overthrow civil government, but rather to establish it upon truer foundations."[92] He never intended, then, by placing Nero or any other tyrant beyond all laws and penalties, to set up cruelest despotism over all mankind. "He intended too," says the same author, "to dissuade from unnecessary and fruitless wars." He does not, therefore, condemn a war taken up against a tyrant, a bosom enemy of his own country, and consequently the most dangerous enemy possible. "It was a common slander in those days that the Apostles were seditious revolutionists who

91. Roman emperors ruling, respectively, in A.D. 54–68 and 41–54.

92. St. John Chrysostom, *Homilies on Romans,* in Philip Schaff, ed., *A Select Library of Nicene and Post-Nicene Fathers of the Christian Church,* 11:511.

did and said everything to overturn the general laws. The Apostle in this chapter stops the mouths of such traducers." So that the Apostles did not write defences of tyrants as you do, but did such things and preached such things as made them suspected of all tyrants—things that in the eyes of such needed to be defended and interpreted.

What the Apostle's design was we have just seen in Chrysostom; let us now examine the words: "Let every soul be subject to the higher powers." These, however, he defined not, for he never intended to do away with the laws and constitutions of all nations, and turn all things over to one man's will and pleasure. Certainly every good emperor acknowledged his authority to be far below that of the laws and the Senate; so among all but barbarous nations it is the law that has been holy above all else. Therefore it is that Pindar, as cited by Herodotus,[93] declared the law king over all. Orpheus in his hymns calls it king not of mortals only but even of immortals:

᾽Αθανάτων καλέω καὶ θνητῶν ἁγνὸν ἄνακτα
Οὐράνιον νόμον.[94]

He gives the reason: for that the law controls single-handed the helm of living things. Plato in *The Laws* says the law is that which ought to have the greatest power in the state.[95] In his epistles he commends that form of government in which the law is ruler and king over men, and not men tyrants over the law.[96] Aristotle is of the same opinion in his *Politics*,[97] and so is Cicero in his *Laws*,[98] that the laws govern the magistrates as the magistrates govern the people. Therefore, since by the judgment of the wisest men and by the constitutions of the best-ordered states the law has always been accounted the

93. Herodotus *Histories* 3.38.
94. "I call heavenly law the holy king of the mortals and of the immortals."
95. Plato *Laws* 4.715.
96. Plato, in the *Eighth Letter*.
97. Aristotle *Politics* 3.14.1287a.
98. Cicero *On the Laws* 3.1 and 3.2.

highest power on earth, and since the teachings of the gospel clash not with reason or with the law of nations, then certainly that man is most truly subject to the higher powers, who heartily obeys the law, and the magistrates so far as they govern according to the law.

St. Paul, then, charges this subjection not only upon the people, but upon kings themselves, who are nowise above the laws. "For there is no power but of God," that is, no way of constituting a state, no lawful ground for rule over men. Nay, the most ancient laws that are known to us were formerly ascribed to God as their author; the law, as Cicero says in his twelfth [99] *Philippic,* "is no other than right reason, derived from the command of the gods, enjoining whatever is virtuous, and forbidding the contrary." So that the establishment of magistrates is from God, and its purpose is that by their governance mankind may live under law. But the liberty to choose whether this form of government or that, and these officers or those, indubitably always belonged to the free nations of men. Hence St. Peter calls kings and governors a human institution or ordinance; [100] and Hosea 8, "They have set up kings, but not by me; they have made princes, and I knew it not." For in the commonwealth of the Hebrews (and there only) where in divers ways they could consult with God, the appointment of a king must by law be referred to him; all we other nations have received no such command.

Sometimes either the very form of government, if it be faulty, or those persons that have the power in their hands, are not of God, but of men, yes and of the devil too, Luke 4: "All this power will I give thee, . . . for that is delivered unto me; and to whomsoever I will I give it." Hence he is called the prince of this world; and in Revelations 13. the Dragon gave to the Beast his power, and his seat, and great authority. Therefore St. Paul must be understood to mean, not all sorts of powers, but lawful ones, of the sort described in what follows; and to mean the powers themselves, not the men, always, in whose hands they are lodged. Upon this passage Chrysostom speaks

99. Actually Cicero's *Eleventh Philippic* 12.28.

100. 1 Pet. 2:13.

plainly. "What!" says he, "is every prince then appointed by God? No such thing. The Apostle speaks not of the person of the prince, but of the thing. He does not say, there is no *prince* but of God; he says there is no *power* but of God." Thus far Chrysostom.[101] The Apostle, then, when he says "The powers that be are ordained, or *ordered,* of God," would have it understood of lawful powers, for 'tis impossible that a thing evil and faulty, being disordered, can be ordered: to say so asserts two contraries at once—order and disorder.

The words "that be" you interpret as "that *now* be," the easier to prove that the Romans ought to obey Nero, who you suppose was then emperor. Content! For then, think as ill as you like of our English Commonwealth, you must needs grant that Englishmen ought to yield obedience to it, for "it now is," and is "ordained of God," like Nero's power of old. And lest you should answer that Nero had got *his* by lawful succession, I say that he no less than Tiberius had seized "by means of his mother's intrigues a power which nowise belonged to him." So that you are all the more unprincipled, and retract your own assertions, in affirming that the Romans owed subjection to the power that then was, and yet denying that Englishmen owe subjection to the power that now is. But, you worthless thing, there are no two things in this world more directly opposite to one another than you nearly always are to your worthless self. What then will become of you, wretch? With this keen wit of yours you have quite ruined the young king, for upon your own theory I will rack you to confess that the power that now is in England is ordained of God, and that all Englishmen within the confines of that Commonwealth are bound to submit to it. Therefore give ear ye critics all! Hands off from this the new emendation of Salmasius upon the Epistle to the Romans! He has discovered for the occasion that the words ought to be rendered not "the powers that be," but "the powers that *now* be"; and all to prove that everybody owed submission to the tyrant Nero, then emperor to wit!

But, my good man, your pitcher is gone once too often to the

101. Chrysostom, *Homilies,* 11:511.

well. As you ruined the king but a moment ago, even thus you now ruin this so pretty emendation. The Epistle which you say was writ in Nero's time was writ in Claudius's, a guileless ruler and no villain: scholars hold this for a certainty upon surest evidence. Besides, there were five years even of Nero's reign that were excellent. So that this oft-obtruded argument, which many have at their tongues' ends, and which has cheated many, to wit, that a tyrant is to be obeyed because Paul urged the Romans to submit to Nero, is found to be the sly invention of some dunce.

"Whosoever . . . resisteth the power," the lawful power, that is, "resisteth the ordinance of God." This principle makes kings liable when they resist the laws and the Senate. But he that resists an unlawful power, or resists a person who goes about to overthrow and destroy a lawful one—does he resist the ordinance of God? In your right wits you would not say so, I trow. The next verse removes any uncertainty that the Apostle speaks here of a lawful power only; for lest anyone mistake, and thence go chasing stupid notions, it explains, by defining bounds and limitations, who are the officers that are the ministers of this power, and why he urges us to submit. "Rulers," says he, "are not a terror to good works, but to evil. . . . Do that which is good, and thou shalt have praise of the same: For he is the minister of God to thee for good . . . He beareth not the sword in vain: for he is . . . a revenger to execute wrath upon him that doth evil." [102] Who but the wicked denies, who but the wicked refuses, willingly to submit to such a power or its minister? And that not only to avoid "the wrath" and the stumbling block, and for fear of punishment, but even "for conscience sake."

Without magistrates and civil government there can be no commonwealth, no human society, no living in the world. But whatever power or whatever magistrate acts contrary to these precepts—neither the one nor the other is in any proper sense ordained of God. Neither to such a power nor to such a magistrate, therefore, is sub-

102. Rom. 13:3-4.

mission owed or commanded, nor are we forbidden to resist them with discretion, for we shall be resisting not the power or the magistrate here excellently described, but a robber, a tyrant, a public enemy. If he is notwithstanding to be called a magistrate just because he holds power, just because he may appear to be ordained by God for our punishment—in this sense the devil too shall be a magistrate!

Certain it is that there can be but one true definition of one and the same thing. So that if Paul here defines a magistrate, which he certainly does, and with careful precision, he could not possibly in the very words of this definition define a tyrant, the exact opposite. Hence the sure consequence: that he would have us submit to such a magistrate only as he himself has writ down and by definition limited, and not to a tyrant, that magistrate's opposite. "For this cause pay ye tribute also":[103] he adds a reason to his command. Hence Chrysostom: "Why pay we revenue to the king? Is it not as we pay hire for protection and care to one who watches out for us? We should have paid him nothing had we not originally come to know that such supervision was good for us."[104] Wherefore I shall repeat what I have said already, that since this subjection is demanded not absolutely but upon an express reason added, that reason will be the true rule of our subjection. Where that reason holds, we are rebels if we submit not; where it holds not, we are cowards and slaves if we submit.

"But," say you, "the English are far from being free men, for they are infamous villains." For my part I will not recount the vices of the French, though they live under a monarchy; neither will I too much excuse those of the English; yet this I say, that the acts which disgrace them are those they learnt under their Pharaohs in Egypt, as it were; nor have they been able to unlearn them at once while yet in the wilderness, though under God's immediate government. But there is good hope of many amongst us—not now to begin an eulogy of those most excellent saintly men and lovers of the truth; whose num-

103. Rom. 13:6.
104. Chrysostom, *Homilies,* 2:513.

ber among us I think not less than where you think there are most such. But "a heavy yoke is laid upon the English nation." What if it be laid upon those that endeavored to lay the yoke upon all their fellow-citizens? What if it be laid upon those that were deservedly subdued? As for the rest, I question not but they are very well content, now the public treasury is exhausted by the civil wars, to bear the burden of maintaining their own liberty at their own expense.

Now he betakes himself again to his piddling rabbins. He asserts that a king is bound by no laws, and yet on their authority proves that "a king may be guilty of lese-majesty if he suffer the rights of his crown to be diminished." So kings are bound by laws, and not bound by laws; they may be criminals and yet not criminals. The man contradicts himself so perpetually that Contradiction herself seems his twin-born sister.

You say that God gave many kingdoms over in slavery to Nebuchadnezzar. I confess he did so for a time, Jer. 27. 7; but do you make appear if you can that he gave the English nation over for a single minute in slavery to Charles Stuart. That God allowed them I would not deny, but I have never heard that he gave them. Or if God be said to give a people into slavery whenever a tyrant prevails over the people, why ought he not as well be said to set them free whenever the people prevail over a tyrant? Shall the tyrant credit and owe his tyranny to God, and not we our liberty? There is no evil in the state that the Lord hath not let in, Amos 3. Famine, plague, sedition, a public enemy—is there a single one of these that the state will not strive with all its might to shake off? Shake them off it surely will if it can, though it know them to be sent by God, unless himself from heaven should command the contrary.

Upon the same reasoning why may not the state rid itself of a tyrant if it be stronger than he? Why should we suppose the uncontrolled passions of this one man to be appointed by God for the common ill, rather than the self-controlled power of the whole state for the common weal? Far be it from all states and all societies of free-born men to maintain principles so senseless, plague-spots of such ignominy, which wipe out the whole life of the state, and, to gratify a tyrant or two, thrust mankind down to the level of four-footed brutes; for tyrants, once lifted up above all law, will wield the same law and sway over men as over cattle.

I pass by those foolish dilemmas of yours, to indulge in which you invent someone's authority for the assertion that "that sovereign power means the people's power"; though for my part I hesitate not to assert that such is the source of all the power that any magistrate has. Hence Cicero in his Oration for Flaccus says: "Our wise and reverend ancestors appointed those things to be bidden and forbidden which the multitude resolved and the sovereign people ordained." [105] Hence too Lucius Crassus,[106] a distinguished orator, and then president of the Senate, whose cause he was pleading with the people, says: "I beseech you, suffer not us to be subject to any but your own entire body, to whom we can and must submit." For though the Senate governed the People, yet it was the People that had given over that very power to regulate and govern themselves unto the Senate. Hence, in our reading we find majesty in those days more frequently ascribed to the Roman people than to kings. Marcus Tullius again in his Oration for Plancius: "It is the condition of free peoples, and especially of this people, chief and lord of all nations, by vote to give or take away, to or from any, what it will. It is for us patiently to submit to the people's wishes. Those that care not much for office have the less obligation upon them to court the people; those that seek office must not grow weary of entreating them." [107] Should I scruple to call a king the servant of his people, when I hear the Roman Senate, which was the master of so many kings, profess itself to be but the people's servant? You will object perhaps that all this is very true under democratic conditions, for that the Lex Regia had not yet transferred the people's power unto Augustus and his successors. But pray

105. Cicero *Pro Flacco* 8.15.

106. Lucius Licinius Crassus, a consul in 95 B.C., praised by Cicero for his understanding of the Roman constitution.

107. Marcus Tullius *Pro Plancio* 4.11.

look at Tiberius, "a tyrant several times over," you say, as he certainly was—who yet, Suetonius says, when someone called him Lord or Master, though after the enacting of that Lex Regia,[108] gave notice that this person must name him so no more, for that it was an insult. Do you hear? That tyrant deemed it an insult to be called Lord. The same emperor addressing the Senate, "I have said," says he, "frequently heretofore, and now I say again, that a good prince and serviceable, whom you have invested with so great and unrestricted power, ought to submit to the Senate, often to the body of the people, and some-times even to particular persons; nor do I repent of having said so: I confess that you have been both good and just masters to me, as well as indulgent ones, and that you are yet so." It will not help you to say that, proficient in the art of hypocrisy as he was, he feigned all this; for does any man desire to *seem* other than he *ought* to be? Hence it was the custom not only for Nero, as Tacitus tells us,[109] but for the rest of the emperors, to do homage to the people at the Circus. Claudian, in his Panegyric upon the Sixth Consulate of Honorius, says of this:

> Authority divine, mysterious,
> Here present visibly unto the people—
> Lo, how it graces them! And they in turn—
> How grand their answering majesty's requital!
> To throngs upon the Circus seats assembled
> The royal purple makes obeïsance,
> And with one crash the adorèd multitude
> Rebellows from the theatre's hollow vale
> Its uproar to the skies.[110]

By this adoration could the emperors of Rome possibly mean any-thing else than to acknowledge that even after the enacting of the Lex Regia the whole body of the people were their masters?

108. *Lex Regia* refers to the law upon which the emperors founded their authority by appealing to the legal fiction that the Roman people had transferred to the emperor their sovereign power. The passage Milton refers to is from Suetonius *Tiberius* 27.

109. Tacitus *Annals* 16.4.

110. Claudian *De sexto consulatu Honorii* 611ff.

I find, as I suspected at first, that you have spent more time and pains in turning over glossaries and pompously publishing laborious trifles than in the careful and diligent reading of sound authors. 'Tis because you have not the slightest tincture of the wisdom of the ancients that you account as new, and as the dream of mere "enthusiasts' delirium," a matter which has been perfectly well known through the opinions of the most eminent philosophers and the words of the most farsighted statesmen. Your Martin Cobbler and William Tanner, whom you so despise, you had better take unto yourself as your partners and guides in ignorance; though indeed they will be able to instruct you, and to solve those stupid riddles of yours, as thus: "Since in a Monarchy the king is supposed to be a servant, is the People supposed to be a servant in a Democracy?—All the People, or a part?" And when they have played Oedipus to you, you have my permission to be Sphinx to them, and go headlong to the devil;[111] else I see no end to your conundrums and follies.

You ask, "When the Apostle says *kings,* does he mean the *people?*" St. Paul does indeed tell us to pray for kings, 1 Tim. 2. 2, but he had already told us, verse 1, to pray for the people. Yet there are some for all that, both among kings and common people, that we are forbidden to pray for; and if a man may not so much as be prayed for, may he not be lawfully punished? What is to hinder? But, you say, "When Paul wrote this epistle, the rulers were the most profligate persons in the world." That is false too, for Ludovicus Capellus[112] proves by the most trustworthy evidence that this epistle likewise was writ in Claudius's time. When St. Paul has occasion to speak of Nero, he calls him not a king but a lion,—that is, a savage beast, out of whose mouth he is glad he was delivered, 2. Tim. 4. So that it is for kings, not for beasts, we are to pray, that under them "we may live a quiet and peaceable life," but, observe, "in all godliness and honesty." What we are here to take account of, clearly, is not so much kings as peace and quiet, godliness and honesty. Yet what nation would not

111. The Sphinx destroyed herself when Oedipus solved her riddle.
112. Louis Cappel, French Hebraist writing in the seventeenth century.

choose, in defense of themselves and their children,—against tyrant or enemy is all one,—to live a life "perturbed and restless," warlike and honorable, rather than under the power of tyrant or enemy to lead a life just as perturbed and restless, but vile into the bargain, in slavery and ignominy? Listen while the Samnites, who had tried both conditions, testify, according to Livy,[113] that they had gone to war again because war, with freedom, was less intolerable than peace with slavery. Nay, listen to your own words; for I often put you on the witness-stand, not to do you honor, but that all men may observe how double-tongued you are, and self-contradictory, and a king's hireling slave. "Who would not rather," say you, "bear with the dissensions that through the rivalries of great men often occur under an Aristocracy, than with the misery and ruin that are sure to come of a monarch accustomed to absolute rule? The people of Rome preferred that condition of their Republic, no matter how much vexed with civil broils, to the unbearable yoke of the Caesars. When a people which to avoid sedition has preferred a monarchy finds by experience that what it wished to avoid is the lesser evil, often it desires to return to its former government." These are your own words, and more you have to this purpose, at page 412 of that discourse concerning bishops, which under the fictitious name of Walo Messalinus you wrote against Petavius the Jesuit—though yourself are more a Jesuit, nay the worst of that crew.

We have already heard the sense of Holy Scripture upon this subject, and are not sorry to have searched it out with all possible care. Therefore perhaps it will not be worth our while to seek after the judgment of the Fathers through all their huge volumes. For if they assert anything which has not been allowed by Scripture, we rightly reject their authority, great though it be. That passage which you cite from Irenaeus,[114] that "Kings are by God's command appointed suitable to the people they then govern" is clear against Scripture. For

113. Livy *Ab urbe condita* 31.14.

114. Second-century Greek father whose work, *Against Heresies,* Milton and Salmasius are citing.

though God himself declared openly that for the government of his own people judges were more suitable than kings, yet he left it wholly to the people's will and decision to exchange, if they would, their government by nobles, which was suitable to them, for one by kings, which was less suitable. And we read that frequently a bad king was given to a good people, and contrariwise, a good king to a bad people. What is most suitable and profitable to a people, then, is something for the wisest men to ascertain; for certain it is that the same form of government is not equally fitting for all nations, or for the same nation at all times; but sometimes one, sometimes another, may be more proper, according as the diligence and valor of the people wax or wane. Yet whoso takes from a people their power to choose what government they wish takes that indeed in which all civil liberty is rooted.

Then you tell us of Justin Martyr's[115] humble and submissive behavior to the Antonines, those best of emperors; as if anybody would not pay deference to princes so excellent, princes so measured in the exercise of their power! "How much worse Christians," you say, "are we in these days than they were! They submitted to a prince of a different religion." Of course they did, being private persons, and far inferior in strength. "But now Papists will not endure a Protestant king," or "Protestants a Papist." As for you, you show yourself to be neither Papist nor Protestant: how discreet of you, and generous too; for you concede of your own accord what we have not now asked of you, that all Christians today agree in that very thing that you alone with so much impudence and wickedness oppose, in a manner too, most unlike those Fathers that you praise. They unto pagan kings kept writing defences for Christians; you write your Defence for a wicked Popish king against Christians and Protestants.

Next you fetch out of Athenagoras and Tertullian[116]—quite ineffectually—quantities of things that had already been said much

115. Second-century Christian father martyred under the prefect Rusticus between 163 and 167.

116. Athenagoras, a second-century Christian apologist; Tertullian (c. 160–230), a father of the Latin Church, apologist, and vigorous controversialist.

more plainly and intelligibly by the Apostles themselves. Tertullian, moreover, is far from agreeing with you that a king is lord and master; as you either knew not, or wickedly pretended you knew not. For he, a Christian, dared in his *Apologeticum* to write to a heathen Emperor that an Emperor ought not to be called Lord. "Augustus himself," says he, "that formed the empire, would not be called 'Lord,' for this is God's title. I will, of course, call the Emperor 'Lord,' but only when I am not forced to call him so in God's place. For the rest, as regards the Emperor I am a free man; my Lord is God alone, etc." And in the same discourse: "He who is Father of his Country, how should he be its Master?"[117] Now take joy to yourself of Tertullian, whom you had better have let alone. But, you say, "the slayers of Domitian he calls parricides." And rightly so, for it was through a conspiracy of Domitian's wife and servants that he was killed, by Parthenius and by Stephanus, a person accused of stealing moneys. If the Senate and the people of Rome had adjudged him a public enemy as erewhile they adjudged Nero, whom then they searched out and put to death,—had they, I say, thus punished Domitian according to the custom of their ancestors, think you Tertullian would have called them parricides? If he had, he would have deserved to be hanged, as you do now.

Unto Origen[118] the same answer will fit as did fit unto Irenaeus.

Athanasius says that it is an abomination to summon the kings of the earth before human tribunals. Who told him so? For in this I hear none of God's Word. And rather than Athanasius I will believe kings and emperors who admit that they have no such exemption. Then you bring in Ambrose, who after he had been a proconsul and then a catechumen at last commenced bishop; you cite, I say, his interpretation of those words of David, "Against thee only I have sinned,"— an interpretation which is ignorant, not to say adulatory. Ambrose was willing all others should be enthralled to the emperor, that he might enthrall the emperor to himself. Everybody knows with what

117. Tertullian *Apologeticum* 34.

118. Origen (c. 186–253) was an Alexandrian church father whose exegetical writings addressed nearly the entire range of biblical books.

a more than high-priestly popish pride and arrogance he treated the emperor Theodosius at Milan, how he took upon himself to declare him guilty of the massacre at Thessalonica, and forbade him to enter the church; and what a raw beginner in Gospel lore he next showed himself to be. When the emperor fell down at his feet, he commanded him to get him out of the church porch; at length when he was received again into the communion of the church, and had made offering, and remained standing at the altar, Ambrose with these words ordered him outside the rails: "Emperor, these inner places are for priests only; it is not lawful for others to come within them."[119] Was this a preacher of the Gospel, or was it a pontifical high priest of the Jewish rite? Yet this man put the emperor to lord it over everyone else, that he himself might lord it over the emperor—quite an usual trick of churchmen. With words to this purpose he put Theodosius back as inferior to himself: "You are ruler over men that are your like and fellow-servants with yourself, for there is one only lord and king and Creator over all." Excellent indeed! This truth, which the craft and flattery of bishops kept hid, was then brought to light by the irascibility, or to speak more mildly, by the ignorant zeal of one of them.

To Ambrose's incompetence you now join your own ignorance or heresy in denying point blank (p. 68) that "under the old covenant there was forgiveness of sins through the blood of Christ at the time when David confessed to God that he had sinned against him only." It is the orthodox belief that any remission of sins there ever was, was but by the blood of the lamb that was offered up from the beginning of the world. I know not whose disciple you are that set up for a broacher of new heresies, but certain I am that that great Divine's disciple whom you so censure was not in error when he said that anyone of David's subjects might have cried upon God, "Against thee only have I sinned," with as much right as David himself.

Then you show off Austin,[120] and trot out an obscure company of Hipponensian divines. What you bring in from Austin makes not

119. Theodoret *Church History* 5.17.

120. St. Augustine (354–430), church father and prolific author of theological and exegetical works.

at all against us; why should we not acknowledge with the prophet Daniel that God changeth times, sets up one kingdom, and pulls down another?[121] Certainly,—yet it is by means of men. If 'twas God alone gave a kingdom to King Charles, God alone took it away, and gave it to the Lords and Commons. If you say it was for that reason our allegiance was due to King Charles, then you must needs say that for the same reason it is due to our present rulers. For you yourself grant that God has given even our rulers such power as he gives wicked kings "to punish the people's sins"; so that, according to your own opinion, our present rulers, being likewise appointed by God, cannot lawfully be removed from office but by God. Thus, as usual, you turn your point against yourself, and are your own assassin. Serves you right too; for you have reached such a pitch of wickedness and shamelessness, of stupidity and madness, that those very persons whom, as you prove with so many arguments, we ought not to lift a finger against, you yourself assert should be hunted down in war by all their subjects.

You tell us that St. Jerome calls Ishmael, who slew Gedaliah the Deputy-Governor, a parricide; and rightly, for it was without cause that Ishmael slew that ruler over Judea, who was a good man.[122] Jerome also in his comment upon Ecclesiastes says that Solomon's counsel "Keep the king's commandment" agrees with St. Paul's doctrine upon the same subject; and he deserves commendation for having made a more moderate construction of that text than did the rest of his contemporaries.

You say you will not "come down to times later than Austin to search out the opinions of the doctors." Yet, for all men (supposing you still had any adherents) to learn that you can more easily lie than say nothing, you do not refrain, after but one sentence more, from coming down at once to Isidore of Seville, Gregory of Tours, and Otto of Freising[123]—even into the midst of mediaeval barbarism. Had you

121. Dan. 2:21.

122. Jer. 41:2.

123. Isidore (570–636), Spanish historian, encyclopedist, and controversialist against the Arians; Gregory of Tours (538–94) wrote a history of the Franks; Otto of Freising was a twelfth-century chronicler of the reign of Frederick I (1123–90).

but known how worthless we consider their authority, you had not told a lie to quote their unintelligible evidence.

Readers, would ye know why he dare not come down to the present time, why he hides away and on a sudden disappears? I will tell you: 'tis because he knows full well that he shall encounter as many keen adversaries as there are eminent divines of the Protestant Church. Let him but put it to the test, and though he strive with all his might, he shall find how easily I will rout and overwhelm him, once I get the Luthers, Zwinglis, Calvins, Bucers, Peter Martyrs, and Pareuses, marshaled out in battle array. I will set against you even your Leyden colleagues, whose University, whose flourishing commonwealth, where freedom dwelt of old—yea not even those fountains and streams of polite learning—could wash away that slavish rust and native barbarism of yours. With not one orthodox divine to take your part (name any you please), stripped, I say, of all Protestant support, you blush not to take refuge in the Sorbonne, a College you know to be utterly given over to the teachings of popery, and of no authority among the orthodox. We surrender so wicked a champion of tyranny: Sorbonne, absorb him!

We will not own a slave so despicable as to maintain that "the whole body of a nation is not the equal of a king the most slothful and cowardly." You labor in vain to unload and lay upon the Pope a doctrine which all free nations and religions and all the Orthodox take unto themselves for their very own. True, the Pope, when he and his bishops were low and of but small account in the world, was the first author of this foul doctrine of yours; 'twas precisely by preaching such doctrine that little by little he got great riches and power into his own hands, and himself turned out to be the worst of tyrants. Yet these tyrants he bound to himself by the closest tie, for he persuaded the nations, whose minds he had long held crushed beneath their superstitions, that it was unlawful to depose a king, though never so bad, unless the Pope absolved them from their oath of allegiance. But you avoid Orthodox writers, and endeavor to bring odium upon the truth by making out the Pope to be the originator of what is a known and common received opinion amongst them. If you did not do it cunningly you would bewray yourself for what you are, neither Papist nor Protestant, but some sort of half-barbarous Edomite Herodian, who worship and adore a monstrous tyrant as if he were a Messiah sent down from heaven.

Your opinions you say you "have proved by the teaching of the fathers that flourished in the first four centuries—teaching which alone should be deemed evangelical and Christian." This man is past all shame. How many things did they say and write which Christ and his Apostles would neither have taught nor have approved? How many things in which all Protestants disagree with them? But what have you proved out of the fathers? Why, "that even evil kings are appointed by God." Allow that they, like all other evils, are, in some sense, by God appointed. What then? why, "therefore they have no judge but God alone; they are above the laws; by no law written or unwritten, law of nature or law of God, can they be indicted by or before their own subjects." But why? Certainly no law forbids it; no law excepts kings; and all reason and right both human and divine requires that all offenders be punished without distinction. Nor have you produced any law whatever, written or unwritten, of God or of nature, which forbids. Then why may not kings be proceeded against? "Because they, even the bad ones, are appointed by God." Had I best call you knave, or fool and blockhead? A vile wretch you must be to dare propagate a doctrine so destructive and pernicious, and a dunce to lean upon such silly arguments. God says, Is. 54, "I have created the slayer to destroy." Then a slayer is above the laws. Weigh and turn it round as much as you will, you shall find this conclusion to be as valid as yours.

For the Pope too is appointed by God just as much as tyrants are, and set up for the punishment of the church, as I have already demonstrated out of your own writings. And yet you say, *Wal. Mes.,* page 412: "Because he has raised his primacy to an insufferable pinnacle of power, so that it is nowise different from a tyranny, both he and his bishops may be more lawfully removed than they were appointed." You tell us that the Pope and the bishops, *though* God in his wrath appointed them, ought to be removed from the church because they are *tyrants;* and yet you deny that *tyrants* ought to be removed from the commonwealth, *because* God in his wrath appointed *them!* How utterly irrelevant and self-contradictory! On the one hand, though the Pope cannot without a man's consent harm even the conscience, which alone is his realm, yet you cry out that he—who in point of fact has not the power to tyrannize—should be removed as a tyrant intolerable; on the other hand you urge that a tyrant indeed, a tyrant that holds all our lives and estates in his grip, and without whose support the Pope himself cannot lord it in the church, must in the commonwealth by all means be borne withal. These assertions compared with one another bewray you as so ignorant and childish a chatterer— whether the thing you say is true or false—that your fickleness and ignorance, your rashness and heedlessness, can be hidden no longer from anybody.

But you allege another reason: "Human affairs would seem turned upside down." They would, and for the better. It would be all over with human affairs if being once at their worst they must be always so. I say they would be changed for the better, for the king's power would revert to the people, by whose will and vote it first proceeded and was conferred upon one of themselves. And most rightfully would the power be transferred from the doer of the wrong to the sufferer; since among all mankind there can be no third party qualified to wield it; for who would submit to the jurisdiction of a foreigner? All men would equally be subject to the laws;—and than such a condition nothing can be more just. There would be then no God of flesh and blood; whoever sets up such among men is an offender no less heinous against the State than against the Church.

Now I mean to turn your own weapons upon you again. To believe that one man sits in Christ's seat, "this," you say, "is the greatest heresy. These two signs mark Antichrist, infallibility in spirituals, and omnipotence in temporals." *Apparat. ad Prim.*, page 171. Are kings infallible? Why then should they be omnipotent? And if they are, why are they not as destructive to temporalities as is the Pope to spiritualities? Does God really concern himself nowise with civil affairs? If he does not, surely he does not forbid us to take care of them. If he does, he would have the same reformation made in the commonwealth as in the church, especially if it has been put to the proof that the assigning of infallibility and omnipotency to man is the identical cause of all the evils in both. In civil affairs God has not enjoined such patience that the state must submit to the cruelties of tyrants, but not the church; nay, rather has he enjoined the contrary; indeed he has left unto the church no arms but patience and innocence, prayer and the teaching of the gospel; but into the hands of the state and its officers altogether he has entrusted not patience, but the sword of the law, avenger of wrong and violence. So this man's upside-down back-foremost mind exposes itself to either astonishment or laughter: in the church he is Helvidius and Thraseas, tyrant-queller out and out; in the state the common slave and lackey of tyrants all. If his doctrine hold, not we only that have cast off our king, but Protestants in general, who against the wishes of their kings have cast off the Pope's supremacy, are rebels all alike.

But long it is ere now that he lies felled by his own shafts. For, let but his enemy's hand not fail, and Salmasius, such is his nature, himself furnishes an overplus of weapons against himself. Nor does any man offer you a handle more easy to refute and ridicule himself withal. You will sooner give over in actual weariness of flogging him, than he of offering his back to the lash.

## CHAPTER IV.

Perhaps you think, Salmasius, that by this Royal Defence you have much ingratiated yourself with kings, and deserved well of all princes and lords of the earth; but if they would reckon their interest and advantage according to truth, not according to your flatteries, they ought to hate nobody worse than you, and banish and keep away nobody farther from their presence. For in the very act of exalting the power of kings above law and beyond measure, you remind most nations that they are under a slavery they had not guessed before, and the more violently drive them to shake off upon a sudden that lethargy in which they kept vainly dreaming they were freemen; for you admonish them what before they recked not, that they are slaves to their kings. And they will count royal government all the less endurable the more you persuade them that it is not by their sufferance and submission that this exorbitant power swelled up, but that from the beginning, even such and so great as it is, it sprang full-grown from the royal right itself. So that whether you convince the nations or not, you and this Defence of yours must needs be to all kings hereafter calamitous and ruinous and accursed. For if you shall persuade a nation that royal right is power without limit, they will no longer endure a monarchy; if you persuade them not, then they will not endure kings who assume so unlawful a power as if it were lawfully theirs.

If kings who are yet uncommitted as to this will heed me, and will suffer themselves to be limited by the laws, then instead of the uncertain, weak, and violent government, full of cares and fears, which now they have, they will secure unto themselves a government perfectly steadfast, peaceable, and lasting. If they slight this counsel, so wholesome to them and their kingdoms, because of its author, then let them know that it belongs less to me than to a very wise king of old. Lycurgus king of the Spartans, who was sprung of an ancient royal stock, observed that his kinsmen in power at Argos and Messene had each turned his rule into a tyranny, and had been the ruin of themselves and their states; thereupon, that he might at once benefit his country and secure the kingly office to his own family as long as possible, he made the senate a partner in his power, and subjected himself, even the king, to the almost censorial office of the Ephors— all this to prop his throne. By this means he handed down the royal power unshaken to his posterity for many generations. Others think it was Theopompus, who ruled over Lacedaemon more than a hundred years after Lycurgus, that adopted this polity, so self-restrained as to set up the popular power of the Ephors above his own, and who thereupon boasted that he had settled the royal power on a sure foundation, and had left it to his posterity much augmented and much more lasting. However this may be, surely the kings of today would have here no base pattern to copy, and distinguished authority too, for a counsel thoroughly safe.

That all men should submit to any one man as superior to law, no law ever did enact, or ever could, for whatever law overthrows all law cannot itself be law. Now, seeing that law spurns you off as an underminer and murderer of law, you try in this chapter to renew the fight by means of examples. Let us make trial, then, of examples, for often they make plain what the laws are silent in, yet hint at.

We will begin with the Jews, whom we suppose to have known most of the will of God, and then, according to your own method, we will "come down to the Christians." But we will make an earlier start, at the time when the Israelites, however they had been subjected to kings, cast that slavish yoke from off their necks. Eglon the king of Moab had made a conquest of them, and had set up his throne at Jericho in the midst of them; he was no contemner of the true God, for at mention of His name he rose from his seat: the Israelites had served him eighteen years, and had sent a present to him, not as to an enemy, but as to their own king.[124] Yet in the very act of publicly making a present to him as their king, they kill him by stratagem as an enemy to their country. To be sure, Ehud, who slew him, is believed to have had a warrant from God for so doing. What greater argument of its being a warrantable and praiseworthy action? God uses not to put men upon deeds that are unjust, treacherous, and cruel, but upon deeds honorable and praiseworthy. But we read nowhere that he had express command from God. "The children of Israel cried unto the Lord";[125] so did we. The Lord raised them up a saviour; so did he for us. Eglon from their neighbor became their inmate, and from their enemy their king. Our gentleman from our king became our enemy, and so no king, for no man can anywise be at once a member of the state and an enemy to it. Antony was never held a consul, Nero an emperor, after the Senate had voted them both enemies.

124. Judg. 3:12–21.
125. Judg. 3:15.

This Cicero tells us unmistakably in his fourth *Philippic:* "If Antony be a consul, Brutus is an enemy; if Brutus is a saviour and preserver of the commonwealth, Antony is an enemy. Who but robbers count him a consul?" By the same reason, say I, who but enemies to their country count a tyrant a king? So that whether or not Eglon was a foreigner, and Charles a countryman of ours, makes no difference, since each was an enemy and a tyrant. If Ehud killed him justly, we too have done justly in putting Charles to death.

Samson, that renowned champion, though his countrymen blamed him (Judg. 15, "Knowest thou not that the Philistines are rulers over us?"), yet made war singlehanded against his rulers; and whether instigated by God or by his own valor only, slew not one, but many at once of his country's tyrants. And as he had first duly prayed to God to be his help, it follows that he counted it no wickedness, but a duty, to kill his masters, his country's tyrants, even though the greater part of his countrymen refused not slavery. Yet, you urge, David, who was both a king and a prophet, refused to take away Saul's life, because he was "the Lord's anointed." David's refusal to do a thing doth not necessarily bind us to the same refusal. It was as a private person that David refused; is that a precedent binding at once upon a Council of State, upon a Parliament, upon a whole nation? David would not kill his private enemy by stealth; shall a public officer therefore not punish a criminal according to law? He would not kill a king; will a Senate therefore be afraid to strike a tyrant? He scrupled to kill the Lord's anointed; must the people therefore scruple to condemn to death their own anointed?—especially one who by so long acting the public enemy was all besmeared with his own subjects' blood, and thus had done away his royal unction, whether sacred or civil. Those kings indeed whom God by his prophets anointed, or by name appointed to some special service, as of old he did Cyrus, Isa. 44, I acknowledge as the Lord's anointed; the rest are in my opinion the people's anointed, or the army's, or the anointed of their own faction only. But that all kings are the Lord's anointed, yet that therefore they are above all laws, and not to be punished no matter what villainies they perpetrate—this you will never force me to grant you.

What if David forbade himself and some private persons to stretch forth their hands against the Lord's anointed? God himself forbade kings to touch his anointed—that is his people, Psal. 105. He preferred the anointing wherewith his people were anointed, before that of kings, if any such there were. Yet shall it not be lawful to punish even God's own believers if they have transgressed against the laws? King Solomon was about to put to death Abiathar the priest, though he were the Lord's anointed too; and did not spare him because he was the Lord's anointed, but because he had been his father's friend. If therefore the Lord's sacred and civil unction could not exempt from death the high priest, the same being in many cases the highest officer of state, how comes a merely civil unction to exempt a tyrant? But you say, "Saul too was a tyrant, and deserved death." What then? It does not thence follow that David, wherever he happened to be, was qualified or empowered to kill King Saul without the people's authority, or the command of the magistracy. But really and truly was Saul a tyrant? I wish you would say so; indeed you do say so, though you had said before in your second chapter, page 32, that "he was no tyrant, but a good king, and chosen of God." Now is there any reason why base informers and perjurers should be publicly branded, and you escape without the same mark of ignominy? For they are wont to practice their falsifications with less treachery and deceit than you are wont to write and to treat even matters of the greatest moment. So Saul was a good king, if that serves your turn; if it suits you not, he shall be, of a sudden, no good king but a tyrant. No wonder; for in so shamelessly pandering to tyrannic power, what do you else than turn good kings into tyrants all? But David, though he would not put to death the king his father-in-law for a number of reasons that we have nothing to do withal, yet in his own defence hesitated not to raise an army, and to take or besiege Saul's cities, and would have defended the town of Keilah against the king's forces, had he not understood that the citizens were ill disposed toward him. Suppose Saul had besieged the city, and set up ladders against the walls, and himself resolved to be the first to scale them; do you think David would straightway have thrown down his arms, and have betrayed all his followers to his anointed enemy? I trow not! Why should he not have done what we did? When his interests so required, he freely proffered aid to the Philistines, the enemies of his country, thus doing against Saul what I am sure we should never have done against our tyrant.

I am ashamed, and have long been weary, of your lies. Falsely you declare it to be a principle of the English "That enemies are rather to be spared than friends, and that because their king was their friend they ought not to spare him." You impudent liar, what mortal ever heard this whimsy before you invented it? Yet we overlook it, for this chapter did not as yet present that most egregious worn-out rhetorical cosmetic of yours, which you now for the fifth time fetch out from the cabinets of your perfumery-shop, and which before the end of your book is to be fetched thence ten times—that stuff about the English being "fiercer than their mastiffs!" The English are not so much fiercer than their own mastiffs as you are hungrier than any mad dog whatsoever, who with your tough guts can bear to return again and again to the cabbage you have so often vomited.

Then you tell us that David commanded the Amalekite to be put to death, who pretended to have killed Saul.[126] But here is no likeness either in the deed or in the persons. There was, in my opinion at least, no motive for David's severe treatment of that man—who professed to have given the king a *coup de grâce* when the king was already at the point of death, and dying in anguish—unless David, because to all appearance he had gone over to the Philistines and joined their army, did the more zealously endeavor to clear himself from all suspicion of plotting the king's murder. The same action all men blame in Domitian, who put to death Epaphroditus likewise for helping Nero to kill himself.[127] Next—another instance of your impudence—you call him not only the "anointed of the Lord," but "the Lord's Christ," whom you had just called a tyrant, and one "driven

126. 2 Sam. 1:13–15.
127. Suetonius *Life of Domitian* 14.

and actuated by an evil spirit." Such base thoughts you have of the name of Christ that you fear not to give that so holy name to a tyrant possessed of a devil.

Now I come to that instance in which whoever sees not that the right of the people is superior to that of kings must indeed be blind. When Solomon was dead, the people assembled at Sichem to make his son Rehoboam king.[128] Thither himself went Rehoboam, as one that stood for the office, that he might not seem to claim the kingdom for his inheritance, or to hold a freeborn people as if they were his father's sheep and oxen. The people propose conditions upon which his royal power shall rest. He desires three days time to advise; he consults with the old men; they advise him nothing about a royal right, but to comply with the people, and speak them fair, it being in their power to make him king or pass him by. Then he consults with the young men that were grown up with him; they, as if stung mad by Salmasius's gadfly, keep dinning in his ears naught but royal right, and urging him to threaten whips and scorpions. Rehoboam answered the people as these advised him. So when all Israel saw that the king "hearkened not unto them," at once with bold words they openly protest their own liberty and the right of the people. "What portion have we in David? To your tents, O Israel! now see to thine own house, David." When the king sent Adoram to them, they stoned him with stones, and perhaps were ready to make an example of the king himself had he not made speed to flee. He raises a great army to reduce the Israelites to their allegiance. God forbids: "Ye shall not go up," says he, "nor fight against your brethren the children of Israel; for this thing is from me." Now consider: heretofore the people had desired a king; God was displeased with them for it, but yet would not interpose against their right. Presently the people reject Rehoboam from ruling them; and God not only leaves the matter in their hands, but forbids Rehoboam to make war against them for it, and stops him; and teaches him withal, that those that had revolted from him

128. 1 Kings 12.

were not on that account to be called rebels, but none the less brethren. Now look to your defences! You say that all kings are of God, and that therefore the people ought not to resist even tyrants. I answer you that the meetings and assemblies of the people, their votes, their acts, endeavors, and decrees, are likewise of God, by the testimony of God himself in this place; and consequently, by the authority of God himself, a king likewise, according to your argument, ought not to resist the people. For as certain as it is that at present kings are of God, and whatever argument thence follows to enforce a people's obedience, so certain is it, that at present free assemblies of the people are also of God, and this affords the same argument for their right of keeping their kings in order, or for casting them off; nor will kings on this account be any more justified than was Rehoboam in making war on their subjects.

Why, then, you ask, did the Israelites not revolt from Solomon? Who but you would ask a question so impertinent in view of the certainty that they did revolt from a tyrant, and with impunity? It is true, Solomon fell into some vices, but he was not therefore a tyrant; he made amends for his vices by many excellent virtues and by deserving greatly of the commonwealth. But admit that he had been a tyrant; yet circumstances are often such that the people will not, and often such that they cannot, depose a tyrant: enough that they did it when it was in their power. "But," say you, "Jeroboam's act was ever had in detestation, and his defection abominated; his successors were ever accounted rebels." Rather I find plenty of passages that blame his defection not from Rehoboam but from the true worship of God; and I remember that his successors are frequently called wicked, certainly, but nowhere rebels.

"From an act that is contrary to law and right," say you, "no right can arise." Pray what then becomes of your right of kings? Thus do you perpetually confute yourself. You say, "Adulteries, murders, thefts are daily committed with impunity." Are you not aware that here you answer your own question how tyrants so often escape unpunished? You say: "Those kings were rebels, and yet the prophets made no attempts to seduce the people from their allegiance." And why do you, you rascally false prophet, endeavor to seduce the people of England from their present magistrates, even supposing these to be rebels as you think? "This English faction of robbers," say you, "allege that they were put upon their wicked impious undertaking by some immediate voice from Heaven." That the English pretend to any such warrant as a justification of their actions is one of those many lies and fictions of yours.

But I proceed to treat you with examples. Libnah, a powerful city, revolted from King Joram, because he had forsaken God: it was the king therefore that revolted, not the city, nor is the city blamed for that revolt, but rather, if the added reason be considered, seems to be approved.[129] "Revolts of this sort are not to be taken as examples," say you. But why did you then so vauntingly promise that throughout this chapter you would contend with me by examples, whereas you can produce no examples but mere denials, which have no validity as proofs, and when we have produced examples that are sure and substantial, you say they are no precedents? For arguing like this who would not hiss you from the platform? You challenged us at precedents; we produced them; and what do you do? you turn your back, and look for byways of escape.

I proceed: Jehu, at the command of the prophet, slew a king; nay, he ordered the death of Ahaziah, his own liege prince.[130] God would not have tyrants put to death by their own subjects, if it were a wicked thing, a thing of bad example, why did God himself command it? If he commanded it, it was lawful, commendable, and glorious. It was not because God commanded it that it was right and lawful to kill a tyrant, but it was because it was right and lawful that God commanded it. Again, Jehoiada the high priest did not scruple to depose Athaliah, and kill her, though she had been seven years in actual possession of

129. 2 Kings 8:22.
130. 2 Kings 9:1–27.

the crown.[131] "But," you say, "she had taken the government when she had no right to it." And did not Tiberius long after assume, as you say, "a sovereignty nowise belonging to him"? And yet you then kept affirming that, according to Christ's teaching, he and other such tyrants ought to be obeyed. It were a most ridiculous thing to imagine, that a king who gets in by usurpation may lawfully be deposed, but one that rules tyrannically may not. But, say you, according to the law, she could not possibly reign, being a woman. "Thou shalt set over thee a king," not a queen. If this comes off, I put it thus: "Thou shalt set over thee a king," not a tyrant. For there is a far greater unlikeness between a king and a tyrant than between a male and a female.

Amaziah a cowardly idolatrous king was put to death, not by a few conspirators, but rather, it should seem, by the nobility and the people.[132] For he fled from Jerusalem, and had none to stand by him, and they pursued him even to Lachish. This counsel against him, says the history, they took "after the time that Amaziah did turn away from following the Lord"; and we do not find that Azariah as a son made any public investigation into his father's death.

And now once more you quote much silly stuff out of the rabbins, to prove that the king of the Jews was superior to the Sanhedrim, but you do not consider king Zedekiah's own words, Jer. 38: "The king is not he that can do anything against you." This is how he addresses the princes, clearly confessing himself inferior to the great council of the realm. "Perhaps," say you, "he durst not deny them anything for fear of sedition." But what does your "perhaps" signify, when your most positive assertion is not worth even the estimation of a hair? For what can be more fickle and shifty and inconsistent than you? How often have I caught you changing sides and colors, disagreeing with yourself, unsaying with one breath what you have said with another?

You make comparisons again betwixt king Charles and some of

131. 2 Kings 11:15−16.
132. 2 Kings 14:19, 14:21.

the good kings of Judah. First you mention David as one to be despised. "Take David," you say, "guilty at once of adultery and murder; no such thing in Charles. Solomon his son, commonly called the wise," etc. Who would not grow indignant at this filthy rascally fool's bandying about the names of worthies, nay of kings, eminent in greatness and piety? Dare you compare King David with King Charles; a most religious king and prophet with a superstitious prince and a mere novice in the Christian religion; a most prudent wise prince with a stupid one; a valiant prince with a cowardly; a most just prince with a most unjust? Can you commend the chastity and self-control of one whom together with the Duke of Buckingham we know to be covered with every kind of infamy? It were to no purpose to inquire into the private actions of his life, who in public at the theatre would wantonly embrace and kiss women, and handle virgins' and matrons' breasts, not to mention the rest. I advise you in your turn, you counterfeit Plutarch, henceforth to abstain from such absurd Parallels, lest I be forced to publish concerning king Charles what otherwise I would fain pass over in silence.

So far it is clear what the People acted or attempted against tyrants, and by what right, in those times when God himself did immediately, as it were, by his word of command govern the Hebrew commonwealth. The ages that succeed do not guide us by their own authority, but, in governing all according to the rule and reason of their forefathers, they only confirm us in our opinion. For after the Babylonish captivity, when God gave no new command concerning the state, though the royal line was not extinct, the people returned to the old mosaical form of government. They were one while tributaries to Antiochus, king of Syria; yet when he enjoined them things that were unlawful, it was under the conduct of their high priests, the Maccabees, that they resisted him and his governors, and by force regained their former liberty.[133] After that, whoever was accounted most worthy of it had the principality conferred upon him, till at last Hyrcanus

133. Antiochus IV ruled Judea as Seleucid king from 175–163 B.C.

the son of Simon, the brother of Judas Maccabaeus,[134] plundered David's sepulchre, and began to keep foreign soldiers, and to invest the priesthood with a kind of regal power; whereupon his son Aristobulus was the first that assumed the crown. Though he was a tyrant, the people stirred not against him, which is no great wonder, for he reigned but one year. And he himself being overtaken with a grievous disease, and repenting of his crimes, ceased not to wish for death, till amid his wishes he breathed his last. His brother Alexander succeeded him; "and nobody rose against him," you say, tyrant though he were. Ah, you might have lied quite fearless of discovery had but Josephus[135] been lost, and only your "Josippus" left extant, from whom you fetch out some ineffectual utterances of the Pharisees. The facts are these: Alexander governed ill, both in war and in peace; and though he kept a great troop of Pisidian and Cilician mercenaries for a bodyguard, yet could he not restrain the people; but even whilst he was sacrificing they fell upon him as unworthy of that function, and had almost smothered him with boughs of palm trees and citron trees. Afterward, for six years, almost the whole nation made war upon him; and when he had slain many thousands of the Jews in this war, and at length desired peace, and asked what they would have him do, they answered with one voice that he should die, nay, that they should hardly pardon him after his death. To get rid by hook or crook of this history, so inconvenient to you, you hid it behind a few trifling sententious Pharisaical speeches—to your own deep disgrace and damage; for you ought either to have let this example quite alone, or to have told the facts;—were it not that, like the old daylight-shunning trickster that you are, you give far more weight to your lies than to your cause. Even those eight hundred Pharisees whom he commanded to be crucified, were of their number that had taken up arms against him; and they and the rest of the people had unani-

134. Judas Maccabaeus led a revolt in reaction to the king's policy of Hellenization.

135. Milton opposes Josephus's *Jewish Antiquities* to Salmasius's tenth-century chronicle by Joseppius, the pseudonym for Joseph Ben Gorion, which some scholars maintain is itself the pseudonym of an anonymous author.

mously protested that they would put him to death if they could defeat him and lay hands upon him. After the death of Alexander, his wife Alexandra seized the crown, like Athaliah of old, not according to law, for (as you have just remarked) the laws of the Jews admitted not a woman to the throne, but partly by force, for she maintained an army of foreigners, and partly by favor, for she had got the support of the Pharisees, who had the greatest influence over the people, upon the understanding that she was to have the royal name, but they the power. Just so in my country the Scotch Presbyterians lately granted Charles the name of king, but for a consideration—namely that they might keep the royal authority in their own hands.[136] After the death of Alexandra, Hyrcanus and Aristobulus her sons were at strife for the sovereignty: Aristobulus, who was more active, and had stronger support, forced his elder brother out of the kingdom. A while after, when Pompey turned aside into Syria from the Mithridatic war, the Jews, thinking that in him they had now found a wholly disinterested arbiter of their liberty, dispatch an embassy to him in their own name; they renounce the rule of both the brothers, and complain that they had been enslaved by them. Pompey deposed Aristobulus, and left to Hyrcanus the priesthood and the royal rank to which ancestral law entitled him: thenceforward he was called High Priest and Ethnarch. Once more, in the reign of Archelaus the son of Herod, the Jews sent fifty ambassadors to Augustus Caesar; made serious charges against Herod that was dead, and Archelaus; deposed the latter as much as in them lay, and petitioned the emperor to let the people of the Jews be without a king. Caesar, somewhat moved at their entreaty, made the appointee not a king but only an Ethnarch. Yet again, in the tenth year of this governorship, the People by their ambassadors to Caesar accused the Ethnarch of tyranny. Caesar heard them graciously, sent for him, and upon his conviction banished him to Vienne. Answer me now: a people that accused their kings, that desired their condemnation, that desired their punishment, would not they themselves rather, if it had been in their power, and that they

136. Charles I had entered into such an agreement with Scottish commissioners in December of 1647.

might have had their choice, would not they themselves, I say, have convicted them, and put them to death? You do not deny that the people and the nobles often took up arms against Roman governors who ruled provinces avariciously or cruelly; but you give a ridiculous reason for this, as usual: "They were not yet accustomed to the yoke." Very likely, under Alexander, Herod, and his son! But, say you, they would not "make war against" Gaius Caesar and Petronius.[137] And very wise of them, too, for they were not able. Will you hear their own words? "Not wishing to make war because we cannot." What they themselves acknowledge to be due to weakness, do you, you hypocrite, attribute to religion?

Next with much ado you do nothing; for you endeavor to prove out of the fathers what you had proved as superficially before, that kings are to be prayed for. That good kings are to be prayed for, no man denies; nay, and bad ones too, as long as there is any hope of them: nay and highwaymen, and our enemies. But how? not that they may lay waste our territory, or slay us with slaughter, but that they may come to their right minds. We pray for both thieves and enemies, and yet who would forbid us to punish the one by law and the other by arms? I value not your "Egyptian liturgies"; but that priest who prayed, you say, "that Commodus[138] might succeed his father," was not praying at all, in my opinion, but did imprecate all the mischiefs imaginable upon the Roman state.

You say "that we have broken our word, which we pledged more than once in solemn assemblies, to preserve the authority and majesty of the king." I wait for you further on, where you speak more fully upon this subject, and shall meet you there again.

You return then to the comments of the fathers; concerning whom take this in short. Whatever they say which is not warranted by the authority of the scriptures, or by good and sufficient reason, shall be of no more regard with me, than if any other and ordinary man had

137. Caligula (Gaius Julius Caesar Germanicus), Roman emperor in A.D. 37–41, directed Publius Petronius, his proconsul in Asia, to set up the emperor's statue in the Temple.

138. Elder son of Marcus Aurelius; he ruled as emperor from 180 to 192.

said it. The first that you quote is Tertullian, who is no orthodox writer, and is notorious for many errors; so that his authority, if he were of your opinion, would yet stand you in no stead. But what says he? He condemns riots and rebellions. So do we. But in saying so, we would not have a premature decision rendered upon all the people's rights and privileges, all the acts and resolutions of senates, and the power of all magistrates, the king alone excepted. The fathers are condemning seditions rashly kindled by the heat of a mad multitude; they speak not of magistrates, of senates, of Parliaments, summoning the people to lawful arms against their tyrants. Hence Ambrose, whom you quote: "Not to resist," says he, "but to weep and groan, these are the Priest's protection and defence. Who is there that, whether alone or among a little number, dare say to the Emperor, 'I do not like your laws'? This is not allowed the priests, and shall laymen pretend to it?" [139] It is evident of whom he speaks, viz., of priests, and of private laymen, not of the magistrates; you see nevertheless by how weak and perverse an argument he carried his torch in the van of the dissensions that were afterwards to arise betwixt the laity and the clergy concerning even civil laws.

But because you think you confute us and press hardest upon us with the examples of the primitive Christians, who, though they were harassed every way, yet "never took up arms against the emperor," I will show in the first place that for the most part they could not; secondly, that whenever they could, they did; and thirdly, that even if they did not when they could, yet in other respects they deserve not that in so many matters we should take pattern after their lives and conduct.

First, as everybody knows, when the republic of Rome ceased, the whole and sovereign power in the empire was settled in the Emperor alone; all the soldiers were under the pay of the Emperor alone; insomuch that if the whole body of the senate, the equestrian order, and all the common people had endeavored a revolution, they might indeed have exposed themselves to massacre, but could accomplish absolutely nothing towards retrieving their lost liberty; for though

139. Milton splices two citations to Ambrose by Salmasius: one to Ambrose's *Oratio in Auxentium de Tradendis Basilicis,* the other to *Epistle XXXII.*

they might perhaps have killed the emperor, the empire would still have continued. This being so, what could the Christians do? It is true there were a great many of them, but they were scattered and un-armed, and were of the common people, generally of the lowest class. How many of them might not one legion easily have kept in subjec-tion? That which many great generals, at the price of their own deaths and the wiping out of armies of tried and seasoned troops attempted in vain, could those rabble manikins expect to accomplish? About A.D. 300, more or less twenty years before Constantine, when Diocle-tian was emperor, only the Theban legion was Christian; and for no other reason it was slain by the rest of the army at Octodurum in Gaul.

The Christians, say you, conspired not "with Cassius, with Al-binus, with Niger";[140] and does not Tertullian count it creditable to them that they poured not out their blood for infidels? It is evident therefore that the Christians could not free themselves from the sway of the Emperors; and it could be no ways advantageous to their in-terest to conspire with infidels as long as heathen emperors reigned.

That afterwards, however, the Christians did make war upon ty-rants, and defend themselves by force of arms, and many times punish tyrants' abominations, I shall now make plain. First of them all, Con-stantine, after his conversion to Christianity, made war upon Licinius his co-emperor, who oppressed the Eastern Christians, and destroyed him. By this act of his he made it clear that one magistrate might pun-ish another, for he for his subjects' sake put to death Licinius, who was as absolute in the empire as himself, and did not leave the ven-geance to God alone; and Licinius might likewise have put to death Constantine if Constantine had likewise crushed the people commit-ted to his government. So then, since the matter is referred by God to men, why did not Parliament stand to King Charles as Constan-tine to Licinius? The soldiers made Constantine what he was; but our laws have made our Parliament equal, nay, superior to our kings.

---

140. Avidius Cassius, governor of Syria, proclaimed himself emperor and was thereupon assassinated. Clodius Albinus and Pescennius Niger were both named emperor by their troops but were defeated by Septimius Severus, the reigning em-peror in the late second century.

---

The inhabitants of Constantinople resisted Constantius,[141] an Arian emperor, by force of arms, as long as they were able, and when he sent Hermogenes with troops to depose Paul the orthodox bishop, they charged him and repulsed him, fired the house whither he had betaken himself, mangled and half-burned him, and at last killed him outright. Constans threatened to make war upon his brother Constantius unless he would restore Paul and Athanasius to their bishoprics. You see how those holy fathers, when their bishoprics were at stake, were not ashamed to stir up their king's own brother to make war upon him. Not long after, the Christian soldiers, who then made whom they would emperors, put to death Constans the son of Constantine because he behaved himself dissolutely and proudly in the government, and turned the empire over to Magnentius. When Julian was not yet apostate, but virtuous and valiant, certain persons saluted him as Emperor, against the will of Constantius their actual emperor. How now? Are they not amongst the number of those primitive Christians whom you place as a pattern for us? When Constantius, by letter openly read to the people, sharply forbade this action of theirs, they all cried out that they had but done what their Provincial and the army and the authority of the commonwealth had decided. The same persons declared war against Constantius, and, as much as in them lay, deprived him of his empire and his life.

What of the inhabitants of Antioch, who were Christians exceedingly? After Julian apostatized, I suppose they prayed for him, when they used to brave him to his face, and defame and revile, and scoff at his long beard and bid him make ropes of it! Think you they used to pray for the health and long life of one upon the news of whose death they offered thanksgivings, made feasts, and gave public demonstrations of joy? Nay, is it not reported that he was killed by a Christian soldier in his own army? Sozomen,[142] a writer of ecclesiastical history, does not deny it, but commends him that did it, if the fact

141. Constantine was an Arian who opposed his three pro-Nicene brothers after the death of their father, Constantine the Great.

142. Sozomen *Ecclesiastical History* 5.2.

were so: "For it is no wonder," says he, "that some one of his own soldiers might think within himself that not only the Greeks but all mankind hitherto had been wont to praise tyrant-killers, who go un-hesitating to death to procure the liberty of all: so that that soldier ought not rashly to be condemned who in the cause of God and of religion was so zealous and valiant." These are the words of Sozomen, a contemporary author, and a good and religious man; by which we may easily apprehend what the general opinion of good men in those days was upon this point. Ambrose himself being commanded by the emperor Valentinian the younger to depart from Milan, refused to obey him, but, hedged about by his people in arms, defended him-self and his basilica against the emperor's officers, and, contrary to his own doctrine, dared resist the higher powers. At Constantinople more than once there was great insurrection against the emperor Arcadius, by reason of Chrysostom's exile. I have now briefly shown how the primitive Christians behaved themselves towards tyrants; how not soldiers only, but the people, yea the very fathers of the church, resisted them, and made or incited war upon them, till Austin's time: for it suits you yourself to go no lower. Therefore I make no mention of Valentinian the son of Placidia, who was slain by Maximus a noble-man, for committing adultery with his wife: nor do I mention Avitus the emperor, whom, because he disbanded the soldiers, and gave him-self wholly to his lusts, the Roman senate immediately deposed; be-cause these things came to pass some years after Austin's death.

But I will make you a present of all this; pretend that I have not set forth any of it; suppose it conceded that the primitive Christians obeyed their kings through thick and thin, and never took or wished to take any action against tyrants; yet as I will now show, they were not such that we ought to rely upon their authority, or can safely fol-low their example. Long before Constantine's time the generality of Christians had lost much of the primitive sanctity and integrity both of their religion and of their conduct. Afterwards, the church, which he had vastly enriched, began to fall in love with offices, absolute rule, and secular power, and then the Christian religion went to wrack.

First luxury and sloth, and then a crew of all the heresies and vices, as if their dungeons had been set open from behind, trooped over into the church; thereupon envy, hatred, and discord overflowed everywhere, and at last they that were linked together into one brotherhood by that dear and gracious bond of religion were as much at variance and strife as the bitterest enemies. No reverence, no consideration of their duty was left: the soldiers and commanders of the army, as oft as they pleased themselves, now created new emperors, now killed good ones and bad ones alike. I need not mention such as Vetrannio, Maximus, Eugenius, whom the soldiers all of a sudden lifted up to the imperial throne; or Gratian, an excellent prince, or Valentinian the younger, none of the worst, whom they put to death. True, these were the deeds of soldiers and camp-followers,—but yet of Christians of that age which you call most evangelical and most to be imitated! Therefore you shall now hear a few words about the clergy. Pastors and Bishops, and sometimes those Fathers whom we admire, each a leader of his flock—those very men, I say, would fight for a bishopric as if for a tyrant's throne; priests and laymen promiscuous would clash swords now throughout the city, now in the very church at the very altar, and keep up their carnage sometimes with great slaughter on both sides. You may remember Damasus and Urcisinus,[143] who were Ambrose's contemporaries. Long it were to relate the notorious insurrections of the inhabitants of Constantinople, Antioch, and Alexandria, especially those instigated and conducted by Cyril, whom you extol as a preacher of obedience; when the monks in that city battle had almost slain Orestes, Theodosius's deputy. Now who would not be stunned at your impudence or your negligence? "Till Austin," you say, "and later than his time, there is no mention extant in history, of any private person, of any commander, or of any number of conspirators, that have put their king to death, or taken up arms against him." Out of well-known histories I have named to you

143. Opposing groups elected Damasus and Urcisinus pope after the death of Liberius in 366.

both private persons and officials that with their own hands slew not only bad but very good kings: whole armies of Christians, many bishops among them, that fought against their own emperors. You produce some of the fathers who with a great multitude of words persuade or boast of obedience to kings, and I on the other side produce both these same fathers and others besides, that by no less multitude of actions refused obedience, even in lawful matters, and defended themselves in arms against the emperor, others that opposed forcibly and wounded his deputies, and others that, being competitors for bishoprics, maintained civil wars against one another. So of course it was lawful for Christians to wage war with Christians, and citizens with citizens, for a bishopric, but unlawful to fight against a tyrant, for our liberty, our wives and children, and our lives! Who would not be out of all patience with such fathers?

You bring in Austin, who, you say, asserts that "the power of a master over his slaves, and of a king over his subjects," is one and the same. But I answer: if Austin has asserted any such thing, he has said what neither Christ nor his Apostles ever said. However, since he apparently recommends upon their authority alone something otherwise manifestly untrue, then even though he say so, yet it hurts not my cause. For concerning a master's power over his slaves he has said, *de Civitate Dei,* Book 19, Chapter 14: "In the house of a righteous man who liveth by the faith, even they who command serve them whom they seem to command." So that if he said the very thing you quote him as saying about "the power of a king over his subjects," and did not contradict himself, then he asserted that even kings, good kings especially, do actually serve whom they seem to command. Meanwhile he has assuredly asserted that the power of an ill king over his subjects, and the power of a highway robber over everyone he meets, is one and the same (*de Civitate Dei,* Bk. 4, Ch. 4): "If righteousness be put away, what are kingdoms but great robbers' dens—for what are robbers' dens themselves but little kingdoms?"—You see how far you have succeeded in deriving out of Austin that grand and glorious right of yours, that royal right to dare do anything they please: so far indeed that the power of kings is found equal and identical not with that of painters or poets, but with that of highway robbers!

That the three or four remaining pages of this fourth chapter are either mere lies or sleepy negligences oft repeated, everyone will perceive for himself from my previous refutations. For what concerns the Pope, against whom you declaim so much without occasion, I am content you should bawl at him till you are hoarse. But as for your attempt to catch the ignorant with the long additional argument that "every Christian yielded entire obedience to kings, whether good or bad, till the papal power began to be acknowledged superior to the royal, and absolved subjects from their oath of allegiance," I have sufficiently proved by many examples "both before and since the age of Austin," that nothing can be more false.

Neither does that seem to have much more truth in it, which you say in the last place; viz., that "Pope Zachary absolved the Frenchmen from their oath of allegiance to their king." For Francis Hotman, both a Frenchman and a lawyer and a very learned man, in the 13th chapter of his *Francogallia*, says that it was not by the Pope's authority that Chilperic was deposed, or the kingdom translated to Pepin; and he proves out of very ancient chronicles of the Franks that the whole affair was transacted in the great national council pursuant to its original authority. That thereafter there was any necessity of absolving the French from their allegiance is contradicted by the French historical documents, and by Pope Zachary himself. The records of the Franks relate, according not only to Hotman, but to Gerard, a very eminent historian of that nation, that the ancient Franks had reserved to themselves from of old an unimpaired right both to choose their kings, and to depose them if they thought fit; and that by custom they swore to the king whom they were putting in office no other oath than that they would perform their word and duty upon condition that the kings for their part would perform what they too, by oath at the same time sworn, did pledge and promise. So that if kings, by misgoverning the state entrusted to their charge, have first broke their own oath, there needs no Pope; the kings themselves by their own breach of faith have absolved their subjects. Finally Pope Zachary himself, in that very letter of his to the Franks, which you yourself quote, disclaimed for himself and ascribed to the people the authority which you say he assumed to himself. For "if a king be liable to punishment by the people through whose favor he holds his royalty; if the people have set up the king and have power to put him down" (the words of that very Pope), it is not likely that the Franks would afterwards by any oath impair that ancient right, or ever tie their own hands so as not to have the same right that their ancestors always had to depose bad kings, as well as to honour and obey good ones; nor would they yield to tyrants that obedience which they thought they were yielding only to good kings. When people are bound by such an oath, a king turned tyrant or rotted with cowardice releases them by breaking his oath; justice herself releases them; the very law of nature releases them; wherefore even by the Pope's own opinion there simply was nothing for the Pope to release.

## CHAPTER V.

I am of opinion, Salmasius, and always have been, that the law of God does exactly agree with the law of nature, and that therefore, if I have shown what by God's law is established with respect to kings, and what has been the practice of the people of God, both Jews and Christians, I have at the same time and by the same attempt shown what is most agreeable to the law of nature. Yet because you think that we "can now be most effectually confuted by the law of nature," I will be content to admit to be necessary, what before I had thought superfluous; so as in this chapter I shall prove against you that nothing is more suitable to the law of nature than that tyrants be punished. Which if I do not demonstrate, I will then not decline to grant you on the spot, that likewise by the law of God they are exempt. I do not purpose to frame a long discourse of nature, and the beginnings of man's political life; that subject has been handled at large by many learned men, both

Greek and Latin. But I shall endeavor to be as short as may be; and my design is not so much that I, who would willingly have spared this pains, may confute you, as that you shall confute yourself and destroy your own position.

I will begin therefore with what you yourself lay down, and shall make it the basis of the following discussion. "The law of nature," you say, "is a principle implanted in all men's minds, to regard the good of all mankind in so far as men are united together in societies. But it cannot procure that common good unless, as there are people that must be governed, it also ascertain who shall govern them." To wit, lest the stronger oppress the weaker, and thus those whom their mutual safety and protection had brought together be disunited and divided by injury and violence, and reduced to a savage life again. This I suppose is what you intended, though you take more words to say it. "Out of the number of those that united into one body," you say, "there must needs have been some chosen, superior to the rest in wisdom or courage, who either by force or by persuasion were to hold to their duty those that were refractory. Often it would so fall out that one single person whose Valour and Discretion was extraordinary might be able to do this, and sometimes several, who would accomplish it together by interchange of advice and counsel. Indeed since any one man cannot order and manage all things himself, he must consult with more, and let others into the governing company. So that whether the supreme power be confined to one person or reside in the body of the people, in either case, since it is impossible that all should administer the affairs of the commonwealth, or that one man should do all, therefore the government does always actually lie upon the shoulders of many." And afterwards you say: "The form of government itself, whether placed in the hands of many, or few, or a single person, is equally natural, for it is derived from the grounds of nature itself, which suffers not one man's single self so to rule that he have no sharers in the government."

Though I might have gathered all this out of the third book of Aristotle's *Politics*, I chose rather to transcribe it out of your own book, for you stole it from him, as Prometheus did fire from Jupiter, to the overthrow of monarchs and destruction of yourself. For search all you will into the law of nature, as just now exhibited by you, you will not find a place in nature for the royal right as you expound it—no, not so much as a trace of it. "The law of nature," you say, "in ordering who should govern others, regarded the good of all mankind." Not then of any one person—of a monarch. Hence the king exists for the people, and consequently the people are above him and to be preferred to him; which being allowed, there can be no right of the king whereby he, the inferior, may oppress or enslave the people, the superior. Since the king has no right to do wrong, the right of the people remains by nature supreme; and therefore, by that right whereby, before kings were instituted, men first united their strength and counsels for their mutual defence, by that right whereby, for the preservation of all men's liberty, peace, and safety, they appointed one or more to govern the rest, by the same right they may punish or depose, for cowardice or folly or dishonesty or treachery, those very persons whom for their valour or wisdom they had advanced to the government, or any others that rule disorderly; since nature hath regarded and doth regard the good not of one, or of a few, but of all in general, whatever become of one man's or of a few men's power.

Now as to the sort of persons whom the people chose. You say they were "superior to the rest in wisdom or courage," to wit, such as by nature seemed fittest for government, "whose extraordinary valour and discretion was adequate" to such an office. Hence there is no right of succession by the law of nature, no king by the law of nature except him who excels all the rest in wisdom and courage; and all kings else are such by force or faction, contrary to nature, being fit rather to be slaves. For unto the wisest man nature gives command over men less wise, not unto a wicked man over good men, a fool over wise men: and consequently they that take the government out of such men's hands, act quite according to the law of nature. To what end nature appoints the wisest man king, you shall hear in your own words; viz., "that he may hold to their duty those that are refractory" against either nature or the laws. But how should he hold others to their duty, that neglects, or knows not, or turns against his own?

Allege now, if you can, any dictate of nature by which we are enjoined to disregard and neglect and hold of no account in matters of human state and polity the wise institutions of the law of nature, when nature herself, rather than lose her end, continually produces great and admirable results in her own province of matters inanimate and non-human. Produce any rule of nature or natural justice by which inferior criminals ought to be punished, but kings and princes to go unpunished for all their evil deeds—nay but, amid their monstrous crimes, be worshiped and revered and held in honor next to God. You grant that "the form of government itself, whether placed in the hands of many, or few, or a single person, is equally natural." So that a king is not by the law of nature more sacred than nobles, or than magistrates chosen from amongst the common people, and as you have granted heretofore that those may be punished, and ought to be if they offend, consequently you must admit the same of kings, who are appointed to rule for the very same end and purpose. For, say you, "Nature suffers not one man's single self so to rule that he have no sharers in the government." It does not therefore suffer a monarch; it does not suffer one single person so to rule as to hold all others in slavery to his single power. In giving the king such partners in his power "that the government does always lie upon their shoulders," you give him colleagues and equals; more, you give them the power to punish, you give them the power to depose him.

So while you go about, not indeed to magnify royal power, but just merely to establish it in nature, you destroy it, as you always do. No greater misfortune, consequently I think, could befall sovereign princes, than to have you to defend them. Poor unhappy wretch! what fog in your wits hath driven you to such a pass of self-deception that you should unwittingly take all these pains to lay bare and open to all men your knavery and ignorance, which until now was long concealed and almost masked; that you should set your labor to hire at the price of your own ignominy, and devote yourself so assiduously to making yourself a laughing-stock? What offence does the wrath of heaven punish you for, in making you appear in public, and with such parade undertake the defence of a hateful cause in the height of impudence and stupidity at once, and, by thus defending it, against your intent and through your ignorance betray it? Who could wish you more forlorn and wretched than you are, when you can be saved from the depth of misery only by an act of shortsighted folly? Since by your unskilful and fatuous defence you have rendered the tyrants whose cause you undertook just so much more odious and detestable (the opposite of what you were expecting) and have unintentionally roused up just so many more enemies against them,—as you have intentionally ascribed to them the greater liberty of doing mischief and tyrannizing with impunity.

But I return to your self-contradictions. Having resolved to be so wicked as to endeavor to found tyranny in nature, you saw yourself compelled to begin by extolling monarchy above other forms of government; which, as is your way, you cannot go about without contradicting yourself. For having said but a little before, "that the form of government itself, whether by more, or by fewer, or by a single person, is equally natural," now you tell us that "of these three, that which is wielded by one person is most natural": nay, though you had said in express terms but lately: "Nature suffers not one man's single self to govern." Now upbraid whom you will with the putting of tyrants to death; since you yourself by your own folly have cut the throats of all monarchs, nay even of monarchy itself. But this is not the place to dispute which form of government is best, by one single person or by many. Many eminent men have indeed extolled monarchy, yet only if the monarch be very excellent and best deserve to reign; without such supposition, no other form of government so easily slips into the worst sort of tyranny.

As for your saying that "it is modeled upon the pattern of the One God"—I ask you who is worthy to hold on earth a power that shall resemble the divine power, save one who, as he far excels other men, is even in wisdom and goodness likest unto God? and such a person, in my opinion, none can be but the Son of God we wait for. As for your forcing a *kingdom* once more into the genus *family,* that you may liken a king to a paterfamilias: a father of course deserves to exercise dominion over his household, all of which he either begot or supports; nothing of the sort with a king, but obviously quite the opposite. Next you set before us for our imitation those animals that live in communities, first birds, and among them bees, since these are birds, on your authority as Physiologus! "The bees have a king." The bees of Trent, that is—do not you remember? All other bees, on your own admission, "have republics." But leave off playing the fool with bees; they belong to the Muses, and hate, and, you see, confute such a beetle as you are. "The quails are under a 'Quail mother'." Lay such snares for your own bitterns; we are not caught by so foolish a fowler.

The next point, however, is not our affair, but yours. "*Gallus gallinaceus,* the cock," you say, "wields imperial power over both males and females." How can that be, since you yourself that are Gallic, and (they say) but too cocky, wield not imperial power over your hen, but she over you? So that if the gallinaceous cock be king over many females, you that are slave to your hen must needs be not Gallus gallinaceus, but some sort of Gallus stercorarius, or dunghill-cock. For the matter of books, in fact, nobody publishes huger dunghills, and you deafen us all with your crowing over them; that is the only point in which you resemble a true cock. I promise to give you many barley-corns if in ransacking this whole dunghill-book of yours you can show me but one jewel. But why should I give barley to you, who, quite unlike the honest plain cock in Aesop, scratched not for barley, but like the good-for-nothing cock in Plautus,[144] scratched eagerly for gold? The outcome, to be sure, was different to this extent, that by scratching you found a hundred gold Jacobuses, though you more deserved to be struck dead with Euclio's club, like that wretched bird in Plautus.

But let us go on: "That same motive—the advantage and safety

144. Plautus *Aulularia* 465.

of all mankind—requires that whoever be once appointed to the sovereignty, be preserved in the possession of it." Who ever questioned this, as long as his preservation is consistent with the safety of all the rest? But can anyone fail to see that the preservation of any one man to the destruction of all others is utterly contrary to nature? But you would at any cost have "even a bad king kept, nay the worst king possible, because the harm that his ill government does the state is less than the disasters produced by the revolts that are raised to get rid of him." But what bearing has this upon the natural right of kings? If nature teaches me to suffer myself to be robbed by highwaymen, or, should I be taken captive, to purchase my liberty with all my estate, rather than fight with them for my life, will you thereupon set up a natural right of robbers? Nature teaches subjects to give way now to the outrages of tyrants, now to times and circumstances; will you upon this forced patience of a nation, upon this compulsory submission, found a natural right even of tyrants? The very right which nature gave to the people for their own preservation, will you affirm that she gave to tyrants for the people's destruction? Nature teaches us of two evils to choose the lesser; and to bear with it as long as needs must; and will you affirm that thence arises a natural right for a tyrant, who for the moment may be the lesser evil, to commit his crimes unpunished? Remember what you yourself formerly wrote against the Loyolite concerning bishops; your words, of a tenor quite the opposite of these, I have quoted above in the third chapter: you there asserted "that seditions, dissensions, and discords of the nobles and commons are a much lighter mischief than sure misery and destruction under the government of one monarch that plays the tyrant." And you said very true, for you were not yet going mad, and being ungilt with Charles his Jacobuses, had not yet got this gold-itch or king's evil. I should tell you perhaps, if you were not who you are, that you ought at length to be ashamed of your disgraceful double-dealing. But you can sooner burst than blush, who long ago cast off shame for profit.

Did you not remember that the Romans had a most flourishing and glorious commonwealth after they had banished their kings?

Could you possibly forget the Dutch, whose Republic, when it had shook off the king of Spain after long but successful wars, bravely and gloriously got its freedom, and keeps you in its pay, knight grammaticaster!—yet with no design that the Dutch youth may learn from you, sophist and double-dealer, such unwisdom as to choose rather to return to the bondage of Spain than inherit their fathers' glorious liberty. Go take along with you your plaguy teaching to utmost Siberia and the Arctic Ocean, and there, while you are about it, you may just as well go to the devil!

Your last example is the English, who put to death their tyrant Charles after he had been taken a prisoner of war, and found incurable. "With their quarrels they defaced and dishonored an island which under its kings was happy and swam in luxury." Yea, when its moral ruin through luxury was almost accomplished that it might the more indifferently bear with enslavement—when its laws were abolished, and its religion bought and sold—then they delivered it from slavery. Behold now a Stoic of the severest, editor of Epictetus [145] with Simplicius's commentary, who considers "an island swimming in luxury" to be happy! I am sure no such doctrine ever came from Zeno's porch. [146] What of that? Shall kings, according to your teaching, have leave to do as they please, and shall not you yourself, Sire du Loup, have leave to send forth whatever philosophy you please from your wolf-bitch's den, as from some strange new Lyceum?

Now begin again to act your part. "Never in any king's reign was so much blood spilt, so many families ruined." All this is to be imputed not to the English nation but to Charles, who had first raised an army of Irishmen against us, had by his own warrant bidden the Irish nation unite in arms against the English, and had by their means slain near two hundred thousand Englishmen in the single province of Ulster; to say nothing of his other crimes—of how he had incited two armies to destroy the Parliament of England and the City of Lon-

145. Epictetus (A.D. 55–135) was a Stoic philosopher. Salmasius had published Simplicius's *Commentaries on the Enchiridion of Epictetus* in 1640.

146. Zeno (335–263 B.C.), founder of the "School of the Porch," or Stoa.

don, and had committed many other acts of war, before the Parliament or the people had enlisted a single soldier to protect the realm.

What principles, what law, what religion ever taught men to consult their ease, to save their money, their blood, nay their very lives, rather than oppose the public enemy—whether foreign or domestic what matter, since both alike threaten bitter calamity and ruin to the nation? All Israel saw that without great bloodshed they could not punish the outrage that had been done upon the Levite's wife;[147] did they therefore think they must be still, or refrain from civil war, though of the cruelest? Did they on that account suffer one poor humble *petite femme* to die unavenged? Certainly if nature teaches us to endure the despotism of a king, no matter how bad, rather than endanger the safety of a great many men in the recovery of our liberty, she must teach us likewise to endure not only a kingly government, which yet is the only one that you argue ought to be submitted to, but even an aristocracy and an oligarchy too—nay, and sometimes a gang of robbers and mutinous slaves! Fulvius and Rupilius must then not have engaged in the Servile War after the Praetorian armies were slain; Crassus must not have marched against Spartacus, after the camp of the ex-consuls was destroyed; nor must Pompey have gone to war against the pirates. Romans, at nature's behest, forsooth, Romans, lest the blood of so many citizens should be shed, must have knuckled down to slaves or to pirates! Nowhere do you show that "nature has imprinted this feeling upon the nations"—or any feeling of the sort; and yet you cannot forbear boding us ill, and denouncing God's vengeance upon us—which may heaven divert upon yourself and all such prognosticators as you!—denouncing it, I say, upon us, though we have done no more than inflict the death that was his due upon him that was our king only in name, but in fact our implacable enemy, and atone for the countless deaths of our good countrymen by punishing the author and cause of them.

Then you tell us that a kingly government appears to be more ac-

147. This grisly story is recorded in Judg. 20.

cording to the laws of nature because "more nations, both in our days and of old, have adopted monarchy than aristocracy and democracy." I answer first that this was not done at the behest of either God or nature. It was only unwillingly that God allowed his own people to be under a king; and what nature and right reason dictates, is best ascertained from the practice not of most nations, but of the wisest. The Grecians, the Romans, the Italians, the Carthaginians, and many others, have in accordance with their own natural temper preferred a government by their aristocracy or by their people rather than by a king; and these nations are proper examples to stand for the rest. Hence Sulpitius Severus reports that "the name of king has always been hateful to nearly all free nations." [148]

But these things concern not our present purpose, nor do the many that come after, which in your empty folly you repeat again and again. I hasten to make plain by examples what I have established already by reason; viz., that it is in the highest degree agreeable to the law of nature, that tyrants should be punished anyhow; and that all nations, taught by nature herself, have punished them; which will expose your impudence, and make it evident to all men that you take a shameful liberty to publish lies. You begin with the Egyptians; and indeed who does not see that you play the gipsy throughout? "In their history," say you, "there is no mention of any king that was ever slain by the people in a popular insurrection, no war made upon any of their kings by their subjects, no attempt made to depose any of them." What think you then of Osiris,[149] perhaps the first king of the Egyptians? Was not he slain by his brother Typhon and five-and-twenty other conspirators? And did not a great part of the body of the people side with them, and fight a great battle with Isis and Orus, the king's wife and son? I pass by Sesostris,[150] whom his brother had well-nigh put to death by treachery, and Chemmis and Chephren,[151] against

148. Sulpitius Severus *Historia sacra* 1.32.

149. Worshipped in the shape of a bull by the Egyptians, Osiris figured in a myth in which he is slain by Typhon. Isis was an earth goddess and Orus the sun.

150. A mythical ruler.

151. Chemmis and Chephren were builders of pyramids.

whom the people were deservedly enraged, and threatened to tear them in pieces after they were dead, being unable to do it while they were alive. Do you think that a people that durst cut off their best kings were restrained either by the light of nature or by any religious scruple from laying hands upon their worst ones? A people that repeatedly threatened to tear their kings, though dead and now at last beyond the power to do harm, from the tomb, where the body of any the meanest pauper is wont to be inviolable—would they, if they had the power, stand back in awe, and fear to punish according to the law of nature kings alive and noxious? I know you would not stick to answer me in the affirmative, how absurd soever it be; but that you may not dare, I will silence you. Know then that many centuries before Chephren's time Ammosis was king of Egypt, and was as great a tyrant as any the greatest; him the people patiently bore with. You exult: this is what you like. But hear what follows, my honest Telltruth. I quote Diodorus: "Weighed down, they bore with him for some while, for they were nowise able to resist them that were more powerful."[152] But as soon as Actisanes king of Ethiopia began to make war upon him, most of them took the opportunity to revolt, and when he was easily subdued, Egypt was added to the kingdom of Ethiopia. You see here that the Egyptians, as soon as they could, took up arms against a tyrant, joined forces with a foreign prince to depose their own king and disinherit his posterity, and preferred a moderate and good king, as Actisanes was, though a foreigner, to a tyrant of their own. These same Egyptians by the hearty consent of them all took up arms against Apries their tyrant, who relied upon his mercenary troops. Under the command of Amasis they conquered and afterwards strangled him, and gave the kingdom to Amasis, who was a noble gentleman. And note this too: Amasis kept the captive king a good while in the palace, and treated him well; at last, when the people complained that he did wrong in maintaining his enemy and theirs, he delivered him over to the people, who put him to death in the manner I have mentioned. These things are related by Herodotus and Diodorus. What

152. Diodorus Siculus *Bibliotēkē Historikē* 1.9.2.

more do you want? Do you think that any tyrant would not choose the axe rather than the noose?

Afterwards, you say, when the Egyptians were "brought into subjection" by the Persians, they "continued loyal to them"; which is utterly false, for they never remained loyal to the Persians, but in the fourth year after Cambyses had subdued them, they rebelled. Afterwards, when Xerxes had tamed them, within a short time they revolted from his son Artaxerxes, and set up one Inarus to be their king. With him they were conquered, but rebelled again, and created Tachus king, and made war upon Artaxerxes Mnemon. Neither were they better subjects to their own king, for they deposed Tachus, and conferred the government upon his son Nectanebus, till at last Artaxerxes Ochus brought them again under subjection to the Persian empire. Even under the Macedonian empire they declared by their actions, as far as in them lay, that tyrants ought to be punished: they threw down the statues and images of Ptolemy Physco, but were unable to kill him, for his mercenary army was too strong. His son Alexander was forced by a popular uprising to leave his country because he had killed his mother. *His* son Alexander likewise, when he lorded it too insolently, the people of Alexandria dragged out of the palace, and killed in the public gymnasium. The same people, finally, deposed Ptolemy Auletes for his many crimes. Now since a learned man cannot be ignorant of such notorious facts, and a man whose profession it is to teach them, and who asks to be believed in matters of such moment, is in duty bound not to be ignorant of them; who would not pronounce it a shame and a disgrace that this person, if so ignorant and illiterate, should to the scandal of true scholarship puff himself about as a great scholar, and solicit pay from kings and commonwealths, or, if such a knave and liar, should not be branded with some special mark of infamy, and banished out of the company and fellowship of all scholars and gentlemen?

Having examined the Egyptians for examples, let us now look at the Ethiopians their neighbors. Their king, chosen, as they think, by God, they worship as a sort of God, and yet whenever the priests condemn him, he kills himself; and on that manner, says Diodorus,[153] they punish all their other criminals: they put them not to death, but send an officer of justice to bid the guilty die.

Next you come to the Assyrians, the Medes, and the Persians, who most revere their kings; and you affirm, contrary to the authority of all historians, that "the royal power there had an unbounded liberty annexed to it of doing what the king listed." In the first place, the prophet Daniel tells us how, when Nebuchadnezzar grew proud beyond excess, they drove him from men, and sent him away to the beasts.[154] The law of those countries was not entitled royal law, but the law of the Medes and Persians, that is, of the people; which law, being irrevocable, bound the kings themselves; insomuch that Darius the Mede, though he earnestly labored to deliver Daniel from the hands of the presidents and princes, yet could not effect it. "Nations in those days," say you, "thought it an impiety to reject a king because he abused that royal right." But in the very writing of these words you are so abjectly stupid that while you are commending the obedience and submissiveness of those nations, you go out of your way to mention that Arbaces deprived Sardanapalus of the crown. Not single-handed, however, for he was helped partly by the priests, who were very well versed in the law, and partly by the people; and he deposed him chiefly upon the ground that he abused his royal right, by way not of cruelty, but only of lust and effeminacy. Run over the histories of Herodotus, Ctesias, Diodorus, and you will find, clean contrary to your assertion, the fact to be "that those kingdoms were destroyed for the most part by *subjects,* and *not* by *foreigners*"; you will find that the Assyrians were deposed by the Medes their subjects, and the Medes by the Persians likewise their subjects. You yourself admit that "Cyrus rebelled, and that in divers parts of the empire despotic governments were seized." Is this how you vindicate the royal right among the Medes and Persians, and their reverence for

153. Diodorus Siculus *Bibliotēkē Historikē* 3.5–6.
154. Dan. 5:20–21.

their kings, which you have set up? What Anticyra[155] can medicine thee thus raving?

You say: "With what power the Persian kings ruled is apparent from Herodotus." Cambyses being desirous to marry his sister, consulted the royal judges, "eminent men chosen from among the people," interpreters of the laws, to whom all difficulties were submitted. What answer had he from them? They told him that they found no law which bids a brother marry his sister, but that they did find another law whereby the king of Persia may do as he likes. Now to this I answer, if the king of Persia were really so absolute, what need was there of any other interpreter of the laws than the king himself? Those superfluous unnecessary judges would have remained anywhere you will but in the palace! Again, if the king of Persia might do whatever he would, it is not credible that Cambyses, eager for power as he was, should be so ignorant as to interrogate those judges concerning his liberties. What was the matter then? Either they designed "to humor the king," as you admit, or they were afraid of what the tyrant might do to them, as Herodotus says,[156] and feigned that they had found a law that would do, and fooled him, which even nowadays is no new thing with judges and gentlemen learned in the law. "But," say you, "Artabanus a Persian told Themistocles[157] there was no better law in Persia than the one which enacted that kings were to be honored and worshiped." An admirable law for you to cite—a law enjoining king-worship!—a law long ago condemned by even the early Fathers! And an admirable person to recommend this law too—Artabanus, who himself a little while after with his own hand slew Xerxes his king! Right king-defenders these you cite—these king-killers! I suspect you have some secret design upon kings!

155. Anticyra was the name of three ancient towns that traded in hellebore, an herb thought to cure insanity.

156. Herodotus *Histories* 3.31.

157. Plutarch *Life of Themistocles* 27.

In the next place, you quote the poet Claudian to prove how obedient the Persians were. But I refer you to their histories and annals, which are stuffed full of the revolts of the Persians, the Medes, the Bactrians, and the Babylonians, and with the murders of their kings. Your next authority is Otanes the Persian, who likewise killed Smerdis his king. While he, out of his hatred of royal government, sets forth the impieties and injurious actions of kings, their violation of the laws, their putting men to death without legal conviction, their rapes and adulteries, you will have all this called the right of kings, and slander Samuel again. You quote Homer, who says that kings derive their authority from Jupiter; to which I have already given an answer. For king Philip of Macedon as an expounder of the right of kings, I had as lief take his interpretation as King Charles's!

Then you quote some sentences from a fragment of Diotogenes the Pythagorean, but you do not tell us what sort of king he speaks of. Observe therefore how he begins, for whatever follows must be understood to have relation to it: "Let him be king," says he, "that of all is most just, and most just is he that acts most according to law"; for without justice no man "can be king, and without law there can be no justice." This is directly opposite to that royal right of yours. And Ecphantas, whom you likewise quote, reasons to the same effect: "Whosoever takes upon him to be king, ought to be naturally most pure and clear from all imputation." And a little after: "He that governs according to virtue is called, and is, a king." He whom you call a king is therefore, in the judgment of the Pythagoreans, no king at all. Hear now, in your turn, what Plato says in his Eighth Epistle: "Let the royal power be liable to be called to account. Let the laws control not only the people but kings themselves, if they do anything not warranted by law." I will mention what Aristotle says in the Third Book of his *Politics:* "Among likes and equals it is neither profitable nor just that any one should be lord and master over all the rest, or should himself be the law, either where there are no laws, or where there are laws; or that a good man should be lord over other good men, or a bad man over other bad men." And in the Fifth Book, says he, "That king whom the people do not wish, is no longer a king but a tyrant." Hear what Xenophon says in Hiero: "Cities are so far from punishing the killing of tyrants, that they confer great honor upon him that kills one, and erect statues of tyrannicides in their temples." Of this I can produce an eye-witness, Marcus Tullius, in his oration *Pro Milone*: "The Greeks," says he, "ascribe divine worship to men who have killed tyrants. What have I myself seen at Athens and in other cities of Greece—what religious observances instituted in their honor—what poems, songs, and hymns in their praise! They are almost consecrated to immortality in adoration and remembrance." And lastly, Polybius, a weighty authority, in the Sixth Book of his History, says thus: "When princes began to indulge their own lusts and avarice, then royal government turned into tyranny, and conspiracies against the lives of the despots were entered into; nor were the instigators the dregs of the citizenry, but the most noble and magnanimous." These few passages I have picked out to taste, for I have store far greater, and am overwhelmed with plenty.

From the philosophers you now appeal to the poets, and I am very willing to follow you. "Aeschylus by himself is enough to inform us," you say, "that kings in Greece held a power not liable to any laws or any judicature; for in the tragedy of *The Suppliants* he calls the king of the Argives 'a ruler not subject to judgment'." Know you (for the greater the variety of your arguments, the more I discern how recklessly uncritical you are), know then, I say, that we must not regard the poet's words as his own, but consider who it is that speaks in the play, and what that person says; for different persons are introduced, sometimes good, sometimes bad, sometimes wise men, sometimes fools, and they speak not always the poet's own opinion, but what is most fitting to each character. The fifty daughters of Danaus, being banished out of Egypt, betook themselves to the king of the Argives as suppliants, and begged him to protect them against the violence of the Egyptians, who were pursuing them with a fleet of ships. The king told them he could not without first imparting the matter to the people.

Ἐγὼ δ' ἂν οὐ κραίνοιμ' ὑπόσχεσιν πάρος
Ἀστῶν δὲ πᾶσι τοῖσδε κοινώσας πέρι.[158]

The women, being strangers and suppliants, and fearing the uncertain suffrages of the people, urge him anew, this time with more flattery:

Σύ τοι πόλις, σὺ δὲ τὸ δήμιον,
Πρύτανις ἄκριτος ὤν.

"Thou standest for city and people, a ruler not to be judged." The king answers:

Εἶπον δὲ καὶ πρὶν, οὐκ ἄνευ δήμου τάδε
Πράξαιμ' ἂν οὐδέπερ κρατῶν—

"I told you before that I could not do it without the people's consent; nay, and though I could, I would not." So he brings the whole matter before the people.

Ἐγὼ δὲ λάους συγκαλῶν ἐγχωρίους
Πείσω τὸ κοινόν.[159]

The people decrees therefore that aid is to be given the daughters of Danaus; whence these words of Danaus in his joy:

Θαρσεῖτε παῖδες, εὖ τὰ τῶν ἐγχωρίων
Δήμου δέδοκται παντελῆ ψηφίσματα.

"Be of good cheer, daughters, for the all-accomplished votes of the people of the country in popular assembly have decided well." Had I not related the whole thing, how rashly would this smatterer have laid down the law concerning the right of kings among the Grecians, out

158. "I would not make promise before I have shared these things with all of the city in a body."
159. "I shall call together the people of the vicinity and I shall persuade them in a body."

of the mouths of women that were both strangers and suppliants, though both the king himself and the very action of the drama lead us to a far different conclusion!

The same conclusion appears from the story of Euripides' Orestes, who being after his father's death himself king of the Argives, was yet brought to trial by the people for the slaying of his mother, pleaded his own cause, and by the people's vote was condemned to die.[160] That at Athens the kingly power was subject to the laws, the same Euripides bears witness in his play likewise called *The Suppliants,* where Theseus, king of Athens, says: "Not ruled by one man, but free, is the city; yet the people reigns."[161] In the same poet's *Heraclidae,* Theseus' son Demophoon, likewise king of the Athenians, says: "For I do not exercise tyrannical power over them, as if they were Barbarians: but if I do right, right is done me."[162] Sophocles in his *Oedipus Tyrannus* shows that anciently in Thebes the right of kings was even so. Hence both Tiresias and Creon answer back courageously to Oedipus. The former says, "I am not your slave"; the latter, "I have some right in this city as well as you."[163] And in the *Antigone,* Haemon tells Creon: "That is no city which belongs to one man."[164]

All men know that the kings of Lacedaemon have been brought to trial, and sometimes put to death judicially. And no wonder, when Lycurgus himself, their lawgiver, might have learned from Homer, whom he had read attentively from beginning to end, that even in the heroic times kings were subject to the very same laws. Homer's Achilles, having found that Agamemnon was himself a pestilence unto his people, who were then suffering under a pestilence, did not, though himself a king, hesitate, in an assemblage of the Greeks fre-

160. Euripides *Orestes* 930 ff.
161. Euripides *The Suppliants* 404–5.
162. Euripides *Heraclidae* 423–24.
163. Sophocles *Oedipus Rex* 410.
164. Sophocles *Antigone* 737.

quent and full, to submit a king to his own subjects for judgment. These are his words (*Iliad* I.):

> King, devourer of the people, since thou rulest over men
> of naught,
> For else, Atrides, hadst thou now committed outrage
> for the last time.

That men of all ranks felt as the heroes did about the royal right, Alcaeus may witness, chief of lyric poets; whose poems, most delightful in themselves, were all the more popular, says Horace, in that they sang the praises of those who had cast out tyrants from their cities: "The shades look on in wonder while the one and the other sing things that deserve to be listened to in reverent silence; but the populace, crowded shoulder to shoulder, drink in yet more with eager ear tales of battles and of tyrants driven out." *Odes* 2.13.29.

To these, in support of the same opinion, let me join Theognis, who was in his prime not so long before the Persian Wars, at a time when there flourished in every part of Greece many worthies distinguished for their wisdom. The teachings which he handed down in his verses he himself avows that he had got from the Wise Men.

> Cast down how thou wilt a king that devours his people:
> For this the gods have no resentment—none.[165]

These instances make clear enough what was the royal right in Greece. Let us consider now the Romans.

First you return to that phrase not of Sallust but of C. Memmius quoted in Sallust, "to do with impunity what you list." This I have answered already. Sallust himself says expressly that "the government of Rome was a government by law, though its name was regal," [166]

---

165. Theognis *Elegies A*. 1181–82.
166. Sallust *Jugurtha* 31.9.

and when "it grew into a tyranny," you know they thrust it out. Cicero likewise in his oration against Piso, "Shall I," says he, "reckon as consul one who reckoned not upon the Senate's existence in the commonwealth? Shall I count as consul him who consults not that without which there could not even be kings at Rome?"[167] Do you hear? At Rome the very king was naught without the Senate. "But," you say, "Romulus, according to Tacitus,[168] had governed the Romans exactly as he pleased." Yes, for, having as yet no foundation of laws, they were a rabble concourse of strangers rather than a state. Of old, before states came into being, all men lived lawless. But, as Livy informs us, when Romulus was dead, though all the people desired a king, not having yet tasted the sweets of liberty, "Yet the sovereign power was allowed to remain in the hands of the people; so that they gave not up more right than they kept."[169] The same author tells us: "That right was afterwards extorted from them" by the Caesars. Servius Tullius at first reigned by indirection, and as it were a deputy of Tarquinius Priscus; but afterwards he referred it to the people "whether they would have him and bid him reign." At last, says Tacitus, "he became the author of laws such as even the kings obeyed."[170] Do you think he would have done such an injury to himself and his posterity, if he had deemed that the right of kings before he did so had been above all laws? Their last king, Tarquinius Superbus, "was the first that put an end to the custom of consulting the Senate about everything"; and for this and other enormities the people annihilated the power of king Lucius Tarquinius, and banished him with his wife and children. To this effect speak Livy and Cicero, than whom you will hardly produce any better expositors of the right of kings among the Romans. As for the dictatorship, that was but temporary, was never applied but in the state's extremities, and was to be laid down within six months.

167. Cicero *In Pisonem* 10.23.
168. Tacitus *Annals* 3.26.
169. Livy *Ab urbe condita* 1.17.2–9.
170. Tacitus *Annals* 3.26.

What you call the right of the Roman emperors was no right, however, but downright force, a power gained through no law but that of arms. "But Tacitus," say you, "that lived under the government of a single person," writes thus: "'The gods have given the sovereign power in human affairs to princes; what has been left to subjects is the honor of submitting.'" But you tell us not where Tacitus has these words, doubtless because you were conscious that you had egregiously put upon your readers; which I smelt out at once, though I could not at once find the place. For those words are not Tacitus's own, who is an approved writer, and the greatest possible enemy to tyrants, but are quoted by Tacitus as the words of M. Terentius, a gentleman of Rome, who being charged with capital crime, amongst other things that he said in fear of death, flattered Tiberius in this manner, *Annals* VI: "The gods have entrusted you with the ultimate judgment in all things; what has been left to us is the honor of submitting." And this you cite as if it were Tacitus's opinion! Whatever your motive—whether you would show off, or are conscious of your weakness—so indiscriminately do you scrape together everything from everywhere, that you would not reject opinions to suit your argument though they were the sweepings of a baker's shop or a barbershop—yes, or of the very gallows! Had you chosen to read Tacitus himself rather than copy too carelessly an extract you found somewhere, he would have taught you whence that imperial right had its origin. "After the victory of Actium," says he, "the whole state of our affairs was turned upside down; nothing of our ancient or uncorrupted manners anywhere; all men put off political equality and began to attend to the orders of the chief of state." This you might have learned out of the third Book of his *Annals,* whence you have all your regal right. "When equality was laid aside, and instead of moderation and self-restraint factiousness and violence stepped in, tyrannical forms of government started up, and fixed themselves in many countries." The same thing you might have learned out of Dio,[171] if your natural levity and unsettledness of judgment would

171. Dio Cassius *History of Rome* 53.28.

have suffered you to apprehend anything above you. He tells us in his fifty-third Book, from which you have quoted, that partly by the violence and partly by the fraud and hypocrisy of Octavianus Caesar, things were brought to that pass that the emperors were loosed from the laws. For though Octavianus promised before the popular assembly that he would lay down the principate, and obey the laws, and even the commands of others, yet under pretence of making war in his provinces he still kept the legions at hand, and so, while in appearance he declined power, he gradually entered upon the possession of it. This was not being duly released from the laws, but breaking forcibly through their bonds, as Spartacus the gladiator might have done; and then assuming to himself the style of *princeps* or *imperator* and αὐτοκράτωρ, as if God or the law of nature had put all men and all laws into subjection under him.

Would you inquire a little further back into the origin of the right of the Caesars? Mark Antony had been made consul at the bidding of Caesar, who by impiously taking up arms against the commonwealth had got all the power into his hands. Now at the celebration of the Lupercalia [172] at Rome, Antony, by previous arrangement it seems, set a crown upon Caesar's head, amid the people's groans and lamentations. Thereupon he caused it to be entered upon the Calendar as a record of the events at the Lupercalia that Marcus Antonius had offered Caesar royal power at the people's instance! Of which action Cicero in his second *Philippic* says: "Was it for this that Lucius Tarquinius was expelled, and Spurius Cassius, Spurius Melius, and Marcus Manlius put to death—that after many generations Mark Antony against the law should make a king in Rome?" Truly you deserve every form of torture and everlasting disgrace even more than Antony himself. Yet be not therefore puffed up, for I compare you not, most contemptible of men, with Antony in aught but wickedness: you that in these unspeakable Lupercalia of yours, most loose-lived Lupercus, or Scare-Wolf, have taken pains to bind about the head not of one tyrant

172. The Lupercal was a sacred cave on the Palatine, the *Lupercalia,* a festival held in February.

only, but of all tyrants, a diadem loosed from all laws, but never to be loosened by any!

Indeed if we must believe the "oracle" of the emperors them-selves—for so the Christian emperors Theodosius and Valens call their edict, Cod. lib. i. tit. 14—the authority of the emperors depends upon that of the law. So that the majesty of the person that reigns, even by the judgment or the oracle of the emperors themselves, must submit to the laws on which it depends. Hence Pliny tells Trajan in his Panegyric, when the power of the emperors was grown to its height: "A principate and a despotism are quite different in their na-ture. Trajan restrains and puts far from him power that is actually royal, and holds the throne as a prince, that there may be no room for a despot." And afterwards: "Whatever I have said of other princes, I said that I might show how our prince moulds anew and straight-ens the way of principates, which by long custom have been cor-rupted and perverted." [173] What Pliny calls the corrupt and depraved customs of principates, are you not ashamed still to keep on calling the right of kings? So much, then, briefly, concerning the right of kings among the Romans.

How they dealt with their tyrants, whether kings or emperors, is generally known. They expelled Tarquin, yes and by ancestral custom even then; for either their neighbor Etruria offered a very ancient precedent in the expulsion of the tyrant Mezentius from the city of Agylla, or Virgil, past master of the fitting and beautiful, meant by that tale in the eighth Aeneid to show even Caesar Octavianus, who then ruled in Rome, what rights kings had among all nations—and this from the utmost antiquity.

"But while the madman yet meditates crimes unspeakable, the citizens, wearied out at last, in armed bands press round both him and his house, and slay his train, and hurl fire upon his rooftree. Slipping away from amid the slaughter, he betakes him to the territory of the Rutuli for refuge, and is defended by the arms of Turnus a stranger.

173. Pliny *Panegyrics* 45.3.

'Twas for this that all Etruria rose up in righteous rage: in open war they claim the king for execution."[174]

Here you see that subjects, fired with righteous wrath, not only sought their tyrant upon a sudden violent impulse to murder him, not only drove him from his kingdom, but when he was a fugitive and an exile made war to get him back again for trial, yea for capital punishment.

"But," say you, "*how* did the Romans expel Tarquin? Did they bring him to trial? No such matter: when he would have come into the city, they shut the gates against him." Ridiculous fool! what could they do but shut the gates, when he was hurrying thither with part of the army? Banished or put to death—what odds, so long as he surely was punished?

Gaius Caesar the tyrant was killed in the senate by the choice and master spirits of that age. This action Marcus Tullius, himself an excellent man, and publicly entitled the father of his country, extols wonderfully in many passages of his works, particularly in his second *Philippic*. I will repeat some of his words: "All good men killed Caesar as far as in them lay. Some lacked the plan, others the courage, others the opportunity; none the wish." And afterwards: "What action ever was performed, oh venerable Jove! not in this city only but in all the world, that was greater, more glorious, and more to be commended to the everlasting remembrance of mankind? Not loath am I to be included in the fellowship that planned it, as with the band of chieftains in the Trojan horse."

That familiar passage of Seneca the tragedian may relate both to the Romans and to the Greeks:

> There can be slain
> No sacrifice to God more acceptable
> Than an unjust and wicked king.[175]

---

174. Virgil *Aeneid* 8.489–95.
175. Seneca *Hercules Maddened* 922–24.

---

For if this be taken as the sentiment of Hercules, who speaks the words, it shows what was the opinion of the most eminent Greeks in that age; if it be taken as the sentiment of the poet, who flourished under Nero (and poets generally put something like their own opinions into the mouths of their best characters), then this passage betokened what both Seneca himself and all good men, even in Nero's time, thought should be done to a tyrant, and how virtuous an action, how acceptable to the gods, they thought it to kill one. So every good man of Rome, as far as in him lay, killed Domitian. Pliny the Younger owns it openly in that Panegyric to the emperor Trajan: "There was pleasure in dashing those overweening looks against the ground, in piercing him with swords, in mangling him with axes, as if he bled and felt pain at every stroke. No man could so moderate his joy, but that he counted it as good as revenge to behold his mangled limbs, his members torn asunder, and at last his grim and horrid statues thrown down and melted in the fire."[176] And afterwards: "They cannot love good princes enough, that cannot enough hate bad ones." Then amongst the enormities of Domitian he reckons this, that he put to death Epaphroditus, who in a way had killed Nero: "Have we ceased to grieve at the vengeance taken but just now for Nero's death? Is it likely that one who was avenging Nero's death would let his life and reputation be ill spoken of?" Pliny actually seems to have thought it almost a crime not to kill Nero, and a very grievous crime to punish his murder.

By what has been said, it is evident that the most excellent of the Romans did not only kill tyrants however and whenever they could, but like the Greeks before them thought the deed most praiseworthy. For whenever they could not proceed judicially against a tyrant in his lifetime, being less powerful than he, yet after his death they would both judge him and by the Valerian Law condemn him; and Valerius Publicola, Junius Brutus his colleague, perceiving that as tyrants were guarded by soldiers they could not be brought to trial, proposed a bill

176. Pliny *Panegyrics* 52.4.

making it lawful to kill them uncondemned any how, and give an account afterwards.[177] Hence, when Cassius had killed Gaius Caligula with a sword, and everybody else had done it with prayers and desires, Valerius Asiaticus, a governor of consular rank, then absent, cried out to the soldiers that began to mutiny because of the Emperor's death, "Would I had been the one to kill him!"[178] The Senate at the same time were so far from being displeased with Cassius that they resolved to extirpate the memory of the emperors, and to raze their temples. When Claudius soon after was saluted Emperor by the soldiers, the Senate forbade him by the tribune of the people to take the government upon him; but the power of the soldiers prevailed. The Senate declared Nero a public enemy, and searched him out to have him punished after the way of their ancestors, which required that he should be stripped naked, his neck thrust beneath the fork, and with rods be whipped to death. Consider now how much more mildly and moderately the English dealt with their tyrant, though many are of opinion that he caused more bloodshed than Nero himself. So the Senate condemned Domitian after his death; they commanded his statues to be publicly pulled down and dashed to pieces, which was all they could do. Commodus, slain by his own officers, was not avenged, but adjudged a public enemy, by both the Senate and the people, who sought out even his dead corpse for mutilation. The Senate's resolution upon this matter is extant in Lampridius: "Let the enemy of his country be deprived of all his titles; let the parricide be drawn, let him be torn in pieces in the gladiators' stripping-place; let the enemy of the gods, the executioner of the senate, be dragged with a hook,"[179] etc. The same persons in a very full session of the Senate condemned the emperor Didius Julianus to death, and sent a tribune to slay him in the palace. The same Senate deposed Maximin, and

177. Valerius Publicola was by traditional belief one of the first consuls (with Junius Brutus). An early version of what would become the *Lex Valeria* was attributed to him.

178. Dio Cassius *History of Rome* 59.30.

179. Lampridius *Historia Augusta* 18.3.

declared him a public enemy. It will be well to read from Capitolinus the Senate's resolution concerning him: "The consul put the question: 'Conscript Fathers, what is your pleasure concerning the Maximins?' They answered: 'They are enemies, they are enemies; whoever kills them shall be rewarded.'" Would you know whether the Roman people and the provinces obeyed the Senate, or obeyed Maximin the emperor? Hear what the same author says: "The Senate sent letters" to all the provinces, requesting them to come to the rescue of the common safety and liberty; the letters were publicly read. Everywhere the friends, the deputies, the generals, the tribunes, the soldiers of Maximin, were slain. Very few cities kept their allegiance to the public enemy.[180] Herodian relates the same thing.[181] What need of more instances from Roman history?

Let us now see what manner of thing the right of kings was in those days among the neighboring nations. Ambiorix king of the Gauls confesses "the nature of his dominion to be such that the people had as much right over him as he over them." Consequently he was always subject to judgment as much as he exercised judgment. Vercingetorix, king likewise, was accused of treason by his own people. These things Caesar relates in his history of the Gallic wars. Nor was "the power of the German kings absolute and unbounded: lesser matters are ordered and disposed by the chiefs, greater matters by all the people. The king or prince is heeded more through the influence of his persuasions than through his power to command. If his opinion has not pleased them, they reject it with a murmur." So says Tacitus.[182] Indeed you yourself now confess that what but of late you exclaimed against as absolutely unheard of has been often done, to wit, that "no less than fifty Scottish kings have been either banished or imprisoned or put to death, nay, and some of them publicly executed." Which having been done over and over again in Britain itself, why do you,

180. Capitolinus *Historia Augusta* 17.4.
181. Herodian *History* 8.5.8–9.
182. Tacitus *Germania* 11.

who spirit your tyrants away like paupers, hugger-mugger, for burial at dusk to conceal their violent deaths, how can you, I say, cry out upon it with so lamentable a voice as a thing unheard of?

You proceed to commend the Jews and Christians for their reverent obedience to tyrants, and with lies to sow a harvest of more lies, which I have so often confuted. A while ago you were praising far and wide the obedience of the Assyrians and Persians, and now you reckon up their rebellions; a little while ago you said they never rebelled at all, and now you give us a great many reasons why they rebelled so often! Then you resume your long-suspended narrative of our king's execution, in order that if perhaps you had not taken care enough to be a ridiculous fool then, you may do it now. You say, "He was led through the members of his court." What you mean by the members of the court, I yearn to know. You enumerate the disasters that the Romans underwent through changing their kingdom into a commonwealth; in which I have shown above how grossly you give yourself the lie. You, who when you wrote against the Loyolite,[183] used to point out that "in an aristocracy or a democracy there could be seditions and tumults only, whereas under a tyrant destruction was sure," dare you now say, you empty-headed and thoroughly corrupt mortal, that "they drank the cup of the ills that arose from their seditions as punishments for banishing their kings aforetime"? To wit, because King Charles afterwards made you a present of a hundred Jacobuses: that is the reason why the Romans expiated the banishing of their kings!

You say it went ill with the murderers of Julius Caesar. Indeed, if I would have had any tyrant spared, it should have been he. He did, to be sure, though a citizen of a republic, forcibly enter upon the exercise of royal power; yet he perhaps more than anyone else deserved it. Nor do I for this reason suppose anyone to have been punished for killing Caesar, any more than Gaius Antonius, Cicero's colleague, was punished for destroying Catiline. Afterward, when he was condemned for other crimes, says Cicero in his oration *pro Flacco,* "Cati-

183. A Jesuit.

line's tomb was decked with flowers," for they that favored Catiline then rejoiced, and "gave out then that Catiline's deeds were righteous," to kindle hatred against those that had cut him off. These are the artifices of wicked men to deter most excellent men from cutting off tyrants, and often from punishing even the most atrocious criminals. I might easily tell against you how often it hath gone well and prosperously with them that have killed tyrants, if from such cases any certain inference might be drawn concerning the outcome of human affairs.

You object further, "that the English put their hereditary king to death not as tyrants use to be sacrificed, but as robbers and traitors are executed." In the first place I do not know what heredity should contribute to impunity for crimes; that it contributes anything is scarcely possible for a wise man to believe. Next, in the conduct which you ascribe to "savage cruelty" there commendably appeared rather our English clemency and moderation; for, though to be a tyrant comprises within itself all sorts of enormities, robberies, treacheries, and treasons, against the whole nation, yet they were content to inflict no greater punishment upon a tyrant than they used of course to do upon any plain highwayman or common traitor!

You hope "that some Harmodius and Thrasybulus[184] will rise up and make expiation" to the tyrant's manes by the slaughter of my fellow-countrymen. But sooner will you run mad with despair, and, as you deserve all good men's curses, will first put an end to a life worthy of yourself by hanging yourself, ere you see Harmodiuses offer the blood of Harmodiuses in atonement to a tyrant! That you will come to such an end is most probable (for who could foretell a more suitable fortune for such a rascal?) but the other thing is an utter impossibility. You mention thirty tyrants that rebelled in Gallienus's time. And what if one tyrant opposes another, must therefore all they that resist or destroy a tyrant be accounted such themselves? You cannot

---

184. Harmodius with Aristogiton killed the Athenian tyrant Hipparchus in 514 B.C.; Thrasybulus first held out against the Four Hundred at Athens, then joined with those who ejected the Thirty Tyrants in 403 B.C.

persuade men into such a belief, you slave-knight, nor can your authority Trebellius Pollio, well-nigh the most inconsiderable of historians.[185] "If any of the emperors were declared enemies by the Senate," you say, "it was done by faction, not law." You put us in mind what it was that first made emperors: it was faction and violence, and to speak plainer, the madness of Antony, and not any law or right, that originally made the emperors themselves take the start in rebelling against the Senate and the people of Rome. "Galba," you say, "was punished for taking up arms against Nero." Tell us likewise how Vespasian was punished for taking up arms against Vitellius! "There was as much difference," you say, "betwixt Charles and Nero, as betwixt those English butchers and the Roman Senators of that age." Gallows-bird! by whom it is scandalous to be commended, and a praise to be evil spoken of: but a few sentences before, discoursing of this very thing, you said: "The Senate under the emperors was in effect but an assembly of toga'd slaves"; and now you say: "the Senate was an assembly of kings." If this be so, why should not kings, according to your own opinion, be considered to be toga'd slaves? Blessed are kings in such a praiser! than whom no man is more a rascal, nor four-footed beast more void of sense, unless this may be said to be his singular property, that none brays more learnedly.

You make out that the Parliament of England is more like to Nero than to the Roman Senate. This itch of yours to paste together utterly inappropriate comparisons forces me to set you right: and I will let you see how like King Charles was to Nero. "Nero," you say, "slew his own mother" with a sword. But Charles murdered with poison one that was both his father and his king. For to omit other evidences: he that snatched from the law the Duke that was charged with the poisoning cannot but have shared the guilt. Nero slew many thousands of Christians, but Charles slew many more. There were those, says Suetonius, that praised Nero after he was dead, that longed to have had him again, that for a long time "used to deck his tomb with spring

185. Trebellius Pollio is thought to be the author of "Tyranni Triginta," in the *Historia Augusta.*

and summer flowers,"[186] and that boded all evils to his enemies. And some there are that with the like frenzy wish for king Charles again, and exalt him with the highest praise; you, Knight of the Halter, lead their troop.

"The English soldiers, more savage than their own mastiffs, erected a new and unheard-of court of justice." Observe this ingenious symbol or adage of Salmasius, now obtruded six times over: "more savage than their own mastiffs." Come all ye orators and schoolmasters; pluck, if you are wise, this elegant flower, which Salmasius is so very fond of; commit to your tablets and cabinets this rhetorical cosmetic of this most eloquent man, lest it perish. Has your madness so destroyed your words that, cuckoo-fashion, you must needs sing the same ill-omened song over and over again? What sort of monstrosity shall I call this? Madness, says the tale,[187] turned Hecuba into a dog; you, Seigneur of St. Wolf, it has turned into a cuckoo.

Now you come out with fresh inconsistencies. You had said before, page 113, that "the prince was loosed from the laws,—not from laws coercive" only, but as well "from laws directory; that there are none at all by which he is held." Now you say that "you will discourse further on of the difference betwixt some kings and others, in so far as some have had more power, some less." By what you call "a most solid argument" you would prove "that kings cannot be judged or condemned by their own subjects"; but it is a very stupid one. You say: "There was no other difference betwixt judges and kings; and yet the reason why the Jews kept asking for a king was that they were weary of the judges, and hated them." Do you think that because they *could* judge and condemn judges for malfeasance in office they were therefore led by hatred and weariness of them to ask for kings, whom they could *not* punish or restrain though they should break through all laws? Who but you ever argued so idiotically? They desired a king, then, for some other reason than that they might have a master whose

186. Suetonius *Lives of the Emperors* 57.
187. Ovid *Metamorphoses* 13.

power should be superior to that of the law; to guess what it was is not to our present purpose. Whatever it was, both God and his Prophet have witnessed that it was ill-advised in the people to desire a king. Once more you fall foul of your rabbins, out of whose writings you said before you had proved that a king of the Jews could not be judged, for saying that a king might be not only judged, but condemned as well to undergo stripes;—which is tantamount to confessing that you had made up out of the whole cloth what you said you had proved out of their writings. Nay, you come at last to forgetting the king's defence, and raising wretched quibbles about the number of Solomon's stables, and how many "mangers he had for his horses."

Finally from a horse-boy you become once more the Knight of the Virtuous Preachments and Identical Repetitions, or rather the sort of monster you were before, a raving distracted cuckoo. You complain that in these "latter ages, the force of order has been slackened, and its rule destroyed"; because forsooth one tyrant loosed from every law is not allowed with impunity to slacken all order, and destroy all men's morals! This doctrine, you say, was introduced by "the Brownists[188] amongst those of the reformed religion"; so that Luther, Calvin, Zwingli, Bucer, and all the most celebrated orthodox divines, are Brownists in your opinion. The English bear your reproaches the more calmly because they hear you rave with nearly the same slanders against the most eminent doctors of the Church, and in effect against the whole Reformed Church itself.

## CHAPTER VI.

After your fruitless and futile mishandling of the law of God and nature, from which you have brought off nothing but the reproach of ignorance and knavery combined, I do not see what you can farther allege in your royal cause but mere trifles. Though I for my part hope

188. Followers of Robert Browne (1550–1633), an early separatist from Anglicanism.

that even should I end my answer here, I have done enough to satisfy fully all men that are neither ignorant nor knavish,—yes, done enough for this noble cause itself,—yet lest others should think that I am retreating from what they suppose your manysidedness and keenness, rather than your immeasurable talkativeness, I will go on as far as you like, but with such brevity as shall make it appear that after having performed all that if not the dignity, yet the urgency of the cause demanded, I now do but comply with some people's expectation or, perhaps, curiosity.

"From now on," say you, "there rises before me another and a grander order of arguments." What! grander arguments than what the law of God and nature afforded? Help, Lucina![189] Mount Salmasius is in labor! It is not for nothing that he was married by a he-wife. Mortals, expect some huge and monstrous birth. "If he that is and is called king might be impeached before another power, this must of necessity be greater than the royal power. But the power that is constituted the greater must be called and be indeed the royal power, for royal power is to be thus defined: the power which is supreme in the state, and unique, and above which no other is acknowledged." A mountainous mouse, and a ridiculous![190] Help, grammarians! help this grammarian in travail! the law of God and nature is safe; but 'tis all up with the dictionary!

What if I should answer you thus? Let names give way to things; to be cautious about the name is not our affair, who have got rid of the thing; let others, who are in love with kings, look to that; we are content with the enjoyment of our liberty. Such would be no unfair answer. But to let you see that I deal fairly and justly with you throughout, I will give you an answer based not upon my own opinion alone, but upon that of the best and wisest men of old, who have thought that both the name and the power of a king are entirely consistent with a greater power in the people and the law. In the first place,

189. Roman goddess of midwives.
190. Horace *Ars Poetica:* "The Mountains gave birth and was born a trifling mouse."

Lycurgus, a man very eminent for wisdom, designing, as Plato says, to provide in the highest degree for the interests of kingly government, could find no other expedient to preserve it than by making the power of the senate and of the Ephors, that is, of the people, superior to it in his own country. Theseus in Euripides was of the same opinion; for he, though king of Athens, yet to his great honor restored the Athenian people to liberty, and advanced the power of the people above that of the king, and left the regal power in that city none the less to his posterity. Whence Euripides, in *The Suppliants,* introduces him speaking on this manner: "I have established the people themselves in sovereignty, having freed this city, which hath an equal right of suffrage." And in another place, to the herald of Thebes: "In the first place you begin your speech, stranger, with a thing that is not true, in asking for the monarch here; for this city is not governed by a single person, but is free; the people is its lord."[191] These were his words, though in that city he yet both was, and was called, king. Another authority on the same point is the divine Plato in his eighth epistle: "Lycurgus introduced the power of the senate and of the Ephors, τῆς βασιλικῆς ἀρξῆς σωτήριον, a thing very preservative of kingly government, which by this means has been kept in great honor for so many ages, because mistress law was made king." Now the law cannot be king, unless there be somebody who, if there should be occasion, may enforce it against the king too. A kingly government so modified and limited, he himself commends to the Sicilians: "Let there be liberty together with royal power; let royal power be ὑπευ-'θυνος, liable to give account; let law prevail even against kings, if they shall act contrary to law." Finally Aristotle says, in the third book of his *Politics:* "Of all royal powers that are governed by laws, that in the Spartan commonwealth seems to be most truly and properly royal." All forms of kingly government, however, he says, were according to laws, but one which he calls παμβασιλείαν, or Absolute Monarchy, and he does not mention that this existed anywhere. Aristotle, then,

---

191. Euripides *Suppliants* 352–53; 403–6.

thought such a kingdom as that of the Spartans to be and deserve the name of a kingdom *par excellence,* and consequently could not deny that such a king as theirs, though the people were above him, none the less was, and was to be called, *par excellence* a king. Now since authors so many and great do upon their faith and credit warrant unto the king that both the name and the substance of his royalty shall be unimpaired, and vouch it safe, even where the supreme power, though generally unused, yet for times of need is kept by the people in their own possession; do you cease with so petty a mind to fear so much for the State of Grammar—of Words, to wit—that rather than the public weal of your word-list should be disturbed, or suffer aught of harm, you would willingly betray the liberty and common weal of mankind. And for the future know that words are subordinate to things, not things to words. By this means you will have more discernment, and not run on "into the infinite and undefined" as you fear!

"In vain then does Seneca," you say, "thus describe those three forms of government." Let Seneca describe in vain, so we enjoy our liberty; and if I mistake not, we are not the sort of men to be enslaved by Seneca's Flowers. Yet Seneca, though he says that the sovereign power resides in a single person, says withal that "the power is the people's,"[192] and by them given to the king in trust for the welfare of the whole, not for their ruin and destruction, and that the people have not given him a property in it, but the use of it. "Kings at this rate," you say, "do not reign by God but by the people." As if God did not so overrule the people that they give the kingdom to whom God wills. The Emperor Justinian in his Institutes themselves openly acknowledges that the Caesars' reign began when "by the Lex Regia the people granted unto them and vested in them all their own power and authority."[193]

But how long shall I keep warming over and over again that stuff of yours which I have so often rejected and refuted? Now once more

---

192. Seneca "On Benefits" 7.4.
193. Milton paraphrases Justinian's *Institutes* 1.2.6.

you push yourself—and it is a thing which reveals your boorish un-
mannerly nature and odious ways—you, a foreign-born outsider,
push yourself inquisitively into our state affairs, which are none of
yours! Come on, then, with an egregious solecism, worthy of such a
busybody. "Every single thing," quotha, "every single thing that those
desperadoes say, are only to deceive the people." Rascal! was it for
this that you, an outlawed grammarian, were so forward to intermeddle with the affairs of our government—that you might stuff us
with your solecisms and barbarisms? But say, how have we deceived
the people? "The form of government which they have set up is not
popular, but military." This is what that gang of renegades hired
you—and hired you cheap—to write; so that I shall not trouble myself to answer you, who babble what you know nothing of, but I will
answer them that hired you. Who "excluded the Lords from Parliament—was it the people?" Ay, it was the people; and in so doing
they threw an intolerable yoke of slavery from off their necks. Those
very soldiers who you say did it were not foreigners, but our own
countrymen, and a great part of the people, and they did it with the
consent and at the desire of almost all the rest of the people, and not
without the authority of Parliament itself. "Was it the people that
maimed the House of Commons by driving away some of the members, etc.?" Yes, I say, it was the people. For whatever the better, that
is, the sounder, part of the legislature did, in which the true power of
the people resided, why may not the people be said to have done it?
What if the majority of the legislature should choose to be slaves, or
to set the government to sale—ought not the minority prevent
this, and keep their liberty, if it be in their power? "But the officers
of the army with their soldiers did it." And thanks are due those
officers for that they failed not the state, but repelled the riotous
workmen and shopkeepers of London, who, like that rabble that appeared for Clodius,[194] had but a little before beset the very parliament
house. The original and proper right of Parliament to look out be-

194. Publius Clodius Pulcher was a scoundrel and demagogue who aided Catiline
and then Caesar against the republic.

fore all else for the people's liberty both in peace and in war— is this what you therefore call "a military despotism"? It is no wonder indeed that the traitors who dictated these passages to you should talk in this strain, for so did that profligate crew of Antony and his adherents use to call the Roman Senate when they took arms against the enemies of their country, "Pompey's Camp." And now I am glad that they of your party looked grudgingly upon Cromwell, that most valiant general of our army, for undertaking the Irish campaign (so acceptable to Almighty God), surrounded with a joyful crowd of his friends, and followed up by the well-wishes of the people and the prayers of all good men; for I question not but at the news of his many victories there they are by this time rotted with spite.

I pass by your quantities of long-winded nonsense about the Roman soldiers. What follows is most notoriously false: "Power ceases to belong to a people," you say, "where it begins to belong to a king." By what law or right is that? For it is very certain that kings in general, throughout the world, receive from the people an authority entrusted to them subject to certain conditions; which if the king abide not by, pray tell us why that power, which was but a trust, should not return to the people, as well from a king as from a consul or any other officer of government. For what you say about "the public safety requiring it" is not to the point; the requirements of safety are identical whether "that power reverts to the people" from a King, or from an Aristocracy, or from a Triumvirate, in case any of them abuse the power entrusted to them; and yet you yourself grant that it may so revert from officers of every sort, a king only excepted. Certainly, if no people in their right wits ever gave power over themselves either to a king or to any magistrates for any other purpose than the common good of all, there can be no reason why, for exactly the inverse purpose, to prevent the utter ruin of them all, they may not take back again the power they gave, and this as well from a king as from other magistrates; nay, and it may with far greater ease be taken from one than from many. And to commit to any mortal creature a power over themselves on any other terms than upon trust were extreme madness; nor is it credible that any people since the creation of the world, who had freedom of will, were ever so miserably silly as either to part with the power absolutely and entirely, or, having once entrusted it to their magistrates, to recall it unto themselves without weightiest reasons. But though dissensions, though civil wars, arise thence, surely no royal right arises thence to withhold by force of arms that power which the people reclaims unto itself for its own.

Whence it follows that what you say, and we do not deny, that "the ruler ought not lightly to be changed," is true with respect to the people's prudence, not the king's right; but it nowise follows that therefore a ruler ought not to be changed ever or for any cause whatsoever. Nor have you hitherto adduced any reason, or produced any right of kings, which ought to hinder the people, when they all concur, from deposing an unfit king, provided it may be done, as it has been often done in your own country of France, without tumult or civil war. Since therefore the safety of the people, not the safety of a tyrant, is the supreme law, and consequently should advantage the people against a tyrant, and not a tyrant against the people; you that have dared invert so sacred and so glorious a law with your jugglings, you who would make this supreme law, which of all laws is most beneficial to mankind, serve only for the impunity of tyrants; let me tell you (since to you we Englishmen so often are "Enthusiasts," "Inspired," and "Prophets") let me, I say, be so far a prophet as to tell you that the vengeance of God and man hangs over your head for so horrid a crime; although your casting down the whole human race under the feet of tyrants, which is naught else than, as far as in you lies, condemning them to be thrown to the beasts of the amphitheatre,— this monstrous wickedness is itself part of its own vengeance upon you; and whithersoever on earth you flee, and wheresoever you wander, will pursue you with its furies soon or late, and drive and harass you with madness yet worse than now you rave with.

I come now to your second argument, which is not unlike the first. If the people may resume their power, "there would be no difference," say you, "betwixt a democracy and a kingdom; but that in a kingdom the appointed governor is one man and in a democracy many." And what if that were true—would the state take any harm of it? But here are some other differences which you yourself bring forward, of "time and succession," to be sure, for "the magistrates in a democracy are generally chosen yearly," whereas kings, if they behave themselves well, are perpetual; and in most kingdoms there is a succession in the same family. But let them differ from one another, or not differ, I regard not those trifles: in this they surely agree, that in either a democracy or a kingdom, when the public good requires it, that power which the people had entrusted to another for the public safety may for the same reason, and without violation of right or law, be recalled by the people unto itself.

"According to the Lex Regia, however, or royal law, so called by the Romans, which is treated in the Institutes, the people of Rome granted all their power and authority to and for the chief of state." Certainly—upon compulsion by the Caesars, who under the honorable pretence of law ratified what was merely their own violence. But of this we have spoken before; and their own lawyers, commenting upon this passage in the Institutes, do not disguise the fact. Doubtless therefore what was not granted by right law or by true consent of the people is revocable. But most reasonable it is to suppose that the people of Rome transferred no other power to the prince than they had before granted to their own magistrates, that is a power to govern according to law, and a power revocable, not unreasonable or tyrannical. Hence it was that the Caesars took over the powers of the Consuls, and of the Tribunes of the People, but after Julius not one pretended to those of a Dictator; in the Circus they used even to adore the people, as I mentioned before, quoting Tacitus and Claudian.

But "as heretofore many a private person has sold himself into slavery to another, so may a whole nation." Jailbird knight from the slaves' prison-house! Slave dealer thyself! Everlasting reproach even to thy native country! The most degraded band of slaves exposed for sale at the block ought to abhor and spit upon so foul a slave-procurer, such a public pander! Certainly if a people had so enslaved themselves to kings, then might kings turn them over to any other master you like, or put them up for sale; and yet certain it is that kings cannot so much as alienate the demesnes of the crown. He then who holds as a grant from the people only the use and enjoyment of the crown (as the phrase is) and of the royal demesne, shall he be owner, as if by purchase, of the people itself? Though you stood forward, a riddled knight with both ears bored[195] and gypsum-whitened feet, exposed for sale, you would not be so much the most contemptible of slaves as now you are, being the author of such a shameful doctrine.

Go on and punish yourself against your will for your rogueries, as now you do. Toward the last you stammer out quantities of things about the right of war and conquest, which have no place here. For on the one hand never did Charles conquer us (and for his ancestors, though it were never so much granted that they did, yet have they again and again renounced their title as conquerors), nor on the other hand were we ever so conquered but that as we swore allegiance to them, so they swore to maintain our laws. When Charles had notoriously violated these, and had first provoked us, we subdued him by force, take him in what capacity you will, as formerly king conqueror or as now king perjurer. But according to your own opinion, "Whatever is acquired by war becomes the property of him that has acquired it." And so in this your argument begin again and be as wordy as you will, be what you were not long ago upon Solinus, a Plinian carping controversialist, of all babblers the wordiest:[196]—whatever you chatter next, whatever uproar you make, whatever you quote from the rabbins, however you shout yourself hoarse even to the end of this chapter, be assured that in the sweat of your brow you have been doing it all, not for the conquered king, but for us, by God's help his conquerors.

195. Exod. 21:6 prescribed these types of wounds as the mark of a slave.

196. Milton refers to a work by Gaius Julius Solinus based on Pliny and newly edited with commentary by Salmasius.

## CHAPTER VII.

To avoid two great inconveniences, and, considering your own weight, very weighty ones indeed, you denied in the foregoing chapter that the people's power was greater than the king's; for if you granted that, then kings must look about for some other name, the appellation "king" being turned over to the people, and certain classifications in your system of politics would be confounded. The first of these consequences would spoil your dictionary, and the second be the death of your Politics. To these I have answered in such wise that a certain consideration might be given first to our own safety and liberty, and after even to your terminology and Politics! Now, say you, "'Tis to be proved by other arguments that a king cannot be judged by his own subjects; of which arguments this shall be the most powerful and most convincing, that a king hath no peer in his kingdom." What? A king hath no peer in his kingdom? What then is the meaning of those old Twelve Peers of France? Are they fables and trumpery stuff of Turpin's invention?[197] Are they called so in vain and in mockery? Have a care how you insult those Princes and Paladins of France! Or is it because they are equal among themselves? As if, forsooth, it were thinkable that of the whole French nobility only twelve were each other's peers, or that this were a reason for calling them Peers of *France!* Nay, if they are not in very truth the Peers of the *King* of France, and this because with him they govern the State by equal right and by conference with him as his equals—look to it lest the dictionary, which is the only thing you are concerned for, be more mocked in the Kingdom of France than in the Commonwealth of England!

But go to, let us hear your demonstration that a king has no peer in his own kingdom. "Because," you say, "the people of Rome, when they had banished their kings, appointed not one, but two Consuls, that if one of them should transgress, he might be checked by his colleague." A sillier argument could hardly have been invented: how

197. Turpin, an eighth-century prelate, was thought to have chronicled Charlemagne's reign and the heroic sacrifice of Roland.

came it to pass then that but one of the Consuls kept the Fasces, and not both, if each had been appointed to check the other? And what if both had conspired against the commonwealth, would the case have been better than if the Romans had not given one Consul a colleague? What is certain, however, is that the Consuls both, and all other magistrates, were bound to obey the Senate, whenever the Senate and the people decided that the interest of the commonwealth so required. For this I have abundant authority in Marcus Tullius's oration for Sestius. Listen at the same time to his concise account of the Roman constitution, which, he always said, was "very wisely framed," and that it behooved all good citizens to be well acquainted with it. And so say I.

"Our ancestors, when they had thrown off the power of the kings, created offices to last one year, but in such wise that over the commonwealth they set the deliberative assembly of the Senate to last forever; that members, however, were to be elected into this assembly by the people as a whole; and that entrance into that exalted body should stand open to the industry and worth of all citizens. They stationed the Senate as the guardian, protector, and champion of the State. This body's authority it was that they would have the magistrates employ, and would have them be, as it were, servants of this most weighty assembly."

The Decemvirs[198] may serve as a shining example: though they were invested with the power of Consuls, and were the chief magistrates, yet the authority of the Senate reduced them all together and at once to order, against their struggles. Nay, we read that some Consuls, before they laid down their office, had been declared public enemies, and arms taken up against them; for in those days no man accounted him a Consul who carried on open war against his country. So, by authority of the Senate, war was waged against Antony, though a Consul; in which being worsted he would have been put to

198. Ten patricians who were granted plenary authority in 451 B.C., then were ejected when they attempted to prolong their office.

death, but that Octavianus Caesar,[199] grasping after empire, joined with him in a conspiracy to subvert the commonwealth.

Your assertion that "it is a property peculiar to kingly majesty that the power resides in a single person" is not less slippery, and is at once contradicted by yourself. "The Hebrew judges," you say, "ruled as long as they lived, and there was but one of them at a time: the Scripture also calls them kings; and yet they were accountable to the Sanhedrim." So it happens that while wishing to be thought to have said all that can be said, you say hardly anything but contradictions. Then I ask what kind of government you call it when sometimes two, sometimes three emperors at once held the Roman Empire? Do you reckon them to have been emperors, that is, kings, or members of an aristocracy, or a triumvirate? Or will you say that the Roman Empire under Antoninus and Verus, under Diocletian and Maximian, under Constantine and Licinius, was not one empire? If these were not kings, your "three forms of government" are endangered by your own cleverness; if they were kings, then it is not an essential property of royal power to reside in a single person. "If one of these offend," say you, "then may the other report upon him to the people, or to the Senate, that he may be accused and condemned." And is it not an act of judging that is performed by the Senate and the people, to whom that second colleague reports? So that if you give any weight to your own statement, there was no need of a second colleague to judge the first. Alas, what a defender!—really to be pitied if you were not rather to be cursed! You lie every way so open to blows that if one were minded for sport's sake to thrust at any part of you, he could hardly miss, were his aim never so ill.

You call it "ridiculous that a king should be supposed willing to appoint judges empowered to condemn him to death." But against you I cite the nowise ridiculous but most excellent Emperor Trajan, who when, as the custom was, he delivered to Saburanus, Captain of

199. The nephew and heir of Julius Caesar who established his hold on the empire by defeating Antony and Cleopatra.

the Praetorian Guard, the dagger which was the badge of his office, frequently thus admonished him: "Take this sword, and use it for me, if I do as I ought; if otherwise, against me; because for the governor and guide of all to go astray is especially unlawful." This Dion and Aurelius Victor say of him. You see here that an admirable emperor appointed one, though not his peer, to be his judge. Tiberius perhaps might have said such words as these out of vanity and hypocrisy; but it is almost a crime to imagine that Trajan, a man most virtuous and blameless, did not speak in all sincerity what he thought true and right and just. Superior to the Senate in power, he might have refused them obedience; how much the more righteous was it that he actually did obey them purely out of consideration for his duty, and acknowledge that they were by law set above him. Pliny tells us in his Panegyric: "The Senate both desired and commanded you to be Consul a fourth time; this, you may trust your own submissiveness, is no word of flattery, but of command"; and a little after: "What you strive for is this,—namely, to recall and restore our liberty."[200] And what Trajan thought of himself, the Senate thought of Trajan, and were of opinion that their authority was indeed supreme, for they who might command their emperor might judge him. So the emperor Marcus Aurelius, when Cassius governor of Syria endeavored to get the empire from him, submitted himself to the judgment of either the Senate or the Roman people, and declared himself ready to lay down the government if they would have it so. How indeed could anyone appraise and determine the right of kings better or more truly than out of the very mouths of the best kings?

Indeed by the law of nature every good king always accounts the senate or the people not only his peers but his betters. But a tyrant being by nature inferior to all men, whoever is stronger than he ought to be accounted equal and superior to him. For even as nature of old taught men from force and violence to betake themselves to law, so wherever the law is set at naught, the same dictate of nature must

200. Pliny *Panegyrics* 78.

necessarily prompt us to betake ourselves to force again. "To be convinced of this," says Cicero *pro Sestio*, "is the part of wisdom; to practice it, the part of courage; but both to think and do it too belongs to manly excellence accomplished in full measure." Let this stand then as a settled maxim of the law of nature, never to be shaken by any tricks or sleights of kings' toadies, that the senate or the people are superior to kings good or bad. This is what yourself do in effect confess, when you tell us that the authority of kings was derived from the people. For that power which they gave the king, they do yet, by nature and a sort of virtue, or, as I may say, *virtually,* even though they have given it to the other party, hold in themselves; for whatever natural causes produce any effect in such outstanding degree still retain more of their own virtue than they impart; nor do they, by imparting to others, exhaust themselves. You see, the closer we approach nature, the more evidently does the people's power stand out above that of the king.

And this is likewise certain, that the people, so the choice be but left free to them, never grant their power to a king in absolute and unconditional ownership, nor by nature can do so; but only for the public safety and liberty, which when the king ceases to take care of, then it is understood that the people have given him nothing at all: for, being warned by nature herself, they gave it him for a certain purpose only; so that if neither nature nor the people can attain this, then their gift or grant will be no more valid than any other void covenant or agreement. These reasons establish unshakably the people's superiority to the king; and so your "most powerful and convincing argument that a king cannot be judged by his people, because in his kingdom he has no peer or superior" melts away. For you take for granted that which we do not grant by any means.

"In a democracy," you say, "the magistrates, being appointed by the people, may likewise be punished by the people for crime; in an aristocracy the nobles may be punished by their colleagues; but it is monstrous that a king in his own kingdom should be forced to plead for his life." What can you conclude but that they who set up a king

over them are the most wretched and foolish of mankind? But pray
what is the reason why the people may not punish a guilty king as
well as a popularly appointed magistracy or the nobility? Do you
think that all peoples who live under kings were so desperately in love
with slavery that when they were free they chose vassalage, and to put
themselves all and entirely under the despotism of one man—often
an evil man, often a fool—and all this in such wise that against a most
outrageous tyrant, if such fall to their lot, they have not left themselves in the laws or in nature herself any protection whatever for their
safety, or asylum for themselves? Why then do they tender conditions
to their kings when these first come to the throne, and even prescribe
laws for them to govern by? Is it that they may suffer themselves to
be the more trampled upon and laughed to scorn? Would a whole
people ever so vilify themselves, so forsake their own interest, and fail
their own cause, as to place all their hopes in one man, usually a most
empty insubstantial one? Why, likewise, do kings swear an oath not
to act anything contrary to law? In order, of course, that wretched
mortals may learn to their deep sorrow that only kings may perjure
themselves with impunity! This is the plain import of your wicked
conclusions: "If a king that is elected promise even upon oath any thing
which if he had not promised perhaps they would not have chosen
him, yet if he refuse to abide by the agreement he cannot be judged
by the people. Nay, though at his election he have sworn to his subjects that he will administer justice according to the laws of the realm,
and that if he do not they shall be discharged of their oath of allegiance and he shall *ipso facto* abdicate, yet if he break his oath it is God
and not man that must exact the penalty." I have transcribed these
lines, not for their elegance, for they are barbarously expressed, nor
because I think there needs any additional answer to them, for they
answer themselves—they explode and damn themselves—by their
barefaced falsehood and loathsomeness, but to recommend you to
kings for your distinguished merits, in order that among so many
places as there are at court they may procure for you some preferment or office that may be fit for you. Some are Chancellors of the

Exchequer, some are cup-bearers, some seneschals and stewards, some Masters of the Revels: you will most fittingly be their Master of the Perjuries. You shall not be, like the famous Petronius,[201] Master of the Royal Literary Graces—you are too ignorant for that—but you shall be Lord High Master of the Royal Treacheries.

Yet, that all men may acknowledge how in you extreme folly is joined with extreme knavery, let us weigh a little more carefully those brilliant propositions which you have just asserted. "A king," say you, "though at his election he have sworn to his subjects that he will govern according to law," and that if he do not "they shall be discharged of their oath of allegiance, and he shall *ipso facto* abdicate," yet cannot be deposed or punished by them. Why not a king, pray, as well as a magistrate in a democracy? Because in a democracy the people do not transfer all their power to the magistrate. But do they then vest it all in a king, to whom they convey royal power over themselves for no longer than he uses it well? Therefore a king sworn to observe the laws, may, if he transgress them, be punished and deposed as well as a democratic magistrate. So you can make no more use of your all-powerful argument that the entire power has been transferred to the king, for it is hoist with your own petard.

Hear now another "most powerful and invincible reason why subjects" cannot judge their king, viz. "because he is bound by no law, being himself the sole lawgiver." But as I have so often proved this to be utterly false, even this invincible argument of yours, as well as the former, comes to nothing. For the rest, if a king is sometimes left unpunished for personal and private crimes, as fornication, adultery, and the like, this is not because the people feel that he ought not in justice be punished, but because they are long-suffering—lest they be more hurt through disturbances occasioned by the king's death and the change of state, than profited by the vindication of individual rights. But when he begins to be injurious and insufferable to everybody, then indeed all nations have believed it lawful to slay the tyrant

201. Petronius Arbiter, literary functionary in Nero's court who committed suicide in A.D. 66.

any how, condemned or uncondemned. Hence Marcus Tullius in his Second Philippic says of those that killed Caesar: "They were the first that ran through with their swords, not a man who affected to be king, but one who was actually settled in the government; which, as it was a glorious and godlike action, so it is set before us for our imitation." How unlike are you to him!

"Murder, adultery, injustice, are not regal and public, but private and personal crimes." Well said, toady! you have obliged all pimps and profligates at court by this expression. How charmingly by a single act do you play at once both parasite and pimp! "A king that is an adulterer or a murderer may yet govern well, and consequently ought not to be put to death, for with his life he must lose his kingdom; and it was never approved by God's laws or man's that for one and the same crime a man was to be punished twice." Shameless disreputable foulmouth! By the same reason the magistrates in a democracy or in an aristocracy ought never to be put to death, for fear of double punishment, nor any corrupt judge or senator, for with their lives they must lose their magistracy too.

As you have endeavored to take all power out of the people's hands, and vest it in the king, so you would all majesty too: a delegated transferred majesty if you will, but surely not their original primary majesty, any more than their original primary power. "A king," you say, "cannot commit treason against his people, but a people can against their king." And yet a king is what he is for the people only, not the people for him. Hence I infer that the whole body of the people, or a majority of them, must needs have greater power than the king. This you deny, and begin to cast up accounts. "He has more power than any one, than any two, than any three, than any ten, than any hundred, than any thousand, than any ten thousand." So be it. "More power than half the people." I will not deny that. "Add now half of the other half, will he not have more power than all those?" By no means!

Go on, o skilful logician, why do you take away the counting-board; do you not understand arithmetical progression? He begins to reckon after another manner, and asks "whether the king together with the nobility have not more power"? No, good Master Chapman Chop-and-Change,[202] I deny that too, if by the nobility you mean the Lords only, because it may happen that among them there may be not one man deserving the name of noble: for it often falls out that among the Commons there are many far better and wiser men than among the Lords. When the majority or the better part of the people joins these, I should not scruple to say that they represent and stand for the whole people. "But if the king is not superior in power to all the people together, he is then king but of single persons, not of all taken together." True; no more he is, unless they are content he should be. Now balance your accounts, and you will find that by miscasting you have lost your principal.

"The English say that the right of majesty by its origin and its nature resides in the people; this would indeed bring on the overthrow of all states." What, of an aristocracy and of a democracy? But you say well, after all, for what if it should overthrow a gynaecocracy too, under which state, they say, you go near to being beaten at home? Would not the English do you a kindness in that, Master Faint-heart? But there is no hope for that; for it is most justly so ordered that since you would impose tyranny upon all mankind abroad, you yourself should live in a shameful impotent unmanly slavery at home.

"It behooves us English to tell you," you say, "what we mean by the word People." There are a great many things which it would more behoove you to be told; for of things that more immediately concern you, you seem altogether ignorant, and never to have learnt or even been able to understand more than the alphabet. But this you suppose you know, that by the word people we mean the common people only, because we "have abolished the House of Lords." And yet this is the very thing that shows that under the word people we comprehend all our citizens, of what order and degree soever; in that we have established a single supreme Commons' House only, in which the

202. In the Latin Milton refers to Salmasius as Vertumnus, the Roman god of incessant changeableness.

lords also have by law the right to vote as a part of the people, not in their own right as they did before, but as representing those constituencies by which they have been chosen.

Then you inveigh against the common people as being "blind and dull, ignorant of the art of governing"; you say there is "nothing more empty and changeable than they, nothing more fickle and excitable." All which is very true of yourself, and it is true likewise of the rabble, but not of the middle sort, amongst whom the wisest men and most skilful in affairs are generally found; the rest are most commonly diverted, on the one hand by luxury and wealth, on the other by want and poverty, from achieving excellence, and from the study of laws and government.

"There are many ways" now, you say, "by which kings are established, so as not to be beholden to the people at all on that score," and first "those who hold their kingdom by inheritance." But those nations must certainly be slaves, and born to slavery, who acknowledge a lord and master so absolute that they believe themselves to have fallen to his lot by inheritance, without any consent of their own. Surely they cannot be held to be citizens, or freemen, or freeborn, nor are they to be accounted as having a body politic, but must be reckoned among the goods and chattels, estates and properties of their owner and his son and heir; for as to ownership I see no difference betwixt them and slaves or cattle. Secondly, you say: "He that carves out a kingdom with his sword cannot acknowledge the people as the originator of the power he has extended or usurped." But what we are talking about now is not a conquering king, but a conquered king; what a conqueror may do, we will discourse elsewhere; do you keep to your subject.

Whereas you repeatedly ascribe to kings the ancient right of the paterfamilias, in order to fetch thence "a model of the unlimited power of kings," I have shown already over and over that there is no likeness at all betwixt them. And that very Aristotle whom you keep prating about would have taught you as much even at the beginning of his *Politics,* if you had read it. There he says that they judge amiss who think there is but little difference betwixt a king and the head of a household: "For a kingdom is different from a household, not in number only, but in kind." For when villages grew to be towns and cities, that right of the king as head of the household vanished by degrees, and was recognized no more. Hence Diodorus[203] in his first book says that anciently kingdoms were transmitted not to the former kings' sons, but to those whose services to the people were most eminent. And Justin says: "Originally the government of peoples and races was by kings, who were exalted to that pinnacle of majesty, not by soliciting the people's support, but for a moderation well-regarded among good men."[204]

Whence it is manifest that in the very beginning of nations, paternal and hereditary government was soon replaced by personal worth and the people's right. This is the most natural reason and cause, and was the true rise of royal power. For it was for this very reason that at first men entered into societies: not that any one might insult over all the rest, but that in case any should injure another, law might not be wanting, and a judge between man and man, whereby the injured might be protected or at least avenged. When men were at first scattered asunder and straying about, some wise and eloquent man brought them over into civil life; "chiefly," say you, "that when he had got them gathered together he might exercise dominion over them." Perhaps you meant this of Nimrod,[205] who is said to have been the first tyrant, or else it is your own wickedness only, which could have no application to those great and high-souled men of yore—a mere fiction of yours, not asserted, as far as I know, by anyone before you. For it is delivered by the memorials of all the ancients that those first founders of cities had in view not any profit or power of their own, but the advantage and safety of mankind.

One thing I cannot pass by, with which I suppose you intended to decorate the rest of this chapter as with some motto in mosaic in-

203. Diodorus Siculus *Bibliotēkē Historikē* 1.43.6.
204. Junianus Justinus *Epitoma Historiarum Philippicarum Pompei Trogi* 1.1.1.
205. Gen. 8:8–10.

lay. "If a Consul," say you, "had been required to come to trial while still in office, there must have been a Dictator created for that purpose;" though at the beginning you had said that "for that very purpose the Consul's colleague was provided." Just so your statements always agree with one another, and reveal on almost every page how whatever you say or write upon any subject is of no weight or importance. "Under the ancient Anglo-Saxon kings," you say, "it was never the custom to call the people to the national councils." If any of our own countrymen had asserted such a thing, I could without much trouble have convinced him that he was in error. But I am not so much concerned at this assertion of yours, which wanders about in foreign parts, and wanders in its mind too about our affairs. This in effect is all you say of the right of kings in general. The many things that remain—for you much too often digress—I omit: things that either rest on no foundation or are nothing to the purpose; for it is not my design to be thought your equal in talkativeness.

### CHAPTER VIII.

If you had published your own opinion, Salmasius, concerning the right of kings in general, without insulting anyone, albeit amid this revolution in England, yet while you did but use your own liberty to write, there was no reason why any Englishman should be displeased with you, nor would you have been less successful in establishing the opinion you maintain. For if it be a positive command both of Moses and of Christ "That all men whatsoever, whether Spaniards, French, Italians, Germans, English, or Scots, should be subject to their kings, whether good or bad," as you asserted before (page 127), what business had you, a foreigner, and unknown, to babble about our *laws*, and read us professorial lectures out of them as if they were your own papers and miscellanies, when all the while you had taught us already in a great many words that our laws, be they how they will, ought to give way to the laws of God?

But now it is apparent that you have undertaken the defence of this royal cause not so much out of your own inclination as because you were hired, partly for payment—and a good round payment too, considering your employer's finances,—and partly by hope of some greater reward hereafter; hired, I say, to rend and tear with your disreputable book the English, who trouble none of their neighbors, and meddle with their own matters only. Were it not so, is it credible that any man should be so shameless and so mad as not to hesitate, though he be a stranger far away, to plunge into our affairs for nothing, and even attach himself to a party? What the devil is it to you what the English do amongst themselves? What would you have, Olus? what do you mean? Have you no concerns of your own at home? I wish you had the same concerns that the much celebrated Olus had in the Epigram;[206] and perhaps so you have; you thoroughly deserve them. Or did that hotspur your wife, who is said to have spurred you— willing horse!—to write all this stuff to please the exiled Charles,— did she bode you some more profitable professorship in England, and God knows what fees, at Charles's return? But assure yourselves, *Madame la femme et Monsieur le mari,* that England has no place for a wolf or for the Seigneur of a wolf. No wonder, then, that you have so often spit so much venom at our English mastiffs! It were better for you to return to those illustrious titles of yours in France: first to that hungerstarved Seigneurie of St. Loup, and next to that *sacré* Council of the Most Christian King;[207] you are too far abroad from your own country for a counsellor. But I see full well that France desires not either you or your counsel, and did not, even when you were back a few years ago, and were beginning to smell out and hunt after a Cardinal's kitchen.[208] She is right, by my troth, she is right, and can willingly allow you, you French capon, with your mankind wife and your desks chock-full of emptiness, to wander about, till somewhere in creation you light upon a dole bountiful enough for a grammarian-

---

206. Martial *Epigrams* 7.10.
207. The King of France.
208. Cardinal Richelieu had offered Salmasius a place at court.

---

cavalier or illustrious hippo-critic,—always supposing any king or state has a mind to bid highest for a vagabond pedant that is on sale. But here am I that will bid for you; whether you are a merchantable commodity or not, and what you are worth, we shall see at once.

You say: "The parricides assert that the kingdom of England is of a composite kind, not purely royal." In the time of Edward the Sixth, Sir Thomas Smith, a countryman of ours, a good lawyer and statesman, whom you will not call a parricide, asserts the same thing near the beginning of his book on the commonwealth of England.[209] He states that it is true not of our government only, but of almost all others— this upon the opinion of Aristotle; and that otherwise no government can subsist. But as if you thought it a sin to say anything without unsaying it, you repeat your former threadbare contradictions. You say: "There neither is nor ever was any nation that did not understand by the name of king that power which is inferior to God alone, and which has God for its sole judge." And yet, a little after, you confess that "The name of king was formerly given to such powers and magistrates as had not a full and unlimited right, but one depending upon the people's will," for example "the sufetes of the Carthaginians, the judges of the Hebrews, the kings of the Lacedaemonians," and, lastly, "of Aragon." Isn't this a pretty piece of self-consistency?

Then you muster out of Aristotle five several sorts of monarchies, only one of which possessed that right which you say is common to all kings. Concerning this I have said already more than once that no instance of it, either cited by Aristotle or anywhere else, has existed. The other four kingships, he clearly shows, were limited by laws, and subject to them. The first of these was that of the Lacedaemonians, which of the four limited monarchies did in his opinion best deserve the name of kingship. The second, of a kind foreign to the Greeks, was lasting only in that it was limited, and that the people willingly submitted to it; for according to Aristotle's own opinion in his fifth book, once the people are unwilling, whatever king retains the throne

209. Sir Thomas Smith, *The Commonwealth of England* (1583 and several subsequent editions), 1.5.

against their will, will instantly be no king, but a tyrant. The same is to be said of his third sort of kings, which he calls Aesymnetes, who were chosen by the people, most commonly for a certain time only, and for certain purposes; such, or nearly such, were the Roman dictators. The fourth is the kind that reigned in the heroic days, upon whom for their extraordinary merits the people of their own accord conferred the government, but yet limited; nor yet did these retain the throne unless the people were willing. And these four sorts of kingship, he says, differ from tyranny in no respect more than in this: that these governments are with the consent of the people, and tyranny against their will. The fifth sort of royal government, finally, called παμβασιλεία, and endowed with the supreme power, which you pretend to be the right of all kings, is utterly condemned by the philosopher, as neither profitable nor just nor natural—unless some people should be able to endure a government of this kind, and withal should confer it upon such as outshine all others in virtue. These things lie open and accessible to anyone in the third book of the *Politics*.

But you, that for once in your life you might appear witty and florid, I suppose, pleased yourself by likening "these five sorts of monarchy to the five zones" of the world. "Between the two extremes of royal power three more temperate kinds appear to be interposed, even as those which lie in the midst between the torrid and the frigid zones." Pretty wit! what lovely comparisons you always make us! Away with you, doublequick, whither you banish "absolute monarchy," to the frigid zone, which after your arrival will be more than doubly frigid. Meanwhile we await from you, our modern Archimedes,[210] that wondrous globe which you describe, in which there be two extreme zones, one torrid and the other frigid, and three temperate ones between.

"The kings of the Lacedaemonians," you say, "might lawfully be imprisoned, but it was not lawful to put them to death." Why not? Is it because the officers of justice and some foreign soldiers, being

210. Archimedes (c. 287–212 B.C.) was a mathematician, a geometer, and an inventor.

surprised at the novelty of the thing, thought it not lawful to lead King Agis to his execution, though condemned to die? Yea, even the Spartan people took his death ill, not because it was a king that was condemned to die, but because he was a good man and beloved by them, and had been hunted to his death by a faction of wealthy men. Says Plutarch: "Agis was the first king that was put to death by the ephors";[211] in which words he tells us only what actually was done, not what lawfully might be done. For it were childish to imagine that they who may lawfully bring a king to trial, and imprison him, may not also lawfully put him to death.

At last you gird yourself up to tackle the law of English kings. "In England," you say, "there was always one king at a time." This you say because you had said before that "unless a king be sole in the government, he cannot be a king." If so, some who I used to think had been kings of England were not really kings; for—to omit many of our Saxon kings, who had either sons or brothers partners with them in the government—it is not disputed that King Henry II, of the Norman stock, reigned jointly with his son.

"Let them show," say you, "any kingdom under the government of a single person who has not absolute power, in some kingdoms, however, more loosened, in others more tightened." Ass, do you show us any absolute power that is loosened; is not that power that is absolute the supreme power? How can it then be both supreme and loosened? Whatsoever kings you shall acknowledge to be invested with a loosened power, those I will clearly prove to have no absolute power; and consequently to be inferior to a people free by nature, which, as it is its own lawmaker, can loosen or tighten the power of the king.

Whether the whole of Britain was anciently governed by kings or no is uncertain; it is most likely that they employed now one form of government, now another, according to the exigencies of the time. Whence Tacitus says: "The Britons anciently were under kings; now

---

211. Plutarch *Life of Agis and Cleomenes* 19.6.

their chiefs distract them into parties and factions."[212] When the Romans left them, they were about forty years without kings; that "perpetual kingship" which you allege had therefore no existence in ancient times. I positively assert that their kingship was not hereditary, which is evident both from the succession of their kings, and from their way of creating them; for the approval of the people is asked in express words. When the king has taken the accustomed oath, the archbishop, stepping to the four sides of the platform erected for the purpose, asks the body of the people four several times in these words, "Will ye consent to have this man your king?"[213] Just as if he said, Roman fashion, "Do ye desire, do ye command, this man to reign?" Which would be needless if the kingdom were by law hereditary.

But with kings usurpation passes very frequently for law and right. You strive to ground Charles's royal right, who was so often conquered himself, upon the right of conquest. William, surnamed "the Conqueror," forsooth, subdued us. But they who are not strangers to our history know full well that the strength of the English nation was not so broken in that one fight at Hastings but that they might easily have renewed the war. Yet they chose rather to accept a king than to endure a conqueror and a tyrant: they swear therefore to William to be his liegemen, and he likewise swears to them at the altar to conduct himself towards them in all respects as a good king ought. When he broke his word, and the English betook themselves again to their arms, William, mistrusting his strength, renewed upon the Gospels his oath to keep the ancient laws of England. Therefore, if after that he miserably oppressed the English, he did it not by right of conquest, but by right of perjury. Besides, it is certain that many ages ago the conquerors and conquered coalesced into one and the same people; so that that right of conquest, if any such there ever were, must needs have been long ago barred by antiquity. His own words at his death, which I report as transcribed from the Caen Book—a

212. Tacitus *Agricola* 12.
213. Coronation oath recorded for Edward II, Richard II, and Henry IV.

thoroughly trustworthy document—remove all doubt. "I appoint no man," says he, "heir of the kingdom of England."[214] By which words that right of conquest and that right of inheritance were at once and together officially bewailed as dead, and buried together with the dead Conqueror.

I see now that you have got a place at court, as I foretold: you are become High Treasurer and Steward of Court Craft; and the following passage you seem to write as if by virtue of your office, magnificent Sir. "If any among preceding kings, being thereunto compelled by factions of great men or seditions among the common people, have remitted somewhat of his right, that cannot hinder a successor from reclaiming it unto himself." A proper reminder! If therefore at any time our ancestors have through neglect lost any thing that was their right, will that hinder us their posterity? If they were willing to promise for themselves to be slaves, they could make no such promise for us, who shall always retain the same right of setting ourselves free that they had of enslaving themselves to any whomsoever.

You wonder "how it comes to pass that a king of Great Britain must nowadays be looked upon as merely a magistrate of the kingdom, whereas they who govern other kingdoms in Christendom wield plenary and unlimited authority." For Scotland I refer you to Buchanan; for your native France (where you seem a stranger), to Hotman's *Franco-Gallia* and Gerard the historian of France: for the rest, to other authors, of whom none as far as I know were Independents: out of whom you might have learned concerning the right of kings a quite other lesson than what you teach.

Not being able to claim for the kings of England a tyrannical power by right of conquest, you now make trial by right of toadyism. Kings proclaim openly, you say, that they reign "by the Grace of God." What of it? What if they were to proclaim that they *are* Gods? They might, I believe, easily get you for a priest! So the Pontiff of Canterbury[215]

214. This quotation appeared in a transcription in William Camden, *Brittania* (1607), and in John Sadler, *Rights of the Kingdom* (1649).
215. William Laud, Archbishop of Canterbury beginning in 1633.

made public pretence to archbishop it "by the Providence of God."
Are you such a fool that you refuse to acknowledge the Pope as king
in the Church in order to establish the king a more than Pope in the
State? But in the statutes of the realm, you say, the king is called "our
Lord the king." Flunkey, doorkeeper slave at the king's levee, you are
turned out on a sudden marvelous skilled in the names in our statutes
that you call out to your royal owner! But what you know not is that
many are called lords who are not lords; you know not how unfair it
is to determine of the right and truth of things from titles of honor,
not to say of flattery. Make the same inference from the Parliament's
being called "the King's Parliament"; for it is called the king's bridle
too, and the king is not on that account any more master of his Parliament than a horse is master of his bridle. But "why is it not a fair
inference that Parliament is the king's, since he summons it?" I will
tell you. The Roman Senate's being summoned by a Consul did not
make him master of that assembly either. And so, too, when the king
summons Parliament, he does it by virtue and in discharge of his duty
and of the office which he has received from the people, that he may
advise even with them he summons, about the difficult business of
the kingdom, not his own; or if any can be called his own, this they
have always been wont to move last, and not at the king's pleasure,
but even at the pleasure of Parliament. And they whom it concerns
to know this, know very well that Parliament anciently might by law
meet twice in the course of a year, whether summoned or not. But
"the laws too are called the king's laws." These phrases, to be sure,
are trappings and gewgaws for a king, but a king of England can of
himself make no law, for he was appointed not to make laws, but to
keep the laws which the people have made.

And you yourself here admit that "Parliament meets to make
laws." Wherefore the law is also called the Law of the Land, and the
Common Law. Whence king Aethelstan in the Preamble to his laws,
speaking to all the people, says: I have bestowed all things "upon you
according to your own law." [216] And in the form of the oath whereby

216. From William Lambarde's *Archaionomia;* Athelstan reigned from 927 to 944.

the kings of England were wont to bind themselves before they were made kings, the people formally demand of them: "Do you grant those just laws which the people shall choose?" The king answers, "I grant." And when you say: "While Parliament is not in session, the king governs the whole state of the kingdom fully and entirely by royal right," you again stray wide of the truth by the length and breadth of all England. For he can determine nothing of much moment with respect to either peace or war; nor even in administering justice can he interfere with the decisions of the courts. It is on this account the judges swear that in performing their judicial functions they will do nothing but according to law, even though the king himself by word, or injunction, yes, or letter under his own seal, should command otherwise. Hence it is that the king is often said in our law to be "an infant," and to possess his rights and dignities only as a child or a ward does his: see the *Mirror of Justices,* Chapter 4, Section 22.[217] Hence too that common saying amongst us, "The king can do no wrong"; which you interpret in this rascally fashion: "That is no wrong which the king does, because he is not liable to be punished for it." From this single interpretation would not anyone see through the man's astonishing impudence and villainy?

"It belongs to the head," you say, "to command, and not to the members; the king is the head of the parliament." Would you argue so flippantly if you were wise in heart or had any gust or savor of wit?

You are mistaken again (but there is no end of your mistakes) in not distinguishing the king's Councillors from the Houses of Parliament; for the king was so bound that he might choose not even all of his Council, and none to be of the House of Lords unless approved by the rest, while as for choosing anyone to the House of Commons, he never so much as pretended to it. They whom the people appointed to that service were chosen severally for their respective constituencies by the votes of all; I speak now of things universally known, and therefore I am the shorter. But you say: "It is false that

217. Andrew Horne, *Mirror of Justices* (1642).

Parliament was instituted by the people, as the worshippers of Saint Independency assert." Now I see why you strive with so much violence to subvert the papacy: you carry another papacy in your belly, as we say. For what else should you be in labor of, you wife of your wife, you he-wolf pregnant by a she-wolf, but either a monster or some new sort of papacy? At least you make he-saints and she-saints at your pleasure, as if you were a genuine Pope; you absolve kings too, of sin; and as if you had laid low the Pope your enemy, you deck and enrich yourself with his spoils. But whereas you have not yet quite prostrated the Pope till the second and third and perhaps the fourth and fifth part of your book de Primatu come out, and whereas this will bore many poor mortals to death ere you shall put down the Pope by it, let it suffice you in the meantime, I beseech you, to climb up to only an Anti-papacy. For besides that Independency that you deride, there is another she-saint that you have canonized in good earnest, that is, Royal Tyranny; you shall therefore be Supreme Pontiff of Saint Tyranny Royal; and that you may want none of the Papal titles, you shall be even "a Servant of the Servants," not of God, but of the court; for that curse pronounced upon Canaan[218] seems to stick as close to you as your shirt.

You call the people "a beast." What are you then yourself? For neither that Sacré Council nor your Holy Wolf can exempt you, its Sire and Seigneur, from being one of the people, nay, of the rabble rout; nor can make you other than the loathsome beast you are. Indeed the Prophets in Holy Scripture shadow forth to us the monarchy and dominion of great kings by the name and under the figure of a great beast.

You say: "There is no mention of a Parliament held under the kings before William." It is not worth while to quibble about a French word; the thing was always in being, and you yourself admit that in Saxon times it used to be called "Concilium Sapientum," Witenagemot, or Meeting of the Wise Men. And there are wise men among

218. Gen. 9:25.

the common people as well as among the nobility. But "in the statute of Merton, in the twentieth of Henry the Third, mention is made of earls and Barons only." Thus you are always imposed upon by words, who yet have frittered away your whole life in nothing else but words. For we know very well that in that age the word Baron was applied not only to the Wardens of the Cinque Ports, and to members from cities, but sometimes even to tradesmen; and doubtless all members of Parliament, though commoners never so much, might then with all the greater reason be called Barons. For the Statute of Marlbridge and most of the other statutes declare in express words that in the fifty-second year of the same king the commoners as well as the lords were summoned. These commoners King Edward the Third, in the Preamble of the Statute Staple, as you very learnedly quote it for me, calls "Comitatuum Magnates," the great men of the counties, those, to wit, "that had come out of the several cities to serve the whole county." And these it was that constituted the House of Commons, and neither were lords, nor could be. Again, a book more ancient than those statutes, called *Modus habendi Parlamenta,* or *The Manner of Holding Parliaments,*[219] tells us that the King and the Commons may hold a Parliament and enact laws though the Earls and the Bishops are absent, but that the King with the Earls and the Bishops cannot do so in the absence of the Commons. And there is a reason given for it, viz., that before any Earls or Bishops were made, kings yet held Parliaments and Councils with their people; then, too, the Earls serve for themselves only, the Commons each for his constituency. Therefore the Commons are felt to be present in the name of the whole nation, and in that name to be more powerful and more noble than the Lords, and altogether to be preferred.

But "the power of judicature," you say, "never was vested in the House of Commons." Nor was it ever vested in the King of England. Remember, though, that originally all power proceeded, and yet does proceed from the people. Which Marcus Tullius excellently well

219. An account written around 1320 purporting to record constitutional custom prior to the Norman Conquest.

shows in his oration *Of the Agrarian Law:* "As it is fitting that all powers, authorities, and commissions proceed from the people as a whole,
this is especially true of those which are ordained and appointed for
the people's benefit and interest. In such a case on the one hand the
people as a whole pick out whoever they think will best advance their
interests, and on the other hand each individual by electioneering
and by his vote may pave the way to receiving the appointment."

Here you see the true origin of Parliaments—one much more
ancient than the Saxon chronicles. Whilst we may dwell in such a
light of truth and wisdom, you labor in vain to spread around us the
gloom of the Dark Ages. Let no one think I say this as if I would
derogate in the least from the authority and prudence of our ancestors, who certainly went further in the enacting of good laws than either those ages or their own wit and learning seem to have been capable of. And though they seldom imposed laws that were not good,
yet, being conscious of the ignorance and infirmity of human nature,
they chose to hand down to posterity as the foundation of all laws,
this principle, which likewise all our lawyers recognize: that if any law
or custom be contrary to the law of God or of nature, or, in fine, to
reason, it shall not be held a valid law. Whence you may learn that
even though you shall perchance succeed in finding in our law some
proclamation or statute whereby tyrannical power is ascribed to the
king, yet this, since it would be repugnant to the will of God, to nature, and to reason, is repealed among us by that general and primary
law of ours which I have cited, and is null and void. But indeed you
will find in our law no such right of kings. Since it is plain therefore
that the power of judicature was originally in the people themselves,
and that the English never did by any Lex Regia part with it to the
king (for the kings of England neither use to judge any man, nor can
do it, otherwise than according to laws already provided and approved:
Fleta, Book 1, Chap. 17),[220] it follows that this power remains yet
whole and entire in the people themselves. For that it was either never

220. *Fleta* is a legal compilation and treatise written in medieval times. John Selden's
edition of 1616 circulated during the seventeenth century.

conveyed away to the House of Peers, or if it were, that it may be re-covered from them again by law, you yourself will not deny.

But "it is in the king's power," you say, "to make a village into a borough, and that into a city, and consequently the king does appoint those that constitute the Lower House." But I say towns and boroughs are more ancient than kings, and the people are the people, though they should live in the open fields.

And now we take huge delight in your Anglicisms, "County Court," "The Turn," "Hundred": you have learnt with amazing do-cility to count your hundred Jacobuses in English!

> "Who provided" Salmasius with his *Hundred,*
> And "taught the magpie to attempt our words?
> His Master of Arts was his guts," and Jacobuses
> One *Hundred,* the guts of the exiled king's money-bag.
> "For if the hope of treacherous coin shall gleam,"
> The very man who but now threatened to puff away
> With a single breath the Primacy of the Pope as Antichrist
> Will of his own accord "sing a tune" to praise a Cardinal.

Next you subjoin a long discourse of the Earls and the Barons, to show that the king created them all; which we readily grant, and for that reason they were most commonly at the king's beck; wherefore we have done well to take care that for the future they shall not be judges of a free people. You affirm that "the power of calling parlia-ments as often as he pleases, and of dissolving them when he pleases, has belonged to the king time out of mind." Whether you, merce-nary foreign buffoon, who transcribe what some fugitives dictate to you, or the explicit words of our own laws are more to be trusted in this matter, we shall inquire hereafter. "But," say you, "there is an-other argument, and an invincible one, to prove the power of the kings of England superior to that of the Parliament. The king's power is continuous and of course, and by itself administers the government without the Parliament; that of the Parliament is out of course, and limited to particulars only, and incapable of enacting anything valid without the king." Where should I say the great force of this argument lies hid? In the words "of course and continuous"? Why, many inferior magistrates, whom we call justices of the peace, have a power of course and continuous. Have they therefore the supreme power? And I have said already that the king's power was committed to him by the people for the definite purpose that by the authority entrusted to him he should see that nothing were done contrary to law, and that he might watch over our laws, not lay his own upon us; and consequently that the king has no power but in and through the courts of the realm; nay, all the ordinary power is rather the people's, who determine all controversies themselves by juries of twelve men. And hence it is, that when a defendant is asked in court, "How will you be tried?" he answers always, according to law and custom, "By God and my country"—not by God and the King or the King's deputy. But the authority of the Parliament, which indeed and in truth is the supreme power of the people committed to that senate, this power, I say, if it may be called extraordinary, out of order, or out of course, must be so called by reason of its eminence only. And another reason: our Estates in Parliament, as everybody knows, are called *Orders*, and therefore cannot properly be said to be out of order; and they have a continuous control and authority, if not in act, or actually, as the phrase goes, yet potentially and virtually, over all courts and ordinary powers,—and this without the king.

And now it seems our barbarous terms grate upon your critical ears, forsooth! whereas, if I had leisure, or it were worth the trouble, I could reckon up so many barbarisms of yours in this one book that if you were to be whipped for them as you deserve, all schoolboys' ferules must surely be broken upon you; nor would you receive so many pieces of gold as that worst of poets did aforetime, but many more boxes on the ear. You say: "It is a prodigy more monstrous than all the most absurd opinions in the world put together, that the madmen should make a distinction betwixt the king's person and his power." I will not quote what every author has said upon this subject; but if by *person* you mean the *man,* then Chrysostom, who was no madman, might have taught you that the person might without absurdity be distinguished from the power; for he explains the apostle's command to be subject to the higher powers, as meant of the thing, the power itself, and not of the man. And why may not I say that a king who acts any thing contrary to law, acts so far forth as a private person or a tyrant, and not as a king invested with legal authority? If you do not know that there may be in one and the same man more persons or capacities than one, and that those capacities may in thought and conception be severed from the man himself, you are altogether ignorant both of Latinity and of common sense. But this you say to absolve kings from all sin, and to make us believe that you are invested with that Primacy you have snatched from the Pope.

"The king," you say, "is supposed incapable of crime, because no punishment follows upon any crime of his." Whoever therefore is not punished offends not: it is not the theft but the punishment that makes the thief! Salmasius the Grammarian commits no solecisms now, because he has pulled his hand from under the ferule! When you have overthrown the Pope, let these, then, be the canons of your pontificate, or at least your indulgences, whether you shall choose to be called the High Priest of Saint Tyranny, or of St. Slavery.—I pass by the foul abusive language which at the last of your chapter you have heaped upon "the state of the English Commonwealth and Church"; it is common to such as you, contemptible varlet, to rail most at those things that are most praiseworthy.

But that I may not seem to have asserted anything rashly concerning the right of the king among us, or rather concerning the people's right over the king, I will not grudge the task to cite from our records themselves a few things indeed of many, yet such as will make it evident that the English lately tried their king according to the settled laws of the realm and the customs of their ancestors. After the Romans quitted this island, the Britons for about forty years were *sui juris,* and without kings; of those whom they first set up, some they put to death. Gildas reprehends them for that, upon a very different ground from yours,—not for killing their kings, but for killing them without trial, or, to use his own words, "without an inquiry into the truth." Vortigern, as Nennius[221] informs us, the most ancient of all historians next to Gildas, was for his incestuous marriage with his own daughter condemned "by St. Germain and a general council of the Britons," and his son Vortimer set up in his stead. This came to pass not long after St. Augustine's death; which easily disproves your unfounded statement that it was a Pope, namely Zachary, who first asserted the lawfulness of judging kings. About the year of our Lord 600, Morcantius, who then reigned in Wales, was by Oudoceus, bishop of Llandaff, condemned to exile for the murder of his uncle, though he bought off the sentence by bestowing certain landed estates upon the church.

Come we now to the Saxons; since their laws are extant I shall quote none of their deeds. Remember that the Saxons were sprung from Germans, who never gave their kings absolute or unlimited power, and who used to hold a council of the whole tribe upon the more weighty affairs of government; whence we may perceive that Parliament, the name itself only excepted, flourished in high authority even among the ancestors of the Saxons. By these it is called, in fact, Council of the Wise Men, all the way from those very times down to the time of Ethelbert, who, says Bede, "with a Council of Wise Men made decrees patterned upon those of the Romans."[222] So Edwin king of the Northumbrians, and Ina king of the West Saxons, made new laws, "having held a Council with their wise men and the elders of the people." Other laws king Alfred likewise promulgated "from an assemblage of his wisest men," and he says: "All of these decreed their observance." From these and many other like passages it is clear as day that chosen men, even from amongst the common people, were members of the supreme councils—unless we must believe that no men but the nobility are wise.

We have likewise a very ancient law-book, called the *Mirror of*

221. An eighth-century scholar thought to have written *Historia Britonum* (1691), a work that Milton has been presumed to have read in some manuscript version.
222. Bede *Ecclesiastical History of the English People* 2.5.

*Justices,* in which we are told that the early Saxons, when they had subdued Britain and set up kings, required an oath of them to submit to the judgment of the law as much as any of their subjects, Chap. 1, Sect. 2.[223] In the same place it is said that it is but just and right that the king have his peers in Parliament to take cognizance of wrongs done by the king or the queen; and that a law made in king Alfred's time required Parliament to be holden twice a year at London, or oftener if need were: which law, when through neglect it grew into disuse, was renewed by two re-enactments in King Edward III's time. And in another ancient manuscript, called *The Manner of Parliament,* we read: "If the king shall dissolve Parliament before it have disposed of all those things wherefore the council was summoned, he is guilty of perjury, and shall be deemed to have broken his coronation oath." For how does he grant, as he is sworn to do, those good laws which the people chose, if he hinders the people from choosing them, either by summoning Parliaments seldomer, or by dissolving them sooner, than the people's business requires? That oath which the kings of England take at their coronation has always been looked upon by our lawyers as a most sacred law. And what remedy can be found for greatest dangers to the state (which is the very end of summoning Parliaments) if that great and august assembly may be dissolved at the pleasure (oftentimes) of a silly and headstrong king?

To absent himself from Parliament is certainly less than to dissolve it; and yet by our laws, as the aforementioned *Manner* reports them, the King neither can nor ought to absent himself from Parliament unless he be quite ill, nor even then unless his body have been inspected by twelve peers of the realm, who may present in Parliament the evidence of his indisposition. Do slaves behave thus to a master? On the other hand the House of Commons, without which Parliament cannot be held, may, though summoned by the King, absent itself, and, having withdrawn, expostulate with the king concerning maladministration, as the same book has it.

223. Horne, *Mirror of Justices,* 7–9.

But—and this is the greatest thing of all—among the laws of King Edward commonly called the Confessor there is a very excellent law relating to the kingly duty: which if the king do not discharge as he ought, then, says the law, "he shall not retain the name of king." Lest these words should not be sufficiently understood, it subjoins the example of Chilperic king of the Franks, whom the people for that cause deposed. That by this law a wicked king is liable to punishment was betokened by that sword of Saint Edward, called Curtana, which the Earl Palatine used to carry in the procession at a coronation, "in token," says our historian Matthew Paris, "that he has authority by law to restrain and control even the king if he go astray": but punishment with a sword is hardly other than capital. This law, together with the other laws of good King Edward, did William the Conqueror himself ratify in the fourth year of his reign, and in a very full council of the English held at Verulam did with a most solemn oath confirm. By so doing he not only extinguished his right of conquest, if he ever had any over us, but even subjected himself to judgment according to the tenor of this very law. His son Henry also swore to the observance of king Edward's laws—this among the rest, and upon those terms only was he chosen king while his elder brother Robert was alive. The same oath was taken by all succeeding kings before they were crowned. Hence, saith our ancient and famous lawyer Bracton,[224] in his first book, Chapter viii,

"There is no king in the case
Where will rules and law takes not place."

And in his third book, Chapter ix. "A king is a king so long as he rules well; he becomes a tyrant when he crushes with despotic violence the people that are trusted to his charge." And in the same chapter, "The king ought to use the power of law and right as God's servant and vicegerent; the power to do wrong is the Devil's, and not God's; when the king turns aside to do wrong, he is the servant of the Devil."

224. Henry de Bracton, *On the Laws and Customs of England* (1640), bk. 1, chap. 8, 5.

Almost these very words hath another ancient lawyer, the author of the famous book called "Fleta." Both of them in fact remembered that true *Lex Regia,* that truly royal law of King Edward, as well as that fundamental maxim in our law which I mentioned before, by which nothing that is contrary to the laws of God and to reason can be accounted a law, any more than a tyrant can be said to be a king, or a servant of the Devil a servant of God. Since therefore the law is right reason above all else, then if we are bound to obey a king and a servant of God, by the very same reason and the very same law we ought to resist a tyrant and a servant of the Devil.

Now because controversies arise oftener about names than about things, the same authors tell us that a king of England, though he have not yet lost the name of king, yet can be judged and ought to be judged like anyone of the common people. Bracton, Book I, Chapter viii; Fleta, Book I, Chap. xvii: "No man ought to be greater than the king in the administration of justice; but he himself ought to be as little as the least in receiving justice, if he offends." Others read: "if he require."

Since our king therefore is liable to be judged, whether by the name of tyrant or of king, it ought not be difficult to say who are his lawful judges. Nor will it be amiss to consult the same authors upon that point. Bracton, Book II, Chap. xvi; Fleta, Book I, Chap. xvii: "The king has his superiors in the government: the law, which made him king, and his court, to wit, the Earls and the Barons. *Comites* (earls) are as much as to say the king's fellows; and he that has a fellow has a master; and therefore, if the king will be without a bridle, that is, lawless, they ought to bridle him." That the Commons are comprehended in the word Barons has been shown already; nay, our old lawbooks tell us quite generally that they were called Peers of Parliament: the *Manner of Parliament,* especially, says: "From all the peers of the realm there shall be chosen five and twenty," of whom there shall be "five knights, five citizens," that is, representatives of cities, "and five burgesses. Two knights of the shire, furthermore, have a greater vote in granting and rejecting than the greatest Earl of England." And it is but reasonable they should, for they vote for some whole county or borough or other constituency, the Earls for themselves only. And who can fail to see that those Earls "by Patent" as you call them, and Earls "by Writ," since we have now none that hold by ancient feudal tenure, are less fit than anyone else to try the king who conferred their honors upon them? Since therefore by our law, as appears by that old book, *The Mirror,* the king has his peers, who in Parliament have cognizance and jurisdiction "if the king have done wrong to any of his people"; and if it is notorious, as it is, that any individual subject may even in inferior courts sue the king for damages, how much more just, how much more necessary is it that if the king have done wrong to his whole people, there should be such as have authority not only to bridle him and keep him within bounds, but to judge and punish him? For that government must needs be very ill and very ridiculously constituted, in which remedy is provided for even private persons in case of the least injuries done by the king, and no remedy, no redress for the greatest, no care taken for the safety of the whole; no provision made but that the king, who by law could not hurt even one of his subjects, may, without any law to the contrary, ruin all of them together!

Yet since I have shown that it is neither fit nor proper for the Earls to be the king's judges, it follows that that jurisdiction does wholly, and by the best possible right, belong to the Commons, who are Peers of the realm, and Barons as well, and are vested with the power and authority of all the people committed to them. Now as we find it expressly written in our law, which I have already cited, that the Commons alone, together with the king, made a good Parliament without the Lords or the Bishops, because Kings used to hold Parliaments with their Commons alone before either Lords or Bishops came into existence; by the very same reason the Commons apart shall have a power that is sovereign, and independent of the king, and capable of judging the king himself; because before there ever was a king, they in the name of the whole body of the nation had been wont to hold Councils and Parliaments, to judge, to pass laws, yea to make kings: not that these might lord it over the people, but that they might manage the people's business. But if the king instead shall try to do them wrong and crush them into servitude, then by the express tenor of our law the name of king remains not in him; he is no king; and if he be no king, why should we have his Peers far to seek? For being then by all good men adjudged already and actually a tyrant, there are none but who are Peers good enough for him, and a court capable enough to pronounce sentence of death upon him.

These things being so, I think that by means of the many authorities and laws which have been cited I have sufficiently proved what I undertook, to wit, that since authority to try the King is by very good right lodged with the Commons, and since they have actually put the king to death for the mischief which without any hope of amendment he had done both in church and in state,—in view of all this, they have acted justly and regularly, for the interest of the State, and in the discharge of their trust, in a manner becoming their dignity, and, finally, according to the law of the land. And here I cannot but congratulate myself upon our ancestors, who founded this State with no less prudence and liberty than did the most excellent of the ancient Romans or Grecians; and they likewise, if they have any knowledge of our affairs, cannot but congratulate themselves upon their posterity, who, when almost reduced to slavery, yet with such wisdom and courage reclaimed that state, so wisely founded upon so much liberty, from a king's outrageous despotism.

### CHAPTER IX.

I think it by this time sufficiently evident that the king of England may be judged even by the laws of England, and that he has his lawful judges; which was the thing to be proved. How do you go on?— for to your mere repetitions I shall not repeat my answers. "Now even from the very business for which Parliaments are wont to be summoned, it appears that the king is above the Parliament. The way to this demonstration," you say, "slopes down steep and easy ahead."

Let it slope as steep as you will, for you shall instantly feel yourself hurled down it headlong. "The Parliament," you say, "is wont to be assembled upon affairs of uncommon weight, wherein the safety of the realm and of the people is concerned." If therefore the king call Parliament to attend to the people's business, not his own, nor to settle even that but by the consent and at the discretion of those he has called, what is he more than the people's servant and agent? For without the suffrages of them that are delegated by the people he cannot resolve the least thing with relation either to others or even to himself. Which also goes to show that it is the king's duty to call Parliaments whenever and as often as the people ask, since it is the people's business, and not the king's, that is to be treated of by that assembly, and to be ordered as the people wish.

For although the king's assent also were asked customarily out of respect, and although in lesser matters, concerning the welfare of private persons only, he might refuse it, and use that form, "The king will advise," yet in affairs that concerned the public safety and the liberty of all the people he had no negative voice whatsoever; for this would have been both against his coronation oath, which was as binding upon him as the most rigorous law, and against the chief article of Magna Charta, chap. 29: "We will not refuse, nor will we delay, right and justice to any man." Shall it be out of the king's power to refuse right and justice, and shall it therefore be in his power to refuse the enacting of just laws? Shall it be out of his power to refuse justice to any man, and shall it therefore be in his power to refuse it to all men? Shall it be out of his power to refuse it in any inferior court, and therefore be in his power to refuse it in the highest court of all? Or can any king be so arrogant as to suppose that he—one person—knows what is just and profitable better than the whole body of the people? Especially, since "he is created and chosen for this very end and purpose, to do justice to all," as Bracton says, lib. iii. c. 9— that is, according to those laws which "the people" have chosen. Hence this passage in our records, 7 H. IV, Rot. Parl. num. 59: "There is no royal prerogative that derogates aught from justice and equity."

And formerly when kings have refused to confirm Acts of Parliament, to wit, Magna Charta, and others the like, our ancestors often have brought them to it by force of arms; nor yet are our lawyers of opinion that those acts are on that account any less valid, or any less the law of the land, since the king was forced to assent to decrees which he ought in justice to have assented to voluntarily. Again, while striving to prove that kings of other nations have been as much under the power of their Sanhedrim or Senate or Council as our kings were, you do not argue us into slavery, but them into liberty. In which you keep on doing over again what you have done from the very beginning of your discourse, and what incompetent practitioners do—argue unawares against their own side of the case.

We grant, you think, that "the king, wherever he absent himself, yet is supposed still to be present in his Parliament by virtue of his power, insomuch that whatever is transacted there is supposed to be done by the king himself." Then as if you had made a great haul, or, for that matter, a pittance either, and tickled as you are with the remembrance of your gold-pieces from Charles, "We take," you say, "what they give us." Take what you deserve, then, a malediction. For we grant not what you were hoping we granted, viz., that thence this follows: "That court possesses no other power than is delegated from the king." For if it is said that the king's power, be it what it will, cannot be absent from Parliament, is it necessarily and immediately said that that power is supreme? Does not the royal power rather appear to be transferred to Parliament, and, as a lesser, to be comprised in its greater? Certainly, if Parliament may rescind the king's acts without his consent and against his refusal, and revoke privileges granted by him to whomsoever; if they may set bounds to the king's own prerogative, as they see cause; if they may regulate his yearly revenue, and the expenses of his court, his very retinue, and, in sum, all the concerns of his household; if they may remove even his bosom friends and counsellors, nay, pluck them from his lap to the scaffold; finally, if unto any soever of the people there is granted by law an appeal in any cause from the king to Parliament, but not so from Parliament to the king—all of which both our public records and the most learned of our lawyers assure us not only can be done, but have been frequently done—I suppose no man in his right wits but will confess Parliament to be above the King. Even in an interregnum the authority of the Parliament is in being, and—than which nothing is more clearly attested in our histories—they have often, without any regard to hereditary descent, appointed by free choice whomever they pleased to be king.

To sum up the whole truth, Parliament is the supreme council of the nation, constituted and appointed by an absolutely free people, and armed with ample power and authority, for this end and purpose: viz., to consult together upon the most weighty affairs; the king was created to take care that there should be executed, obedient to their vote and resolution, all the acts and decrees of those Orders, Estates, or Houses.

Which things after the Parliament themselves had lately declared in a public edict of theirs,—for such is the justice of their proceedings that of their own accord they have been willing to give an account of their actions,—look! here from his hovel appears this man of no standing or influence or property or credit, this home-born Burgundian slave, and accuses the supreme Senate of England, when it is asserting by a public instrument its own and its country's right, "of a detestable and horrible imposture!" Your country shall be ashamed, you rascal, to have brought forth so prodigiously impudent a midget.

But perhaps you have somewhat to tell us that may be for our good: go on, we are listening. "What laws," say you, "can be enacted by a Parliament in which not even the order of Bishops is present?" Did you then, you madman, go about to uproot the Bishops out of the Church, that you might transplant them into Parliaments? A wicked wretch! who ought to be delivered over to Satan, and whom the church ought not fail to excommunicate as a hypocrite and an atheist, and no civil society of men to take in, being a common plague-sore to the liberty of mankind. Nay, and besides he struggles to prove out of Aristotle and Dionysius of Halicarnassus,[225] and next from papistical statutes of the most corrupt ages, that the King of England is the head of the Church of England, a thing not to be proved at all if it be not proved from the Gospel:—all this to the end that he may once more, as far as in him lies, set up over God's holy Church those bishops, grown of late his intimates and boon-companions, whom God himself thrust out; set up them, I say, to be robbers and tyrants anew, whose whole order, as in his formerly published books he had noisily maintained, ought to be exterminated root and branch as the bane of the Christian religion. What apostate did ever so shamefully and wickedly desert as this man has done, I do not say his own doctrine, for he has none that is settled, but the Christian doctrine which he had formerly asserted?

"The Bishops being removed, who under the king and by his permission had jurisdiction of ecclesiastical causes, upon whom," ask you, "will that jurisdiction devolve?" O villain! have some regard at least to your own conscience; remember before it be too late, unless indeed this admonition of mine be already too late, remember that this mocking of God's Holy Ghost is the unpardonable sin, and will not be left unpunished. Stop at last, and set bounds to your madness, lest the wrath of God that you have provoked lay hold upon you suddenly,—you that are fain to deliver Christ's flock, and God's untouchable anointed, to be crushed and trampled again by those same enemies and cruel tyrants from whom God's wonder-working hand did lately stretch out and set them free. Yes, and from whom you yourself maintained that they ought to be set free, I know not whether for any good of theirs, or to the hardening of your own heart and the furthering of your own damnation. If the bishops have no right to lord it over the church, certainly much less have kings, whatever human statutes may be to the contrary. For they that have tasted the

225. Dionysius of Halicarnassus was an authority on rhetoric and an historian of the late first century B.C.

Gospel more than lip-deep know that the government of the church is altogether divine and spiritual, not civil.

Whereas you say that "in secular affairs, the king of England has always had the highest jurisdiction," our laws do abundantly show this to be false. Our courts of justice are erected and suppressed, not by the King's authority, but by that of the Parliament, and yet in them the meanest subject might go to law with the King. Nor did the judges seldom give judgment against him, which if the King should endeavor to obstruct by any prohibition, charge, or letter, the judges were bound by law and by their oaths not to obey him, but rejected such charges, and held them for naught. The king could not imprison any man, or seize his estate as forfeited; he could not inflict the penalty of death upon any man who had not first been summoned to appear in some court where not the king but the ordinary judges gave sentence; and this, frequently, as I have said, against the king. Hence our Bracton, book 3, ch. 9: "The royal power is a power according to law, not a power to do wrong; and the king cannot do anything else than what he can do lawfully." Those pettifoggers you have consulted, men that have lately fled their country, insinuate something else to you—something, to be sure, based upon certain statutes, not very ancient ones, made in the reigns of Edward IV, Henry VII, and Edward VI. But they overlooked the fact that what power soever those statutes granted the king was granted all by Parliament—begged for as a favor, so to speak—and revocable by the same power that conferred it. How could sagacious you let yourself be so put upon that you thought you were proving the king's power to be absolute and supreme by the very argument which most convincingly proves that it depends upon Acts of Parliament? Also our records of great authority declare that our kings owe all their power, not to any right of inheritance, of conquest, or of succession, but to the people. So in the Parliament Rolls of the first of Henry IV, number 108, we read that such a kingly power was granted by the Commons to Henry IV, and before him to Richard II, just as any king customarily grants to his commissioners their governorships and official charges by edict and patent. Thus the House of Commons ordered expressly to be entered upon record "that they had granted to King Richard" to use "the same good liberty that the Kings of England before him had." And because that king abused it to the subversion of the laws, and "contrary to his oath at his coronation," he was by these same Commons bereft of his kingdom. The Commons, as also appears by the same Roll, publish in Parliament that, having confidence in the prudence and moderation of Henry IV, "they will and enact that he be in the same great royal liberty that his ancestors possessed." Had the former, however, been other than wholly a trust, as the latter was, then indeed not only must those Houses of Parliament have been foolish and vain to grant what was none of their own, but those Kings too that were willing to receive as a grant from others what was already theirs, must have been too injurious both to themselves and to their posterity; neither of which can be believed.

"A third portion of the royal power," say you, "concerns the forces; this portion the kings of England have handled without peer or competitor." This is no truer than the rest that you have written in reliance upon what the renegades told you. In the first place, both our own histories and those of foreigners that have been in the least exact touching our affairs declare that the making of peace and war always did belong to the Great Council of the realm. And the laws of St. Edward, which our kings are bound to swear that they will maintain, put this beyond dispute in the chapter "De Heretochiis," [226] viz. "That there were certain officers appointed in every province and county of the realm, that were called Heretochs, in Latin *ductores exercitus,* commanders of the army," that were to command the forces of the several counties, not "for the honor of the crown" only, but "for the good of the realm." And they were chosen "by the common council, and by the several counties in full public assemblies of the inhabitants, as sheriffs ought to be chosen." Whence it is evident that

226. St. Edward, *Ancient Laws and Institutes of England,* Commissioners of the Public Records, 2:456.

the forces of the kingdom, and the commanders of those forces, were anciently, and ought to be still, not at the king's command, but at the people's; and that this most just law obtained in this our kingdom no less than heretofore it did in the Roman republic. Concerning which it will not be amiss to hear what Cicero says, *Philipp.* 10: "All the legions, all the forces, wheresoever they are, belong to the Roman people. For not even those legions that deserted Antony when he was Consul are said to have belonged to Antony rather than to the Commonwealth." That law of St. Edward, together with the rest of his laws, did William, called the Conqueror, at the desire and command of the people, confirm by oath, yes and added over and above, chap. 56: "All cities, boroughs, and castles to be so guarded every night, as the Sheriff, the Aldermen, and the other officers placed in command by the Common Council shall think meet for the safety of the realm." And in the 62d law, "Castles, boroughs, and cities were built for the protection of the folks and peoples of the realm, and therefore ought to be maintained free, entire, and unimpaired, by all ways and means." How then? Shall towns and places of strength in times of peace be guarded against thieves and evildoers no otherwise than by the Common Council of each place; and shall they not be defended in dangerous times of war, against enemies both domestic and foreign, by the Common Council of the whole nation? If this be not granted, they surely cannot be guarded and maintained "free" or "unimpaired" or "by all ways and means"; nor shall we obtain any of those ends for which the law itself tells us that towns and fortresses are founded in the first place. Indeed our ancestors were willing to put anything into the king's power rather than their arms and the garrisons of their towns; conceiving that that would be as if they went about to hand over their liberty to the unrestrained cruelty of their kings. Of which there are so very many instances in our histories, and those so generally known, that it would be superfluous to mention any of them here.

But "the king owes protection to his subjects; and how can he protect them unless he have men and arms at command?" But, say I, he had all this for the good of the kingdom, as has been said, not for the destruction of his people and the ruin of the realm. In Henry III's time, one Leonard, a learned man, in an assembly of the Bishops, wisely answered Rustand, the Pope's Nuncio and the king's Chancellor, in these words: "All churches belong to My Lord the Pope, as we say all things belong to a prince, for protection, not for his use and enjoyment or his property," as the phrase is; for defence, "not for destruction." The aforementioned law of St. Edward is to the same purpose; and what is this but a power in trust—not a power absolute? Now, though the commander of an army in the field has much this same sort of power—delegated, that is, and not absolutely his own—yet he is generally none the slower to defend both at home and abroad the people that chose him. Vainly had our Parliaments contended of old with our kings about liberty and St. Edward's laws, and surely it had been an unequal match, had they been of opinion that the power of the sword must belong to the king alone; for how unjust laws soever the king would have imposed upon them, in vain would they have defended themselves against his sword by a "Charter," however "Great"!

But, you ask, "What shall it profit Parliament to have command of the forces, since towards the maintenance of them they cannot without the king's assent raise a farthing from the people?" Let not that trouble you! In the first place you go upon the false supposition that the Estates in Parliament "cannot without the king's assent impose taxes upon the people"—the very people who send them, and whose side they are taking! In the next place it cannot have escaped you—so busy an inquirer into other people's business—that the people by melting down their gold and silver vessels raised a great sum of money of their own accord toward the carrying on of this war against the king.

Then you recount the large annual revenues of our kings; you rattle on about nothing less than "five hundred and forty thousands"; you have heard, and greedily, that "those of our kings that have been eminent for their bounty and liberality" have used to give "large boons out of their own patrimony." Greedily you heard this; it was by this allurement that those traitors to their country enticed you to their side, as the wicked Balaam was enticed of old, so that you dared to curse the people of God and to clamor against the divine judgments. Fool! what, pray, did such boundless wealth profit that unjust and violent king? What did it profit you? For I hear that nothing whatever of all you had been devouring with your huge expectations did reach you, beyond that one paltry purse wrought with glass beads and stuffed with a hundred gold pieces. Balaam,[227] take your wages of unrighteousness that you loved, and much good may it do you!

You go on playing the fool. "The setting up of the standard," that is, "of the signal of battle, is a prerogative that belongs to the king only." Why? Why because

"Turnus set up an ensign of war on the top of the tower of Laurentum."[228]

Do you really not know, Grammarian, that this very thing is the office of any commander of an army in the field? But "Aristotle says that the king must always have a guard to help him defend the laws, and therefore it behooves the king to have greater military strength than the whole body of the people."[229] This man twists conclusions as Ocnus[230] does ropes in Hell; which are of no use but to be eaten by asses. For a guard given by the people is one thing, and the control of all the forces is quite another thing; the latter, Aristotle judges, in the very passage which you have cited, should not belong to kings. It behooves the king, says he, to have so many armed men about him "as to make him stronger than any one man, or many men together,

227. Num. 22:5–34.

228. Virgil *Aeneid* 8.1.

229. Aristotle *Politics* 3.15.1286b.

230. A mythological criminal condemned in Hades, Ocnus was forced to make a rope of straw, which was continuously devoured by an ass as soon as he had spliced it.

but not stronger than the people." *Pol.* Book 3, ch. 11. Else, under
show of protecting them, he could subject both people and laws to
himself. This indeed is the difference betwixt a king and a tyrant: a
king, by consent of the senate and the people, has about him a sufficient guard against public enemies and seditious persons. A tyrant,
against the will of the senate and the people, strives to get as great a
guard as he can, either of public enemies, or of profligate subjects,
against the senate and the people. Parliament therefore granted the
king, as they granted whatever he had besides, the "setting up of the
standard"; not that he might give hostile signals to attack his own
people, but that he might defend them against such as the Parliament
should declare enemies to the state. If he acted otherwise, he was
to be accounted an enemy himself, for according to that same law of
St. Edward, or, what is more sacred, the very law of nature, he lost
the name of king. Whence Cicero in his *Philippic* aforesaid: "He who
attacks the state with an army and his official powers forfeits all right
to the command and to his office."

As for "tenants by knight-service," the King was not allowed to
summon them to a war which the authority of Parliament had not
resolved upon; as is evident from many statutes. The same is true of
Tonnage and Poundage and Ship Money;[231] these the king could not
exact from his subjects without an Act of Parliament; as was publicly
resolved by the ablest of our lawyers about twelve years ago, when the
king's authority was at its height. And, long before them, Fortescue,
an eminent lawyer, and chancellor to Henry the Sixth, was of the same
opinion. The king of England, says he, can neither alter the laws, nor
lay taxes without the people's consent.[232]

231. Parliament granted Charles I customs (or "Tonnage and Poundage") for one
year (the tax dates back to 1347), but Charles extended the levy, prompting Parliament to declare the taxes illegal in June 1641. Ship Money was levied upon the sea-
side counties in 1634 and extended inland the next year. An Act abolishing Ship
Money was passed by Parliament in July 1641.
232. Sir John Fortescue, *De Laudibus Legum Angliae* (1616). Fortescue (1394?–
1467?) was chief justice of the King's Bench.

Nor can any testimonies be brought from antiquity to prove "the government of the realm of England an unmixed monarchy." "The king," says Bracton, "has jurisdiction over all his subjects"; that is, in his courts of justice, where justice is administered in the king's name indeed, but according to our own laws. "Everyone is subject to the king"—that is, every private individual; and so Bracton explains himself in the passages that I cited before.

What follows is but turning the same stone over and over again— a sport at which I believe you able to tire out Sisyphus[233] himself— and is sufficiently answered by what has been said already. For the rest, if our Parliaments have sometimes offered deference to good kings with expressions as generous as they could be this side of flattery and servility, this should not be understood as offered in like measure to tyrants, or in prejudice of the people; for liberty is not impaired by proper deference. As for what you cite out of Sir Edward Coke[234] and others, "that the realm of England is an absolute power," so it is with regard to any foreign king, or to the Emperor, or, as Camden says, "because it is not among the dependents of the Empire": but each of them adds, besides, that this power dwells not "in the king" alone, but "in the body politic." Whence Fortescue says, *de Laud. Leg. Ang.* ch. 9: "The king of England" governs his people "not by an unmixed royal power, but by the power of a State; for the English people is governed by those laws which" it makes. Foreign authors were not ignorant of this: hence Philippe de Comines, a weighty authority, says in the Fifth Book of his Commentaries: "Of all the kingdoms of the earth that I have any knowledge of, I think there is none where government is carried on under more restraint, or where the king is allowed less power against his people, than in England."

Finally you say: "Ridiculous is the argument they adduce—that kingdoms existed before kings; which is as much as to say there was

233. Sisyphus was eternally condemned to push a rock to the top of a hill only to have it roll back down.

234. A chief justice who resisted James I, Coke (1552–1634) was one of the foremost authorities on English law.

light before the sun was created." But, my good Sir, we do not say that kingdoms, but that the people, were before kings. In the mean time, whom shall I call more ridiculous than you, in denying (as if *it* were ridiculous) that light came into being before the sun? Thus while you would be inquisitive in other men's matters you have un-learned your very rudiments! You wonder, in the last place, "how they that have seen the King at a session of Parliament sitting upon his throne under the golden and silken heaven of his canopy of state, should so much as make a question whether the majesty resided in him or in the Parliament." Hard of belief indeed are they, whom so bril-liant an argument, prayed down from "heaven," especially a "golden and silken heaven," cannot convince. Which golden heaven, you, like a Stoic, have so devoutly and singly gazed upon, that you seem to have quite forgot the heaven of Moses and the heaven of Aristotle; for you have denied that in Moses's heaven "there was any light before the sun"; and in Aristotle's you have exhibited three temperate zones. How many zones you observed in that golden and silken heaven of the king's I know not, but so much I know: you got one money-belt—one zone well tempered with an hundred golden stars—by this your heavenly contemplation!

## CHAPTER X.

Since this whole controversy, whether concerning the right of kings in general, or that of the king of England in particular, has been ren-dered more difficult by partisan obstinacy than by the nature of the thing itself, I hope that for those who prefer the pursuit of truth be-fore the interest of faction I have produced out of the law of God, the laws of nations, and the municipal laws of my own country, such abundance of proofs as shall leave it beyond question that a king of England may be brought to trial and put to death. With the rest, whose minds fanaticism possesses wholly, or whose wit has been so blunted by premature admiration of royal splendor that they can see nothing glorious or magnificent in true magnanimity and liberty—with these whether we strive either by reason and arguments or by examples, we strive in vain.

In fact, Salmasius, absurdly as you seem to do all else, you seem to fill up the measure of absurdity in this, that while you cannot give over heaping all manner of abuse upon all Independents, you assert that the very king you defend was the most Independent of all, for that he did not "owe his sovereignty to the people, but to his descent."

Next, whereas in the beginning of your book you vehemently bewailed him for being "forced to plead for his life," now you complain "that he perished unheard." But if you have a mind to look into his whole defence, which is very correctly published in French,[235] it may be you will be of another opinion. Whereas Charles certainly was afforded for some days together the fullest opportunity to say what he could for himself, he made no use of it—not he—to clear himself of the crimes laid to his charge, but utterly to spurn his judges and their jurisdiction. Now whenever the accused either is mute, or always says nothing to the purpose, then, if his guilt is evident beyond all doubt, there is no injustice in condemning him even unheard.

If you say that Charles "died a death fully answerable to his life," I agree with you; if you say that he died piously, holily, and "composedly," remember that his grandmother Mary, an infamous woman, died on the scaffold with as much outward show of piety, holiness, and constancy as he did. And lest you should ascribe too much to that very strong impression of courage which any common malefactors often give at their death, let me tell you that despair or a hardened heart many times puts on a certain look and mask, as it were, of fortitude, and stupidity many times a show of tranquillity of mind. The worst of men desire to appear good, undaunted, innocent, and sometimes holy, not only in their life, but at their death as well. In going to their death for very villainies, they are wont to make a last parade

---

235. Claude Salmasius *Histoire entière & véritable du Procez du Charles Stuart* (1650).

of their hypocrisy and deception as handsomely as they can, and, as is the way of foolish poets or stageplayers, hanker after applause even when the play is over.

Now you say you are "come to that part of the inquiry where you must discuss who were the chief movers of the king's condemnation." Whereas it ought rather to be inquired into how you, a foreigner and a French vagabond, came to hold an inquiry into our affairs, so strange to you? And bought with what price? That, however, is well enough known. But who at last satisfied your curiosity about our affairs? Even those deserters and traitors to their country that got hold of your eminent emptiness and easily hired you to speak ill of us. Then there was handed you some paltry account of the state of our affairs, written either by some crazy half papist chaplain or by some cringing courtier, and you were given the job of turning it into Latin. Out of that you took those made-up stories of yours, which, if you please, we will examine a little.

"Not the hundred thousandth part of the people consented to this sentence of condemnation." What were the rest of the people then, that suffered so great a deed to be done against their will? Were they stocks and stones, were they mere trunks of men only, or such utterly inert creatures as those in Virgil's tapestry?

Britons interwove hold up the purple hangings.[236]

For methinks you mean to describe no true Britons, but some sort of painted Picts, or even gentlemen embroidered in needlework! Since therefore it is a thing incredible that a warlike nation should be subdued by so few, and these of the dregs of the people, which is the first thing that occurs in your narrative, that is manifestly quite false.

"The Lords Spiritual were turned out by the Parliament itself." The more deplorable is your madness therefore—for you are not yet sensible that you rave—to complain that Parliament turned out those who, as you yourself say in a lengthy book, ought to be turned out of

236. Virgil *Third Georgic* 25.

the Church. "A second Estate of Parliament, to wit, the Lords Temporal, consisting of dukes, earls, and viscounts, was cast down from its place." And deservedly, for, not being returned by any constituency, they represented themselves only. They had no right over the people, but by a sort of old-established custom of their own used for the most part to oppose the people's rights and liberties. Created by the king, they were his companions, his servants, and, as it were, his shadows; and, the king once got rid of, they must needs be reduced to the body of the people, from whom they rose.

"One part of the Parliament, and that the worst of all, ought not to have assumed unto itself that power of judging kings." But I have shown you already that the House of Commons was not only the chief part of our Parliament, even while we had kings, but made in and by itself a Parliament in all respects perfect and lawful, even without the Lords Temporal, much more the Lords Spiritual. But "not even the whole House of Commons itself was admitted to vote at the king's trial." True, for the part that was not admitted had in sentiment and counsel openly revolted to Charles—to one whom, though they deemed him their king in words, they had yet in their deeds so often deemed an enemy. The Estates of the Parliament of England, and the deputies sent from the Parliament of Scotland, had written to the king on the 13th of January, 1645, in answer to his request for a deceitful truce and for a conference with them at London, that they could not admit him into the City till he had made satisfaction to the state for the civil war that he had raised in the three kingdoms, and for the deaths of so many of his subjects slain by his order, and till he had in writing provided and taken order for a true and firm peace upon such terms as the Parliaments of both kingdoms had offered him so often already, and should offer him again. He for his part had either rejected their very just requests by answering that he refused to listen, or by ambiguous answers had evaded them, though most humbly presented to him seven times over. After so many years' patience, the Houses at last, lest the deceitful king, even in prison, should by his temporizings ruin that Commonwealth which he had not the strength to subdue in the field, and by gathering the sweet fruit of our divisions be restored, though a public enemy, and triumph unexpectedly over his conquerors,—this to prevent, the Houses resolve that for the future they will pay no attention to the king, send him no more requests, and receive no more from him. After this resolution there were yet found even some members of Parliament who hated that invincible army, envied its glorious deeds, and, after it had deserved so well of the nation, desired to disband it in disgrace. They were under the thumb of a certain number of seditious ministers, by whom they were governed like miserable slaves. They found their opportunity when many whom they knew to be far otherwise minded than themselves were absent in the provinces, sent by the House itself to put down the Presbyterian rising which had already begun to spread. With a strange levity, not to say perfidy, they vote that that inveterate enemy of the state, king in name only, though he had given scarce any security or satisfaction, should be brought back to the City and restored to his throne and sovereignty, exactly as if he had deserved excellently well of the nation. So that they preferred the king before their religion, their liberty, and that Covenant of theirs which so often they had vaunted. Meantime what of those who were sound themselves, and saw such pestilent councils on foot? Ought they to have been wanting to their country, and have failed to provide for the safety of their countrymen, because the infection had spread even into their own House?

But who excluded those unsound members? "The English army," you say. So it was not an army of foreigners, but of most valiant and faithful citizens, officered for the most part by the very members of Parliament whom those excluded Honorable Members had thought fit to exclude from their very country, and send far away into Ireland![237] The Scots, meanwhile, acting in what had by now become very dubious good faith, were occupying with large forces the four English counties nearest their border, were keeping garrisons in the strongest towns of those parts, and were holding the king himself in

237. Milton refers to a project promoted by Denzil Holles in 1647 for disbanding the New Model Army and sending a force to Ireland.

custody. They also encouraged here and there in both city and country factions and uprisings of their own countrymen, which were more than threatening to Parliament, and which soon after broke out into not only our Civil War but the Scottish War as well.

If it has been always counted praiseworthy in private men to succour the state by advice or arms, there surely is no reason why our army can be blamed, who being by authority of Parliament summoned to the City, obeyed orders, and quelled with ease an uprising of the royalist faction which more than once threatened the House itself. Things had been brought to such a pass indeed, that of necessity either we must be crushed by them, or they by us. On their side were most of the London hucksters and handicraftsmen, and generally the most factious of the ministers; on ours an army known for its great loyalty, moderation, and courage. It being in our power by their means to keep the liberty, the safety, of our state, do you think that all ought to have been surrendered and betrayed by negligence and folly?

The leaders of the Royalist party, when subdued, had unwillingly laid down their arms indeed, but not their hatred; and they had flocked to town, watching all opportunities of renewing the war. With these men (though their greatest enemies) the Presbyterians, seeing themselves not admitted to civil as well as ecclesiastical despotism over everybody, had begun to make common cause, secret and most unworthy of what they had formerly both said and done. They went on to such a degree of bitterness that they would rather enthral themselves to the king again than admit their own brethren to that portion of liberty which they too had purchased with their own blood, and would rather try being lorded over once more by a tyrant dyed in the gore of so many of his own subjects, and burning with rage and with the vengeance he already imagined against the survivors, than endure their brethren and friends to share and share alike with them. Only those who are called Independents knew from first to last how to be true to their cause, and what use to make of their victory. They would not—and wisely, in my opinion—that he who when he was king had made himself the state's enemy should ever, from being the state's enemy, be king any more; nor were they on this account averse to peace, but they very prudently dreaded either new war or perpetual slavery wrapped up in the name of peace.

To slander our army the more fully, you begin a dry disorderly narrative of our affairs; in which though I find many things false, many things frivolous, many things laid to our charge which ought rather to be credited in our praise, yet I think it will be to no purpose for me to set over against it another narration from the opposite side. For our contest is by reasonings, not by narrations, and both sides will believe the former, but not the latter. And indeed the nature of the things themselves is such that for their weight and worth they cannot be related as they deserve but in a right history; so that I think it better, as Sallust said of Carthage,[238] rather to say nothing at all about things of such weight and importance than to say too little. Nor will I so much offend as to interweave in my book the praises not of great men only, but above all of Almighty God, which in this wonderful course of affairs ought to be most often repeated, to interweave these, I say, amongst your slanders and reproaches. I will therefore, as is my wont, pick out only such things as seem to have any color of argument.

You say: "The English and the Scots by solemn covenant promised to preserve the majesty of the king." But you omit upon what terms they promised it—to wit, if it might consist with the safety of their religion and their liberty; to both of which that king was so hostile and treacherous, even unto his last breath, that it was evident their religion would be endangered, and their liberty would perish if he lived.

But now you come back to the movers of the king's execution: "If the thing be considered according to the influences that decided it, the conclusion of this abominable action must be imputed to the Independents in such a way that the Presbyterians may justly claim the glory of its beginning and progress." Hark, ye Presbyterians, how does it help, how does it profit your reputation for innocence and

238. Sallust *Jugurtha* 19.2.

loyalty that ye seemed so much to abhor putting the king to death? According to this everlasting talkative advocate of the king, your accuser, ye "went more than half-way"; "to the fourth act and beyond ye were beheld twittering and stammering while ye turned this tragedy into a circus feat of jumping or straddling two horses at once." But meanwhile, o wielder of far-fetched rhetoric, why imitate so readily those whom you accuse so toilsomely—being yourself so often "beheld" in this *Royal Defence* "twittering and stammering" while you "straddle two horses at once!"

But, once more, O Presbyterians! ye "may justly be charged with the crime of killing the king, since ye paved the way to killing the same." "Ye, and no others, struck the accursed axe upon his neck." Woe to you before all others, if ever Charles's stock recover the crown of England; upon my word, ye are like to pay the piper! But make your prayers to God, and love your brethren your deliverers, who have hitherto kept that calamity and sure destruction from you, though against your wills. Ye are accused likewise for that "some years ago ye endeavored by sundry petitions to lessen the king's authority; that in the very papers ye presented to the king in the name of Parliament, ye inserted and published some expressions abusive of the king": to wit, "in that Declaration of the Lords and Commons of the 26th of May, 1642, ye declared openly, in some mad proposals that breathed rebellion, what ye thought of the king's authority. Hotham, by order of Parliament, shut the gates of Hull against the king": ye "aimed by this first act of rebellion to make trial how much the king would bear." What could be said more perfectly adapted to reconcile the minds of all Englishmen to one another, and estrange them wholly from the king? For hereby they may understand that if ever the king come back, they shall be punished not only for his father's death, but for petitions they made long ago, and Acts passed in full Parliament for putting down the Bishops and the Book of Common Prayer, and for the Triennial Parliament,[239] and what was else enacted with the people's

239. The Triennial Act of February 1641 required that in the absence of a royal summons the Parliament must meet every three years for fifty days.

fullest consent and applause—all these as seditious and "mad proposals of the Presbyterians"!

But this slight fickle fellow changes his mind all of a sudden; and what but of late "when he reckoned the thing itself aright" he thought was due wholly to the Presbyterians, this, now that "he turns over from on high" the very same "thing," he thinks is due wholly to the Independents. A moment ago he was averring that the Presbyterians "advanced against the king with overt force of arms," and that by them the king was "defeated, taken, and put in prison." Now he says this whole "theory of rebellion" belongs to the Independents. Such trustworthiness and consistency in the man! What need is there now of a counter-narrative to this of yours, that has so shamefully failed to meet its own obligations?

But if anyone should question whether you are an honest man or a knave, let him read these following lines of yours: "It is time to explain whence and at what time this sect of enemies to kingship first broke out. Why truly these charming Puritans began in Queen Elizabeth's time to issue forth out of the darkness of Hell, and thenceforward to disturb the Church, yea and the State itself too; for they are no less plagues to the State than to the Church." Now your very speech bewrays you right Balaam; for where you designed to vomit out all the venom of your bitterness, there unwittingly and against your will you have pronounced a blessing. For it is notorious throughout all England that if any endeavored, after the pattern of those churches, whether French or German, which they accounted more truly reformed, to follow a purer type of divine service, which our Bishops had almost universally defiled with their ceremonies and superstitions, or if any, in fine, excelled the rest either in piety toward God or in purity of conduct, such persons were by the Bishops' party termed Puritans. These are they whose principles you so loudly declare to be unfriendly to kings; nor are they alone in this, for "the majority of Protestants, who have not adopted the rest of their principles," you say, "yet seem to have approved of this only, which opposes royal despotism." So that while you inveigh bitterly against the Independents, you praise them in deriving their descent from the most pure and uncorrupted family of Christians; and a principle which you everywhere affirm to be peculiar to the Independents, you now confess that "the majority of Protestants have approved." Nay, you are arrived to that degree of temerity, impiety, and apostasy, that even the Bishops, who, you formerly maintained, ought to be uprooted out of the church, as so many plagues and Antichrists, you now aver "ought to have been protected by the king" in order not to "impair his coronation oath"! Beyond your present villainy and shame there is no step you can take but one alone—to abjure as soon as possible the Reformed religion which you taint with your presence. Whereas you say we "tolerate all sects and heresies," you ought not to find fault with us for that as long as the Church tolerates you, impious wretch and empty-headed lying slanderer for hire, you Apostate who have the impudence to say that the most saintly Christians, and even the majority of Protestants—a majority which happens to be opposed to you—issue forth out of the darkness of Hell!

Why should I not pass by the telltale rascalities upon which you spend a great part of the rest of your chapter, and those prodigious tenets that you ascribe to the Independents, to render them odious? For they concern not at all this disputed question about kings, and are for the most part such as deserve anybody's laughter or contempt rather than refutation.

## CHAPTER XI.

You seem to me to approach this eleventh chapter, Salmasius, though still unashamed, yet with some sense of your inefficiency. For whereas you proposed to yourself to inquire in this place "by what authority" sentence was given against the king, you add immediately something which nobody expected of you, that "it is in vain to make any such inquiry," to wit, because "the quality of the persons that did it leaves hardly any room for such a question." And therefore as the conviction of meddlesomeness and impudence of which you have been found guilty in the undertaking of this cause is now matched by your present guilty consciousness of your own impertinent garrulity, I shall give you the shorter answer. To your question then "by what authority" the House of Commons either condemned the king themselves, or delegated that power to others, I answer: "the highest in the land." How they came to have the highest authority, you may learn from what I said before, when I was refuting your persistent nonsense upon this very subject; for if you believed yourself capable of ever saying the sufficient and satisfactory thing, you would not have the habit of so often and so tediously repeating the same old singsong. And the House of Commons might delegate their judicial power in the same way in which you say the king, who himself likewise received all he had from the people, may delegate his. Hence in that Solemn League and Covenant that you have brought against us,[240] the Estates of England and Scotland solemnly protest and engage to each other to punish traitors in such manner as "the supreme judicatories of both Kingdoms respectively, or others having power from them for that effect, shall judge convenient." Now you hear the Parliaments of both nations with one voice bearing witness that they may delegate their judicial power, which they call "supreme"; so that the controversy you raise about delegating this power is vain and frivolous.

"But," you say, "with those judges that were chosen from the lower House were joined even judges from the army; soldiers never, though, had a right to sit in judgment upon a citizen." I will turn the edge of your argument in a very few words; for remember that we are not now talking of a citizen, but of an enemy. Suppose such an enemy taken prisoner, and to be dispatched at once if duly sentenced; now if the commander of the army with his officers should decide to try him before a Court Martial, would he be deemed to have done aught contrary to martial law and custom? An enemy to a state, made a prisoner of war, cannot be looked upon to be so much as a citizen

240. Milton refers to the fourth article of the Solemn League and Covenant, a Presbyterian device created in 1647 to consolidate the power of the sect in Parliament and to advance the Presbyterian form of worship and church government.

in that state, much less a king. This is the purport of the sacred law of St. Edward, which declares that a bad king neither is a king, nor ought to be called a king.

To your objection that it was "not a whole" House of Commons, but a house "maimed and mutilated, that tried and condemned the king," take this answer. The number of them who gave their votes for putting the king to death was far greater than is lawfully necessary—even in the absence of the rest—to transact any business whatsoever in Parliament. Now since they were absent through their own fault, nay guilt (for their hearts' desertion to the common enemy was the worst sort of absence) they could not delay the rest, who had continued faithful to the cause, in the work of preserving the state, which, when it was tottering and almost quite reduced to slavery and utter ruin, the whole body of the people had before all else committed to their fidelity, prudence, and courage. And they acted their parts like men; they set themselves against the unruly wilfulness, the rage, the secret designs of an embittered king; they held the common liberty and safety before their own; they outdid all former Parliaments, they outdid all their ancestors, in wisdom, magnanimity, and steadfastness to their cause. Yet a great part of the people, though it had promised full fidelity, support, and assistance, did ungratefully desert these men in the midst of their undertaking. This part was for slavery and peace, with sloth and luxury, upon any terms; the other part, however, kept demanding liberty, and no peace but what was sure and honorable. What was the Parliament to do now? Ought it to have defended the part that remained sound and faithful to it and to the country, or to have sided with the one that deserted both? I know what you will say it ought to have done, for you are not Eurylochus, but Elpenor,[241] a miserable Circean beast, a filthy swine, accustomed to foulest slavery even under a woman; so that you have not the least relish of manliness or of the liberty which is born of it. You would have all men slaves, because you feel not in

241. In Ovid's account (*Metamorphoses* 14), Eurylochus alone of Odysseus's crew resisted Circe's enchantments while Elpenor was one who succumbed.

your heart aught magnanimous or free; you say nothing, you breathe nothing, but what is mean and servile.

You raise another scruple, to wit, "that he whom we condemned was the king of Scotland too." As if he might therefore do what he would in England! But that you may conclude this chapter, which of all others is the most dry and doddering, at least with some witty quirk, "There are two little words," you say, "consisting of the same letters and the same number of them, and differing only in the position of them, but differing enormously in meaning, to wit, VIS and IVS (might and right)." Of course it is no great wonder that you, being a man of three letters ( *fur,* a thief ), should make such a clever little quibble upon three letters; much more wonderful is this which you affirm throughout your book: that two things "differing" so much in all other respects should yet be one and the same thing in kings. For did kings ever perpetrate a royal violence which you do not affirm to be their royal right?

In nine long, long pages these are the matters that I could observe worth answering. The rest are either matters which, having been again and again repeated, have been more than once refuted, or matters which have no bearing upon this discussion. So that my more than usual brevity should not be counted against my diligence, which, though I be irked in the extreme, I let not slack, but against your everlasting talk, so void and vacant of matter and sense.

## CHAPTER XII.

In order that no one shall by any chance get the impression that I am unfair or too severe to King Charles, now he has fulfilled his destiny and borne his punishment, I for my part, Salmasius, wish you had passed over in silence this whole passage concerning "his crimes," as it had been more advisable for yourself and your party to do. But since it has pleased you rather to talk copiously and over-confidently upon them, I will make you clearly perceive that you could not have done a more inconsiderate thing than to save up the worst part of your cause,—namely the tearing open and searching those old wounds, the king's crimes—to the last. For when I shall have proved them to have been actually committed and most heinous, they will not only render his memory repulsive and hateful to all good men, but leave in your readers' minds as well an intense final hatred of you as his defender.

"The indictment against him," you say, "may be divided into two parts: one is concerned with censure of his way of life; the other with faults he might commit as king." I will be content to pass by in silence the life he spent amid banquets, plays, and bevies and troops of women; for what can there be in luxury and excess worth relating? And what would those things have been to us if he had been only a private person? but he would act the king; consequently, as he could not live unto himself alone, so neither could he sin unto himself alone. For in the first place, he did his subjects much mischief by his example; in the second place, all the time—and it was very much— that he spent upon his lusts and sports, he stole away from the State which he had undertaken to govern; lastly, he squandered away upon the luxury of his household boundless wealth, uncounted sums of money which were not his own but the public revenue of the nation. So it was in his private life at home that he first began to be an ill king.

But let us rather "pass over to those crimes that he is charged with having committed in misgoverning." Here you lament his being condemned as "a tyrant, a traitor, and a murderer." That in this he was not wronged shall now be shown. First, however, let us define a tyrant, not according to the notions of the crowd, but according to the judgment of Aristotle and of all learned men. A tyrant is one who regards his own welfare and profit only, and not that of the people. So Aristotle defines one in the tenth book of his *Ethics,* and elsewhere, and so do many others. Whether Charles regarded his own advantage or the people's, these things, which I shall only touch upon, and which are only a few out of many, will serve to show.

When his crown property and royal revenue could not defray the expenses of the court, he laid very heavy taxes upon the people, and having squandered these, invented new ones—not for the benefit, honor, or defence of the state, but that he might hoard up in one house, or in one house fritter away, the riches of nations more than one. When in this fashion he had unlawfully scraped together an incredible amount, he attempted either wholly to do away with Parliament, which he knew was the only thing that could bridle him, or to summon it no oftener than suited his convenience, and to make it accountable to himself alone. This bridle being once cast off himself, himself put another bridle upon the people: he had German horse and Irish foot stationed in many towns and cities as if to garrison them, though in time of peace. Do you think he does not begin to look like a tyrant? In this very thing, as in many others which I have exhibited above upon occasion given me by you—in this, I say, though you scorn to have Charles compared with so cruel a tyrant as Nero, he resembled him extremely, for Nero likewise often threatened to abolish the Senate.

Meanwhile the king bore extremely hard upon the consciences of godly men, and compelled all to use certain ceremonies and superstitious worships which he had brought back into the Church again from the midst of popery. Them that would not conform he banished or imprisoned; and he made war upon the Scots twice[242] for no other cause than that. So far he may seem to have surely deserved the name of tyrant at least "once over."

Now I will tell you why the word traitor was put into his indictment. While he had again and again assured this Parliament by promises, by proclamations, by imprecatory oaths, that he had no design against the state, at that very time either he was recruiting levies of Papists in Ireland, or by secret embassy to the king of Denmark[243] he was begging arms, horses, and troops, expressly against the Parliament, or he was endeavoring to raise an army, first of Englishmen, and then of Scots, by bribes. To the English he promised the plunder of the City of London; to the Scots, that he would annex the four

242. In 1639 and again in 1640.
243. Christian IV (1588–1648).

northern counties to Scotland, if they would but help him get rid of the Parliament by any means soever. These projects not succeeding, he gave one Dillon,[244] a traitor, secret instructions to the Irish to fall suddenly upon all the English colonists in Ireland. These are the proofs of his treasons, and they are not gathered out of idle reports, but are certainties found in letters under his own hand and seal.

Finally, I suppose no man will withhold the name of murderer from him by whose order the Irish took arms and put to death with most exquisite torments five hundred thousand English, who in a time of profound peace apprehended nothing of the kind; nor will any man, I suppose, deny that he who raised so great a civil war in the other two kingdoms was a murderer. I add that at the conference held in the Isle of Wight the king openly took upon himself the guilt of this war and the blame for it, and in his confession known of all men cleared the Parliament.[245] Thus you have in short why King Charles was adjudged a tyrant, a traitor, and a murderer.

But you ask "why was he not so adjudged before by either the Presbyterians or the Independents," either in that "Solemn League and Covenant," or afterwards when he was surrendered, but rather "was received as became a king to be received, with all reverence?" This very point is sufficient to convince any man of good understanding that only at long last, and after they had borne all things, and tried all things, and steadfastly endured all things, were the Estates resolved to depose the king. That which to all good men will evidence their extreme patience, calmness, self-control, and perhaps overlong forbearance with the king's pride, you alone maliciously seize upon as a reproach.

But "in the month of August before the king suffered, the House of Commons, which already ruled alone and was controlled by the

244. Thomas Dillon, a viscount.

245. Milton refers to Charles's withdrawing his objection to Parliament's public statement that it had been obliged to undertake a war in "just and lawful defence" (September 25, 1648).

Independents, wrote a letter to the Scots[246] protesting that it had never had in mind an alteration of the form of government which had obtained so long in England under King, Lords, and Commons." See now how little the deposing of the king is to be ascribed to the principles of the Independents! They, who are not wont to dissemble their principles, profess even then, when they have the sole management of affairs, that they "had never had in mind an alteration of the form of government." But if a thing which at first they had not in mind afterwards came into their mind, why might they not take the course which seemed to lead straighter to the common weal? Especially when they found that Charles could not possibly be entreated or anywise moved to assent to those just demands which they presented, and which were always the same from the beginning. Those froward opinions with respect to religion and his own right which he had all along maintained, and which were so destructive to us, in these he persisted, nothing changed from that too-well-known Charles who both in peace and in war had done us all so much mischief. If he assented to anything, he gave intimations not obscure both that he did it against his will, and that as soon as he should have his own way he would hold it null and void. The same thing his son openly declared by a published writing, when in those days he ran away with part of the fleet, and so did the king himself by letter to certain of his party in town.

In the mean time, against the open disapprobation of Parliament, he had in secret struck up a peace upon base dishonorable terms with the Irish, our most savage and inhuman enemies; but whenever he invited the English to negotiations for peace—which he kept asking for, and which were always bootless—at those very times he was making every effort to prepare for war against them. In this situation, which way should they turn who were charged with the common weal? The safety of us all, with which they were entrusted—should

246. On May 6, 1648, the Houses sent to Scotland an assurance they did not seek to alter "the fundamental Government of the Kingdom by King, Lords, and Commons."

they betray it to our most bitter adversary? Should they leave us another seven years of almost exterminating war to bear again to the bitter end, not to forebode worse? God gave them a better mind, to prefer, pursuant to that Solemn League and Covenant, the common weal, and religion, and liberty, before their former thoughts of not dethroning the king (for they had not come to a vote); all which they saw—later indeed than behooved them, but still some time!—could not stand firm if and while the king stood. Surely Parliament ought never to be otherwise than entirely free and uncommitted, to provide in the best possible way for the good of the nation as occasion requires, nor so bound to their former opinions as to scruple to change—though God have given them the understanding and the means—to wiser ones thereafter for their own or the nation's good.

But "the Scots are of another opinion; for in a letter to the younger Charles they call his father a most sacred king, and the putting him to death a most execrable villainy." Take care to say no more of the Scots, whom you know not; we know them, and know the time when they called that very king a "most execrable" murderer and traitor; and the putting the tyrant to death a "most sacred" deed.

Then you pick holes in the sentence we drew up against the king, as not being properly drafted, and you ask "why we needed to add to the count of tyrant the titles of traitor and murderer, since the name tyrant includes all evils," and then you actually explain to us grammatically and lexicographically what a tyrant is! Off with your trifles, pedant, which that definition of Aristotle's that has lately been cited will alone easily blow away, and teach you, teacher, that the word *tyrant* (for you care not to understand aught but words) may well fall short of treason and murder.

But "the laws of England do not declare it treason or lese-majesty in the king to stir up sedition against himself or his people." Nor, say I, do they declare that Parliament can be guilty of lese-majesty, or hurting majesty, in deposing a bad king, or ever was guilty, though it has often deposed one in times past; but our laws do plainly declare that a king may indeed hurt his own majesty, and diminish it, yes and wholly lose it. For that expression in the law of St. Edward, of "losing the name of king," signifies neither more nor less than being deprived of the kingly office and dignity; as befel Chilperic king of France, whose example the law itself mentions in the same passage for the sake of illustration. There is not a lawyer amongst us who can deny that high treason may be committed against the kingdom as well as against the king. I appeal to Glanville himself, whom you cite: "If any man attempt to put the king to death, or raise sedition in the realm, it is high treason."[247] Thus that machination whereby certain Papists were making ready to blow up the Parliament-house with the Estates themselves in a single explosion of gunpowder was by King James himself and both Houses of Parliament adjudged to be "high treason" not against the King only, but against the Parliament and the realm. Where the truth is so clear, of what use is it to quote, as I yet could easily, more of our precedents established? For the thing itself is highly ridiculous, and contradictory to reason itself, that treason can be committed against the king, and cannot be against the people, on account of whom, for whose sake, by the grace of whom, and by whose good leave, so to speak, the king is what he is. So that you babble in vain over so many statutes of ours; in vain you torment yourself and steep yourself in our ancient law-books; for the laws themselves Parliament always had power to confirm or repeal; and to Parliament alone it belongs to declare what is treason, what lese-majesty. And I have often shown that this majesty never has so far deserted the people for the king, as not to be visibly more lofty and august in Parliament.

Who can yet endure to hear such an insipid French mountebank as you expound our laws? But you, English deserters! so many bishops, doctors, and lawyers, who proclaim that all learning and literature is fled out of England with yourselves, did not one of you know how to defend the king's cause and his own with sufficient vigor and Latinity, and submit it to the judgment of other nations? Did you fall so far short that this crackbrained purse-snatcher of a Frenchman

247. Ranulf de Glanville, *De Legibus et Consuetudinibus Regni Angliae* (1554), 1.2.

must needs be fetched out for hire to take sides with you, and undertake the defence of a helpless poverty-stricken king, attended though he was with so much infantry of speechless priests and doctors? Even for this too, believe me, your dishonor will blaze forth notorious among foreigners; and all men will consider that you deserved to fail at any rate in a cause which you availed not even to uphold by words, much less by force of arms and valor.

Now, goodman speechifier, I come to you again,—if at least you are come to yourself again; for here, so near the end of your book, I catch you snoring, and sleepily yawning out an irrelevant something-or-other about voluntary death. Then you deny "that it can occur to a king in his right wits to embroil his people in seditions, betray his own forces to defeat by enemies, and raise factions against himself." All which things having been done by many kings, and particularly by Charles himself, you can no longer doubt, especially being a Stoic, that, like all profligate villains, all tyrants too are downright mad. Hear what Flaccus says: "Whoever is led blindly on by malign stupidity and by whatsoever ignorance of truth, him doth Chrysippus' porch and school account a madman. This saying comprises great kings, this whole nations, except the wise man only."[248] So that if you would clear King Charles from the imputation of acting like a madman, you must rid him of wickedness first, before you can rid him of insanity.

But you say: "The king could not commit treason against such as were his own vassals and subjects." In the first place, since we are as free as any nation of mankind, we will not endure any barbarous custom to our hurt. In the second place, suppose we had been the king's "vassals"; even so we were not bound to endure a tyrant to lord it over us. And as for our being "subjects," all such subjection, as our own laws declare, is limited to what is "honorable and beneficial." Leg. Hen. I. Cap. 55. All our lawyers tell us that this engagement is "mutual" upon condition that the lord shall give, as the phrase goes, "liege protection and defense"; but if the lord be too harsh to his tenant, and

248. Horace *Second Satire* 2.3.

do him some cruel hurt, "all bond of homage is dissolved and utterly extinguished." These are the very words of Bracton and Fleta.[249] Hence there are situations in which the law itself arms the vassal against the lord, and delivers the lord over to be killed, if it so fall out, by the vassal in single combat. If a whole state or nation may not lawfully do the same to a tyrant, the condition of freemen will be worse than that of slaves.

Then you strive to excuse king Charles's murders, partly by murders committed by other kings, and partly by instances of right action on their part. For the matter of the Irish butchery, you "refer the reader to the king's well-known work the *Eikon Basilikė,*" and *I* refer *you* to *Eikonoklastes.* "The taking of La Rochelle," the betrayal of its townsmen, "the making a show of assistance instead of giving it them," you will not have laid at Charles's door, nor have I anything to say as to whether it deserves to be; he did mischief enough and more than enough at home, so that I need not take the trouble to follow up his misdemeanors abroad.[250] (But you in the mean time would make out all the Protestant churches that have at any time defended themselves by force of arms against kings who were professed enemies of their religion, to have been upon this one ground guilty of rebellion. Let these churches themselves consider how important it is for the preservation of ecclesiastical discipline and of their own integrity, not to pass by this insult offered them by their own nursling and disciple.) What troubles us most is that we English were betrayed in that expedition. He who had long designed to convert the government of England into a tyranny thought he could not accomplish his plan till the flower and strength of his subjects' military power were cut off.

Another of the king's crimes was the causing some words to be struck out of the usual coronation oath before he would take it. Unworthy and abominable action! Him that did it I call wicked; what

249. Bracton, *On the Laws and Customs of England,* bk. 2, chap. 35, 12; *Fleta,* bk. 3, chap. 16, 23–35.
250. Lord Buckingham led an assault upon the Isle of Rhe off Rochelle which failed and resulted in heavy losses to the English.

shall I call him that defends it? For by the eternal God, what breach of faith and violation of the laws can possibly be greater? What ought to be more sacred to him, next to the holy sacraments themselves, than that oath? Which, pray, is guiltier, he that offends against the law, or he that endeavors to make the law his accomplice in offending, or rather, destroys the law that he may not seem to offend against it? Look you: that oath, which he ought most scrupulously to have sworn to, this king of yours did violate; but that he might not seem openly to violate it, he craftily adulterated and foully corrupted it, and lest he might be said to have perjured himself, turned the very oath into a perjury. What else could be expected than that one who began his reign with so detestable a wrong, and dared as a first step to adulterate that law which he thought his only hindrance from perverting all the laws, would rule most unrighteously, craftily, and disastrously? But that "Oath" (thus you justify him) "cannot bind kings more than do the laws; and kings pretend that they will be bound by laws, and live according to them, though actually they are unbound by them." To think that anyone should express himself so impiously and sacrilegiously as to assert that a most solemn oath, sworn upon the Holy Evangelists, may without cause be unbound as if in itself it were the merest trifle! Scoundrel, monster, you are refuted by Charles himself, who, thinking that oath no trifle, chose rather by stealth to evade, or by artifice to elude, its binding force, than openly to violate it, and chose rather to be a corrupter and falsifier of the oath, than visibly a perjurer.

"The king indeed swears to his people, as the people do to him; but the people swear fealty to the king, not the king to them." Pretty invention! Does not he that promises and engages under oath faithfully to perform something, bind his fidelity to them that require the oath of him? To the performance of what he promises, every king does in fact swear to the people his "fealty, service, and obedience." Then you come back to William the Conqueror; yet even he was forced more than once to swear to perform not what was agreeable to him, but what the people and the great men of the realm demanded of him.

If many kings "receive the crown" without the usual solemnity, and accordingly reign without taking an oath, the same thing may be said of the people, a great many of whom never have taken the oath of allegiance. If the king by not taking an oath be unbound, the people are so too. And that part of the people that swore, swore not to the king only, but to the realm and the laws by which the king came to his crown, and to the king so far only as he should act according to those laws which "the common people," that is, the commonalty or House of Commons, "should choose." For it were folly always to wish to turn the phraseology of our laws into purer Latin. This clause, "which the commons shall choose," Charles before he was crowned procured to be razed out of the form of the royal oath. "But," say you, "without the king's assent the people can choose no laws"; and for this you cite two statutes, one 37 Henry VI, Chap. 15, and the other 13 Edward IV, Chap. 8. But either of the two is so far from appearing in our statute-books, that in the years you mention neither of those kings enacted any statute at all! Now that you are fooled, go and complain of the bad faith of those renegades in dictating to you statutes that never were heard of; while other people stand astonished at the combination of presumption with empty-headedness in you, who were not ashamed to pretend to be thoroughly versed in books which you have so clearly shown you have never looked into or so much as seen.

As for that clause in the coronation oath, which you, brazen-faced jack-pudding, dare to call "fictitious," you yourself say: "The king's defenders say that possibly" it may be extant in some ancient copies, "but that it fell into disuse because it had no satisfactory meaning." But precisely on this account did our ancestors put that clause into this oath, that it might have a meaning which would forever be *not* satisfactory to tyranny! If it had really fallen into disuse, however, which yet is utterly false, who would deny that there was the greater need of reviving it? But even that would have been to no purpose, according to your doctrine; for that custom "of taking an oath, as kings nowadays generally use it, is only ceremonial." Yet the king, when it behooved him to put down the bishops, pretended that he could not do it by reason of this same oath. Consequently that sacred solemn oath, according as it serves the king's turn or not, will be something genuine and immovable, or merely something empty and "ceremonial."

Englishmen, take notice of this, I adjure you, again and again, and consider what manner of king ye are like to have, if he ever come back! For it would never have entered into this rascally foreign grammarian's head to wish to write, or to think himself able to write, of the law of the English crown, had not Charles's banished son, deep-dyed in his father's teachings, together with those profligate prompters of his, eagerly supplied what they would have him write. 'Twas they dictated to him "that Parliament as a whole was liable to be charged with treason against the king" even for this alone, that "without the king's assent it declared all to be traitors who have taken arms against the Parliament of England; for that Parliament is the king's vassal"; but that the king's coronation oath is "merely a matter of ceremony." Then why not the vassal's oath too? So that no reverence for laws, no binding force of an oath, or scruple to break it, will avail to protect your lives and fortunes either from the cupidity of a king unbridled, or from the revenge of a king embittered, who from childhood has been taught to think that laws, religion, nay, and his own promise, ought to be his vassals, and subject to his will and pleasure. If you desire riches, liberty, peace, and empire, how much more excellent, how much more becoming yourselves would it be, resolutely to seek all these by your own virtue, industry, prudence, and valor, than under a royal despotism to hope for them in vain? They who think that these things cannot be compassed but under a king and lord—it cannot well be expressed how meanly, how dishonorably (I do not say how unworthily!) they think of themselves; for what do they other than confess that they themselves are lazy, weak, wanting in intelligence and prudence, and born to be slaves body and soul? All manner of slavery indeed is disgraceful to a man freeborn; but for you, after recovering your liberty with God to warrant and your own arms, after so many brave deeds done, and so notable an example made of a most mighty and puissant king, for you to desire, against your very destiny, to return again into bondage, will be not only most shameful, but a thing sinful and wicked. And your wickedness will be like unto the wickedness of them who were seized with desire of their former Egyptian bondage, and were at length divinely cut off with many and divers destructions, paying to God their deliverer the penalty for so slavish a mind.

You who would persuade us to become slaves, meanwhile what say you? "The king," you say, "had power to pardon treason and other crimes; which sufficiently proves that the king himself was not bound by the laws." The king might indeed pardon treason, not against the kingdom, but against himself, as anybody else may pardon a wrong done to himself; and he might perhaps pardon some other offenders, though not always. But does it follow that one who sometimes has some right to save an evildoer, shall therefore necessarily have any right whatever to destroy all good men? If the king be impleaded in an inferior court, he, like any one of the people, to be sure, is not obliged to answer but by his attorney; shall he therefore, when summoned by all of his subjects to appear in Parliament, refuse to come—refuse to answer in person?

You say that we "endeavor to justify our action by the example of the Dutch"; and hence, fearing to lose the pay with which the Dutch support such a murrain and pest as you, you would fain show "how unlike are their actions and ours," lest in defaming the English you should appear also to defame the Dutch who support you. I shall omit this comparison of yours, though some things in it are quite false, and other things reek flattery lest perchance you should not bring an acceptable offering unto your wages. For the English think they need not justify their actions by the example of any foreigners whatever. They have their laws of the land, which they have followed—laws which in this matter are the best in the world; they have for their imitation the examples of their ancestors, great and gallant men who never gave way to the unrestrained power of kings, and who put many of them to death when their government became insupportable. They were born free; they stand in need of no other nation; they can make unto themselves what laws they desire. One law in particular they venerate before the rest, a very ancient one enacted by nature itself, which measures all human laws, all civil right and government, not according to the lust of kings, but, above all else, according to the safety and welfare of good men.

Now I see nothing left over but rubbish and fragments of your earlier chapters; yet as you have raised an huge great heap of these at the end, I cannot imagine what other design you could have than to forebode the ruin of your whole fabric. At last after unmeasured talk you shut off the stream, "calling God to witness that you undertook the defence of this cause not only because you were asked, but because your conscience prompted you that you could defend no better cause." Merely because you were asked, would you intermeddle with our affairs, so utterly foreign to you, when we ourselves did not ask you? Would you rend with insults undeserved, would you in a disreputable book libel and defame, the supreme magistracy of the English nation, when according to the authority and power to them entrusted they do but their duty within their own jurisdiction—and all this without the least injury or provocation from them, for they did not even know that you were born? By whom, though, *were* you asked? By your wife, I suppose, who, they say, exercises the royal right over you, and, like the notorious Fulvia in the obscene epigram[251] from which a while ago (p. 320) you patched together a cento, cries to you whenever she has a mind: "Either" *write* "or we must fight!" Wherefore you preferred to write rather than the trumpets should sound the charge! Or were you asked by the younger Charles and that profligate crew of vagabond courtiers, like a second Balaam solicited by a second King Balak, to deign to restore by curses and ill writing a king's desperate cause that was lost by ill fighting? That may well be, except there was something like this difference: when *he* came to

251. Martial *Epigrams* 11.20.

curse, he was a clever man sitting upon a talkative little ass; you are a very talkative ass yourself, sat upon by a woman, and being overgrown with the healed heads of the bishops that heretofore you had wounded, you seem to present a sort of miniature portrait of that beast in Revelation.[252]

But they say that you repented yourself of this book a little after you had written it. It is mighty well; and therefore to witness your repentance unto all men, the first thing you ought to do will be, instead of so long a book, to make only just one proper long letter of yourself. For it was so Judas Iscariot repented himself, whom you resemble. Young Charles found it out too, and he sent you the purse, that badge of traitor Judas, precisely because he had heard before, and knew afterward by experience, that you were an apostate and the Devil. That other Judas betrayed Christ, and you betray Christ's Church. You had taught heretofore that Bishops were Antichrists; you have deserted to them. You have undertaken the cause of them that you had damned to Hell. Christ delivered all men; you have attempted to drive all men back into slavery. Never question, since you have been such a wicked wretch to God, to the Church, and to every nation of men, that the same fate awaits you as erewhile befel your double: out of despair rather than repentance, and utterly weary of yourself, to hang at last upon the gallows-tree, and burst asunder as he did; and to send beforehand that faithless and treacherous conscience of yours, that persecutor of good and holy men, to the place of torment that is sooner or later prepared for you.

And now I think, through God's good help, I have finished the work I undertook at the beginning, namely to defend both at home and abroad the noble actions of my countrymen against the brainsick envious rage of this mad sophist, and to assert the people's common rights against the unrighteous despotism of kings,—and this not out of any hatred of kings, but of tyrants. Nor have I knowingly left unanswered any argument or example or document alleged by my adver-

252. Rev. 13:1.

sary, that seemed to possess any solid substance or power to convince. Perhaps I have been nearer the opposite fault, that by rather too often answering also his sillinesses and threadbare quibbles as if they were arguments, I may seem to have given them an importance that they nothing deserved.

One thing yet remains, haply the greatest, and that is, that ye too, my countrymen, yourselves refute this adversary of yours, which to do I see no other way than by striving constantly to outdo all men's bad words by your own good deeds. Your vows, your burning prayers, when, crushed beneath more than one kind of slavery, ye fled to God for refuge, he hath graciously heard and granted. Gloriously hath he delivered you before all other nations from what surely are the two greatest mischiefs of this life, and most pernicious to virtue—Tyranny and Superstition; he hath inspired you with the greatness of soul to be the first of mankind who, after having conquered their own king, and having him delivered into their hands, have not hesitated to judge him with a judgment that yet resounds in men's ears, and to condemn him, and pursuant to that condemnation to put him to death. After so glorious a deed, ye ought to think, ye ought to do, nothing that is mean and petty, nothing but what is great and sublime. This praise that ye may attain, there is but one path to tread: as ye have subdued your enemies in the field, so ye shall prove that unarmed and in the midst of peace ye of all mankind have highest courage to subdue what conquers the rest of the nations of men—faction, avarice, the temptations of riches, and the corruptions that wait upon prosperity; and in maintaining your liberty shall show as great justice, temperance, and moderation as ye have shown courage in freeing yourselves from slavery. By these arguments and documents only can ye prove ye are not such as this libeler reproaches you with being—"Traitors, Robbers, Assassins, Parricides, Madmen"; that what ye did was not the slaughtering of a king because ye were driven by factiousness, or desire to usurp the rights of others, or mere quarrelsomeness, or perverse desires, or fury or madness, but was the punishing of a tyrant because ye were aflame with love of your liberty and your religion, of justice and honor, yea—and is not this the sum and end of all these?—with dear love of your country.

But if ye prove to be of other mind—which may the good God forbid forever!—if as ye have been valiant in war, ye should grow debauched in peace, if ye that have had such visible demonstrations of the goodness of God to yourselves, and of his wrath against your enemies, have not learned by so eminent and memorable an example before your eyes, to fear God and work righteousness, I for my part shall verily grant and confess, for I cannot deny, that the worst which slanderers and liars now speak or think of you is true. And in a little time ye will find God far more wrathful against you than either your adversaries have found him embittered, or ye have found him aforetime gracious and favorable beyond all other nations at this time on earth.

It is now several years since I published the foregoing, in haste, as reason of state then required, for I kept thinking that if ever I might take it in hand again at leisure, as occasionally happens, I might thereupon smooth out, or remove, maybe, or add somewhat. This I now judge that I have accomplished, though more briefly than I used to count upon doing it: a memorial which, such as it is, I see will not easily perish. Though someone may be found who may have defended civil freedom more freely than here it is defended, yet there shall hardly be found anyone who hath defended it in a greater and more glorious example. If, then, an action of example so high and illustrious is believed to have been as successfully accomplished as not without God's prompting undertaken, let this be reason good for thinking that in these my praises too it hath even by the same Might and Inspiration been glorified and defended. Indeed I had much rather all men thought so, than that any other success, whether of wit or judgment or industry, were allowed me. Yet as that famous Roman Consul,[253] upon retiring from office, swore in the popular assembly that the state and the city owed their safety to his single efforts, even so,

253. Cicero, referring to his struggle to expose Catiline's conspiracy.

as I now put the last touches to this work, so much only I dare assert, calling God and man to witness: that in this book I have indicated and brought to light, from the highest authors of wisdom both divine and human, matters whereby, I trust, not only the English people has been adequately defended in this cause, to the everlasting reputation of its posterity, but numerous other human beings as well, hitherto deluded by foul ignorance of their right and by false show of religion,—multitudes of men, I say, except such as themselves prefer and deserve to be slaves—have been quite set free. Now the oath of that Consul, great as were its claims, was in that same assembly ratified by oath of the whole Roman people with one mind and one voice; this conviction of mine, I have long understood, is fully ratified by the most excellent not only of my fellow-citizens, but of foreigners too, with the loud voice of nations everywhere.

This my zealous labor's fruit—the highest that I for my part have set before me in this life—I gratefully enjoy; yet therewith too consider chief how I may bear best witness—not only to my own country, to which I have paid the highest I possessed, but even to men of whatever nation, and to the cause of Christendom above all—that I am pursuing after yet greater things if my strength suffice (nay, it will if God grant), and for their sake meanwhile am taking thought, and studying to make ready.

# SECOND DEFENCE OF
# THE PEOPLE OF ENGLAND

*The work now generally referred to as* Second Defence of the People of England *was written in Latin (*Joannis Miltoni Angli Pro Populo Anglicano Defensio Secunda*) and directed against a proroyalist diatribe also in Latin composed anonymously and entitled* The Cry of the Royal Blood to Heaven Against English Parricides. *A Frenchman, Alexander More, was known to be the editor of the piece considered by Milton's party offensive to their cause. More was an itinerant scholar who had recently been ejected from an academic post in Middleburg for misconduct—apparently the sort of misconduct of which Milton makes More the butt of his ridicule in the pamphlet before us. Beyond the hearty invective, however, lie the important issues of the revolution, the case against Charles, the defense of Commonwealth policy, Milton's measured brief for Cromwell, and of great interest for the modern student of the poet-pamphleteer, Milton's own apologia for his political conduct as well as his account of his project for the furtherance of liberty on several fronts—personal, domestic, ecclesiastical, and civil.*

John Milton an Englishman His

# SECOND DEFENCE OF THE PEOPLE OF ENGLAND

Against
The Infamous Anonymous Libel, Entitled,
The Cry of the Royal Blood to Heaven,
Against the English Parricides.

As it is the first of duties, throughout the life of man, and in every condition, to be ever thankful to God, and mindful of his benefits; and as it should be our earliest and especial care, when events have been prosperous beyond our hopes and even our wishes, to return, on that account, our peculiar and solemn thanks— this I now feel incumbent on myself; and chiefly for three reasons. First, that I was born in those times of my country, when the effulgent virtue of its citizens—when their magnanimity and steadiness, surpassing the highest praise of their ancestors, under the inspection of God first implored, and under his manifest guidance, setting examples and performing deeds of valour, the greatest since the foundation of the world—delivered the Commonwealth from a grievous domination, and religion from a most debasing thraldom. And secondly, when there suddenly appeared many, who, as is customary with the vulgar, hatefully calumniated deeds nobly done; and when one,[1] above the rest, inflated and confident with literary pride, and with the opinion entertained of him by those of his own herd, nefariously undertook the defence of all tyrants, in a book beyond ex-

---

1. Claudius Salmasius (Claude de Saumaise); see headnote for the *First Defence,* p. 98.

ample scandalous, levelled against us—that I, rather than another, deemed not unequal to an adversary of so great a name, nor to speaking on so great a subject, accepted, of those very deliverers of the country, and by general consent, the part spontaneously assigned me; namely, to defend publicly (if any one ever did) the cause of the people of England, and thus of liberty itself. Lastly, I return thanks to God, that, in a task so arduous, so full of expectation, I neither disappointed the hopes nor the opinions of my fellow-citizens, nor failed to satisfy no small number of foreigners, as well among the learned, as among persons conversant with public affairs; that I even so completely routed my adversary, though of the most audacious order, that he retired with his spirit broken, his reputation shattered; and for the three years which he afterwards lived, much as in his rage he threatened, he gave us no farther trouble, than to solicit, for his support, the secret services of certain persons of the vilest character, and to suborn I know not what senseless and unconscionable applauders, to patch up, if possible, his unexpected and recent ignominy. This will immediately appear. As I conceived these fortunate, and even great events to have happened to me from above, and indeed, that they were particularly suited not only to discharge my debt of gratitude to the Deity, but to supply the most favourable omen for my proposed work, I thought it behoved me to begin, as I do, with the reverend mention of them. And who is there who considers not the honourable achievements of his country as his own? And what can be more for the honour or glory of any country, than liberty, restored alike to civil life, and to divine worship? What nation, what city has struggled for it, in both kinds, more successfully or more courageously? Indeed as courage shines out not exclusively in war and arms, but displays its intrepid power equally against every species of fear, those Greeks and Romans, whom we most admire, brought along with them, for the expulsion of tyrants from their states, scarcely any other virtue but zeal for liberty, accompanied with ready arms, and eager hands. The rest they achieved from the impulse thence derived, amid the general shout, applause, and joyous circumstance. They were even less eager for dangerous and uncertain enterprise, than for the trial of virtue fair and glorious, and for rewards and crowns, and the certain hope of immortal fame. For, the sovereign authority was not yet consecrated to tyrants. Tyrants, suddenly transformed into viceroys, forsooth, and vicars of Christ, could not yet exercise their power through royal grace; had not yet fortified themselves by the blind superstition of the vulgar. The lower orders, stupefied by the wicked arts of priests, had not yet degenerated into a barbarism viler than what disgraces the Indians, dullest of mortals: for these merely worship as gods those malignant demons they are unable to put to flight; while those, that they might not cashier tyrants when they had it in their power, exalted them into gods most impotent to rule over them—deifying the pests of the human race for their own destruction. Now against all these close embattlements of long-received opinions, religions, slanders, and terrors, more dreaded far by others than the enemy himself, had Englishmen to contend; and being better taught, and without doubt inspired from heaven, such was their confidence in their cause, such their firmness and strength of mind, that all these they overcame. Hence, though, in number, they were indeed a great people, yet were they, in spirit, so erect and lofty, that they were no longer a mere populace; even Britain herself, which heretofore has been said to be a land fruitful in tyrants, shall henceforth deserve the perpetual celebration of succeeding ages, as a country far more fruitful in deliverers. These men were never let loose, by a contempt or violation of the laws, to an unreigned licence; they were inflamed by no delusive vision of virtue and of glory, or by any foolish emulation of the ancients for the empty name of liberty; they were taught the straight and only way to true liberty, by innocence of life and sanctity of manners; they were compelled by necessity to arm in the just defence of the laws and of religion. Thus, confident of the divine aid, they drove out slavery in their glorious warfare. Of this glory, though I claim no share for myself, it is easy for me to defend myself against the charge, if any such be brought against me, either of timidity or of cowardice. For, if I avoided the toils and the perils of war, it was only that I might earnestly toil for my fellow-citizens in another way, with much greater utility, and with no less peril. In doubtful postures of our affairs, my mind never betrayed any symptom of despondence, nor was I more afraid than became me of malice, or even of death. Devoted even from a child to the more humanizing studies, and always stronger in mind than in body, I set an inferior value upon the service of the camp, in which I might have been easily surpassed by any ordinary man of a more robust make, and betook myself to those occupations, where my services could be of more avail; that, if I were wise, I might contribute my utmost power, from the higher and more excellent, not from the lower parts of my nature, to the designs of my country, and to this transcendent cause. I thought, therefore, that if it were the will of God those men should perform such gallant exploits, it must be likewise his will, that when performed, there should be others to set them forth with becoming dignity and ornament; and that the truth, after being defended by arms, should be alike defended by reason—the only defence which is truly and properly human. Hence it is, that while I admire those men, unconquered in the field, I complain not of the part allotted to myself; nay, I may rather congratulate myself, and once again return my highest thanks to the heavenly bestower of gifts, that such a lot has fallen to me, as may be viewed, with much greater reason, as a subject of envy to others, than in any way as a cause of repentance to myself. It is not my wish, however, to make a comparison of myself with any one, not even with the humblest; nor is it from any arrogant feeling that I have spoken a single word in my own behalf. But when I turn my mind to that cause, of all others the most noble and most renowned, and to this splendid office of defending even the defenders—an office assigned me by their own suffrages and judgments, I confess it is with difficulty I restrain myself from soaring to a more daring height than is suitable to the purpose of an exordium, and from casting about for something of more grandeur, to which I may give utterance: for, to whatever degree I am surpassed (of which there can be little doubt) by the ancient, illustrious orators, not only as an orator, but also as a linguist (and particularly in a foreign tongue, which I employ of necessity, and in which I am often very far from satisfying myself) I shall surpass no less the orators of all ages in the nobleness and in the instructiveness of my subject. This it is, which has imparted such expectation, such celebrity to this theme, that I now feel myself not in the forum or on the rostrum, surrounded by a single people only, whether Roman or Athenian, but, as it were, by listening Europe, attending, and passing judgment. I feel that I addressed myself in my former defence, and that I shall again address myself in this, to all sittings and assemblies, wherever are to be found men of the highest authority; wherever there are cities and nations. I imagine myself to have set out upon my travels, and that I behold from on high, tracts beyond the seas, and wide-extended regions; that I behold countenances strange and numberless, and all, in feelings of mind, my closest friends and neighbours. Here is presented to my eyes the manly strength of the Germans, disdainful of slavery; there the lively and generous impetuosity of the Franks, worthily so called; on this side, the considerate virtue of the Spaniards; on that, the sedate and composed magnanimity of the Italians. Wherever there are natures free, ingenuous, magnanimous, either they are prudently concealed or openly professed. Some favour in silence, others give their suffrages in public; some hasten to receive me with shouts of applause, others, in fine, vanquished by truth, surrender themselves captive. Encompassed by such countless multitudes, it seems to me, that, from the columns of Hercules to the farthest borders of India, that throughout this vast expanse, I am bringing back, bringing home to every nation, liberty, so long driven out, so long an exile; and as is recorded of Triptolemus[2] of old, that I am importing fruits for the nations, from my own city, but of a far nobler kind than those fruits of Ceres; that I am spreading abroad among the cities, the kingdoms, and na-

2. Ovid's *Metamorphoses* (5.643−50) tells of Ceres's sending Triptolemus in her chariot to sow the lands with wheat.

tions, the restored culture of citizenship and freedom of life. But if I am he, who laid low that redoubted satellite of tyrants,[3] hitherto deemed invincible in the general opinion, and in his own conceit; if I am he, who, when he disdainfully defied us and our embattled might, (and our chief men turning their eyes first upon me) engaged him in single combat, and with this stylus, the weapon of his choice, stabbed the reviler to the heart, and bore off abundant spoils;—unless I should choose to discredit, and wholly to disparage the estimates and opinions of hosts of intelligent readers on all sides, far from being devoted or under obligations to me; if I am he, I say, I shall return as one not utterly unknown, perhaps even not unwelcome. That all this is true, without any extravagant talking, is most clearly proved even from the following circumstances: when Salmasius, or Salmasia (for of what sex he was, was rendered extremely doubtful, from his being plainly ruled by his wife, alike in matters regarding his reputation, and in his domestic concerns) when Salmasius, or Salmasia, then, had indeed the honour of being invited by the most serene, the queen of Sweden[4] (than whom there lives not, I think, nor has ever lived one, who has more studiously cultivated the liberal arts, or who is a more generous patroness of men of letters) and when arrived in that country, of being treated, though a foreigner, with great distinction—he was there surprised, while dreaming of no such thing, by our Defence—an event which I must think could not have happened but by the will of God. Here it was immediately perused by no small number; and the queen, who was among its first readers, attentive only to what became her own dignity, remitted nothing, indeed, of her former grace and munificence towards her guest. For the rest, if it be allowable to disclose what I have often heard, and which is no secret, so remarkable a change was suddenly wrought in the sentiments of people, that the man, who, of yesterday, blossomed in the meridian beams of favour, is to-day almost withered; and on his leaving Sweden, which he did, with good leave, not long after, it became a matter of doubt

3.   Again, Milton's opponent Salmasius.

4.   Christina, who, however, subsequently invited Salmasius to return.

with many persons, whether his arrival was attended with more honour, or his departure with more contempt. It sufficiently appears also, that his reputation sustained no less injury in other places. But as to all these matters, I am not so situated as to be forced to trumpet my own praises. This is not at all necessary. I would only show more clearly that I had no light reasons for beginning, as I did, with giving my especial thanks to God most high and most excellent; I would show that this proem, in which I am able to evince by so many proofs, that I and my concerns (though in no wise free from the ills of humanity) are under the care of the Deity—must redound to my honour and fair fame; I would show that I am aided by the divine favour and help, in undertakings of the greatest magnitude, planned for the needed service of my country, and tending to be of the highest use to society and to religion, not in respect of one people only, much less of one unprincipled man, but rather of the universal race of man, against the enemies of man's freedom—addressing myself, as it were, to the multitudes of all nations gathered together and crowded into one vast congregation. It is not possible for me, nor can it ever be my desire, to ascribe to myself any thing greater or more glorious. Wherefore I implore the same immortal God, that as, upheld solely by his wonted aid and goodness, I have both justly and intrepidly defended deeds hitherto unparalleled, I may not be deficient in vindicating with the same or even greater, integrity, diligence, fidelity, and even success the authors, and myself also, conjoined as I am with so many others, in unmerited reproach and calumny, for purposes of ignominy instead of honour. And if there be any one who thinks that these things would have been better passed over in contempt, I do not dispute it, admitting these things to have been scattered among those who have understood us rightly; but how shall it be made appear at last to the rest of mankind, that the lies which our adversary has told are not truths? Yet, as we shall do our endeavour, which is no more than just, that however far slander has gone before, so far the avenger truth shall follow after, it is my belief that those who have been deceived will cease to think wrongfully of us, and that the adversary will peradventure be ashamed of his lies; and if he is not ashamed, that then it would at last be better to treat him with contempt. Meanwhile, I should have prepared a suitable reply to him with more despatch, if he had not all along entrenched himself in delusive rumours; giving out every now and then his menacing warnings, that Salmasius was sweating at the anvil, and fabricating new volumes against us, which he was even on the point of publishing.[5] By all this he merely effected that the punishment he would suffer for his slanderous tongue should be deferred: for I thought it behoved me to wait, that I might reserve my strength entire against the more potent adversary. But with Salmasius I imagine my battling is now at an end, for he is among the dead. And how he died I shall not undertake to say: for I will not impute to him his death as a crime, as he did to me my blindness. There are not wanting, however, those who lay the guilt of his death upon me, and upon those stings of mine which were but too sharp; and which, by resisting, he caused to sink the deeper. And while he saw the work he had in hand advance slower and slower; saw that the time for reply was gone by; saw that the grace of his work was no more: stung, moreover, by the recollection, that his fame, his estimation had perished; in fine, that the favour shown him by princes had abated, by reason of his poor defence of the royal cause—he is said, after three years of chagrin, to have died, worn away by sickness of mind, more than from any bodily disease. But however this may be, if I must engage him a second time—if I must wage even a posthumous war with an enemy, who is now sufficiently well known to me, as I have found no difficulty in sustaining the ferocity of his most vigorous charge, I can have no reason to dread his feeble and dying efforts.

5.    A reply was published after the death of Salmasius, not, however, the work to which Milton is here replying, which Milton attributes to Alexander More (1616– 70), a professor of ecclesiastical history at Amsterdam.

Today scholars agree that the work Milton targets in *Second Defence* was actually written by Peter Du Moulin, an Anglican priest, and that More arranged publication and inserted a preface. It is not clear whether Milton really believed or merely pretended to believe in More's authorship.

But, at length, let us now proceed to the personage, such as he is, who raises this cry against us. I hear the cry indeed, not of the royal blood, as the title would make us believe,[6] but of some skulking scoundrel: for the crier himself I no where find. Ho there! who are you? A man, or nobody? Certainly of the most beggarly order of men; for slaves even are not without a name. Shall I for ever be concerned with the nameless? Such, however, would be accounted king's men in a degree above their fellows. I should wonder if they persuaded kings of this. The followers and the friends of kings are not ashamed of kings. How then are these men friends to kings? They make no presents; on the contrary, they are far more ready to receive them. Those are not the men to expend their fortunes upon the royal cause, who venture not to bestow even their names. What then? They bestow words; but they have not enough good-will to persuade themselves, they have not enough constancy to have the courage to subscribe their names, and thus to bestow even words upon their kings for nothing. But ὦ ἄνδρες ἀνώνυμοι, anonymous Sirs! (for I may be allowed to address you in Greek, as I find no name for you in Latin) since your Claudius had undertaken to write, without a name, on the right of kings, a subject truly gracious, I might have followed his example, but that I was not so much ashamed either of myself or of my cause: besides, I thought it dishonorable to go to a subject of such grandeur, without openly declaring my name. How is it, that what I am seen to do openly against kings, in a commonwealth, you have not the spirit to attempt, unless secretly and by stealth, against a commonwealth in a kingdom, and under the patronage of kings? Why cast a cloud over the supreme power, the sovereign grace, by this invidious and suspicious timidity?—timorous when in safety, dark in the midst of light. Are you afraid lest kings should be too weak to protect you? Thus cloaked, thus muffled up, by Jove, one would think you come not as defenders to assert the right of kings, but as thieves to rob the treasury. Now what I am, I openly profess to be. The right

6. The anonymous attack against the *First Defence* was entitled *The Cry of the Royal Blood to Heaven Against the English Parricides*.

which I deny to kings, I would boldly persist in denying, in any legitimate kingdom. No monarch could injure me, without first condemning himself, by the confession that he was a tyrant. If I inveigh against tyrants, what is that to kings? between whom and tyrants I make the widest difference. As much as a good man differs from a bad, so much, do I maintain, that a king differs from a tyrant. Whence it follows, that a tyrant is not only no king, but is ever the most irreconcilable enemy to a king. And in fact, he who runs over the records of history will find that more kings have been overpowered and displaced by tyrants, than by the people. He who affirms, therefore, that tyrants ought to be displaced, affirms not that kings are to be displaced, but the bitterest foes to kings—foes, which, above all others are most hostile to kings. On the other hand, the right which you give to kings, that whatever they may choose to will, *that* shall be right, is not right, but wrong, but iniquity, but perdition itself. By a gift thus poisonous, instead of salutary, you become yourselves the murderers of those, who as you affirm, should be above all violence and all danger: you make a king and a tyrant identical, inasmuch as you ascribe the same right to both. And admitting that a king makes no use of this right of his (which he never will, as long as he shall be simply a king, and no tyrant) this is to be attributed not to the king, but to the man. Now what can be imagined more absurd than this kingly right, which if any king uses, that is, whenever he would be a king, he would cease to be a good man; whenever he should choose rather to be a good man, he would prove himself to be no king? What greater contumely can be cast upon kings? He who teaches this right must himself be most unjust—yea, the worst of his kind: for how can he be worse, than by first becoming himself such a one, as he thus moulds and fashions others. But if every good man is a king, as a certain sect of the ancients[7] magnificently philosophized, it follows, by parity of reason, that every bad man, according to his proportion, is a tyrant: and that he may not be puffed up with this name let it be

7.  The followers of Plato and the Stoics presumably.

observed, that a tyrant, so far from being anything great, is the meanest of earthly things; that as far as he surpasses all in the elevation of his rank, so far is he the vilest of all, and the most a slave. For others are the willing slaves, only of their own vices; he is obliged to be the slave, even against his will, not of his own vices only, but of the most importunate profligacies of his ministers and satellites; he is obliged to yield the subordinate branches of his tyranny to the most worthless of his creatures. Tyrants, therefore, are the most abject of slaves; they are slaves even to their own slaves. Hence, this name may be correctly applied even to the most insignificant pugilist of tyrants—nay to this crier; the reason of whose vociferating so furiously, in this tyrannous cause, will sufficiently appear from what has been already said, and from what shall be said presently; as likewise, the reason of his being anonymous. For either he is basely hired, like Salmasius, and has sold this cry of his to the royal blood; or it were nothing strange, if, smitten with a fearful consciousness of the infamy of its doctrine, or if, from his flagitious and scandalous life, he is desirous of concealment; perhaps even he places himself in such a position, as to snuff a more promising hope of gain from another quarter, that he may be free, in his own conscience, to desert kings at a future time, for some commonwealth, though yet to be established: and even in this case, he would not be without an example in his great Salmasius,[8] who, captivated by the glittering reward, revolted in his old age, from the orthodox to the bishops, from the popular party to the royalists. We are at no loss then to discover, who you are—crier as you are, from some paltry hovel; it is in vain you try to lurk unknown; be assured you shall be dragged to light, nor shall that Pluto's helmet[9] any longer protect you: I will make you swear to the latest day of your life, either that I am not blind, or at least that I am not purblind in respect of you. Listen now, if you have time (and it is a sort of Milesian,

8. Milton refers to Salmasius's traduction of his earlier attack upon Episcopacy in a work published in 1641.

9. Pluto's helmet was held to confer invisibility.

or Baian tale[10]) while I relate who he is, whence sprung, influenced by what expectation, by what allurements, coaxed by what panderly offices, he came to this cause of kings.

He is one "More," part Scot, part Frenchman, (that one nation or country may not lie under the whole infamy of his character) an unprincipled fellow, who, according to general report, and what is of most weight, according to the testimony of his friends (whom from fast friends he has made his greatest enemies) is without fidelity, without veracity, without gratitude; an evil-speaker, an unceasing slanderer of men, as likewise of women, whose modesty he is as little accustomed to spare, as their good name. This personage, to pass over the obscurity of his early life, first made his appearance as teacher of Greek at Geneva; and though he often explained to his scholars the meaning of his own name, Morus, in Greek,[11] he could not himself unlearn to be a fool and a profligate; besides, his being conscious of so many crimes, though perhaps not yet detected, served the more to work him up to such a pitch of madness, that he felt no horror at becoming a candidate for, and at defiling with his scandalous manners, the office of pastor in the church. But he could not long escape the censure of the presbyters. A trifler, and given to women, marked also for various other offences, convicted of numerous aberrations from the orthodox faith, which he was so base as to recant on oath, and so impious as to retain, he last of all turns out a notorious adulterer. He happened to be seized with a lawless passion for a servant girl of his host; and though the girl was married not long after to another, he still followed her; the neighbours had frequently observed them enter together a small lodge in the little garden. This amounts not, it may be said, to adultery; he might have been employed about something else. True, he might have been talking with her, for example, on the sub-

10. Brief and lewd erotic tales of the sort written by Aristides (c. 100 B.C.).

11. The Greek *Morus* translates as "fool." *Morus* in Latin means a mulberry tree, or in its diminutive *morillus* a little mulberry tree, which in turn allows Milton to indulge a witticism upon the story of Pyramus and Thisbe in Ovid at the expense of More's alleged sexual misadventure with Pontia.

ject of gardening; he might have taken occasion from gardens, from those of Alcinous,[12] suppose, or of Adonis,[13] to introduce certain lecturings of his to the woman, who might have been a prodigy of understanding, and eager to listen. He might now have praised the parterres; might even have wished for nothing more than shade; might have been allowed no other liberty than to engraft a mulberry in a fig, thence to raise, with the utmost dispatch, a line of sycamores — a most delectable walk. Then he might have shown the woman the manner of engrafting. All these things and many more he might have done; who denies it? But all these things would not satisfy the presbyters, but they must smite him with their censure as an adulterer, and sentence him as totally unworthy of the pastoral office. The heads of these and of similar charges are still preserved in the public library of that city. In the meantime, while these proceedings were not publicly known, he receives by the influence of Salmasius, from the Gallican church at Middelburg, an invitation to Holland; and to the great offence of Spanheim (a man truly learned, and a pastor of the first character, who had known him well before at Geneva,) contrived to obtain of the Genevese, but on condition only of his quitting Geneva, letters testimonial, as they are called, (and these, to tell the truth, were rather cold); though, at the same time, there were some who thought it not to be borne, that a man of his description should be graced with the testimony of the church; while others again were of opinion, that anything was to be borne, rather than the man himself. On his arrival in Holland, and going to pay his respects to Salmasius, he cast his wanton eyes on the servant-girl of Salmasius's wife, whose name was Pontia: for the fellow's lust always lights upon waiting-maids. From this, he began to pay court to Salmasius with his utmost assiduity, and, as often as he could, to Pontia. I know not, whether Salmasius, pleased with his adulation and struck with the thought of using him

12. Odysseus encounters miraculously the abundant gardens of King Alcinous in the fifth book of the *Odyssey*.

13. *Gardens of Adonis* were small containers of plants stimulated to rapid growth but short-lived.

for his convenience, or whether More, thinking to contrive a desirable opportunity of meeting Pontia the more frequently, was the first to begin the conversation on the subject of Milton's Answer to Salmasius. However this may be, More undertakes to defend Salmasius, and Salmasius on his part promises to procure for More the divinity-chair in that city: and More promises himself both this, and the additional douceur of Pontia's stolen embraces. On pretence of consulting Salmasius about that work, he frequents his house day and night; and as Pyramus of old was transformed into a mulberry tree, so the mulberry now fancies itself suddenly changed into Pyramus— the Genevan into the Babylonian. But exceeding that youth in good fortune as much as he exceeds him in wickedness, he has now the liberty of speaking with his Thisbe, his Pontia, whenever he pleases, under the same roof; there is no need of searching for a chink in the wall. He promises her marriage: and with this delusive hope debauches her; in committing which crime (I shudder with horror while I relate it, but it must be related) a minister of the holy gospel defiles even the house of his host. From this connection, there followed, in due time, something strange and monstrous—out of the common course of nature. Not the female only, but the male conceived; Pontia a Moreling which, for a long time after, served to exercise the Plinian exercitator,[14] Salmasius; More this addle and windy egg, from which burst forth that tympany—the *Cry of the Royal Blood.* This was thought at first a most delicious sup for our hungry royalists in Belgium; but now the shell is broken, they turn with loathing from the rotten and offensive contents. As for More, inflated in no small degree with this birth of his, and thinking he had deserved well of the whole Orange faction, he was already seizing, in his presumptuous expectations, new professorial chairs; and like a scoundrel as he is, had already deserted his poor, humble Pontia, she being only a waiting maid, and now great with child. Thus despised and deluded, she complained to the synod and magistrates, imploring their pro-

14. *Plinian exercitator:* An allusion to Pliny the Elder, the author of a vast compendium of horticultural lore in his *Naturalis historia,* written in the first century.

tection. Hence the affair at length became public, and long furnished a subject for mirth and derision at almost all convivial meetings and parties. This gave occasion to somebody (and whoever he was, he had no contemptible genius for wit) to write the following distich:

As your belly, Pontia, 'gins to swell,
From tread of the Gallican;
That under More, you've been Mored, well,
Deny it not a man.


Pontia alone is not seen to smile; but she gained nothing from complaint: for the cry of the royal blood easily drowned the cry of her violated chastity, and the lamentation of a poor defiled girl. Salmasius too, full of vexation at the injury and dishonour brought upon himself and household, and that he had been thus made the sport of his friend and panegyrist; that he was thus again at the mercy of his adversary—this new misfortune, added to his former ill-success in the royal cause, was perhaps the circumstance which not long after brought him to his end. But of this by and by. In the meantime, Salmasius, not unlike in fate to Salmasis, (for as the name, so the tale is not inapt) unconscious that More, whom he had associated to himself, was an hermaphrodite, alike capable of procreation and of parturition, not aware of what More had begotten at home, he fondles in ecstasy what he had brought forth—namely the book in which he found himself so often styled great; being, no doubt in his own estimation, worthily praised, though certainly, in the estimation of others, most absurdly and ridiculously. However, he goes with all haste in search of a printer; and struggling in vain to keep hold of the fame which had been so long deserting him, those praises, or rather those gross flatteries, which he had pitifully coveted, through this man and others, he lends his obstetric services for bringing into the world. For this business one Vlaccus is found to be the fittest of all others. Him he easily persuades not only to print the said book, which nobody could have blamed; but also to profess himself, by subscribing his name, the author of a letter addressed to Charles, full of reproaches and contumelies upon me, who had never any knowledge of the man. That no one, however, may feel surprise, that he suffered himself so easily to be prevailed upon to set upon me with such insolence without cause, and to think it, as he does, so trifling a matter thus to become a proxy for venting other people's fury, I shall show (for I have made the discovery) how he has conducted himself towards the rest of mankind.

This Vlaccus, whose country I know not, is a sort of vagabond bookseller, a spendthrift, and a practised impostor. For some time, he carried on a clandestine trade, as a bookseller, in London; from which city, after innumerable frauds, he fled for debt. At Paris, the whole of the Rue St. Jacques knew him for his total want of credit, and for his dishonest practices; and having been formerly a fugitive from this city also, he dares not approach it within many parasangs. At this time, if any one has need of a venal and most incorrigible rogue, he shows himself newly furbished up as a printer at the Hague. Now, that you may know what he is saying, or what he is doing; how totally without business he is; that there is nothing so sacred which he would not regard as of less value than even the most trifling gains; and that it was from no public consideration, as any one would have thought, that he raged so furiously against me—I shall produce himself as an evidence witnessing against himself. He no sooner observed that some booksellers had got money by what I had written against Salmasius, than he writes to certain friends of mine to use their interest with me, that, if I had any thing to print, it might be thrown into his hands; assuring them it should be printed in far better type than what had been used by my former printer. I replied, through the medium of those friends, that at present I had nothing to print. But behold! not long after, he comes forth as the author (the suppositious one indeed) of a production full of the grossest abuse against the very man to whom lately he had so officiously offered his services. My friends express their indignation. The fellow, unrivalled in impudence, writes in answer, that he is astonished at their simplicity and ignorance of the world, in expecting or even in desiring any regard to duty or honesty from him, seeing by what business he got his livelihood; that he had received the said letter, together with the book, from Salmasius himself, who asked him, as a favour, whether he would do what he has actually done; that if Milton, or any one else, should think proper to reply, and chose to make use of his labour, he had no scruple: that is, either against Salmasius, or against Charles: for in such reply, this was the only thing which he could expect to happen. I need say no more; you see the man.

I now proceed to the rest: for there were more than one concerned in getting up this tragedy, as they would make it, of the royal cry. Here then in the beginning, according to custom, you have the *dramatis personae:* The cry, by way of prologue; Vlaccus, a paltry rogue; or if you will, Salmasius, disguised as the rogue Vlaccus; two poetasters, drunk with stale beer; More, adulterer and whore-master. Admirable set of tragedians, truly! the battle in array with which I have to encounter! But as our cause could hardly be expected to have different adversaries, let us now attack them, such as they are, one after another; only premising, that if any one should think our refutation deficient in gravity, he should consider that we have not to do with a grave adversary, but with a herd of players; to which, while it was necessary to accommodate the nature of the refutation, we thought it proper to have in view not always what would be most suitable to decorum, but what would most suit them.

## THE CRY OF THE ROYAL BLOOD TO HEAVEN AGAINST THE ENGLISH PARRICIDES

If, More, you had shown that blood to have been unjustly shed, your account might have worn an appearance of plausibility. But, as in the early periods of the reformation, the monks, from their weakness in argument, were used to have recourse to all manner of spectres and imaginary monsters; so you, after all other things have failed, resort to cries which were never heard and to arts of despicable friars, which are grown out of date. You would be far enough from giving credit to any one of our party, who should affirm that he had heard voices from heaven; though I should have little difficulty in believing (with which you charge me) that you had heard cries from hell. But tell us, I beseech you, who heard this cry of the royal blood? You say that you heard it: trash! for in the first place, you are never favoured in what you hear; and the cry which ascends to heaven, if heard by any but God, is heard, as I must think, by the just and the upright alone; inasmuch as they being themselves void of offence, are authorized to denounce the wrath of God on the guilty. But to what end should you hear it?—That, lecher as you are, you might write a satire? For it appears, that at the very time you were forging this cry to heaven, you were slyly playing the wanton with Pontia. You have many impediments, More, you have many things ringing within and without, which will not suffer you to hear things of that nature which have reached to heaven; and if you had nothing else to prevent you, the loud cry which is raised to heaven against yourself, would certainly be sufficient. That strumpet of yours of the garden, who has complained, that what most of all led to her seduction was the example of yourself her own pastor, is crying, whether you know it or not, against you; the husband whose bed you violated is crying against you; Pontia is crying, with whom you broke your nuptial compact; and if any one is crying, that little infant is crying, whom you begot in shame, and abandoned a helpless babe. If you hear not all these cries to heaven against yourself, you never could have heard the cry of the royal blood. At the same time, this libel, instead of being called the cry of the royal blood to heaven, may be more properly inscribed—More's lascivious neighing for his Pontia.

The prolix and stale epistle which follows is devoted in part to Charles, in part to Milton, to extol the one, and to vilify the other. From the very beginning, you may form your judgment of the author. "The dominions of Charles (says he) have fallen into the sacrilegious hands of parricides, and (because proper words could not be found, we are abused in a word from Tertullian[15]) of deicides." Whether his rant is to be referred to Salmasius, to More, or to Vlaccus, let us pass it by. But what he says a little after—"That there lives not the man who is more studious to promote the happiness of Charles," though only ridiculous to others, must rouse the indignation of Charles. And is there no one alive more studious of his happiness than you, who have offered to the enemies of Charles, your services in the very same way—that is, to write a letter, and afterwards to print it? Well might you call the king miserable, in being thus deserted by his friends, when a rascally printer can presume to rank himself among the few more intimate friends which remain: miserable indeed, when his most faithful friends do not surpass in faith and studious regard the perfidious Vlaccus. What could he say more arrogant, as it respects himself, or more contemptuous, as it regards the king and his friends the royalists? Nor is it less ridiculous to introduce an illiterate mechanic philosophizing on the weightiest subjects, and on the virtues of kings; uttering sentiments, such as they are, which could not have been bettered either by Salmasius or More. To tell the truth, I have discovered Salmasius, here, as often elsewhere, and by no obscure signs, to be a man, though of great reading, of an unexercised and puerile judgment. Though he must have read—that the chief magistrates in the excellently modelled commonwealth of Sparta, if any wise saying happened to fall from a worthless character, ordered it to be taken from him, and conferred by lot upon some man of virtue and prudence—he was yet so ignorant of every thing that is called decorum, as to do quite the reverse—as to suffer opinions, which he thought becoming in an honest and prudent person, to be put into the mouth of a man who is an arrant scoundrel. Be of good cheer, Charles: the scoundrel Vlaccus, "from his trust in God," bids you be of good cheer. "Don't throw so many sufferings away": Vlaccus, the most prodigal of spendthrifts, who has thrown away his whole sub-

15. Quintus Septimus Florens Tertullianus (c. 160 – c. 240), a Christian apologist and rhetorician noted for his vehement polemical style.

stance, if he ever had any, counsels you not to throw away your sufferings. "Make use of fortune, who is thus acting towards you as a
stepmother." And can you avoid making use of her, especially when
you have such an adviser, who, for so many years, has been in the
habit, right or wrong, of using other people's fortunes? "You have
drunk deep of wisdom; drink on": so counsels, so directs the drunken
Vlaccus, the unrivalled preceptor of kings, who, amidst his fellow-
workmen and pot-companions, seizing the leathern flaggon with his
inky hands, drinks a mighty draught to your wisdom. Such are the
goodly counsels, to which your Vlaccus ventures to put his name, and
which Salmasius and More, with the rest of your champions, are either too timid, or too proud to acknowledge: that is, whenever you
require to be advised or defended, they are always wise or brave, not
in their own name, but in the name of another, and at another's hazard. Whoever this personage may be, therefore, let him cease idly to
vaunt his "bold and manly eloquence," when the man, who is eminent (please the gods) for the elegance of his genius, was afraid to give
up "his very celebrated name." The book, in which he has avenged,
as he says, the royal blood, he dared not even dedicate to Charles, but
through his confident and deputy Vlaccus; meanly content to signify,
in the words of his printer, "that, with your permission, O king, he
was going," without a name, "to dedicate the book to your name."

Having thus dispatched Charles, he is now preparing, with no
little blustering, his attack upon me: "After these preludes, the wonderful Salmasius will blow the terrible trumpet." You prognosticate
health, and give us notice of a new kind of musical harmony: for
when that terrible trumpet shall be blown, we can think of no fitter
accompaniment for it than a reiterated crepitation. But I would advise Salmasius not to inflate his cheek overmuch: for you may take
my word for it, that the more it is swollen out, the fairer will he present it for slaps, in musical response, while both his cheeks ring again,
to this modulated tone of the wonderful Salmasius, with which you
are so delighted.—You continue to croak. "Who has neither an equal

nor a second in the whole circle of literature and of science." Can you believe it, ye learned, whoever you are, can you believe it, that this book-worm of a grammarian, whose whole ability and hope turned upon a glossary, does thus indeed rank above you all? A man whom the devil might well take as the hindermost, if compared with men truly learned.—But the assertions which follow are so foolish, that they could never have been made, but by some low fellow, and infatuated to a degree even below Vlaccus: "And who has now brought to your majesty's cause an erudition stupendous, infinite, conjoined with a celestial genius." If you recollect what I have told you above, that it was Salmasius himself who brought this epistle, together with the book, to be printed; that it was written either by himself, or by some person who was nameless; that he entreated the obsequious typographer to put his name to it, as the author himself would not— you will judge him to be a man of a mind most weak and abject; thus pitifully spreading his sails to catch the breeze of his own panegyric, thus artfully endeavouring to entrap the immoderate praises of so senseless an encomiast!—"In vain do a few buffet the immortal work; the lawyers cannot sufficiently admire, that a Frenchman should so soon make himself master of English affairs, laws, acts of parliament, instruments, and disentangle them," &c. Nay, what nonsense he has talked, what a mere parrot he has been, on the subject of our laws, we have abundantly shown, and in the opinion too of our lawyers.— "But soon, he himself, in another impression which he is meditating upon the rebels, will at once stop the mouths of the Theons, and chastise Milton for us according to his deserts." You yourself, then, like the little fish which goes before the whale as a client his patron, are merely the harbinger of the whale Salmasius, who is threatening an invasion of our shores! We sharpen our harpoons and instruments of iron, that we may secure whatever oil or pickle may be obtained from that invasion and meditated castigation of us. Meanwhile, we admire the more than Pythagorean benevolence of the great man, who, compassionating even animals, and above all fish, to whose flesh even Lent

shows no indulgence, could have destined so many volumes to en-
wrap them decently, and out of so many thousands of poor tunnies,
may be, or herrings, could have bequeathed a papercoat for each!

> Rejoice ye herrings, and ye fish beside,
> That, the winter chill, in cold friths abide;
> For the good Salmasius, that piteous knight,
> Of paper liberal, saddens at your plight;
> Your nakedness to clothe, he'll frocks prepare,
> The insignia, name, and honours that shall bear
> Of Claude Saumaize; that through the fishy mart,
> You all may wear your paper liveries smart,
> As clients of the knight; a prize to those,
> Who on their tunic's sleeve do wipe their nose.

I wrote these lines on the long-expected edition of this far-famed
work; and while, as you tell us, Salmasius was meditating this impression, you, More, were contaminating his house, by a most shameless
commerce with Pontia. It appears indeed, that Salmasius long applied
himself, and with great earnestness, to finish the work: for, a few days
before his death, when a certain literary man, from whom I had the
account, sent to inquire of him, when he intended to publish the second part of what he had prepared against the pope's supremacy, he
replied, that he should not return to that work, till he had completed
what he had still in hand against Milton. And so, I am even preferred
to the pope for refutation. That pre-eminence which he denies him
in the church, he spontaneously concedes to me in his enmity. It seems
then I have made a timely diversion for the supremacy of his holiness,
since it was to have been overturned without delay. I have diverted
from the walls of Rome this new Catiline,[16] though not invested in
the consular robe, as of old the consul Tullius, nor was it done in a
dream, but in a very different manner; and shall merit for this service
something beyond a mere cardinalship; I even suspect that the Roman

---

16. Catiline led an abortive conspiracy to overthrow the late republic. His attempt
was exposed by Cicero, the "Tullius" mentioned in the next clause.

pontiff, transferring to me the title of our kings, will hail me as defender of the faith. You see what an artificer of envy Salmasius has been to me; yet, it is his place to see to it, who, basely deserting so honorable an office to mix in strangers' controversies, withdrew himself from the cause of the church, to political and foreign concerns, with which his own had nothing to do; who made a truce with the pope; and what was baser than all, became reconciled to the bishops, after declaring open war against them.

Let us come now to the charges against me. Can he find any thing to blame in my life or manners? Clearly nothing. What does he do then? He does what none but a brute and barbarian would have done; he upbraids me with my person, and with my blindness.

A monster horrid, ugly, huge, and blind.

I certainly never thought I should have to contend with the cyclops for the point of beauty! But he immediately corrects himself. "He is not huge, it is true: for nothing can be more lean, bloodless, and shrivelled." Though it is to little purpose for a man to speak of his beauty; yet at last, as I have reason, in this particular also, for giving thanks to God, and am able to confound liars, lest any one should haply think me some monster with a dog's head, or a rhinoceros (as the Spanish vulgar, trusting but too much to their priests, imagine of heretics) I will say a few words.

No one, who has only seen me, has ever to my knowledge, thought me ugly: whether handsome or not, is a point I shall not determine. My stature, I own, is not tall; but may approach nearer to the middle than to the small size. And what if small, as many men have been, who were of the very first rank, both in peace and war; and why should that stature be called small, which is large enough for every virtuous purpose? But it is not true, that I am thus lean beyond example; on the contrary, I possess that spirit and strength, that, when my age and manner of life so inclined me, I was neither unskilled in handling my sword, nor unpractised in its daily use. Armed with this weapon, as I commonly was, I thought myself a match for any man, though far my superior in strength, and secure from any insult which one man could offer to another. At this day, I have the same spirit, the same strength, my eyes only are not the same; yet, to external appearance, they are as completely without injury, as clear and bright, without the semblance of a cloud, as the eyes of those whose sight is the most perfect. In this respect only am I a dissembler; and here, it is against my will. In my countenance, than which, as he has said, there is "nothing more bloodless," there still remains a colour so very opposite to the bloodless and pale, that, though turned of forty, there is scarcely any one who would not think me younger by nearly ten years. It is equally untrue, that either my body or my skin is shrivelled. In these particulars, were I guilty of any falsehood, I should deservedly expose myself to the ridicule of many thousands of my countrymen, who know me personally, and even of foreigners not a few. Now if this man be detected of telling such impudent and unfounded falsehoods, on a subject it was not at all necessary for him to meddle with, you may form a correspondent conjecture as to the rest.

Thus much have I been even constrained to say of my person. Of your person, though I have understood it to be most contemptible, and the living image of the wickedness and malice which dwell within you, I neither care to speak, nor do others care to hear. Would it were equally in my power to confute this inhuman adversary on the subject of my blindness! but, it is not. Then, let us bear it. To be blind is not miserable; not to be able to bear blindness, that is miserable. But why should I be unable to bear that which it behoves every one to be prepared to bear, should the accident happen to himself, without repining? Why should I be unable to bear what I know may happen to any mortal being,—what I know has actually happened to some of the most eminent and the best of men, on the records of memory? Or shall I mention those old poets, ancientest and wisest, whose calamity the gods are said to have recompensed with far more excelling gifts, and men to have honoured with that high honour, as to choose rather to blame the gods themselves, than to impute their blindness to them as a crime. What is handed down of the augur Tiresias is well known.[17] Of Phineus thus sang Apollonius in his Argonautics:

> Not Jove himself he feared; his daring ken
> With truth disclosed the will of fate to men;
> With length of years did Jove him hence requite,
> But his eyes bereft of the day's sweet light.

But God himself is truth; and the more closely any one adheres to truth, in teaching it to mankind, the more nearly must he resemble God, the more acceptable must he be to him. It is impious to believe God to be jealous of truth, or to be an enemy to the utmost freedom of its communication to men. It does not appear, therefore, that it was for any crime, that this ancient sage, who was so zealous to enlighten human kind, and that many among the philosophers, were deprived of light. Or, should I mention those men of old, so deserving of admiration for their civil wisdom, as also for their great actions? And first, Timoleon of Corinth[18]—the deliverer of his own city, and of all Sicily—than whom, a better man or more revered in the commonwealth no age has produced. Next, Appius Claudius, who, by nobly declaring his sentiments in the senate, delivered Italy from Pyrrhus, a formidable enemy; but himself delivered not from blindness.[19] Then Caecilius Metellus[20] the high-priest, who lost his eyes, in saving from the flames not the city only, but the Palladium, on which hung the destiny of the city, as also the most sacred of the religious mysteries; though on other occasions it is certain that God has declared that his favour attends a devotedness so extraordinary, even

17. Although blinded by an irate Hera, Tiresias was renowned for the reliability of his foresight and for the accuracy of his prophecies.

18. See the account of Timoleon's life in Plutarch's *Lives of the Ancient Grecians and Romans,* chap. 37.

19. Plutarch *Life of Pyrrhus,* chap. 18.

20. *Lucius Caecilius Metellus,* consul in 251 B.C., saved a sacred statue of Minerva, the *Palladium.*

among the Gentiles. What therefore has happened to such a man, I can hardly think should be considered as an evil. Why should I add others of later times—as Dandolo[21] prince of Venice, the first man by far of all his compatriots; or Ziska[22] the gallant duke of Bohemia, champion of the orthodox faith? Why divines of highest name, Hieronymus Zanchius,[23] with some others? When it is well known, that the patriarch Isaac himself, than whom no mortal was ever more dear to God, lived blind no small number of years; and for some time, perhaps Jacob also his son, of God no less beloved; when, in fine, it is beyond all doubt, from the divine testimony of Christ our Saviour, that the man whom he healed had been blind even from the womb, for no sin either of himself or of his parents. As for myself, I call thee, O God, to witness, the searcher of the inmost spirit, and of every thought, that I am not conscious of any offense (though, to the utmost of my power, I have often seriously examined myself on this point, though I have visited all the recesses of my heart) recently committed or long ago, the heinousness of which could have justly caused, could have called down this calamity upon me above others. Whatever I have written, yea, at any time (since the royalists in their exultation imagine I am now suffering for it, by way of atonement, as they will have it) I call the same God to witness, that I have written nothing, which I was not persuaded at the time, and am still persuaded, was right, and true, and pleasing to God; and this without being moved by ambition, by lucre, or by glory; but solely by a sense of duty, of grace, and of devotion to my country; that, above all, I have done this, with a view not only to the deliverance of the commonwealth, but likewise of the church. Hence, when that office against the royal defence was publicly assigned me, and at a time when not

21. Enrico Dandalo (1120–1205), although he was blind since his youth, led an army that rescued the famous bronze horses of St. Mark.

22. John Zisca, blinded in war, continued to win victories in the civil conflicts that beset the German states in the first part of the fifteenth century.

23. Jerome Zanchius was a sixteenth-century convert to Protestantism who held a chair of theology in Strasbourg.

only my health was unfavorable, but when I had nearly lost the sight of my other eye; and my physicians expressly foretold, that if I undertook the task,[24] I should in a short time lose both—in no wise dismayed at this warning, methought it was no physician's voice I heard—not the voice even of Aesculapius[25] from the shrine of Epidaurus—but of some diviner monitor within; methought, that, by a certain fatality in my birth, two destinies were set before me, on the one hand, blindness, on the other, duty—that I must necessarily incur the loss of my eyes, or desert a sovereign duty. Nor did I fail to recollect the two-fold destiny, which the son of Thetis[26] reports that his mother brought back concerning himself, when she went to consult the oracle at Delphi:

> Two fates conduct me to the realms of night:
> If staying here around Troy-town I fight,
> I return no more; but my glory fair
> Shall shine immortal, and my deeds declare:
> If to my dear and native land I'm led,
> Long is my life; but my glory is fled.
>
> *Iliad 9.*

Hence I thought with myself, that there were many who purchased a less good with a greater evil; for example—glory, with death. On the contrary, I proposed to purchase a greater good with a less evil; namely, at the price of blindness only, to perform one of the noblest acts of duty; and duty, being a thing in its own nature more substantial even than glory, ought on that account to be more desired and venerated. I decided, therefore, that, as the use of light would be allowed me for so short a time, it ought to be enjoyed with the greatest possible utility to the public. These are the reasons of my choice;

---

24. Milton wrote his reply to Salmasius and saw it through the press barely a year and a half after the publication of his rival's work.
25. The god of medicine.
26. Achilles.

these the causes of my loss. Let the slanderers, then, of the judgments of God cease their revilings; let them desist from their dreamy forgeries concerning me; in fine, let them know, that I neither repine at, nor repent me of my lot; that I remain fixed, immovable in my opinion; that I neither believe, nor have found that God is angry; nay, that in things of the greatest moment I have experienced, and that I acknowledge his mercy, and his paternal goodness towards me; that above all, in regard of this calamity, I acquiesce in his divine will, for it is he himself who comforts and upholds my spirit—being ever more mindful of what he shall bestow upon me than of what he shall deny me; last of all, that I would not exchange my own consciousness of what I have done, for any act of theirs however well performed, or lose the recollection of it, which is always so calm and delightful to me. As to blindness, I would rather at last have mine, if it must be so, than either theirs, More, or yours. Yours, immersed in the lowest sense, so blinds your minds, that you can see nothing sound or solid; mine, with which you reproach me, deprives things merely of their colour and surface; but takes not from the mind's contemplation whatever is real and permanent in them. Besides, how many things are there, which I should choose not to see; how many which I might be unwilling to see; and how few remaining things are there which I could desire to see! Neither am I concerned at being classed, though you think this a miserable thing, with the blind, with the afflicted, with the sorrowful, with the weak; since there is a hope, that, on this account, I have a nearer claim to the mercy and protection of the sovereign father. There is a way, and the Apostle is my authority, through weakness to the greatest strength.[27] May I be one of the weakest, provided only in my weakness that immortal and better vigour be put forth with greater effect; provided only in my darkness the light of the divine countenance does but the more brightly shine: for then I shall at once be the weakest and the most mighty; shall be at once blind, and of the most piercing sight. Thus, through this infirmity should I

27. Heb. 11:34.

be consummated, perfected; thus, through this darkness should I be enrobed in light. And, in truth, we who are blind, are not the last regarded by the providence of God; who, as we are the less able to discern any thing but himself, beholds us with the greater clemency and benignity. Woe be to him who makes a mock of us; woe be to him who injures us; he deserves to be devoted to the public curse. The divine law, the divine favour, has made us not merely secure, but, as it were, sacred, from the injuries of men;[28] nor would seem to have brought this darkness upon us so much by inducing a dimness of the eyes, as by the overshadowing of heavenly wings; and not unfrequently is wont to illumine it again, when produced, by an inward and far surpassing light. To this I attribute the more than ordinary civilities, attentions, and visits of friends; of whom there are some, with whom, as with true friends, I may hold the dialogue of Pylades and Orestes:

> *Orest.* Go slowly on, and be the rudder of my feet.
> *Py.* Precious is my charge.
>
> *Eurip. in Orest.*[29]

And in another place:

> Give your hand to your friend and helper.
> Throw your arm about my neck, and I will be your guide.
>
> *Id. in Her. furent.*[30]

For they do not suppose that by this misfortune I am rendered altogether a nullity; they do not suppose that all which belongs to a man of sense and integrity is situated in his eyes. Besides, as I am not grown torpid by indolence, since my eyes have deserted me, but am still active, still ready to advance among the foremost to the most arduous struggles for liberty; I am not therefore deserted even by men

28. Deut. 27:18.
29. Euripides *Orestes* 796.
30. Euripides *Hercules Maddened* 1398–1402.

of the first rank in the state. On the contrary, such men, considering the condition of humanity, show me favour and indulgence, as to one who has completed his services; and readily grant me exemption and retirement. They despoil me of no dignity, they deprive me not of any public office I before held; they disparage not the benefit which may have accrued from that particular service; and though they are aware that they are now to confer their favours upon one who is become less useful, they think it ought to be done with no less benignity; indeed, with the same honour, as if, like the Athenians in ancient times, they had decreed a maintenance for me in the Prytaneum.[31] Thus, while I can derive consolation in my blindness both from God and man, let no one be troubled that I have lost my eyes in an honorable cause; and far be it from me to be troubled at it; far be it from me to possess so little spirit as not to be able without difficulty to despise the revilers of my blindness, or so little placability, as not to be able, with still less difficulty, to forgive them.

I return to you, whoever you are, who, with no little inconsistency, will one while have me to be a dwarf, another while, an Antaeus.[32] But, at last, you express a wish: "Nothing better could befall the united provinces of Holland, than that they may make an end of this war as easily and as successfully, as Salmasius will make an end of Milton." In which wish I shall readily acquiesce, and am of opinion, that I am neither presaging ill nor praying ill for our success, and for the cause of England.

But hark! again some strange and cackling cry! I suppose a flight of geese is on the wing, coming from some quarter or other! Oh, I now perceive what it is. I remember that it is the clamour of a tragedy. The chorus makes its appearance. See, two poetasters; either two or one; but there are two different shapes and colours. Shall I call it a sphinx, or that poetical monster of Horace, with a woman's head, an

31. The public eating hall.

32. Mythical giant overcome by Hercules. The war mentioned a few lines later is a naval conflict begun in May of 1651 and concluded in April of 1654 with a British victory.

ass's neck, arrayed in motley plumes, and with limbs borrowed from different animals?[33] Aye, that is the very thing: that is, some rhapsodist, covered from head to foot with centos and patches; whether he is one or two is doubtful, as he also is without a name. Now poets who are truly so called, I love and reverence; and it is one of the most frequent and delightful of my pleasures to listen to their song. Besides, I know that most of them, if I pass them in review from the very first down to our Buchanan,[34] are the sworn foes of tyrants. But who can endure these pedlers of verse?—a race of mortals than which nothing can be more foolish, more vain, corrupt, or lying. They praise or blame, without choice, without discrimination, without judgment or measure, now princes, now plebeians, alike the learned and unlearned, honest men and knaves, as prompted by caprice,—as inspirited and transported by the bottle, by the hope of getting a little money, or by their own senseless fury; heaping together from all sides inconsistencies, both in words and things, so threadbare and of colours so incompatible, that it would be better far for the person praised to be passed by in silence, and to live, as the saying is, on the sneers of contempt than to be thus praised: nay, he who has incurred their blame, may take it to himself as no ordinary honour, that he is not a favorite with these dull and paltry scoundrels. The foremost of them, if there are really two, I am in doubt whether to call a poet or a mason, so unconscionably does he bedaub the person of Salmasius,—so like a perfect wall does he plaster and whitewash it. He introduces the giant-warring hero in a sort of "triumphal" car, brandishing his "spears and clubs," and I know not what trumpery armour, with the whole host of the learned following on foot in the rear, but at an awful distance; like "the coming," forsooth, "of any God, in seasons of danger, for the salvation of the world: for at length the time was come, for kings to be covered with such a shield by the parent," God wot, "of right and dominion." Surely, Salmasius must have been mad and twice a

33. Milton is recalling the three opening lines of Horace's *Epistula ad Pisones*.
34. George Buchanan (1506–82), Scottish historian and satirist.

child, when he could not only be flattered with bepraisings so fulsome, but when he could use his utmost diligence to get them printed with all possible dispatch! The poet too must have been a sorry poet, and unobservant of decorum, who could dignify with such immoderate eulogiums a grammarian,—a description of person, who has ever been a menial—merely subservient to poets. The other, so far from making verses indeed, is absolutely beside himself—the maddest of all the enthusiasts, whom he persecutes with so much fury. As if he were executioner to Salmasius, a son of Syrus or Dama, he invokes the slave-whippers, and Cadmus;[35] then, drunk with hellebore, he vomits out a whole sink of foul abuse collected, with the help of an index to Plautus,[36] from the mouths of slaves and mountebanks. You would think he was speaking Oscan[37] instead of Latin, or croaking like one of the frogs of the marshy plains in which he swims. Then, to show you what an adept at iambics he is, he makes two false quantities in one word, making the one long where it ought to be short, and the other short where it ought to be long.

Hi trucidato rege per horrendum nefas.[38]

Away with your panniers "of emptiness," you ass! and at last utter three words, if you can, like a man in his sound and sober senses, if that pumpkin head, if that "thick head" of yours be capable of common sense even for a moment. In the meantime I hand you over, you Orbilius[39] you, to be flogged by your own scholars. Go on, and revile me in this way, as being, in your eyes, "worse than Cromwell": for it is impossible for you to bestow upon me higher praise. But am I to consider you as a friend, or as a blockhead, or as an insidious

---

35. Milton employs typical slave names (Syrus and Dama) from the time of Horace; Cadmus is the name of an executioner mentioned in Horace's *First Satire*.

36. Plautus (254–184 B.C.) was a Roman comic dramatist.

37. Primitive Latin dialect as distinguished from proper Latin.

38. Milton's point is that the metrics are forced.

39. A brutal schoolmaster in Horace's *Epistles*.

enemy? That you are not a friend is certain: for your words betray you for an enemy. How then came you to be so great a blockhead, as to take it into your head to prefer me for your accusation to so great a personage? Do you imagine, that what you do not comprehend, I also do not comprehend?—namely, that the more inveterate you discover your hatred to be against me, the greater do you proclaim my merits to be towards the commonwealth?—That with my own party your manifold reproaches do but declare my praise? For if you hate me to a degree beyond all others, it is plain that I, of all others, have galled you the most severely; that it is I, who have the most humbled you; that it is I, who have done the most mischief to your cause. If this be the fact, then it is I also, who have deserved the most highly of my fellow citizens: for the testimony or judgment of an enemy, though in other respects abundantly trivial, is the weightiest of all on the subject of his own pain. Do you not remember, when Ajax and Ulysses contended for the arms of the dead Achilles, that the poet, by the counsel of Nestor, chose the judges not from among the Greeks who were their countrymen, but from the Trojans, who were their enemies?

Hence let the impartial Trojans judge the strife.[40]

And a little after:

Now they a righteous judgment will declare,
As nor to one nor t'other love they bear;
For all the Greeks they hold in equal hate;
Darkly remembering their ruined state.

Thus far the Smyrnaean, or Calaber. It follows, then, that you must be insidious, and labour to cast an odium upon me, since, by wicked arts, and with the purpose of inflicting a deeper injury, you pervert and deprave that kind of judgment which is usually unbiassed and

40. Milton cites the continuation of Homer, the *Posthomerica,* by the fourth-century poet Quintus of Smyrna.

sincere in an enemy: hence, you are not merely the most depraved of men, but the most depraved of enemies. But, my good man! I will render frustrate none of your endeavours: for though I could most ardently wish that I were Ulysses, that is, that I had deserved the most highly of all of my country; yet, I covet not the arms of Achilles; I seek not to carry before me the heavens painted on my shield, which others may look to in a contest, though I do not; it is my endeavour to bear on my shoulders, a real not a painted burden, to be felt by myself, rather than by others. Indeed, as I have no private malice or enmity against any man, nor, as far as I know, has any man against me, I am the less concerned at the torrent of abuse which is cast upon me, at the numberless reproaches which are hurled against me, as I bear all this not for myself, but for the sake of the commonwealth. Nor do I complain, that by far the least share of the reward and of the advantages thence proceeding and that by far the greatest share of the reproach, have attached to me; content to have had in view and to have prosecuted without reward, those things which were honorable to be done, for their own sakes alone. This is what others should look to, and as for yourself, know that I have not so much as touched those "good things," "that wealth" with which you reproach me, nor am made one half-penny the richer by that name, on account of which you bring your chief accusations against me.

Here More begins again, and in the second epistle gives his reasons for writing: and for writing to whom?—To "the Christian reader," forsooth, the adulterer and fornicator More writes, greeting. You lead us to expect a truly pious epistle: come let us hear your reasons. "The minds of the nations of Europe and most of all our French protestants, were roused to become acquainted with the parricide and with the parricides," &c. The French, even the Protestants themselves, have engaged in wars against the laws; what farther they would have done, if they had had the like success with ourselves, cannot now be known. It is certain, that their own kings, if any credit is to be given to the records of those transactions, stood in no less apprehension from them, than our king from us: nor was this without reason, when they considered the spirit and multitude of the writings even of those reformers, and how often they had gone so far as to threaten. They were unwilling, therefore, whatever you pretend, to promise too splendidly of themselves, or to think unjustly of us.—He goes on with his reasons. "Indeed, such have been my habits of intimacy with Englishmen of the better note";—Those who in your eyes are of the better note, are, in the eyes of men of virtue, of the worst note;—"That I might undertake to say I know those monsters of men in heart and in grain." I thought you knew nobody but your adulteresses, and strumpets; and you also know monsters in heart and in grain.—"The Englishmen with whom I had intercourse easily prevailed upon me to suppress my name." And, in truth, not without a crafty policy: for in this way, they had the hope of being indulged with a larger measure of your impudence, and that you would do less mischief to the cause by your character, which was bad even at that time. For they had known you of old; had known what an excellent keeper of gardens you had formerly been; and though now a priest all shaven and spruce, that you could not keep your hands off not even from Pontia Pilate; nor without reason indeed: for if *carnifex* (an executioner) be supposed to be derived a *conficienda carne* (from dispatching flesh) why should you think it less likely, that from a priest you should be made *pontifex* (a high-priest) *conficiendo Pontiam,* (from dispatching Pontia)? though these stories about you were no secrets to other people; though it is impossible but that yourself must have been conscious of them; yet with an impiety which is scarcely credible, and which deserves execration, you dare openly to profess that "you are seeking only and vindicating only the glory of God"; and at the very time you yourself are pursuing the most scandalous courses, accuse others "of covering their crimes under the mask of piety"; though no man was ever more manifestly and more wickedly guilty of this than yourself.—"For the order of transactions (you say) you derived great assistance from other writers, and especially from *A View of the late Troubles in England.*" You are indeed a trifling fellow: for though you raise so great a clamour, you can bring nothing that is your own; you could produce against us the writers only who are devoted to the royalist faction—authors, for that very reason justly suspected—and whose credit once invalidated, you would be unable to proceed. We shall therefore refute those writers, and if necessary, one view by another: as we see occasion, we shall reply not to them through you, but to you through them. In the meantime, it behoves you to be prepared to defend what you have brought forward of your own; the nature of which, as it proceeds from a name evidently impious and atheistic, let all religious persons now hear, and tremble with horror. "The love of God commands,—the keenest sense of the injury done to his sacred name compels us, to lift up our suppliant hands to God." Hide, O hide those polluted hands, which, grovelling as you are in ambition and lust, you have the presumption to lift up, lest you dare also to pollute heaven itself with the touch that has already contaminated the sacred mysteries of religion. But that divine vengeance, which you rashly and absurdly imprecate upon others, you will find hereafter you have called down upon your own guilty head.

Thus far we have been listening merely to the preludes of the cry; now (for the cry gets the principal, and almost the only part, in this drama) the mouth is opened to its utmost yawn, as the cry is to reach to heaven; and if it arrive thither, it will, in truth, cry out against no one more sharply than against the crier, More himself. "Since the majesty of kings has, in all ages, been held sacred," &c. Indeed, More, you clamour many things against us, in your vulgarity, many in your malice, which are nothing to the purpose: for the murder of a king, and the punishment of a tyrant, are not the same, More, they are not the same; they differ most widely, and will differ, as long as sense and reason, right and wrong, the power of distinguishing straight from crooked, shall be allowed to men. But as to these things enough has been often said already, enough defended. You who can do us no injury with all your mighty blustering, shall not put an end to us at last by serving up your hash again. You have some fine things about patience; then about piety. But,

You preach of virtue, while of flesh you're frail;
What fear, though now as erst you wag your tail?

"All protestants, you say, especially the Dutch and the French, were struck with horror at what we have done"; and immediately after—"good men were no where at liberty to speak what they thought." But for you to contradict yourself is a trifling matter; what follows is of a far more disgraceful and atrocious character: "In comparison of our wickedness (say you) the wickedness of the Jews in the crucifixion of Christ was nothing, whether we consider the intention of the men, or the effects of the crime." Maniac! and do you, a minister of Christ, make so light of the horrible crime committed against Christ, as, whatever might have been "the intention" or "the effect," to dare to pronounce, that to kill any king is equally sinful? The Jews, from the clearest signs, might certainly have recognized the Son of God; but it was impossible that we, in any way, should have been made to comprehend that Charles was not a tyrant. To mention the accidental consequences with a view to diminish a crime, is most absurd. But I always remark this in a royalist; according as he is the more acrimonious, does he make less account of any offence committed against Christ, than against the king; and though he teaches that the king ought to be obeyed chiefly for the sake of Christ, he plainly makes it appear, that himself is no true follower either of Christ, or of the king; but that, having other selfish objects in view, he makes a display of this his incredible fidelity and devotion to his king, from ambition, or from other passions which he conceals.—"Salmasius, therefore, the great prince of letters, came forward." Don't persist, More, in this manner in calling such a man great. Though you should repeat it a thousand times, you would never persuade any man of sense that Salmasius was a great man; but rather that More is a most little one, a worthless manikin, who, from his ignorance of propriety, abuses thus absurdly the epithet of great. To grammarians and critics, whose highest praise consists either in editing the works of others, or in correcting the blunders of transcribers, we readily allow industry indeed and the knowledge of languages, with the credit and rewards of a learning by no means to be despised; but we do not bestow upon them the title of great. He alone deserves the appellation of great, who either achieves great things himself, or teaches how they may be achieved; or who describes with suitable dignity the great achievements of others. But those things only are great, which either make this life of ours happy, or at least comfortable and agreeable as far as is consistent with honesty, or which lead to another and a happier life. Now what has Salmasius done of such things as these? Clearly nothing. And what has he taught or written that is great? Unless perhaps what he wrote, against the bishops and the pope's supremacy, which, being recanted by his subsequent conduct, and by other writings in opposition to us and in favour of episcopacy, he has rendered null. He, therefore, who had either never written any thing great, or who basely disclaimed the best thing he ever wrote, is not entitled to be called a great writer. He has my permission to be "the prince of letters," and of the alphabet too; but in your apprehension he is not merely the "prince of letters," but "the patron of kings," and "a patron truly worthy of clients so illustrious." Indeed, you have consulted admirably for kings, when, in addition to their other notable titles, you would have them to be styled the clients of Claudius Salmasius. By the law, surely, that if you deliver yourselves up, ye kings, to the patronage of Salmasius the grammarian, if you humble your sceptres to the rod, you are absolved from all other laws.—"As long as the world shall stand, kings will owe to him the vindication of their dignity and safety." Hear, O ye princes! the man who has defended you so scurvily, nay, who has defended you not at all, for he had nobody to oppose him, affirms, that for your dignity and safety you are indebted to him! Now this is all they have gained, who have assisted the haughty grammarian, while, in a court of moths and book-worms, he sustained the cause of kings.—"Nor will the church owe him less than the cause of royalty." It is not praise, then, that the church will owe him, but a richly deserved mark of infamy, for deserting her cause.—Now you would lavish your encomiums upon the royal defence; you admire "the genius, the learning, the acquaintance with things little short of infinite, the profound knowledge of the canon and civil law, the vigour of elevated language, the eloquence, the grace of that golden work"—of all which qualities I maintain that the man was wholly destitute (for what had Salmasius to do with eloquence?) But, that the work was a golden work, this I acknowledge a hundred times over: for so many pieces of gold did Charles count out; not to mention what the prince of Orange also bestowed upon the same work.—"Never did a great man appear greater; never did Salmasius": yes indeed, he was so much greater that he burst: for how great he was in that work we have already seen; and if he has left any posthumous work, as is reported, on the same subject, we shall perhaps see again. Now I do not deny, that, after the publication of that book, Salmasius was in everybody's mouth, and that he pleased the royalists to a miracle; that "he was invited, and amply rewarded, by the most august the queen of Sweden"; nay, that, in the whole of that contest, Salmasius had every thing in his favour, and I almost every thing against me. In the first place, of his erudition, the opinion of mankind could go no higher, which opinion he had been collecting for many previous years, by writing a multitude of books, and of no small bulk; not books of general utility, but on the abstrusest subjects, and stuffed with scraps of citation from eminent authors; than which nothing sooner excites the wonderment of the literary vulgar. On the contrary, who I was, scarcely any one in those parts had ever heard. He, by applying a more than ordinary diligence to the work, the subject being of such magnitude, had awakened in respect of himself great expectation; while it was not in my power to awaken any. Nay, as I should be a raw recruit engaging with a veteran, there were many who dissuaded me from the undertaking, partly out of envy, lest, whatever the issue, I should gain glory from a contest with an enemy so illustrious; partly, from apprehension for me and for the cause, lest I should retire vanquished, to the heavy disgrace of both. Lastly the specious and plausible nature of his cause, the rooted opinion of the vulgar, or which is more properly called superstition, and the pre-possession in favour of the royal name, had given additional vigour and spirit to Salmasius—circumstances which all made against me. Hence when our defence soon after made its appearance, it is less to be wondered at, that it was seized with avidity by most persons, as they had an eager curiosity to see who could be so rash as to presume to enter the lists with Salmasius, than that it should give such pleasure and satisfaction to many; insomuch that as respect was no longer had to the author, but to truth itself, Salmasius, who was lately seated on the summit of honour, now, as if the mask which disguised him had been taken off, suddenly fell from his renown and from his confidence; and though he strained every nerve to recover himself, he was unable to accomplish it as long as he lived.

But you, most serene queen of the Swedes![41] and that nice discernment of yours, he could not long deceive. You have stood forth the princess and the authoress little less (shall I say?) than heavenly, of preferring truth to the partialities of faction. For although you invited and loaded with honours the man, who, at that time, was celebrated above his fellows for pre-eminent learning, and for his defence of the royal cause, yet, after that answer had appeared, which was perused by you with singular equanimity, and you had discovered that Salmasius was convicted of talking to no purpose, and of palpable misrepresentation; that he had said many things which are frivolous, many which are extravagant, some which are false, others which go against himself, and are contrary to his former sentiments, and that when called into your presence, as the report goes, he could give no satisfactory reasons for all this—your mind underwent so visible a change, that, from that time, it was plain to everybody, that you neither paid the same attention to the man as before, nor made much account of his genius and learning; and what was altogether unexpected, showed an evident inclination to favour his adversary. For you denied that what was spoken against tyrants could have any reference whatever

41. Milton is praising Christina (1626–89), the daughter of Gustavus Adolphus, who began her reign in 1644.

to you; and by this you gained, with yourself the fruit, with others the reputation, of a most upright conscience. As it is sufficiently plain from your actions, that you are no tyrant, this open declaration of your sentiments shows, in a still clearer light, that you are utterly unconscious of the thing. Happy am I! happy even beyond my highest hope! (for I boast of no other eloquence than that persuasion which is inherent in truth itself;) who, when I had fallen upon those times of my country, in which I was constrained of necessity to engage in a cause at once so arduous and invidious, that I must seem to impugn all regal right, have found a witness and an interpreter of my integrity so illustrious, so truly royal, as to interpret and bear witness for me, that I have spoken not a syllable against kings, but against the underminers and pests of kings—against tyrants only. But how magnanimous, Augusta, how secure on all sides must you be, fortified as you are with a virtue and wisdom clearly divine! when you could not only peruse with such equanimity, such calmness, with a candour of mind so unexampled, with a serenity of countenance so perfect, what might have seemed written against your own right and dignity; but could adopt an opinion of this nature against your own advocate himself, so as to be commonly thought even to award the palm to his adversary! In what honour, in what veneration, must you ever be held by me, when your exalted virtue and greatness of spirit, not only glorious to yourself, but auspicious and fortunate for me, have freed me, as it respects other kings, from all suspicion and disgrace, and, by this signal and immortal benefit, have bound me to you for ever! With what favour must foreigners have thought, with what favour must your own people have both thought and hoped of your equity and impartiality, when, at a time in which your own concerns, in which your majesty itself seemed to be the subject of contention, they saw you delivering your judgment, with as little emotion, with no less composure, on your own rights, than you had been accustomed to do on the rights of the people! Besides, it was for no idle purpose that you collected from all parts such multitudes of choice volumes, so many monuments of learning! It was not that from these things yourself might learn any thing, but that from them your own citizens might learn to know you, that they might be able to contemplate the pre-eminence of your virtue and of your wisdom; and unless the very image of the goddess of wisdom had sat before your inmost spirit, unless she had appeared, as it were, in a visible form before your eyes, she could never have raised in you, by any book-learning, such an ardent love of herself. This makes us admire the more your vigour of mind manifestly ethereal, as if the purest particle of the breath divine had fallen upon those remote regions—a particle, which that melancholy and cloudy sky, with its freezing cold, could neither extinguish nor oppress; nor could that horrid and rugged soil, which is wont to harden also the minds of its inhabitants, create in you any thing unequal or rough; nay, this very land, so fertile in divers metals, though to others a stepmother, being certainly to you a fostering parent, seems to have exerted her utmost powers to produce you entirely of gold. I would address you as the daughter of Adolphus, as the only descendant of that invincible and famous king, if, Christina, you did not outshine him as much as wisdom exceeds strength, as much as the arts of peace surpass the stratagems of war. Henceforward, not the queen of the south alone shall be celebrated in story.[42] The north has now also his queen, and worthy too, not merely to go and listen to that wisest king of the Jews, or to any other, should any ever more arise like him, but to be herself the heroine to be visited by others, flocking from all quarters as to the brightest pattern of royal virtue; and who should confess that there is no dignity upon earth equal to her praises and merits; of which they would see that the least is, that she is a queen—the monarch of so many nations. Again, it is not the least, that she herself thinks this the least of her honours, and meditates upon something far greater and more sublime, than to reign; meriting to be valued, on this very account, above innumerable kings. Hence, she may abdicate the kingdom, should such a misfortune await the Swedish nation; but that she, who has proved herself worthy of

42. Milton is alluding to the Queen of Sheba, described in 1 Kings 10:1–13.

the empire, not of Sweden only, but of the world, should divest herself of the queen, can never be in her power!

There is no one I trust, who, so far from blaming, would not commend me for this digression to an eulogium of the queen so well deserved; an eulogium which, though others were silent, I could not omit without a heavy charge of ingratitude; since, I know not by what chance, though certainly by a most happy one, or whether by some hidden consent or guidance of the stars, or of spirits, or of things—I, who the least of all men expected, who the most of all wished such a thing, have found, in the remotest regions, an arbitress so illustrious, so impartial and favorable to me.

We must now return to the remaining part of the work, of however different a nature. By your account, "we were in the utmost agitation at the news of the royal defence; and looked around for some hungry pedagogue, who would employ his venal pen in defence of parricide." This, in your unrivalled malice, is what has been invented by you, from your recollecting that the royalists, when they looked around for a crier for their lies and their slander, applied to the grammarian Salmasius, who, if not hungry, was at least not a little thirsty of gold; who fairly sold them not merely his present work, but his good intentions, if he ever had any, for the future—from your recollecting that Salmasius, his fame now wept over and gone, when he looked around for some one who should repair, at any rate, his abased and shattered reputation, by the just retribution of God, lighted upon you; who were now no longer the minister of Geneva, from which place you were driven out, but the bishop of Lampsacus—in other words, Priapus[43] from the garden, the defiler of his own house. Whence, loathing such tasteless bepraisings, purchased with so much dishonour, he became, from a friend, an irreconcilable enemy, and died with many a curse upon you his own eulogist.—"One John Milton, a great hero doubtless, was found, to be opposed to Salmasius." I did not know that I was a hero, though you, for ought I know,

43. The Roman god of male sexual potency.

may be the son of some frail heroine; for you are one entire mass of corruption. That I was the only one who was found to defend the cause of the people of England, if I consider the interests of the commonwealth, is a subject of real concern to me; if I consider the glory, it is not willingly that I suffer any one to share it with me. Who and whence I am, say you, is doubtful. So also was it doubtful, in ancient times, who Homer was, who Demosthenes. The truth is, I had learnt to be long silent, to be able to forbear writing, which Salmasius never could; and carried silently in my own breast what if I had chosen then, as well as now, to bring forth, I could long since have gained a name. But I was not eager for fame, who is slow of pace; indeed, if the fit opportunity had not been given me, even these things would never have seen the light; little concerned, though others were ignorant that I knew what I did. It was not the fame of every thing that I was waiting for, but the opportunity. Hence, it happened, that I was known to no small number of persons, before Salmasius was known to himself; now he is more known than the pack-horse Andremon.[44] —"Whether he is a man or a worm." In very truth, I had rather be a worm, a confession which king David also makes of himself,[45] than conceal within my breast that worm of yours that shall never die.— You proceed—"It is said, that the man was expelled from the university of Cambridge for his debaucheries, and that, flying from his disgrace and his country, he shifted his quarters to Italy." It may be conjectured even from this, what credit is due to those, from whom you received your information of our affairs: for, that both you and they are guilty of a most impudent falsehood, in this particular, is well known to all who know me, and shall presently be shown more at large. Now, after being expelled from Cambridge, why should I shift my quarters to Italy, rather than to France or Holland? where you, who are covered with debaucheries out of number, and a minister of the gospel, not only live with impunity, but preach; but, to the utter

44. Milton is alluding to Martial *Epigrams* 10.9.
45. Ps. 22:6.

disgrace of that church, defile with your filthy hands even the holy ministeries. Why then to Italy, More? like another Saturn, I suppose, I fled to Latium, to find a hiding place![46] But I fled to Italy, not, as you imagine, as to the skulking corner, or the place of refuge to the profligate, but because I knew, and had found before, that it is the retreat of civility and of all polite learning.—"On his return, he wrote his book on divorce." I wrote nothing more than what Bucer before me wrote at large on the kingdom of Christ, than what Fagius on Deuteronomy, Erasmus on the first epistle to the Corinthians— works intended for the particular benefit of Englishmen[47]—than what many other very celebrated men have written for the good of mankind in general. Why that should be charged upon me in particular as a fault, which nobody finds fault with in them, I cannot comprehend. I could wish only that I had not written in the vernacular tongue; for I had not fallen upon vernacular readers, with whom it is usual to be unconscious of their own good fortune, and to ridicule the misfortune of others. And is it for you, base seducer, to make a clamour about divorce, who have been guilty of the most cruel of all divorces with Pontia, the waiting maid, whom you engaged in marriage, and with this lure debauched her? And yet this servant of Salmasius was an Englishwoman, as it is said, attached the most warmly to the royal party; in short, miscreant, you loved her as a royal thing and left her as a public thing; but take care you are not found to be the author of her conversion, the thought of which you seem so unable to endure; take care, I say, lest by utterly overturning Salmasia's sovereignty, you do not convert Pontia into a republic. In this way, indeed, you are said to have founded, though yourself a royalist, many republics in the same city, or, to administer them, as public minister, after they have been founded by others. Such are your divorces, or as

46. Deposed by his son Jupiter, Saturn fled to Italy bringing to the people there a golden age of peace and prosperity.

47. Milton here refers to Martin Bucer's *De Regno Christi* (1577); Paulus Fagius (1504–49) was a professor of Hebrew at Cambridge; Erasmus had urged a relaxation of canon law regarding divorce for incompatibility.

you would rather have it, your diversions, from which you have come out against me, a very Curius.[48]—You now return to your lies. "When the decapitation of the king was agitated by the conspirators, he wrote to them, while yet wavering, and urged them to the horrid deed." Now I neither wrote to them, nor was it possible that I should urge those, who had already resolved upon the thing, without even an intention of consulting me. But I shall speak of what I wrote upon that subject hereafter, as also of the *Eikonoklastes*.

Since this man (though I am in doubt whether I should call him a man, or merely the refuse of a man) from his corruption of maid-servants, has proceeded to corrupt all truth, and by heaping upon me lies without number, has endeavoured to render my name infamous among foreigners, let me intreat that I may not be misinterpreted, that I may not excite ill-will, that I may not give offence, if I have spoken before, and if I shall speak again more of myself than I could wish; that, if I cannot rescue my eyes from blindness, my name from oblivion or calumny, I may at least be able, in open day, to redeem my life from that dimness which is produced by a stain. This will be necessary for me on more accounts than one. And first, that so many excellent and learned men, throughout the neighbouring nations, who are now reading my writings and are disposed to think favourably of me, may not feel regret and shame on my account; but may be convinced, that I am not such a one, who has ever disgraced fair words by foul deeds, or the language of a free man by the actions of a slave; and that my life, by God's help, has been ever far removed from all baseness and loose behaviour. Secondly, that those praise-worthy and illustrious men, whose eulogies I undertake to pronounce, may know it to be my opinion, that there could be no greater cause for shame, while myself was vicious and deserving of reproof; in fine, that the people of England, to whose defence, whether it was my destiny or my duty, I was impelled by their own virtue, may know, that if I have ever led a life free from shame and dishonour, my defence (whether

48. Curius was a Roman public officer of the third century B.C. famous for his incorruptible integrity. Milton taunts More with posing as such a figure.

it may redound to their honour and ornament I know not) can certainly never prove to them a cause of shame or disgrace. Who, then, and whence I am I will now make known.

I was born at London, of respectable parents. My father was a man of the highest integrity; my mother, an excellent woman, was particularly known throughout the neighbourhood for her charitable donations. My father destined me from a child for the pursuits of polite learning, which I prosecuted with such eagerness, that after I was twelve years old, I rarely retired to bed from my lucubrations till midnight. This was the first thing which proved pernicious to my eyes, to the natural weakness of which were added frequent headaches. But as all this could not abate my instinctive ardour for learning, he provided me, in addition to the ordinary instructions of the grammar school, masters to give me daily lessons at home. Being thus instructed in various languages, and having gotten no slight taste of the sweetness of philosophy, he sent me to Cambridge, one of our two national colleges. There, aloof from all profligate conduct, and with the approbation of all good men, I studied seven years, according to the usual course of discipline and of scientific instruction—till I obtained, and with applause, the degree of master, as it is called; when I fled not into Italy, as this foul miscreant falsely asserts, but, of my own free will, returned home, leaving behind me among most of the fellows of the college, who had shown me no ordinary attention, even an affectionate regret. At my father's country house, to which he had retired to pass the remainder of his days, being perfectly at my ease, I gave myself up entirely to reading the Greek and Latin writers; exchanging, however, sometimes, the country for the town, either for the purchase of books, or to learn something new in mathematics, or in music, which at that time furnished the sources of my amusement. After passing five years in this way, I had the curiosity, after the death of my mother, to see foreign countries, and above all, Italy; and having obtained permission of my father, I set out, attended by one servant. On my departure, I was treated in the most friendly manner by Sir Henry Wotton, who was long ambassador from king James to

Venice, and who not only followed me with his good wishes, but communicated, in an elegant letter, some maxims of the greatest use to one who is going abroad. From the recommendation of others, I was received at Paris with the utmost courtesy, by the noble Thomas Scudamore, Viscount of Sligo, who of his own accord introduced me, accompanied by several of his suite, to the learned Hugo Grotius, at that time ambassador from the queen of Sweden to the king of France, and whom I was very desirous of seeing. On my setting out for Italy some days after, he gave me letters to the English merchants on my route, that they might be ready to do me any service in their power. Taking ship at Nice, I arrived at Genoa; and soon after at Leghorn and Pisa, thence to Florence. In this last city, which I have always valued above the rest for the elegance of its dialect and of its genius, I continued about two months. Here I soon contracted a familiar acquaintance with many persons eminent for their rank and learning, and regularly frequented also their private academies—an institution which deserves the highest commendation, as calculated to preserve at once polite letters and friendly intercourse: for, the pleasing, the delightful recollection I still retain of you Jacobo Gaddi, of you Carolo Dati, Frescobaldi, Coltellino, Bonmatthei, Clementillo, Francini, and many others, no time will efface. From Florence I pursued my route to Sienna, and then to Rome; and having been detained about two months in this city by its antiquities and ancient renown, (where I enjoyed the accomplished society of Lucas Holstenius and of many other learned and superior men) I proceeded to Naples. Here I was introduced by a certain hermit, with whom I had travelled from Rome, to John Baptista Manso, Marquis of Villa, a man of the first rank and authority, to whom the illustrious Italian poet, Torquato Tasso, addressed his book on friendship. By him I was treated, while I stayed there, with all the warmth of friendship: for he conducted me himself over the city and the viceregent's court, and more than once came to visit me at my own lodgings. On my leaving Naples, he gravely apologized for showing me no more attention, alleging that although it was what he wished above all things, it was not in his power in that city, because I had not thought proper to be more guarded on the point of religion. As I was preparing to pass over also into Sicily and Greece, I was restrained by the melancholy tidings from England of the civil war: for I thought it base, that I should be travelling at my ease, even for the improvement of my mind abroad, while my fellow-citizens were fighting for their liberty at home. As I was about to return to Rome, the merchants gave me an intimation, that they had learnt from their letters, that, in case of my revisiting Rome, the English Jesuits had laid a plot for me, because I had spoken too freely on the subject of religion: for I had laid it down as a rule for myself, never to begin a conversation on religion in those parts; but if interrogated concerning my faith, whatever might be the consequence, to dissemble nothing. I therefore returned notwithstanding to Rome; I concealed from no one, who asked the question, what I was; if any one attacked me, I defended in the most open manner, as before, the orthodox faith, for nearly two months more, in the city even of the sovereign pontiff himself. By the will of God, I arrived safe again at Florence; revisiting those who longed no less to see me, than if I had returned to my own country. There I willingly stopped as many months as before, except that I made an excursion for a few days to Lucca; when, crossing the Apennine, I made the best of my way, through Bononia and Ferrara, to Venice. Having spent a month in getting a survey of this city, and seen the books shipped which I had collected in Italy, I was brought, by way of Verona, Milan, and the Paenine Alps, and along the lake Lemano, to Geneva. This city, as it brings to my recollection the slanderer More, makes me again call God to witness, that, in all these places where so much licence is given, I lived free and untouched of all defilement and profligate behaviour, having it ever in my thought, that if I could escape the eyes of men, I certainly could not escape the eyes of God. At Geneva I had daily intercourse with John Deodati, the very learned professor of divinity. Then, by the same route as before, I returned through France, to my own country, after an absence of a year and about three months. I arrived nearly at the time that Charles, breaking the pacification, renewed the war, called the episcopal war, with the Scots,[49] in which the royal forces were routed in the first engagement; and Charles, now finding the whole English nation enraged, and justly, to the last degree against him, not long after called a parliament; though not by his own will, but as compelled by his necessities. Looking about me for some place in which I might take up my abode, if any was to be found in this troubled and fluctuating state of affairs, I hired, for me and my books, a sufficiently spacious house in the city. Here I returned with no little delight to my interrupted studies; leaving without difficulty, the issue of things more especially to God, and to those to whom the people had assigned that department of duty. Meanwhile, as the parliament acted with great vigour, the pride of the bishops began to lose its swell. No sooner did liberty of speech begin to be allowed, than every mouth was open against the bishops. Some complained of their personal vices, others of the vice of the order itself. It was wrong, they said, that they alone should differ from all other reformed churches; that it was expedient the church should be governed by the example of the brethren, and above all by the word of God. I became perfectly awake to these things; and perceiving that men were in the right way to liberty; that, if discipline originating in religion continued its course to the morals and institutions of the commonwealth, they were proceeding in a direct line from such beginnings, from such steps, to the deliverance of the whole life of mortal man from slavery—moreover, as I had endeavoured from my youth, before all things, not to be ignorant of what was law, whether divine or human; as I had considered, whether I could ever be of use, should I now be wanting to my country, to the church, and to such multitudes of the brethren who were exposing themselves to danger for the gospel's sake—I resolved, though my thoughts were then employed upon other subjects, to transfer to these the whole

49. The Scots invaded England in August of 1640, besieged Newcastle, and despite Charles's attempt at relief, captured the city not long after winning a victory at the Battle of Newburn. Puritans resented Charles's efforts toward enforcing religious conformity upon the Scots.

force of my mind and industry. Accordingly, I first wrote *Of the Reformation of the English Church,* in two books, to a friend. Next, as there were two bishops of reputation above the rest,[50] who maintained their own cause against certain leading ministers; and as I had the persuasion, that on a subject which I had studied solely for the love of truth and from a regard to Christian duty, I should not write worse than those who contended for their own lucre and most iniquitous domination; to one of them I replied in two books, of which one was entitled *Of Prelatical Episcopacy,* the other *Of the Reason of Church Government;* to the other, in some *Animadversions,* and soon after, in an *Apology;* and thus, as was said, brought timely succour to those ministers, who had some difficulty in maintaining their ground against the bishops' eloquence: from this time too, I held myself ready, should they thenceforward make any reply. When the bishops, at whom every man aimed his arrow, had at length fallen, and we were now at leisure, as far as they were concerned, I began to turn my thoughts to other subjects; to consider in what way I could contribute to the progress of real and substantial liberty; which is to be sought for not from without, but within, and is to be obtained principally not by fighting, but by the just regulation and by the proper conduct of life. Reflecting, therefore, that there are in all three species of liberty, without which it is scarcely possible to pass any life with comfort, namely, ecclesiastical, domestic or private, and civil; that I had already written on the first species, and saw the magistrate diligently employed about the third, I undertook the domestic, which was the one that remained. But as this also appeared to be three-fold, namely, whether the affair of marriage was rightly managed; whether the education of children was properly conducted; whether, lastly, we were to be allowed freedom of opinion—I explained my sentiments not only on the proper mode of contracting marriage, but also of dissolving it, should that be found necessary: and this I did according to the divine law which Christ has never abrogated; and much less has

50. James Ussher (1581–1656), archbishop of Armagh, and Joseph Hall (1574–1656), bishop of Norwich.

he given a civil sanction to any other, that should be of higher authority than the whole law of Moses. In like manner I delivered my own opinion and the opinion of others concerning what was to be thought of the single exception of fornication—a question which has been also copiously elucidated by our celebrated Selden,[51] in his *Hebrew Wife,* published some two years after. Again, it is to little purpose for him to make a noise about liberty in the legislative assemblies, and in the courts of justice, who is in bondage to an inferior at home,—a species of bondage of all others the most degrading to a man. On this point, therefore, I published some books,[52] and at that particular time, when man and wife were often the fiercest enemies, he being at home with his children, while she, the mother of the family, was in the camp of the enemy, threatening slaughter and destruction to her husband. I next treated, in one little work, of the education of children, briefly it is true, but at sufficient length, I conceived, for those, who apply themselves to the subject with all that earnestness and diligence which it demands—a subject than which there can be none of greater moment to imbue the minds of men with virtue, from which springs that true liberty which is felt within; none for the wise administration of a commonwealth, and for giving it its utmost possible duration. Lastly, I wrote, after the model of a regular speech, *Areopagitica,* on the liberty of printing, that the determination of true and false, of what ought to be published and what suppressed, might not be in the hands of the few who may be charged with the inspection of books, men commonly without learning and of vulgar judgment, and by whose licence and pleasure, no one is suffered to publish any thing which may be above vulgar apprehension. The civil species of liberty, the last which remained, I had not touched, as I perceived it drew sufficient attention from the magistrate. Nor did I write any thing on the right of kings, till the king, pronounced an enemy by the parliament, and vanquished in war, was arraigned as a captive be-

51. John Selden (1584–1654), scholar, jurist, and leader in the parliamentary faction, published the book Milton mentions in 1646.

52. Four tracts on divorce were produced by Milton between 1643 and 1645.

fore judges, and condemned to lose his head. But, when certain presbyterian ministers, at first the bitterest foes to Charles, unable to endure that the independent party should now be preferred to them,
and that it should have greater influence in the senate, began to clamour against the sentence which the parliament had pronounced upon
the king (though in no wise angry at the deed, but only that themselves had not the execution of it) and tried to their utmost to raise a
tumult, having the assurance to affirm that the doctrine of protestants,
that all the reformed churches shrunk with horror from the atrocity
of such a sentence against kings—then indeed, I thought it behoved
me openly to oppose so barefaced a falsehood. Yet even then, I neither wrote nor advised any thing concerning Charles; but simply
showed, in general, what may be lawfully done against tyrants; adduc-
ing, in confirmation, the authorities of no small number of the most
eminent divines; inveighing, at the same time, almost with the zeal
of a preacher against the egregious ignorance or impudence of those
men, who had promised better things. This book[53] was not published
till after the death of the king, being intended rather to compose the
minds of men, than to settle any thing relating to Charles; that being
the business of the magistrates instead of mine, and which, at the time
I speak of, had been already done. These services of mine, which were
performed within private walls, I gratuitously bestowed at one time
upon the church, at another, upon the commonwealth; while neither
the commonwealth nor the church bestowed upon me in return any
thing beyond security. It is true, that I gained a good conscience, a
fair repute among good men, and that the deeds themselves rendered
this freedom of speech honorable to me. Some men however gained
advantages, others honours, for doing nothing; but no man ever saw
me canvassing for preferment, no man ever saw me in quest of any
thing through the medium of friends, fixed, with supplicatory look
to the doors of the parliament, or clung to the vestibules of lower assemblies. I kept myself commonly at home, and supported myself,

53. *The Tenure of Kings and Magistrates* was published in February of 1649.

however frugally, upon my own fortune, though, in this civil broil, a great part was often detained, and an assessment rather disproportionate, imposed upon me. Having dispatched these things, and thinking that, for the future, I should now have abundance of leisure, I undertook a history of the nation from its remotest origin; intending to bring it down, if I could, in one unbroken thread to our own times. I had already finished four books,[54] when lo! (Charles's kingdom being reduced to a commonwealth) the council of state, as it is called, now first constituted by authority of parliament, invited me to lend them my services in the department more particularly of foreign affairs[55]—an event which had never entered my thoughts! Not long after, the book which was attributed to the king made its appearance, written certainly with the bitterest malice against the parliament. Being ordered to prepare an answer to it, I opposed the *Iconoclast* to the *Icon;* not, as is pretended, "in insult to the departed spirit of the king," but in the persuasion, that queen truth ought to be preferred to king Charles; and as I foresaw that some reviler would be ready with this slander, I endeavoured in the introduction, and in other places as far as it was proper, to ward off the reproach. Next came forward Salmasius; and no long time, as More reports, was lost in looking about for some person to answer him, so that all, of their own accord, instantly nominated me, who was then present in the council.—It is chiefly, More, for the sake of those good men, who have otherwise no knowledge of me, that, to stop your mouth and to confound your lies, I have so far given an account of myself. I tell you, then, foul priest, hold your peace, I say: for the more you revile me, the more fully will you compel me to explain my own conduct; from which you could gain nothing yourself, but the reproach, already too heavy, of being a liar; and would lay open for me a still wider field for the commendation of my own integrity.

I had censured Salmasius, as being of another country, and of

54. Milton's *History of England* was eventually published (in six volumes) in 1670.
55. Milton was appointed Secretary for the Foreign Tongues to the Council on March 13, 1649.

foreign extraction, for intermeddling with our affairs. You insist, "that this defence concerns those most, who have no concern with England." And why? "Englishmen (you say) may be supposed to be strongly actuated by the spirit of faction; whereas, it is likely, that the French took more account of the thing, than of the men." To this I make the same retort as before; that no man, who is a foreigner and at a great distance, like yourself, will embroil himself with the affairs of another country, especially when those affairs are in a state of distraction, unless he is corrupted. I have before shown that Salmasius was bribed; it appears that yourself, through the medium of Salmasius and of the Orange faction,[56] made interest for a professorial chair; and what is still worse, you are next falling foul of the parliament, while you are playing foul with Pontia. But the reason you give why these things rather concerned foreigners is perfectly ridiculous: for if the English are carried away by party feelings, what is it that you, who follow them exclusively, transfer to yourselves, if not their passions only? Hence, if those Englishmen are not to be believed in their own cause, surely much less are you to be believed, who know nothing of our affairs, or at least believe nothing, but what you have received from these very persons, and who, even in your own judgment, are scarcely worthy of credit.—Here again you break out in encomiums upon the great Salmasius. To you he was great indeed, you having employed him as a sort of pimp to procure his servant girl. You praise him nevertheless; but he praises not you; nay, before his death it was well known that he held you in abomination, and reproached himself a thousand times for not giving credit to that venerable divine Spanheim,[57] who warned him of your impiety.—Now you have worked yourself up into a fury, as if bidding adieu to reason: "Salmasius," it seems "has been dead long ago in reason"; you ask for yourself the part only of crying and raving; and yet you give the first in reviling also to Salmasius; "not because he is outrageous in his lan-

56. The Orange faction was the royalist group in Holland.

57. Frederick Spanheim (1600–49) was a German theologian and an inveterate enemy of Salmasius and More.

guage, but because he is Salmasius." Babbler! for these smart things I suppose we are indebted to the more-bearing Pontia. It is hence your cry has learnt to be witty, as well as to lament in whining tone; it is hence also, in your bullying way, you thus threaten us: "The time shall come, ye foul beasts, when ye shall be made to feel what the style can do." Shall we be made to feel you, maid-hunting miscreant— shall we be made to feel you, lecher, or your style, which is formidable only to maid-servants? When, if any one should only show you a radish-root or a mullet, by Hercules, you would think yourself well off, to escape without having your breech cut in sunder, and without the loss of that salacious style of yours.—"Indeed (you remark) my head is not so empty as to attempt a task which had been undertaken by Salmasius": a task, however, which he had never undertaken, unless his head had been deplorably empty. It is truly amusing, for you to rank the great Salmasius before yourself in emptiness of head.— "To raise the cry of the royal blood to heaven," "it being the duty" even "of the illiterate"—you mean, I suppose, is your duty. Cry, vociferate, bellow; go on to play the hypocrite, to have words of sanctity in your mouth, to live in the worship of Priapus! Be assured, the time shall come, when the God of vengeance, to whom you so often cry, shall arise; he shall arise, and it shall be his first care to root out you, minister of the devil! the unutterable disgrace and pest of the reformed church. To the multitudes who condemn the abuse of Salmasius, you reply,—"It is thus that parricides, of all monsters the most abominable, deserve to be treated." I commend you; for you furnish us with weapons; and instruct us opportunely in what way it is proper that yourself as well as your adversaries should be dealt with; at the same time that you absolve us from blame. Finding you can do nothing with reason, afraid to venture upon the general ground of the right of kings, which had been pre-occupied by Salmasius, and having alleged every thing that has relation to reason to be found in him, you now tack about from contumely and fury to some wretched narratives, though being destitute of any rational purpose, you merely continue the same clamour with which you set out. These narratives you have partly dressed up from Salmasius, and partly copied from that anonymous and most refutable view, the author of which has forsaken not his country only, but his name; to their chief points having already replied at sufficient length, either in *Eikonoklastes,* or in my answer to Salmasius, I cannot, I think, well say more, at lesser length than a regular history. Shall I for ever be compelled, every now and then, to tread the same round, and, at the noise of every low fellow, to repeat what I have so often said before? I will not do it; I will not make so ill a use either of my labour or of my time. If any one thinks these mercenary cries, these ready-made lamentations of a hireling mourner, these contemptible speechifyings, the spurious progeny of concubinage with a waiting maid, and born at a litter with the little bastard More—if any one thinks these things of sufficient account to be believed, I, for my own part, shall make no attempt to hinder him from thinking so still; indeed, from any one so credulous and thoughtless, I can in truth have nothing to fear. I will touch, however, upon a few things, which will answer the purpose of many, from which you will learn in a few words of what description the author is, as well as what he says; and likewise what is to be thought of the rest.

This alien having talked a good deal of nonsense about the reduction of the Lords and Commons to a single house (a demand which no man in his senses would blame) remarks, "that, having established equality in the state, they might proceed to introduce the same into the church: for at the time I speak of, the bishops yet remained: if this be not rank anabaptism, I do not see what is." Who could ever have expected this from a divine and a minister of the Gallic church? He who sees not what anabaptism is, unless this be it, I should really think can see as little what baptism is. But, if we would call things by their right names, equality in the state is not anabaptism, but democracy, a thing far more ancient; and as established in the church, is the discipline of the apostles. But "the bishops remained." Granted; they remained too at Geneva, when that city expelled, on account of religion, its bishop, who was at the same time its legitimate prince. Why should that be considered as disgraceful in us, which in them was re-

garded as honourable? I am not at a loss, More, to know what you
would be at; you would revenge the votes of the Genevese, by which
it is yet a question, whether you were dismissed with ignomy, or
ejected from the Genevese church. That you, therefore, as well as
Salmasius, are become a renegado from this evangelical institution,
and are gone over to the bishops, (if it be of any consequence whither
you go) is manifest.—"Then the state passed (you say) to the equality of the ministers of our persuasion: for it is known to every body,
that the same spirit then prevailed, which at last, in the eighth year,
put an end to the business by the atrocious parricide of the king." It
appears, then, that the same spirit by which the ministers of your persuasion were constituted, also executed the parricide. Go on as you
have begun, to belch out your ravings, which comport well with an
apostate.

"There were only three petitions (you say) which demanded
punishment on the king": which is well known, and which I myself
remember, to be utterly false. Indeed, those among us who have
charged their memories with these circumstances, remember not three
petitions only of this kind, but many from different counties of
England; and that, for the space of nearly a month, three a day were
presented by the regiments of the army. You see what grave deliberation the parliament must have bestowed upon this subject, when the
people, suspecting them of excess of lenity, thought it right, by their
numerous petitions, to put an end to their lingering. How many thousands were there, do you suppose, who were unanimous in thinking
it officious or superfluous to urge the parliament to a measure, which
was then under their serious consideration? Of this number I myself
was one, though what was my wish it is not hard to divine. What if
all men had been silent, in amazement at the magnitude of the thing?
Would the senate have been more at a loss how to decide in so great
a matter? Was the nod of the people to be waited for, on which to
hang the issue of counsels so important? In truth, if the supreme
council of the nation, which is employed by the whole body of the

people as a check upon the wild domination of the king, after having made the king a prisoner of war, he being found in open violence and resistance, were obliged to recur to the commands of the people, and to ask their orders to punish a captive enemy—what else would those men, who with so much courage had rescued the commonwealth, have appeared, in fact, to have done, but, with the countenance of the people, if they had haply obtained it, to have rashly thrown themselves into the toils of the tyrant? Or if, after having accepted the sovereign power to decide on things of the highest moment, on things especially which are above the capacity of the vulgar, they had been compelled again to refer, I do not say to the people, (for though invested with this power, they are themselves still the people) but to the multitude, who, from feeling their own ignorance, had before referred every thing to them—what would have been the end of this referring forward and backward? In fine, what resting place had there been in this Euripus?[58] Amidst these petitions proceeding from so many fantastical heads, what settlement, what safety could there have been for the shaken fabric of society? What if they had demanded that Charles should be restored to the kingdom? That there were some petitions of this description, not however, of a petitionary but of a menacing nature, must be confessed, from seditious persons, whose hatred one while, and whose complaining another, was, for the most part, equally absurd and malicious: and were such to obtain notice? who according to your account, "to procure a conference with the king, left their villages and flocked to the doors of the parliament house in great numbers; of whom very many were cruelly murdered by the military, who were admitted by the members." You mention also the country people of Surrey—mere peasants, who, whether instigated by the malice of others, or by their own licentious inclinations, I am not informed, paraded through the city with a petition, being in a state of intoxication, and more prepared for carousing than for pe-

58. The name of the strait separating Euboea and Boeotia known for its rapidly shifting tides.

titioning.[59] Soon, in a body they beset the doors of the parliament-house in a riotous manner; turned the soldiers who were stationed there from their posts; killed one at the very parliament doors, without having received the slightest provocation by word or deed; and "breathing" drunkenness rather than "liberty," they were very properly driven thence and roughly handled, though not more than two or three of them were killed.—You every where concede that "the Independents were the most powerful, not in number, but in counsel and military virtue." And I contend, that they were hence also justly and deservedly superior: for there is nothing more agreeable to nature, nothing more just; nothing more useful or more for the interest of man, than that the less should yield to the greater; not number to number, but virtue to virtue, and counsel to counsel. Those who excel in prudence, in their experience in business, in industry and virtue, will, in my opinion, however few, prove to be the majority, and will prevail more in the suffrages of mankind than any number, however great.

You intersperse a good many things about Cromwell, and of what description we shall see hereafter. As to the rest, we have long since replied to them as urged by Salmasius. You do not forget also the judgment passed upon the king, notwithstanding this has been pitifully declaimed over by your great rhetorician. The nobles (you say) that is, the king's courtiers, and courtly ministers, as most of them were, shrunk with horror from judging the king. That this is of little weight, we have shown in another work.—"Next, the judges of the courts were struck out: for they when appealed to had returned for answer, that it was contrary to the laws of England, that the king should be put upon his trial." I know not what they then answered; but I know what they now approve and defend. It is no new thing for judges to be timorous, though in them of all men it is the least becoming.—"For this despicable and accursed court there was chosen

59. One of the several popular commotions directed against Commons on behalf of the king. This march upon Westminster mounted on May 16, 1648, was dispersed by Cromwell's troops.

a suitable president—an obscure and insolent scoundrel." Now for you who have been guilty of so much impurity and wickedness—for you who are nothing but one mass of foulness and of crimes, to have brought such a callus upon your mind and senses (if your mind be not rather one entire callosity) as towards God to be an atheist and a defiler of the sacred rites, towards man a savage, a calumniator of the undertakings of every man of eminent character,—what is it but to be near of kin to Iscariot and to the devil? But though your censure is the highest praise, yet, far be it from me to be so wanting to that preeminent personage, at whom you are barking, and who is a friend of my own, of all others, the most deserving of my reverence, as not to defend him from the audacious tongues of the fugitives and the Mores, which but for the commonwealth he never had felt.

John Bradshaw[60] (a name which liberty herself, wherever she is respected, has commended for celebration to everlasting memory) was sprung, as is well known, from a noble family; and hence, spent the early part of his life in the diligent study of the laws of his country. Becoming afterwards a skilful and eloquent pleader, a zealous defender of liberty and of the people, he was admitted to the higher offices in the state, and several times discharged the function of an incorrupt judge. At length, on a request from the parliament that he would preside on the trial of the king, he refused not the dangerous office: for to skill in the law, he added a liberal mind, a lofty spirit, with manners unimpeached, and beholden to no man. This office, therefore, which was great and fearful almost surpassing all example, marked out as he was by the daggers and threats of so many ruffians, he executed and filled with such steadiness, such gravity, with such dignity and presence of mind, that he seemed destined and created by the deity himself for this particular act—an act which God in his stupendous providence had pre-ordained should be exhibited among this people—and he so far surpassed the glory of all tyrannicides, as it

60. John Bradshaw (1602–59), a lawyer and chief justice of Chester, was appointed to preside over Parliament's High Court upon its establishment. He heard the case against Charles and delivered the sentence.

is more humane, more just, more full of majesty, to try a tyrant, than to put him to death without trial. He was otherwise neither gloomy nor severe, but mild and gentle. Yet, at all times equal to himself—the consul, as it were, not of a single year—he supported the high character which he took upon him with a becoming gravity; so that you would think him sitting in judgment upon the king, not on the tribunal only, but every moment of his life. He is above all men indefatigable in counsel, and in exertions for the public—he alone is equal to a host. At home, he is, according to his means, hospitable and splendid; the most faithful of friends, and, in every change of fortune, the most to be relied upon. No one sooner or more willingly discovers merit, wherever it is to be seen, or acts towards it with greater favour. At one time he aids the pious, at another the learned, or men known for any species of skill; now he relieves, from his private fortune, brave men of the military profession who have been reduced to want; and if they are not in want, he yet receives them with a willing courtesy, a friendly welcome. It is his constant practice to proclaim the praises of others, and to conceal his own: and among his political enemies, if any has happened to return to his right senses, which has been the case with many, no man has been more ready to forgive. But if the cause of the oppressed is to be openly defended; if the favour and the power of the mighty is to be resisted; if the public ingratitude against any meritorious character is to be reproved; then indeed, no one could find in this man any want of eloquence or of firmness; no one could even desire an advocate, or a friend, more able, more intrepid, more eloquent: for he has found one, whom no threats can turn aside from rectitude, whom neither intimidation nor bribes can bend from his duty and virtuous purpose, can move from an unshaken steadiness of mind and of countenance. By these virtues, he has made himself deservedly dear to most men, and not to be despised by his greatest enemies. And when you, More, and those who are like you, shall be utterly confounded, he shall spread the renown of his country's noble deeds among all foreign nations, and with posterity to the end of time.

But we must proceed. The king was condemned to lose his head. "Against this outrage, almost all the pulpits in London began to thunder." You will not fright us much with this wooden thunder; we are nothing afraid of these Salmoneuses; the time will come when they will suffer for this counterfeit thunder, which they have had the presumption to wield.[61] Now these are authorities truly grave and sincere, when but a little before, and from the very same pulpits, they thundered with a noise equally horrific against pluralists and non-residents; and soon after, one seizing upon three, another upon four, to his own share, of the benefices of the prelates, whom with their thundering they had driven out, and thus of necessity becoming non-residents themselves, they were guilty of the same crime as that against which they thundered; so that each was struck with the lightning which proceeded from his own thunderclap. Nor do they yet feel any shame. Now they are struggling tooth and nail in defence of tithes; and if their thirst of tithes is so great, why I would let them have tithes enough in all conscience; they should have not the tenth only of the fruits of the earth, but the tenth waves of the sea. The same persons were the first to advise war against the king, as against an enemy devoted to destruction: by and by, when we had gotten the enemy into our hands—an enemy who had been so often condemned by themselves as the cause of the slaughter and bloodshed, they would spare him forsooth as being a king. Thus, in their pulpits, as if in a tradesman's shop, they sell whatever wares, whatever trumpery they please, to the poor, silly people; and what is worse, they reclaim what they have sold as often as they think proper.—Again—"The Scots earnestly demanded that the king should be set at liberty; they mention the promises of the parliament after they had delivered up the king to the English." Now I can prove from the confession of the Scots themselves, that there were no public promises at all, when the king was delivered up; and disgraceful indeed had it been to the English, if their own king was not to be given up by the Scots, who were mer-

61. Salmoneus was thrown into Tartarus by Jupiter for his impiety in attempting to imitate Jupiter's thunder and lightning.

cenaries in the pay of England, unless on conditions: nay, the very answer itself of the parliament to the stipulations of the Scots, which answer was made public on the 15th of March 1647, clearly denies that any assurance had been given as to the point, how the king was to be treated. Indeed, the parliament thought it a disparagement of their dignity, that they should be unable to obtain their right of the Scots, but on such a condition.—But "they earnestly demanded that the king should be set at liberty." The gentle souls began no doubt to relent; they could no longer bear the yearning of their spirits towards their king: and yet, from the beginning of these commotions in Britain, these same men had more than once brought forward a motion in parliament on the subject of the right of kingship, and had unanimously resolved, about the year 1645, that there were three main reasons for which a king may be deprived of his kingdom—his proving to be a tyrant, his alienation of the royal demesnes, and his desertion of his people. In the parliament held at Perth, they proceeded to collect the sentiments of the house on the question, whether a king, who was plainly an enemy to the saints, might not be interdicted from the communion of the church? But before they came to any determination on this point, the assembly was thrown into confusion by the approach of Montrose[62] to that city at the head of his forces. The same men, in their answer to general Cromwell, in the year 1650, acknowledge that the king was justly punished; that the form only of the trial was reprehensible, and because themselves were not invited to act a part in it. This transaction, then, having taken place without them, is atrocious; if themselves had had a share in it, it would then have been glorious; as if right and wrong depended upon their nod, and just and unjust must be defined agreeably to their dictate. Suppose the king had been set at liberty, would themselves, let me ask, have been more lenient in their resolutions respecting him?—But "the Scottish delegates had received for answer before from the parliament of

62. James Graham, Marquis of Montrose (1612–50), one of the ablest commanders of Royalist forces.

England—that it was not their intention to alter the form of the English government; though they afterwards answered, that they had no intention at that time; but that now they had such an intention, as the safety of the state required it." And they answered well. But what is your remark upon this? "This subterfuge, you say, overturns all treaties, intercourse, and common sense itself." It overturns your common sense, it seems, since you know not the difference between an unconditional promise, and the obligation of a treaty. Concerning the form of the future government, a view of which it was unnecessary to present to the Scots, the English gave a frank reply, according to the best of their judgment at the time. Now, the safety of the state calls for different measures, if they would not forfeit their faith and solemn oath to the people. Which do you imagine to be of the most sacred obligation, an unconditional promise given the Scottish commissioners concerning the future form of the government, or an oath originating in necessity, and an assurance of the most solemn kind given their own countrymen, that they would provide for the safety of the state? But that a parliament or senate is at liberty, according to expediency, to change its counsels, I would have you learn, since every affirmation of ours is, in your eyes, anabaptistical and monstrous, from Cicero's oration for Plancius.[63] "We should all take our stand as it were in some circle of the commonwealth; and since this circle turns round, we should make choice of that particular point of it, to which we may be directed by its advantage and safety." He proceeds to say that he does not consider it any mark of inconstancy, for a man to regulate his opinion, as if a sort of ship and a ship's course, by the political atmosphere. "Indeed, I have learnt, I have observed, I have read—the writings of the wisest and most illustrious men in this republic and in other states have recorded for our use, that the same men are not always bound to defend the same opinions, but such as may be required by the state of the nation, the bent of the times, and

63. A speech delivered in 54 B.C. in which Cicero defends his friend against charges of corrupting elections.

by a regard to union." Thus Marcus Tullius; but you, More, would prefer Hortensius.[64] Such are the maxims of those ages, which flourished most in civil prudence—maxims, which, if the anabaptists follow, they are in my judgment, wise. How many more could I produce, which, by these trashy ministers and their Salmasius, a man absolutely without learning, if we consider things rather than words, are condemned as anabaptistical!—Again, you say, "the most potent, the united states of Holland could do no more: for they struggled hard, through the medium of their ambassadors, both by entreaty and rewards, to ransom the sacred head of the king." Now to wish thus to bribe justice, was the same thing as not to wish that the king might be saved. But they have found, that all men are not merchants; that the parliament of England is not so eager to sell.—Upon the sentence of the king you remark, "In how many respects did Charles, in his sufferings, resemble Christ! the soldiers made their incessant mocks at him." In truth, Christ resembled malefactors in his sufferings more than Charles resembled Christ; and many things of this sort were every where bandied about by those who, on account of this act, made it their business to stir up the greater malice, to invent all manner of falsehood, and to retail what they found invented to their hands. But suppose the common soldiers did behave with insolence; it does not immediately follow, that this is to be placed to the account of the cause. "That some man was actually murdered at the feet of the king, as he was passing along, for praying that God would have mercy on him," is what I never heard before; nor could I ever yet meet with any one who had heard it: nay, I caused an inquiry to be made, as to this matter, of the colonel who commanded the guards during the whole time of the execution, and who scarcely moved a step from the king's side; and he positively affirmed that he had never heard this before, and that he knew for certain that it was wholly without foundation. From this we may learn what credit is due to your narratives; nay, what foundation there is for credit even in the other parts of your

64. Hortensius, Cicero's chief rival as a pleader, lived from 114 to 50 B.C.

work: for in soliciting for favour and even for adoration, if you can
obtain it, for Charles after his death, you will be found to have paid
not much more regard to truth, than in your iniquitous attempts to
kindle hatred against us.—"The king (you say) on the fatal scaffold,
was heard to say twice to the bishop of London, remember! remember!" This, to be sure, made the king's judges anxious to know, to
what last request this word, thus repeated, could have reference; and
the bishop was sent for, as you report, and ordered, with threats, to
declare what this reiterated "remember" meant. He, it seems, was at
first squeamish, as had been pre-concerted (for a fiction of this sort
was expedient) and refused to disclose it, as if it had been some great
secret. But upon their becoming more urgent with him, he at length,
with much ado, made known, but in such a manner as if it had been
wrested from him by intimidation and against his will, what in reality, he would have had divulged at any price. "The king (said he) ordered me, if I could ever get to his son, to carry him this last command
of a dying father, that, should he ever be restored to his kingdom and
his power, he would pardon you the authors of his death: this is what
the king charged me again and again to remember." Shall I say now,
that the king was the more pious, or that the bishop was the more
leaky, when he could so easily be won upon, to blab a thing entrusted
to him with so much secrecy on the scaffold! But O miracle of taci-
turnity! Charles had long ago entrusted this very same thing to his
son, among other precepts, in the *Icon Basilike;* which book, it sufficiently appears, was written, for the express purpose of divulging to
us a little after, with all diligence, even against our wish, that secret,
and with the same parade with which it had been counterfeited. But
I see plainly that you are determined to impose upon the inexperi-
enced, if not this Stuart, at least some Charles Stuart who is the mirror of all excellence, some hyperborean and fabulous Charles, whom
you draw in whatever false colours may happen to hit your fancy.
Thus you have fantastically got up this fable, as if for scenic representation, bravely embellished, after what mimic I know not, with dialogue and pithy sentences, as baits for vulgar ears. Now I do not mean

to deny that the bishop might have been incidentally questioned, as to this point, by some one or another of the commissioners; but I do not find that he was sent for, that either the council or that body of judges paid any particular attention to it, as if they had been at all apprehensive on that account, or that they made any anxious inquiry about the matter. But let us now give your account of the business. Charles, on the scaffold, gave these last commands to the bishop, to be carried to his son, that he should pardon the authors of his death. And in this, what has he done that is so extraordinary, so different from what others have done who have been brought to the same situation? Who is there among those who die on a scaffold, who when about to finish the drama of life, and seeing the vanity of things mortal, would not act in the same way? and willingly lay aside, or at least pretend so to do, his enmities, his angers, his hatreds, as if now making his exit from the stage, that he may leave behind him in the minds of men a feeling of compassion, or a conviction of his innocence? That Charles dissembled; that he never from his heart, from the sincere purpose of his mind, gave such a command to his son, as "that he should pardon the authors of his death"; or that if he gave this command in public, he gave a different in private, may be proved by no light arguments: for there can be no doubt that the son, who was, in other respects, over-obsequious to the father, would have paid obedience to the last and the most solemn of his father's injunctions, delivered to him with such religious care by the bishop. But in what manner has he paid obedience to it, when either by his order or by his authority, two of our ambassadors, one in Holland, the other in Spain, have been murdered; the latter without even the slightest suspicion of being accessary to the king's death? When, in fine, he has more than once, by a public declaration in writing, made known to all men, that it is not his intention, on any account, to pardon those who put his father to death? It is for you to consider, therefore, whether you could wish this pretty narrative of yours to be true, when in proportion as it applauds the father, it condemns the son.

You now lose sight of your main object, and feign cries, not of the royal blood to heaven, but of the people against the parliament—you, who, next to Salmasius, are the most odious of meddlers in other people's affairs, while at home no man manages his own so shamefully. Shall the people employ your voice in their defence, you mass of impurity, from whose very breath, tainted with venereal corruption, every clean person would turn with loathing? You take the voice of the beggarly refugees for the voice of the people; and like a foreign mountebank to the crowd, imitate the voices only of the vilest of animals. Now who denies that times may often occur, when a large majority of the citizens may be unprincipled—citizens, who would make choice of Catiline or Antony for their leader, in preference to the sounder part of the senate; but it will not less behove good citizens to strive against them on that account, and to do bravely, more regardful of their duty, than of the smallness of their number. This dainty piece of declamation therefore, of yours, in behalf of our people, I would advise you, that the paper might not be wholly wasted, to insert in the annals of Volusius.[65] As for ourselves, we do not stand in need of so paltry, so goatish, so rank a rhetorician.

We are next accused of injuries to the church. "The army is the Lerna[66] of all heresies." Those who do not calumniate our army, acknowledge it to be not only the bravest of armies, but the most modest and religious. Other camps are usually distinguished for drunkenness, for indulgence in various lusts, for rapine, gaming, swearing, and perjury: in ours, the leisure which is allowed is spent in the search of truth, in diligent attention to the holy scripture; nor is there any one who thinks it more honorable to smite the foe, than to instruct himself and others in the knowledge of heavenly things—more honorable to engage in the warfare of arms, than in the warfare of the gospel. And indeed, if we consider the proper use of war, what can

65. An allusion to a witticism of Catullus, who refers to the writings of a certain Volusius as used toilet paper.
66. Lerna was a swamp; the Lernean Hydra was a many-headed monster.

be more becoming in soldiers, who are enlisted and embodied for the express purpose of being the defenders of the laws, the guardians of justice in martial uniform, the champions of the church? What is there which can make it more incumbent upon men to be, not ferocious and barbarous, but courteous and humane, whose duty it is not to sow and reap war, but to cultivate peace and safety for the race of man, as the true and proper end of their labours? But if any of those who aspire to these noble designs should be led astray by the errors of others, or by their own infirmity, we should not in savage rage proceed against them with the sword, but should struggle against them with reason, with admonition, and with prayer poured forth to God, with whom alone it rests to dispel all errors from the mind, and to impart to whom he wills the heavenly light of truth. Nevertheless, we approve no heresies which are justly so called; nor do we even tolerate all; we wish them extirpated, but by such means as are suitable—that is, by precept and sounder doctrine: for as they are seated in the mind, they are not to be cut out with the sword and lash, as if their seat had been in the body.—Again; "Another and no less injury of ours is in the temporal foundation of the church." Ask the Dutch, or even the protestants of Upper Germany, whether they have ever abstained from the property of the church, when the Emperor of Austria seeks for no other pretence for making war against them, than that he may order the possessions of the church to be restored. But the truth is, that those possessions were not the property of the church, but of the ecclesiastics only, who in this sense especially may be called clergy, or more properly, holoclergy, inasmuch as they had seized upon the whole patrimony. Indeed, most of them deserve to be called wolves, rather than any thing else; and what crime was there in transferring the property of wolves,—or rather the accumulated plunder, obtained from the superstition of preceding times, of which for so many ages they had made their advantage,—to the purposes of a war kindled by themselves, when there was nothing else left to supply the heavy and daily expences of that war? But, "it was expected that a law would be made for bestowing the wealth wrested from the bishops upon the pastors of the churches." I know that they expected and coveted that all should be poured upon themselves: for there is no gulf so deep which may not sooner be filled than the avarice of the clergy. In other places perhaps the provision for the ministers is inadequate; ours were already provided for well enough and more than enough. They should be called sheep rather than shepherds: for they are fed more than they feed. With them all things are usually full of fatness, their intellects even not excepted: for they are pampered with tithes, a custom which is disallowed by all other churches, and are so distrustful of God, as to choose rather to extort them from their flocks by the magistrate and by force, than to owe them either to divine providence, or to the kindness and gratitude of the churches. And besides all this, they are so often feasting with their disciples both male and female, that they scarcely know what it is to dine or sup at home. Hence most of them live in luxury, rather than in want; and their children and wives vie, in extravagance and finery, with the children and wives of the rich. To have increased this luxury by new and large possessions would have been precisely the same thing, as if some new poison had been poured into the church—a pest, which of old under Constantine was deplored by a voice from heaven.[67]—The next thing is for us to give an account of the injuries towards God, of which three are specified, namely, our confidence in the divine aid, "our prayers, and our fastings." Now out of thine own mouth, most corrupt of mortals, will I condemn thee; and that expostulation of the apostle, which thou hast produced, I will retort against thee: who art thou that "judgest another man's servant?" Before our own master let us stand or fall. I will add that passage also from David the prophet:[68]

67. Apparently alluding to the voice mentioned by the poet John Gower in his *Confessio Amantis,* Milton has in mind the so-called Donation of Constantine once supposed to convey from Constantine I to Pope Sylvester rulership of Italy and the Western provinces of the Roman Empire.

68. Ps. 69:10.

"When I wept and chastened my soul with fasting, that was to my
reproach." Were I to follow in detail your other delirious gabblings
on this subject, which no one can read twice, I should myself be
chargeable with no light offence.—Nor is what you so tediously prate
about our successes, less foreign to the purpose. Take care, More, take
care, that after your Pontian sweats, you do not contract a gravedo in
your head or a polypus in your nose. It is to be feared, that, like the
once great Salmasius, you may chill the warm baths. Now as to our
success, I reply in these few words; that a cause is neither proved to
be good, nor shown to be bad, by success: we demand not that our
cause should be judged of by the event; but the event by the cause.—
You now undertake to handle political considerations, chaired slave
as you are, and even cathedralized our injuries, against all kings and
people. What injuries? for nothing of this sort had been laid to our
charge. We have merely done our own business; we have not meddled
with other people's business. If any good has overflown upon our
neighbours from our example, we have no invidious feelings on that
account; or if any thing of a different description, we do not believe
it has happened by our fault, but by the fault of those who have
abused us. And after all, who made you, such a pitiful fellow as you,
interpreter of the injuries whether of king or people? Certain it is,
that when their ambassadors and lieutenants-general have had audience in the council, so far from complaining of their injuries, I have
often heard them, as others have heard them in the senate, soliciting,
of their own accord, our friendship and alliance; congratulating us
besides, in the name of their kings and princes, on our affairs; and
even praying for our prosperity, and wishing us peace and length of
duration, and a continuance of the same auspicious success. These are
not the words of enemies; these are not, as you report, the words of
those who hated us: it follows then of necessity, that either you are
convicted of a lie, which in you is a very trifling matter, or kings
themselves of deceit and wicked arts, which in them would be most
dishonorable. But you object to our writings, since in them we con-

fess, "that we have set an example salutary to all people, to be dreaded by all tyrants." You tell of a mighty crime no doubt; pretty much the same thing, as if any one had said:

Advised, learn justice, and revere the Gods.[69]

Could any thing be said more pernicious? "This is what was written by Cromwell to the Scots, after the battle of Dunbar." And which was worthy of himself and of that noble victory. "The infamous pages of Milton are strewn with sesamum and poppy of a like description." You always join me with some illustrious colleague, and in this affair, you make me evidently Cromwell's equal, sometimes even his superior—a name by which, above all others, I think you honour me most, if any thing honorable can proceed from you.—"But those pages (you say) were burnt by the hangman at Paris, by order of the parliament." So far from this being the work of the parliament, I find it was done by one of the city officers, (and whether he held a civil or an uncivil office I know not) at the instigation of some of the clergy, those laziest of animals, who, from scattered and distant auguries, prognosticated for their own bellies, what I pray may one day fall upon them. Do you imagine that we also could not have burnt, in our turn, the royal defence of Salmasius? If I had thought such an insult deserving of any other revenge than contempt, I could myself have easily obtained this from our magistrates. In your hurry to put out one fire by another, you have raised an Herculean pile, from which I may rise up in greater brightness.[70] We have more wisely thought that the chilliness of the royal defence should not be warmed. But this I wonder at, that the people of Toulouse should have become so unlike their ancestors (for I find I have been also burnt at Toulouse) as now to burn the defence of liberty and religion in the very city, in which, under

69. Milton is paraphrasing Virgil's *Aeneid* 6.620.

70. Hercules immolated himself upon a pyre and was then by some accounts translated to the abode of the gods.

the counts of Raimond, both liberty and religion had been before so signally defended. "Would! (you exclaim) that the writer also had been burnt!" And is this indeed your wish, slave? You have taken especial care, that I shall not return you a like compliment, as you have been long since consuming in far blacker flames. You are burnt by your adulteries, you are burnt by your fornications, you are burnt by your perjuries, by the aid of which perjuries you perfidiously shook off the woman who became betrothed to you by the sacrifice of her honour; you are burnt by your outrageous madness, which has impelled you, miscreant as you are, to covet the holiest of functions, and as a priest, to pollute with adulterous hands the undiscerned body of the Lord. Under the pretence of sanctity also, you would denounce, in this cry of yours, every thing that is direful against pretenders to sanctity, though you must bring your own accursed head into the snare, as being condemned even by your own sentence. With these crimes, with these infamies are you all on fire; in these furious flames are you scorching day and night, and suffering a punishment for us, than which no enemy could imprecate on you one more grievous. Meanwhile, these burnings of yours injure not, they touch not me; and against such disgraces I have many things to oppose which are grateful, which are delightful to my spirit. Under the influence of bad auspices, I have been burnt by one court, perhaps by a single Parisian executioner. But, in spite of this, how many excellent and learned men are there, throughout all France, who read, approve, embrace? How many throughout the spacious tracts of Germany, the domicile, as it were, of liberty, and in other regions, wherever any traces of liberty are yet visible: and even Greece herself—Athens the eye of Greece, revived as it seems once more, has contributed her applause by the voice of one of her sons—the noble Philaras.[71] This, moreover, I can truly say; at the time when our defence was first published, and readers were all glowing with attention to it, there was not an

---

71. Leonard Philaras (1600–73), a native of Greece, served as ambassador of the Duke of Parma and visited the blind Milton in 1654. He expressed admiration for the *First Defence*.

---

ambassador from any prince or state at that time in the city, who did not congratulate me either on an accidental meeting, who did not desire my company at his own house, or who did not visit me at mine. But it were an injury to forget your departed spirit, Adrian Paul,[72] who, with the high dignity of ambassador to us, and the glory and ornament of Holland, were solicitous to make known to me by frequent messages, though I never happened to see you, your great and distinguished kindness towards me. It is also pleasing to me to dwell frequently upon the circumstance, and which, it is my belief, could never have happened without the especial favour of God, that I, who, as it seemed, had been writing in opposition to kings, have obtained the approving nod even of royal majesty itself,[73] and its testimony, only not divine, to my integrity, and to the superior truth of my opinion. And why should I scruple to say this as often as I think of that most august queen, whose high praises are the theme of every tongue? Indeed, not even that wisest Athenian, between whom and myself, however, I make no comparison, can I think more graced by the testimony of the Pythian himself, than me by her opinion. And if I had happened to have written what I have, when a young man, and the same liberty were allowed to orators as to poets, I should in truth not have hesitated to prefer my fortune to that of some among the gods; forasmuch as they, being gods, contended only for beauty, or in music, before a human arbiter; and I, being a man, with a goddess for my arbitress, have come off victorious in the noblest far of all contests. Thus highly honoured, no one but an executioner would dare to treat me with disrespect, whether by ordering it to be done, or by doing it himself.

Here you labour hard to prevent our defending what we have done by the example of the exploits of the Dutch in favour of liberty—a point which has been fruitlessly laboured also by Salmasius. I would return the same answer to you now, as I did then to him: that he who

72. Adrian de Pauw, ambassador of Holland to England, on mission in June and early July of 1652.

73. Milton refers once more to his favor with Sweden's Queen Christina.

thinks our struggles have been occasioned by the example of any one, is mistaken; that, of necessity, we, who have often aided and encouraged the exploits of the Dutch in favour of liberty, could never have been their rivals; and that, if any thing is to be done bravely for liberty, we, being our own masters, are accustomed to lead the way, not to follow others. But you, vile orator, by the absurdest of arguments, worthy of a paltry fellow like you, also incite the French to war against us: "The spirit of the French, (you say) will never bear to receive our ambassadors." But, what is more, the spirit of the French has already borne to send their own, three or four times, and of its own accord, to us. The French, then, are generous as usual; while you, degenerate and spurious, are found to be ignorant and mistaken as to your political considerations.—You next try to make it appear, that the negotiation was purposely spun out to a great length by the United States; and that they were desirous neither of a treaty nor of a war with us. Surely it concerns the States not to suffer their counsels to be thus exposed, and, as I may say, falsified by a Genevese fugitive who is got housed among them, and who, if tolerated much longer, will not merely, as it seems, bring prostitution upon their servant maids, but upon their public counsels: for they themselves are all sincerity and brotherly kindness, and have now, agreeably to the wish of every good man, renewed with us a perpetual peace. "It was amusing (says he) to see, with what scoffs, with what perils, those gallows ambassadors," namely of the English, "had daily to contend, not only from the English royalists, &c. but most of all from the Dutch." If we had not long since discovered on whom was to be charged the murder of Dorislaus our first ambassador, and the injuries received by our two succeeding ambassadors, here would be an informer, who accuses even falsely his hosts and supporters. And do you suffer this man, Hollanders, to be fostered among you, who is not merely a debauchee-minister of the church, but a sanguinary instigator to the violation of all right, and the false and traitorous informer, when the violence has been committed?

The last title of the accusations is—"Our injury towards the re-formed churches." Now how have we injured them, more than they have injured us? If you urge, by our example, I reply, that if you ex-amine into records, beginning from the Waldenses, and people of Toulouse, and proceeding downwards to the famine of Rochelle,[74] we shall be found to be the last of all the churches who have taken up arms against tyrants, though the first who have condemned one to a capital punishment: and in truth, because we were the first who had it in our power. What they would have done, if they had had the same power, is not very well known, I apprehend, even to themselves. In short, my opinion is, that (if a man has any use of his reason) he, against whom we make war, is considered by us as an enemy; that, to put an enemy to death has always been lawful, by the same right as we oppose him; and as a tyrant is not simply our enemy, but the general enemy as it were of the whole human race, that, by the same right as he may be resisted by arms, may he likewise be put to death. Nor is this my opinion alone, or any new opinion; the same was sug-gested, whether by prudence or common sense, to others in ancient times. Hence Marcus Tullius for Rabirius: "If it was unlawful for Saturninus to be put to death, arms could not, without a crime, have been taken up against Saturninus; if you admit that arms were justly taken up, you necessarily admit that he was justly put to death."[75] I have said more on this subject above, and often elsewhere; besides, the thing is not dark in itself. Whence, you may judge what the French themselves would have done, if the same opportunity had been given them. I moreover add: those who oppose a tyrant with arms, do all they can to put him to death; nay, they have already put him to death, whatever they may absurdly wish to persuade themselves or others.

74. The Waldenses dissented from the Roman Church from the twelfth century onward; the city of Toulouse freed itself from feudal taxes in the twelfth century; La Rochelle was the center of Huguenot resistance to the French crown until forced by famine to yield in 1628.

75. From Cicero's *Pro Rabirio,* delivered in 63 B.C.

But this doctrine belongs no more to us, than to the French, whom you would willingly exempt from this heinous crime: else, whence that Francogallia, if not from Gaul?[76] Whence those *Vindications against Tyrants*—a book commonly ascribed to Beza[77] himself? Whence other books mentioned by Thuanus?[78] And yet you say, "This is the point which Milton is labouring with such busy zeal," as if I were the only one, "and whose atrocious fury I would have received as it deserved." You would have received, you villain? whose nefarious profligacies if the church of Middelburg which has the misfortune and infamy of having you for a pastor, had received as they deserved, it had long ago have sent you to the devil; if the magistrates had received as they deserved, you would long ago have expiated your adulteries on a gallows. To tell the truth, you seem very likely to make an expiation ere it be long: for, as I am lately informed, your church of Middelburg has watched you narrowly, has consulted its own reputation, and has sent you about your business, that you may go and be hanged—goatherd of a pastor as you are, nay, the rankest of goats. Hence too, the magistrates of Amsterdam laid an interdict for you on the pulpit, which is your stage; and forbad that shameless face of yours to be seen from that place, to the utter scandal of all good men; forbad that impious voice to be heard in public on a sacred subject. At this time, your professorship of Greek alone remains; and this also is soon to be taken away, all but that single letter, of which, however, you will not be the professor, but ere long deservedly the disciple pensile from the top. Nor do I forebode these things for you in anger, but simply speak what is right: for, so far from being offended at such revilers as you, we could even wish to have always such; and are persuaded that it is through the divine favour it has happened, that those

---

76. *Franco-Gallia* was the chief work of Francis Hotman (1524–90), who taught history and law at several Protestant universities.

77. Theodore Beza (1519–1605) was a French religious reformer and close associate of Calvin.

78. Jacobus Augustus Thuanus (1553–1617) was the author of *Historia Sui Temporis* (1620).

---

who have raised the most virulent clamours against us, have always been eminently such, whose abuse is no infamy, but honour, but applause: for certain it is, that their praise would have been a reproach. But as you are so courageous a fellow, what has checked your late violence? "Unless (you say) I had been religiously scrupulous not to invade the province of the great Salmasius, to whom shall be left the substantial part of the victory over his great adversary, forsooth." Since you now seem to think *me* great as well as him, I shall perhaps be found to be a province the more difficult to be invaded, especially as he is dead. I am little solicitous about the victory, provided only truth be the victor.—Meanwhile, you pursue your clamour: "They convert parricide into a doctrine; and this they would fain do, with the consent of the reformed churches; they dare not defend it openly. This was the opinion also, says Milton, of the most eminent divines, the very authors of the reformation in the church." It was, I say; and this I have shown abundantly in the book, in our own tongue, entitled *The Tenure of Kings and Magistrates,* second edition; and in other places. What I have done so often, I feel a reluctance to do again. In that work, I have cited word for word the very passages from Luther, Zuinglius, Calvin, Bucer, Martyr, Paraeus, and lastly from that Knox, "the only Scot (you say) I have of my side, and who was condemned, as to this matter, by all the Protestants of that age, especially by the French." On the contrary, he himself affirms, as is there related, that he drew this doctrine expressly from Calvin, and from other eminent theologians of that time, with whom he had familiar intercourse. You will there find also more upon the same subject taken from the sincerer part of our divines, in the reigns of Mary and Elizabeth. But at length you impiously conclude in a tedious ready-made prayer to God, deserving of execration; and hardened in iniquity, offer up that adulterous mouth to heaven. I have no difficulty in suffering you to proceed without interruption: for your impiety could receive no accession.

I now return to what I promised above, and will here bring forward to public view the chief crimes which are laid to the charge of Cromwell; that it may be seen how light they must have been when scattered, when, in a body, they have no weight against him. "He declared it, before numerous witnesses, to be his intention to overturn all monarchies, to exterminate all kings." What credit is due to your narratives, we have often seen already. One of the refugees, perhaps, told you that Cromwell had said so; of those numerous witnesses, you name not one; so that, that abuse of yours which is without authority, falls by its own default. Cromwell is not a man who has been ever heard, by any one, to boast of the achievements he has actually performed; and equally far is he from making insolent promises and threats, as to those he intends to perform, especially achievements of such difficulty. Indeed, those who told you all this, if they had not been wilfully and naturally liars, rather than from deliberation, would at any rate, not have invented a forgery, which is totally foreign to his character. But when kings, whom you frequently admonish to take care of themselves, look out for their own safety, they will not be obliged to snatch at any trivial tittle-tattle, but will be at liberty to despise so ignorant an adviser as you, and to listen to plans of policy worthy of themselves, and by which they may more easily discern their true interests.—Another crime is, that Cromwell persuaded the king "to retire privately to the Isle of Wight." It is well known, that king Charles had rendered his affairs desperate from various other causes, and three times by flight: first, when he fled from London to York; secondly, when he fled to the Scotch mercenaries in England; and lastly, when he fled to the Isle of Wight. But it was Cromwell who persuaded him to this last flight. Very well; and yet, in the first place, I cannot but admire those royalists, who persist in affirming, that Charles was a paragon of prudence, when he scarcely ever had a will of his own: when, whether among his friends or enemies, in the court or in the camp, he was almost always at the disposal of others; at one time of his wife, at another of the bishops, now of the courtiers, then of the military, and lastly of his enemies: when, for the most part, he followed the worst counsels, and those commonly of the worst men; and Charles is persuaded, Charles is imposed upon, Charles is played upon, he is smitten with fear, he is deluded with vain hopes; when Charles was driven and carried about, the common prey, as it seemed, of all; of friends as well as of enemies. Let them take away these things from their writings, or cease to extol the sagacity of Charles. Again, though it is an excellent thing to excel in prudence and in counsel, yet, when the commonwealth is torn with factions, it is not without its inconveniences; and renders the man of the greatest capacity and experience the more obnoxious to the calumnies of both parties. This is what has frequently happened to Cromwell. Hence the presbyterians, his enemies, for that reason, impute not to the parliament in general, but to Cromwell alone any measure which they may think harsh towards themselves; and even, when themselves, through their own inprudence, conduct any business unsuccessfully, they have the effrontery to ascribe this also to the wiles and artifices of Cromwell. Every fault is fathered upon him; it is he who must bear the blame of every thing. And yet, it is beyond all doubt, that King Charles's flight to the Isle of Wight, happened as suddenly and unexpectedly to Cromwell, he being at the time some miles distant, as to the member of parliament then in the city, to whom he communicated it as a thing the most unexpected in the world, of which he had just been informed by letter. The truth of the matter is this: the king, terrified at the outcry of the whole army, (who, as he failed to alter his conduct for the better in consequence of any offices or promises of theirs, began, even at the time I speak of, to demand his punishment,) resolved to provide for his own safety by flying in the night, with two attendants, the only persons privy to his escape. But more determined to fly than rightly knowing whither—at a loss where to seek refuge through the inexperience or timidity of his attendants, he made a voluntary surrender of himself to Hammond, governor of the Isle of Wight, in hopes of being able to procure a ship privately, in which he might get an easy passage from that island into France or Holland. I had this account of the king's flight to the Isle of Wight from those who had the best possible opportunity of being acquainted with the whole affair thoroughly.—And it is likewise a crime, it seems, that, through Cromwell, "the English gained a great victory over the Scots." Not *parti sunt,* More; but, without the solecism, *pepererunt,*[79] gained for themselves a splendid victory. Imagine now, what a bloody battle that must have been to the Scots, when you could not even mention it, without knocking your professorial head, made giddy by fear, against Priscian's[80] desk! But further; let us see what great crime it was in Cromwell to have conquered, in the noblest battle which had been fought for many ages, the Scots who were meditating an irruption, and already promised themselves the supreme sway over the English. "Amidst this confusion, while Cromwell is absent with his army": Yes, while Cromwell, seeing the enemy advanced into the heart of England, threatening even the parliament, was conquering and gloriously dispersing that enemy; while he was harassing himself in reducing the revolted Welsh to obedience, and by a long siege— the presbyterians "began to be tired of Cromwell." Here you speak the truth. While he is repelling the common enemy at the hazard of his life, while he is engaged in war for themselves and bravely fighting in the field, these men are accusing him at home of fabricated crimes, and suborn one captain Huntingdon,[81] to charge him with a capital offence. Who can even listen with patience to such baseness of ingratitude! At the instigation of the same persons—a most worthless and insolent set of fellows—the apprentices from the shops in great numbers beset the doors of the parliamenthouse; and with their clamour and threats, compel the parliament to resolve whatever they choose to dictate; and what could be a greater indignity than this? And

79. Milton complains of a Latin construction in More's work (actually Du Moulin wrote this portion of *The Cry of the Royal Blood*) that by placing the verb in the passive denies the full efficacy of the British initiative in seizing their victory.

80. Priscianus Caesariensis (491–518) was a grammarian at Constantinople.

81. Maj. Robert Huntingdon, one of Cromwell's closest lieutenants, appeared before the House of Lords August 2, 1648, to accuse Cromwell of bad-faith dealing with Charles and of plotting to acquire supreme authority.

when returned, the bravest of conquerors, from the Scots, we should have seen our Camillus[82] sent into banishment, or suffering the most unmerited of punishments, if general Fairfax[83] had not thought it was not to be borne that such disgrace should be inflicted on his invincible lieutenant; if the whole army, which was likewise treated with sufficient ingratitude, had not put a stop to conduct so atrocious. Cromwell, therefore, having entered the city, soon reduced the citizens to order, and deservedly turned out of the parliament the partisans of the hostile Scots; the rest, now freed from the insults of the shopkeepers, rescinded the treaty which in contradiction to the vote of parliament, and a public declaration, had been entered into with the king, in the Isle of Wight. His accuser Huntingdon, left in impunity and to his own disposal, at length repented, and of his own accord asked forgiveness of Cromwell, and without solicitation, confessed by whom he had been suborned. These are the chief crimes, with the exception of those to which I have replied above, with which this magnanimous deliverer of his country has been reproached; and of what weight they are you now see.

But I shall have done nothing, if I only make it appear that this great man, who has deserved so highly of the commonwealth, has done nothing wrong; when it concerns not the commonwealth alone, but myself in particular, conjoined as I am so closely with him in the same infamy, to show forth to the nations, and as far as I am able, to all ages, his transcendent merit, his sovereign worthiness of all praise.— Oliver Cromwell was sprung from a noble and illustrious family. The name was famous of old under the kings for skill in the administration of public affairs; and it grew more famous in consequence of the orthodox or reformed religion being at the same period established

82. Marcus Furius Camillus went into exile after being accused of cornering spoils in his capture of Veli. He was recalled to lead the Romans against two invasions by the Gauls.

83. Thomas Fairfax (1612–71), Cromwell's ablest and highest-ranking field commander.

among us for the first time. He grew up in the privacy of his own family, and till his age was quite mature and settled, which he also passed in private, was chiefly known for his strict attendance upon the purer worship, and for his integrity of life. He had cherished his confidence in God, he had nursed his great spirit in silence, for some extraordinary times. When a parliament was at last called by the king, he was returned member for his own town; and immediately became conspicuous for the justness of his opinions, and the firmness of his counsels. When the appeal was made to arms, he was appointed, by his own choice, to a troop of horse; and as his force was augmented by the eager zeal of the good, who flocked from all quarters to his standard, he soon surpassed almost the greatest generals in the grandeur of his achievements, and in the rapidity with which they were executed. Nor is this to be wondered at: for, he was a soldier, above all others the most exercised in the knowledge of himself; he had either destroyed, or reduced to his own control, all enemies within his own breast—vain hopes, fears, desires. A commander first over himself, the conqueror of himself, it was over himself he had learnt most to triumph. Hence, he went to encounter with an external enemy as a veteran accomplished in all military duties, from the day he first entered the camp. It would not be possible for me, within the limits of this discourse, to follow him with all suitable dignity, through so many captured cities, so many battles, and those of the greatest order, in none of which was he ever conquered or put to flight; but he traversed the whole circle of Britain in one continued series of victories—victories, which demand the great work of a regular history; another field, as it were, on which they may be told; a space for narration equal to the things to be described. To evince his extraordinary, his little less than divine virtue, this mark will suffice; that there lived in him an energy whether of spirit and genius, or of discipline, established not by military rule only, but by the rule of Christ and of sanctity, that he drew all to his camp, as to the best school both of military science, and of religion and piety—nay those who were already good and brave, from all parts, or made them such principally by his own example;

and although there were many who opposed him, retained them in their duty, (and yet retains,) during the whole period of the war, sometimes even of an intervening peace, through so many changes of minds and of circumstances, not by largesses and military licence, but by his authority and their pay alone: and greater praise than this we are not wont to bestow either upon Cyrus, Epaminondas,[84] or upon any of the first generals of antiquity. Hence it is, that no one ever raised for himself a larger or better disciplined army in shorter time, obedient in all things to the word of command, welcome to the citizens and beloved by them; to its enemies in arms terrible indeed, but when reduced to peaceable subjection, the objects of their admiration: for so far from being oppressive and mischievous, when quartered in their fields, and their houses, when those enemies recollected the violence, the drunkenness, the impiety and lust of their own royalists, they were happy at the change, and now thought themselves visited not by enemies, but by guests; a protection to the good, a terror to the evil, the encouragers to all virtue and piety.

Nor must I forget you, Fairfax, in whom nature and the divine favour have conspired to unite the greatest modesty, the most exemplary sanctity of life, with the highest courage. Your merit and your right entitle you to be called forth to receive your share of these eulogies; though in your present secession, like that Scipio Africanus[85] of old at Liternum, you hide yourself, as much as possible, from the public view. It is not the enemy alone, you have conquered; you have conquered ambition, and what itself conquers the most excellent of mortals, you have conquered glory; and are now enjoying, in the most delightful and glorious of retirements, your virtues and illustrious deeds, which is the end of all labours, of the greatest even of human actions—a retirement, which when the ancient heroes enjoyed after their battles and famous exploits no greater than yours, the poets who

84. Cyrus the Great in the sixth century B.C. conquered widely in the Near East; Epaminondas (420–362 B.C.) was a Theban famed for his generalship.

85. Publius Cornelius Scipio (236–183 B.C.) retired to his estate in Liternum after a distinguished and lengthy war career.

attempted their eulogies, despaired of being able to describe with appropriate dignity, but by fabling that they were received up into heaven, and sat at table with the gods. But whether you have withdrawn on account of your health, which I am most inclined to think, or whether from any other motive, of this I am fully persuaded, that nothing could have torn you from the service of the commonwealth, if you had not seen what a protector of liberty, what a firm and faithful pillar, what a rampart of England's prosperity you have left in your successor. For, while you, Cromwell, are in safety, he shows not a sufficient confidence in the supreme, who has any fears for the prosperity of England; seeing, as he must, that God so manifestly favours you, that, in all things he is your helper. But you were now left to yourself, and had to engage in a fresh struggle of battles.

But what need of many words? I will recount your principal exploits as briefly, if I can, as you are accustomed to achieve them rapidly. All Ireland was lost, with the exception only of one city, when you transported an army, and immediately, in a single battle, broke the power of the Irish. What remained to be done you were dispatching daily, when you were suddenly recalled to the war in Scotland. Quitting Ireland you advance, unwearied, against the Scots, who, with their king, were preparing for an irruption upon England; and in about one year, reduced, and added to the dominion of England a kingdom, which all our kings, during a period of eight hundred years, had been unable to subdue. The remains of their forces, which however were in high condition and well-equipped, marched, in their utmost despair into England, which at that time was almost destitute of garrisons. You pursued them with forced marches, and overtaking them when they had advanced as far as Worcester, fell upon them suddenly, and destroyed them in a single battle; taking the chief part of their national nobility prisoners. There was now, at home, a profound peace: and it was then we felt, but not then for the first time, that your power was not less in counsel than in the arts of war. In the parliament, it was your daily care to see, either that the faith of the treaty entered into with the enemy should be maintained, or that without delay such resolutions should be adopted as might be for the benefit of the state. But perceiving that delays were artfully contrived; that every one was more attentive to his private interest than to the interest of the public; that the people complained they were disappointed in their expectations, and circumvented by the power of a few, you put an end to their arbitrary authority, which they, though so often advised to it, had refused to do. A new parliament is called; the privilege of voting is allowed to those only, to whom it was proper to allow it; the elected meet; do nothing; and having harassed one another for a while with their dissentions and altercations, and most of them being of opinion that they were unfit persons, and not equal to undertakings of such magnitude, they dissolve themselves. Cromwell, we are deserted; you alone remain;[86] the sovereign authority of the state is returned into your hands, and subsists only in you. To your invincible virtue we all give place, all but such, who without equal ability are desirous of equal honours; who look with envy upon the honours bestowed upon others more worthy than themselves, or who know not, that there is nothing in human society more pleasing to God, or more agreeable to reason; that there is nothing more just in a state, nothing more useful, than that the most worthy should possess the sovereign power. That you are such, Cromwell, that such have been your deeds, is acknowledged by all—you, who are the greatest and most glorious of our citizens, the director of the public counsels, the leader of the bravest of armies, the father of your country: for by this title do all good men hail you with spontaneous voice sent forth from the heart. Other titles, though merited by you, your actions know not, endure not; and those proud ones, deemed great in vulgar opinion, they deservedly cast from them. For what is a title, but a certain definite mode of dignity? Your achievements surpass every degree even of admiration, and much more do they surpass every title;—they rise above the popular atmosphere of titles, as the tops of

86. Milton refers here to Cromwell's dismissing of the Rump Parliament, which he immediately replaced with members nominated by Independent congregations or by the army.

pyramids hide themselves in the clouds. But though it can add nothing to dignity, yet as it is expedient, for virtues even the most exalted to be finished and terminated by a sort of human summit, which is counted honour, you thought it right, and suffered yourself, for the public benefit, to assume something like a title, resembling most that of *pater patriae,* the father of your country;[87] you suffered yourself not to be raised indeed, but to descend so many degrees from on high, and to be forced as it were into the ranks; despising the name of king for majesty far more majestic. And justly so: for if, after becoming so great, you should be captivated with a name, which, as a private man, you were able to subjugate, to reduce to a cipher, it would be all one, as if, after subduing, by the help of the true God, an idolatrous nation, you were to worship as gods those whom you had brought under subjection. Go on therefore, Cromwell, in your wonted magnanimity; it fits you well. Your country's deliverer, the founder of our liberty, and at the same time its protector, you can assume no other character more dignified or more august; for your exploits have surpassed not merely those of kings, but even those which have been fabled of our heroes. Consider often, how precious a thing you hold deposited with you, and by a parent how dear—liberty, commended and entrusted to your care by your country! who, what she before expected from the choicest men of the whole nation, now expects, and hopes to attain through you alone. Respect this high expectation of you, this only hope of your country. Respect the countenances and the wounds of so many brave men who, under your conduct, have fought so zealously for liberty, and the departed spirits of those, who have fallen in the struggle. Respect also what foreign nations think and say of us; what great things they promise themselves from our liberty, which has been won with so much bravery, from our commonwealth, which has sprung up with so much glory; and which, if it should vanish as soon as it has arisen, no equal disgrace and shame could fall upon this nation. Last of all, respect yourself, and suffer not

87. That is, Lord Protector.

that liberty, which you have gained with so many hardships, so many dangers, to be violated by yourself, or in any wise impaired by others. Indeed, without our freedom, you yourself cannot be free: for such is the order of nature, that he who forcibly seizes upon the liberty of others, is the first to lose his own, is the first to become a slave: and nothing can be more just than this. But if the patron himself of liberty, and as it were, her tutelary genius—if he, than whom none is esteemed a more just, a holier, or a better man, should at last offer violence to her whom he has defended, this must, of necessity, be destructive and deadly not to himself alone, but, in a manner, to the very cause of all virtue and piety. Honour and virtue themselves will appear to have faded away; henceforward, religious faith will be narrowed; reputation will be a poor thing indeed; and a deeper wound than this, after that first, it would not be possible to inflict upon human kind. You have taken upon you by far the heaviest burden, which will try you thoroughly; it will search you through and through, and lay open your inmost soul; it will show what is the predominant disposition of your nature, what is your strength, what is your weight; whether there is indeed in you that living piety, that faith, justice, and moderation of mind, for which we have thought that you above all others deserved, by the will of God, to be elevated to this sovereign dignity. To rule by your counsel three most potent nations; to be desirous of leading the people from corrupt institutions to a better plan of life and of discipline than they had before; to send out your anxious mind, your thoughts, to the remotest parts; to watch, to foresee, to cavil at no toil, to despise all the blandishments of pleasure, to shun the pomp of wealth and of power,—these are those arduous things, in comparison of which war is a play-game; these will drive against you like a mighty wind, and shake your steadiness; these require a man who is upheld by divine help, who is admonished and taught by little less than divine converse. All these things and more, I doubt not, you frequently meditate, and revolve in your mind; as likewise, by what means you may give effect to those momentous considerations, and restore to us our liberty safe, and augmented. This, in my judgment, you could in no way be more likely to accomplish, than by associating those, as you do, among the first, in your counsels, whom you had first as companions of your labours and of your dangers—men distinguished alike for their modesty, their integrity, and their courage; whom the sight of such multitudes of deaths, such multitudes of slaughters, has not taught cruelty or hardness of heart, but justice, and reverence of God, and compassion for the lot of humanity; but, in fine, to be tenacious of their liberty in proportion to the danger to which they have exposed their lives for her sake. These men were not taken from the refuse of the people, or of foreigners; they are no mob of men, but most of them citizens of the better note, either of a noble origin, or of an origin not disreputable; possessed, some of ample, others of moderate fortunes. And what if some be recommended even by their poverty? These were not called together by the hope of plunder, but were excited to the deliverance of the commonwealth from tyranny, by the difficulty of the times, when the situation of affairs was eminently critical, often adverse; prepared not only to talk and interchange opinions, in a place of safety, or in the parliament, but to join in close fight with the enemy. And unless we are to be for ever in pursuit of vague and idle hopes, I see not in what men we can at last rest and confide, if we are not to have confidence in these, and such as these. Of their fidelity we have a certain, an undoubted pledge, in their not refusing to meet even death, if such should be their destiny, for the public good: of their piety, in their having been accustomed, after humbly imploring the assistance of God and being often signally assisted by him, to ascribe all the glory of their success to him whom they had asked for succour: of their justice, in their having brought even the king to judgment, and refused to spare him when condemned; of their moderation, since this we have ourselves long experienced; besides, if the peace which they have obtained for themselves should be broken, through their own fault, they themselves would be the first to feel the evils which would thence arise, would receive on their own bodies the first wounds, would have to fight again for all those fortunes and ensigns of dignity which they had so happily won before: last of all, of their courage; for, in the recovery of their liberty, no men ever showed greater courage, or had greater success: and let us not suffer ourselves to think that there are any who can preserve it with greater diligence.

My speech is impatient to commemorate the names of men who have risen to distinction: and first you Fleetwood,[88] whom I have known to have been always the same in the humanity, gentleness, and benignity of your disposition, from the time you first entered upon the profession of a soldier to your obtainment of these military honours, the next only to the first; and whom the enemy has found of dauntless valour, but the mildest of conquerors: and you Lambert,[89] who, when a young man, at the head of a mere handful of men, checked the progress of the duke of Hamilton, attended with the flower and strength of the Scottish youth, and kept him at check: you, Desborow,[90] and you, Whalley,[91] whom, whenever I heard or read of the fiercest battles of this war, I always expected, and found, among the thickest of the enemy: you Overton,[92] who have been connected with me for these many years in a more than brotherly union, by similitude of studies, and by the sweetness of your manners: in that memorable battle of Marston Moor, when our left wing was routed, the chief officers looking back in their flight beheld you keeping your ground with your infantry, and repelling the attacks of the enemy, amid heaps of slain on both sides: and afterwards, in the war in Scotland, no sooner were the shores of Fife occupied, under the auspices of Cromwell, with your troops, and the way opened be-

88. Charles Fleetwood (1618–92) led the English force in Ireland at this time. After a cessation of hostilities he functioned as virtual governor of the island.

89. John Lambert (1619–84) led parliamentary forces against a Scot invasion in 1648 and established himself as third in command after Cromwell and Fairfax.

90. John Desborough (1608–80), member of Council of State and treasurer at the time of writing.

91. Edward Whalley, a regimental commander who for a time was entrusted with charge over the defeated king.

92. Robert Overton (1609–68), governor of Hull from 1653 to 1654 and publicly critical of the Protectorate.

yond Stirling, than both the western and the northern Scots acknowledged you for the humanest of enemies, and the farthest Orcades for
their civilizing conqueror. I will yet add some, whom, as distinguished
for the robe and arts of peace, you have nominated as your counsellors, and who are known to me either by friendship or reputation:
Whitlocke; Pickering; Strickland; Sydenham; and Sidney (an illustrious name, which I rejoice has steadily adhered to our side); Montague;
Lawrence[93]—both men of the first capacity, and polished by liberal
studies: besides numberless other citizens, distinguished for their rare
merits, some for their former senatorial exertions, others for their
military services.

   To these accomplished men and chosen citizens you doubtless
might properly commit the care of our liberty; indeed, it is not easy
to say, to whom it could more safely be committed or confided. After this, I could earnestly wish that you should leave the church to itself, and have the prudence to relieve yourself and the magistrates
from that burden, which is one half, and at the same time, most remote from your own province; and that you should not suffer the two
powers, the ecclesiastical and the civil, which are so totally distinct,
to commit whoredom together, and, by their intermingled and false
riches, to strengthen indeed, in appearance, but in reality to undermine, and at last to subvert one another. I could wish, that you should
take away all power from the church—and power will never be
wanting as long as there shall be money, the poison of the church, the
quinsy of truth; as long as there shall be hire for preaching the gospel,
coercively collected even from those who have no disposition to pay

93. Bulstrode Whitlocke (1605–75) was a long-term M.P. and an ambassador to
Queen Christina; Sir Gilbert Pickering (1613–68) was an M.P. in both the Short
and Long Parliaments and served on the Council of State; Walter Strickland served
on various commissions to Holland and as a member of the Council of State under
the Protectorate; William Sydenham (1615–61) served in Cromwell's Parliaments
and in the Army Council of Thirteen; Algernon Sidney (1622–83) distinguished
himself as a military leader in the Civil War and served as an M.P. although he opposed abolition of monarchy, lords, and Cromwell's establishing the Protectorate;
Edward Montague (1625–72) fought for Parliament, was elected M.P. in 1645, and
held a place on the Council of State in 1653; Henry Lawrence (1600–64) was Lord
President of the Council of State throughout the Protectorate.

it; that you should cast out from the church those money-changers, who sell not doves, but the dove, the holy spirit itself. Again, I could wish, that you should introduce fewer new laws, than you abrogate old ones: for there are often to be found in a state men, who have a sort of diseased itching for the enaction of a multiplicity of laws, like that of versifiers for the fabrication of a multitude of verses; but laws are commonly bad, in proportion as they are numerous—acting not as warnings to men, but as rocks on which they must split. You should retain only those which are necessary; should enact others; yet not such as would bring the good and the bad under the same yoke, or such as, while they provided against the knavery of the unprincipled, should, at the same time, prohibit what, to honest men, should be free from all restraint; but such as should punish only actual crimes, and not forbid things, in themselves lawful, for the fault of those who abuse them: for laws have been provided only to restrain malignity; to form and increase virtue, the most excellent thing is liberty. Next, I could wish you should make a better provision for the education and morals of youth, than has been yet made; and that you should feel it to be unjust, that the teachable and unteachable, the diligent and the idle, should be maintained at the public charge; and that you should reserve the rewards of the learned for those who are already proficients in learning, for those whose merit is already established.— Again, it is my earnest wish, that you would give permission to those who are inclined to freedom of inquiry, to publish what they have to communicate at their own peril, without the private inquisition of any magisterial censor: for nothing could contribute so much to the growth of truth; nor would all science be for ever measured out to us in the bushel, and be bestowed at the good pleasure of the half-learned, whether arising from their censure, their envy, their narrow-mindedness, or from their having detected superstition in others. Lastly, it is my fervent wish, that you should not be afraid to listen either to truth or falsehood, of whatever description that may be; but that you should listen the least of all to those, who never fancy that themselves are free, unless they deprive others of their freedom; who labour at nothing with so much zeal and earnestness, as to enchain not the bodies only, but the consciences of their brethren; and to introduce into church and state the worst of all tyrannies—the tyranny of their own misshapen customs and opinions. May you ever take part with those, who think it just, that not their own sect or faction alone, but all the citizens alike should have an equal right to be free. Should any one think this liberty, which may be dispensed by the magistrates, to be not enough, such a man seems to me to have his thoughts employed more about ambition and disturbance, than a generous liberty; and the more, as, notwithstanding the people have been agitated with so many factions, as after a tempest before the waves have yet subsided, he refuses to admit so desirable and perfect a state of things.

And as for you, citizens, it is of no small concern, what manner of men ye are, whether to acquire, or to keep possession of your liberty. Unless your liberty be of that kind, which can neither be gotten, nor taken away by arms; and that alone is such, which, springing from piety, justice, temperance, in fine, from real virtue, shall take deep and intimate root in your minds; you may be assured, there will not be wanting one, who, even without arms, will speedily deprive you of what it is your boast to have gained by force of arms. Many were made greater by the war, whom the peace has again made less. If, after putting an end to the war, you neglect the arts of peace; if war be your peace and liberty, war alone your virtue, your highest glory, you will find, believe me, that your greatest enemy is peace itself; peace itself will be by far your hardest warfare, and what you think liberty will prove to be your slavery. Unless by real and sincere devotion to God and man, not an idle and wordy, but an efficacious, an operative devotion, you drive from your minds superstition, which originates in an ignorance of true and substantial religion, you will not want those who will sit upon your backs and upon your necks, as if you were beasts of burden; who, though you are the victors in the war, will sell you, though by no military auction, as their plunder to the highest bidder; and will make an excellent market of your ignorance and superstition. Unless you banish avarice, ambition, luxury from your thoughts, and all excess even from your families, the tyrant, whom you imagined was to be sought abroad, and in the field, you will find at home, you will find within, and that a more inexorable one; yea, tyrants without number will be daily engendered in your own breasts, that are not to be borne. Conquer these first; this is the warfare of peace; these are victories, hard, it is true, but bloodless; more glorious far than the warlike and the bloody. If ye are not the victors here also, that enemy and tyrant, whom you so late have conquered in the field, you have either not conquered at all, or have conquered to no purpose: for, if, to be able to devise the subtlest expedients for filling the treasury; if, to furnish out sea and land forces, with the utmost expedition; if, to treat warily with the ambassadors of foreign states; to enter, with dexterity, into coalitions and treaties, be accounted by you more grand, more useful, more wise in a state, than to administer uncorrupted justice to the people; than to succour the oppressed, and those who are injuriously afflicted; than to give to every man his free, unshackled right—when you have suddenly found those grand things to be delusive, and the things which are now thought little and are neglected by you shall prove adverse and destructive; it will then be too late for you to discover how great has been your error. Again, the fidelity of the armies and adherents, in whom ye confide, is uncertain, unless it be maintained by the authority of justice alone: and wealth and honours, the objects of pursuit to most men, easily change masters. Where virtue, where industry, and patience of labour are in greatest vigour, thither do they take their flight; the indolent they forsake. Thus nation presses on nation; or the sounder part of a nation thrusts out the more corrupt. Thus have you thrust out the royalists. If you suffer yourselves to turn aside to the same vices; to imitate them; to follow the same courses; to hunt after the same vanities, you will, in effect, be royalists yourselves, and in your turn will lay yourselves open to these, either to the same as have been hitherto your enemies, or to others; who, trusting to the same prayers to God, the same patience, integrity, and skill, by which you first prevailed, will deservedly bring you under the yoke, corrupted as you then will be, and sunk into royalist excess and folly. Then, as if God had utterly repented him of you, which is a miserable thing, you will appear to have passed through the fire only to

perish in the smoke; and then you will become as much the contempt
of mankind, as you are now their admiration; and will leave behind
you this only salutary lesson, which hereafter may haply be useful to
others, though not to yourselves,—how great achievements true virtue and piety could perform, when the false counterfeit of these qualities, merely well dissembled, could, in your case, attempt so much and
succeed so far in their attempt. But if, either through your inexperience, or inconstancy, or want of principle, achievements so splendid
have turned out unfortunately, they will not be the less feasible, on
that account, or the less likely to succeed, for the time to come, in
the hands of better men. But no man, not Cromwell himself, not the
whole nation of those deliverers the Brutuses,[94] if it should revisit us,
either could, if it would, or would, if it could, deliver you again, if
you are thus easily corrupted. For, to what purpose, in such a case,
would any one stand up in your behalf, for freedom of suffrage, and
for the privilege of returning whom you please to parliament?—that
every candidate may entertain the men of his own party in the cities?
or, that you may elect the man, however unfit, who should treat you
with the most lavish feastings, or the farmers and countrymen, in
the borough-towns, with the greatest quantity of drink? Thus would
faction and cramming, not prudence and authority, create for us the
men who are to watch over the state; and we should have victuallers
and hucksters from the city-shops, and herdsmen and graziers from
the villages, for our senators. That is, the concerns of the public would
be entrusted to those, to whom nobody would entrust his private
concerns—the treasury and taxes to such as had shamefully squandered their own substance, the public revenue to those who would
be guilty of peculation, who would convert public into private property. Can men become all at once the legislators of a nation, who have
never learnt what law means, what reason, what is right or wrong,

94. Junius Brutus, who helped found the Roman republic by leading a revolt
against the tyrant Tarquinius Superbus, and Marcus Brutus, who led the conspiracy against Julius Caesar.

lawful or unlawful? Who think that all power consists in violence; dignity, in pride and haughtiness? Whose first acts in the parliament, are to confer corrupt favours on their friends, and to take care to thwart their enemies? Who appoint in the provinces their relations and dependents to superintend the assessments, and to sequester property—most of them men of worthless character and desperate fortunes, who from being the purchasers at their own auctions, amass immense sums of money, which they convert to their own use, and thus defraud the public, plunder the provinces, enrich themselves, and from the beggary and meanness of yesterday, suddenly emerge to opulence and pride? Who can bear such thievish servants, their masters deputies? Who would believe that the very masters and patrons of thieves could be proper guardians of liberty, or think himself made one jot the more free by such administrators of the state (though the customary number of five hundred should be returned, after this manner, from the counties and towns) when there would be so few among the very guardians of liberty, and by whom it is guarded, who could either know how to use, or could be worthy to enjoy it? But last of all, it is not to be forgotten, that those who are unworthy of liberty are commonly the first to show their ingratitude towards our deliverers. Who would now fight, or incur the least danger, for the liberty of such men? It does not suit, it does not fall to the lot of such men to be free. However they may bawl and boast about liberty, they are slaves both at home and abroad, and yet perceive it not; and when they shall at length perceive it, they will disdain the curb like headstrong horses, and from the impulse of pride and little desires, not from a love of genuine liberty (which a good man alone can properly attain) they will try to shake off the yoke. They may make the same attempt by arms again and again; but they will make no progress: they may change their slavery perhaps; but they will never be able to shake it off. This is what very frequently happened even to the ancient Romans, after they had become effeminate and unnerved through luxury: and much more did it happen to the modern Romans, when, after a long interval they affected—under the auspices of Crescentius Nomentanus, and afterwards of Nicolaus Rentius,[95] who got himself nominated tribune of the people—to renew their ancient glory, and to restore the republic. For know, that you may not feel resentment, or be able to blame any body but yourselves, know, that as to be free is precisely the same thing as to be pious, wise, just and temperate, careful of one's own, abstinent from what is another's, and thence, in fine, magnanimous and brave—so, to be the opposite of these, is the same thing as to be a slave; and by the wonted judgment, and as it were by the just retribution of God, it comes to pass, that the nation, which has been incapable of governing and ordering itself, and has delivered itself up to the slavery of its own lusts, is itself delivered over, against its will, to other masters—and whether it will or no, is compelled to serve. For this we have the sanction of law, and of nature herself; since he who has no command of himself, who, either through imbecility or derangement of mind, is unable to manage properly his own affairs, is not left at his own disposal; but, like a ward, is given up to the direction of another; and much less is he set to manage other people's affairs, or the affairs of a state. Do you, therefore, who have the wish to continue free, either begin with being wise, or repent without delay. If it be hard, if it be against the grain, to be slaves, learn to obey right reason, to be masters of yourselves; in fine, keep aloof from factions, hatreds, superstitions, injuries, lusts, and plunders. Unless you do this to the utmost of your power, you will be thought neither by God nor man, not even by those who are now your deliverers, to be fit persons in whose hands to leave liberty, the government of the commonwealth, and what you arrogate to yourselves with so much eagerness, the government of others, when like a nation in pupillage, you would then want rather a tutor, and a faithful and courageous superintendent of your own concerns.

As for myself, to whatever state things may return, I have performed, and certainly with a good will, I hope not in vain, the service

95. Crescentius seized power in 983 upon the death of the emperor Otto II yet was deposed and executed when Otto III marched on Rome; Cola di Rienzi (1313–54) sought to revive Roman glory but maintained only a brief hold on power and left Rome much as he had found it.

which I thought would be of most use to the commonwealth. It is not before our own doors alone that I have borne my arms in defence of liberty; I have wielded them on a field so wide, that the justice and reason of these which are no vulgar deeds, shall be explained and vindicated alike to foreign nations and to our own countrymen; and by all good men shall no doubt be approved; and shall remain to the matchless renown of my fellow-citizens, and as the brightest example for after-ages. If our last actions should not be sufficiently answerable to the first, it is for themselves to see to it. I have celebrated, as a testimony to them, I had almost said, a monument, which will not speedily perish, actions which were glorious, lofty, which were almost above all praise; and if I have done nothing else, I have assuredly discharged my trust. But as the poet, who is styled epic, if he adhere strictly to established rules, undertakes to embellish not the whole life of the hero whom he proposes to celebrate in song, but, usually, one particular action of his life, as for example, that of Achilles at Troy, or the return of Ulysses, or the arrival of Aeneas in Italy, and leaves alone the rest; so likewise will it suffice for my duty and excuse, that I have at least embellished one of the heroic actions of my countrymen. The rest I pass by: for who could do justice to all the great actions of an entire people? If, after achievements so magnanimous, ye basely fall off from your duty, if ye are guilty of any thing unworthy of you, be assured, posterity will speak, and thus pronounce its judgment: The foundation was strongly laid, the beginning, nay more than the beginning, was excellent; but it will be inquired, not without a disturbed emotion, who raised the superstructure, who completed the fabric! To undertakings so grand, to virtues so noble, it will be a subject of grief that perseverance was wanting. It will be seen that the harvest of glory was abundant; that there were materials for the greatest operations, but that men were not to be found for the work; yet, that there was not wanting one, who could give good counsel; who could exhort, encourage; who could adorn, and celebrate, in praises destined to endure forever, the transcendent deeds, and those who performed them.

*The End.*

# THE READIE AND EASIE WAY TO
# ESTABLISH A FREE COMMONWEALTH

*Soon after the execution of Charles I the Rump Parliament had abolished the office of king, declaring it dangerous to liberty, unnecessary, and burdensome. Eleven years later England seemed to be on the point of restoring a king in the person of the son of the lately deposed monarch. On February 21, 1660, the Rump, at the instigation of Maj. Gen. George Monk, readmitted members who had been purged by Colonel Pride in 1648. Thus swollen with new members tending to Presbyterianism and monarchy, Parliament appeared ready for a return to monarchial government, and the question of the qualifications for voting on new M.P.s set for April 26 loomed with some urgency. Milton first wrote an open letter to General Monk calling upon him to support a republican regime strengthened by a perpetual grand council. Then, after Monk had entered London on February 6, Milton wrote and hastily had published the first version of* The Readie and Easie Way to Establish a Free Commonwealth; And the Excellence Therof Compar'd with the Inconveniencies and Dangers of Readmitting Kingship in This Nation. *Even after it had become certain that the impending parliament would be composed of those favorable to the return of royalty, Milton rushed through the press an enlarged edition of* Easie Way *just prior to the return of Charles II in May of 1660. Failing as he had to avert the reversion of his country to its pre-Commonwealth status, Milton nevertheless left in this appeal to republicans his most detailed plan for consolidating the gains of the revolution in a regime at once popularly based and arranged as an early version of the federal system of compound government later to be adopted in the American Constitutional Convention.*

# THE READIE AND EASIE WAY TO ESTABLISH A FREE COMMONWEALTH;

---

### And the Excellence Therof Compar'd with the Inconveniencies and Dangers of Readmitting Kingship in This Nation

A lthough since the writing of this treatise, the face of things hath had som change, writs for new elections have bin recall'd, and the members at first chosen, readmitted from exclusion,[1] yet not a little rejoicing to hear declar'd the resolution of those who are in power, tending to the establishment of a free Commonwealth,[2] and to remove, if it be possible, this noxious humor of returning to bondage, instilld of late by som deceivers, and nourishd from bad principles and fals apprehensions among too many of the people, I thought best not to suppress what I had written, hoping that it may now be of much more use and concernment to be freely publishd, in the midst of our Elections to a free Parlament, or their sitting to consider freely of the Government; whom it behoves to have all things represented to them that may direct thir judgment therin; and I never read of any State, scarce of any tyrant grown so incurable, as to refuse counsel from any in a time of public deliberation; much less to be offended. If thir absolute determination be to enthrall us, before so long a Lent of Servitude, they may permitt us a little Shroving-

---

1. Milton refers to the readmission of members who had been ejected in Colonel Pride's purge of 1648.

2. Before dissolving, the Rump Parliament had provided for free elections to Parliament to be held on April 26, 1660.

---

time[3] first, wherin to speak freely, and take our leaves of Libertie. And because in the former edition through haste, many faults escap'd, and many books were suddenly dispersd, ere the note to mend them could be sent, I took the opportunitie from this occasion to revise and somwhat to enlarge the whole discourse, especially that part which argues for a perpetual Senat. The treatise thus revis'd and enlarg'd, is as follows.

The Parliament of *England,* assisted by a great number of the people who appeerd and stuck to them faithfullest in defence of religion and thir civil liberties, judging kingship by long experience a government unnecessarie, burdensom and dangerous, justly and magnanimously abolished it;[4] turning regal bondage into a free Commonwealth, to the admiration and terrour of our emulous neighbours. They took themselves not bound by the light of nature or religion, to any former covnant, from which the King himself by many forfeitures of a latter date or discoverie, and our own longer consideration theron had more & more unbound us, both to himself and his posteritie; as hath bin ever the justice and the prudence of all wise nations that have ejected tyrannie. They covnanted *to preserve the Kings person and autoritie in the preservation of the true religion and our liberties;*[5] not in his endeavoring to bring in upon our consciences a Popish religion, upon our liberties thraldom, upon our lives destruction, by his occasioning, if not complotting, as was after discoverd, the *Irish* massacre,[6] his fomenting and arming the rebellion, his covert leaguing with the rebels against us, his refusing more then seaven times, propositions most just and necessarie to the true religion and our liberties, tenderd him by the Parlament both of *England* and *Scotland.* They made not

3. Shrove Tuesday was the day before the beginning of the Lenten fast and hence a time of indulgence during the Catholic era.

4. The monarchy was abolished by an act of Parliament on February 7, 1649.

5. Here and in the previous citation of a covenant, Milton refers to the Solemn League and Covenant of September 25, 1643.

6. Irish revolts occurring in October of 1641 and in 1643 were ascribed to the instigation of Charles I.

thir covnant concerning him with no difference between a king and a god, or promisd him as *Job* did to the Almightie, *to trust in him, though he slay us:*[7] they understood that the solemn ingagement, wherin we all forswore kingship, was no more a breach of the covnant, then the covnant was of the protestation before, but a faithful and prudent going on both in the words, well weighd, and in the true sense of the covnant, *without respect of persons,* when we could not serve two contrary maisters, God and the king, or the king and that more supreme law, sworn in the first place to maintain, our safetie and our libertie. They knew the people of *England* to be a free people, themselves the representers of that freedom; & although many were excluded, & as many fled (so they pretended) from tumults to *Oxford,*[8] yet they were left a sufficient number to act in Parlament; therefor not bound by any statute of preceding Parlaments, but by the law of nature only, which is the only law of laws truly and properly to all mankinde fundamental; the beginning and the end of all Government; to which no Parlament or people that will throughly reforme, but may and must have recourse; as they had and must yet have in church reformation (if they throughly intend it) to evangelic rules; not to ecclesiastical canons, though never so ancient, so ratifi'd and establishd in the land by Statutes, which for the most part are meer positive laws, neither natural nor moral, & so by any Parlament for just and serious considerations, without scruple to be at any time repeal'd. If others of thir number, in these things were under force, they were not, but under free conscience; if others were excluded by a power which they could not resist, they were not therefore to leave the helm of government in no hands, to discontinue thir care of the public peace and safetie, to desert the people in anarchie and confusion; no more then when so many of thir members left them, as made up in outward formalitie a more legal Parlament of three estates[9] against them. The best

7.  Job 13:15.

8.  Milton refers to the 175 members from both Houses who fled to set up a Royalist Parliament in Oxford at the king's military headquarters in January 1644.

9.  Bishops, nobles, commons.

affected[10] also and best principl'd of the people, stood not numbring or computing on which side were most voices in Parlament, but on which side appeerd to them most reason, most safetie, when the house divided upon main matters: what was well motiond and advis'd, they examind not whether fear or perswasion carried it in the vote; neither did they measure votes and counsels by the intentions of them that voted; knowing that intentions either are but guessd at, or not soon anough known; and although good, can neither make the deed such, nor prevent the consequence from being bad: suppose bad intentions in things otherwise welldon; what was welldon, was by them who so thought, not the less obey'd or followd in the state; since in the church, who had not rather follow *Iscariot* or *Simon* the magician, though to covetous ends, preaching, then *Saul*,[11] though in the uprightness of his heart persecuting the gospell? Safer they therefor judgd what they thought the better counsels, though carried on by some perhaps to bad ends, then the wors, by others, though endevord with best intentions: and yet they were not to learn that a greater number might be corrupt within the walls of a Parlament as well as of a citie; wherof in matters of neerest concernment all men will be judges; nor easily permitt, that the odds of voices in thir greatest councel, shall more endanger them by corrupt or credulous votes, then the odds of enemies by open assaults; judging that most voices ought not alwaies to prevail where main matters are in question; if others hence will pretend to disturb all counsels, what is that to them who pretend not, but are in real danger; not they only so judging, but a great though not the greatest, number of thir chosen Patriots, who might be more in waight, then the others in number; there being in number little vertue, but by weight and measure wisdom working all things: and the dangers on either side they seriously thus waighd: from the treatie,[12] short fruits of long labours and seaven years warr; securitie

10. *Best affected:* favorably disposed to the Commonwealth.

11. For the Iscariot reference, see Matt. 26:15; for Simon, see Acts 8:9. Saul would become the Christian Paul; see Acts 26:4.

12. Milton refers to the Treaty of Newport of October 27, 1648, offering proposals that were rejected by Parliament.

for twenty years, if we can hold it; reformation in the church for three
years: then put to shift again with our vanquishd maister. His justice,
his honour, his conscience declar'd quite contrarie to ours; which
would have furnishd him with many such evasions, as in a book
entitl'd *an inquisition for blood,*[13] soon after were not conceald: bishops
not totally remov'd, but left as it were in ambush, a reserve, with ordination in thir sole powr; thir lands alreadie sold, not to be alienated,
but rented, and the sale of them call'd *sacrilege;* delinquents few of many
brought to condigne punishment; accessories[14] punishd; the chief
author, above pardon, though after utmost resistance, vanquish'd; not
to give, but to receive laws; yet besought, treated with, and to be
thankd for his gratious concessions, to be honourd, worshipd, glori-
fi'd. If this we swore to do, with what righteousness in the sight of
God, with what assurance that we bring not by such an oath the whole
sea of blood-guiltiness upon our own heads? If on the other side we
preferr a free government, though for the present not obtaind, yet
all those suggested fears and difficulties, as the event will prove, easily
overcome, we remain finally secure from the exasperated regal power,
and out of snares; shall retain the best part of our libertie, which is
our religion, and the civil part will be from these who deferr us, much
more easily recoverd, being neither so suttle nor so awefull as a King
reinthron'd. Nor were thir actions less both at home and abroad then
might become the hopes of a glorious rising Commonwealth: nor
were the expressions both of armie and people, whether in thir publick declarations or several writings other then such as testifi'd a spirit
in this nation no less noble and well fitted to the liberty of a Commonwealth, then in the ancient *Greeks* or *Romans.* Nor was the heroic
cause unsuccesfully defended to all Christendom against the tongue
of a famous and thought invincible adversarie;[15] nor the constancie

13. James Howell, *An Inquisition of Blood, to the Parliament and the Army* (1649).

14. One cannot be sure whether to identify Laud and Strafford or such later Loyalists as Sir Charles Lucas and Sir George Lisle, who were also executed during the
war, as the "accessories" to whom Milton refers.

15. Milton refers to his own vindication of the revolution in the *First Defence,*
written in reply to the famed Salmasius.

and fortitude that so nobly vindicated our liberty, our victory at once against two the most prevailing usurpers over mankinde, superstition and tyrannie unpraisd or uncelebrated in a written monument, likely to outlive detraction, as it hath hitherto convinc'd or silenc'd not a few of our detractors, especially in parts abroad. After our liberty and religion thus prosperously fought for, gaind and many years possessd, except in those unhappie interruptions, which God hath remov'd, now that nothing remains, but in all reason the certain hopes of a speedie and immediat settlement for ever in a firm and free Commonwealth, for this extolld and magnifi'd nation, regardless both of honour wonn or deliverances voutsaf't from heaven, to fall back or rather to creep back so poorly as it seems the multitude would to thir once abjur'd and detested thraldom of Kingship, to be our selves the slanderers of our own just and religious deeds, though don by som to covetous and ambitious ends, yet not therefor to be staind with their infamie, or they to asperse the integritie of others, and yet these now by revolting from the conscience of deeds welldon both in church and state, to throw away and forsake, or rather to betray a just and noble cause for the mixture of bad men who have ill manag'd and abus'd it (which had our fathers don heretofore, and on the same pretence deserted true religion, what had long ere this become of our gospel and all protestant reformation so much intermixt with the avarice and ambition of some reformers?) and by thus relapsing, to verifie all the bitter predictions of our triumphing enemies, who will now think they wisely discernd and justly censur'd both us and all our actions as rash, rebellious, hypocritical and impious, not only argues a strange degenerate contagion suddenly spread among us fitted and prepar'd for new slaverie, but will render us a scorn and derision to all our neighbours. And what will they at best say of us and of the whole *English* name, but scoffingly as of that foolish builder, mentiond by our Saviour, who began to build a tower, and was not able to finish it.[16] Where is this goodly tower of a Commonwealth, which the English boasted they would build to overshaddow kings, and be

16. Luke 14:28–30.

another *Rome* in the west? The foundation indeed they laid gallantly; but fell into a wors confusion, not of tongues, but of factions, then those at the tower of *Babel;* and have left no memorial of thir work behinde them remaining, but in the common laughter of *Europ.* Which must needs redound the more to our shame, if we but look on our neighbours the United Provinces,[17] to us inferior in all outward advantages; who notwithstanding, in the midst of greater difficulties, courageously, wisely, constantly went through with the same work, and are setl'd in all the happie enjoiments of a potent and flourishing Republic to this day.

Besides this, if we returne to Kingship, and soon repent, as undoubtedly we shall, when we begin to finde the old encroachments coming on by little and little upon our consciences, which must necessarily proceed from king and bishop united inseparably in one interest, we may be forc'd perhaps to fight over again all that we have fought, and spend over again all that we have spent, but are never like to attain thus far as we are now advanc'd to the recoverie of our freedom, never to have it in possession as we now have it, never to be voutsaf't heerafter the like mercies and signal assistances from heaven in our cause, if by our ingratefull backsliding we make these fruitless; flying now to regal concessions from his divine condescensions and gratious answers to our once importuning praiers against the tyrannie which we then groand under: making vain and viler then dirt the blood of so many thousand faithfull and valiant *English* men, who left us in this libertie, bought with thir lives; losing by a strange aftergame of folly, all the battels we have wonn, together with all *Scotland* as to our conquest, hereby lost, which never any of our kings could conquer, all the treasure we have spent, not that corruptible treasure only, but that far more precious of all our late miraculous deliverances; treading back again with lost labour all our happie steps in the progress of reformation; and most pittifully depriving our selves the instant fruition of that free government which we have so dearly purchasd, a free Commonwealth, not only held by wisest men in all ages the

17. The Netherlands.

noblest, the manliest, the equallest, the justest government, the most agreeable to all due libertie and proportiond equalitie, both human, civil, and Christian, most cherishing to vertue and true religion, but also (I may say it with greatest probabilitie) planely commended, or rather enjoind by our Saviour himself, to all Christians, not without remarkable disallowance, and the brand of *gentilism* upon kingship.[18] God in much displeasure gave a king to the *Israelites,* and imputed it a sin to them that they sought one:[19] but *Christ* apparently forbids his disciples to admitt of any such heathenish government: *the kings of the gentiles,* saith he, *exercise lordship over them;* and they that *exercise authoritie upon them, are call'd benefactors: but ye shall not be so; but he that is greatest among you, let him be as the younger; and he that is chief, as he that serveth.* The occasion of these his words was the ambitious desire of *Zebede's* two sons, to be exalted above thir brethren in his kingdom, which they thought was to be ere long upon earth. That he speaks of civil government, is manifest by the former part of the comparison, which inferrs the other part to be alwaies in the same kinde. And what government coms neerer to this precept of Christ, then a free Commonwealth; wherin they who are greatest, are perpetual servants and drudges to the public at thir own cost and charges, neglect thir own affairs; yet are not elevated above thir brethren; live soberly in thir families, walk the streets as other men, may be spoken to freely, familiarly, friendly, without adoration. Wheras a king must be ador'd like a Demigod, with a dissolute and haughtie court about him, of vast expence and luxurie, masks and revels, to the debaushing of our prime gentry both male and female; not in thir passetimes only, but in earnest, by the loos imploiments of court service, which will be then thought honorable. There will be a queen also of no less charge; in most likelihood outlandish and a Papist; besides a queen mother such alreadie; together with both thir courts and numerous train: then a royal issue, and ere long severally thir sumptuous courts; to the multiplying of a servile crew, not of servants only, but of nobility and gen-

18. Thus Milton interprets Mark 10:42–43.
19. 1 Sam. 8:11–18.

try, bred up then to the hopes not of public, but of court offices; to be stewards, chamberlains, ushers, grooms, even of the close-stool; and the lower thir mindes debas'd with court opinions, contrarie to all vertue and reformation, the haughtier will be thir pride and profuseness: we may well remember this not long since at home; or need but look at present into the *French* court, where enticements and preferments daily draw away and pervert the Protestant Nobilitie. As to the burden of expence, to our cost we shall soon know it; for any good to us, deserving to be termd no better then the vast and lavish price of our subjection and their debausherie; which we are now so greedily cheapning,[20] and would so fain be paying most inconsideratly to a single person; who for any thing wherin the public really needs him, will have little els to do, but to bestow the eating and drinking of excessive dainties, to set a pompous face upon the superficial actings of State, to pageant himself up and down in progress among the perpetual bowings and cringings of an abject people, on either side deifying and adoring him for nothing don that can deserve it. For what can hee more then another man? who even in the expression of a late court-poet, sits only like a great cypher set to no purpose before a long row of other significant figures. Nay it is well and happy for the people if thir King be but a cypher, being oft times a mischief, a pest, a scourge of the nation, and which is wors, not to be remov'd, not to be contrould, much less accus'd or brought to punishment, without the danger of a common ruin, without the shaking and almost subversion of the whole land. Wheras in a free Commonwealth, any governor or chief counselor offending, may be remov'd and punishd without the least commotion. Certainly then that people must needs be madd or strangely infatuated, that build the chief hope of thir common happiness or safetie on a single person: who if he happen to be good, can do no more then another man, if to be bad, hath in his hands to do more evil without check, then millions of other men. The happiness of a nation must needs be firmest and certainest in a full and free Councel of thir own electing, where no single person, but rea-

20. Bargaining over.

son only swaies. And what madness is it, for them who might manage nobly thir own affairs themselves, sluggishly and weakly to devolve all on a single person; and more like boyes under age then men, to committ all to his patronage and disposal, who neither can performe what he undertakes, and yet for undertaking it, though royally paid, will not be thir servant, but thir lord? how unmanly must it needs be, to count such a one the breath of our nostrils, to hang all our felicity on him, all our safetie, our well-being, for which if we were aught els but sluggards or babies, we need depend on none but God and our own counsels, our own active vertue and industrie; *Go to the Ant, thou sluggard,* saith *Solomon; consider her waies, and be wise; which having no prince, ruler, or lord, provides her meat in the summer, and gathers her food in the harvest.*[21] Which evidently shews us, that they who think the nation undon without a king, though they look grave or haughtie, have not so much true spirit and understanding in them as a pismire: neither are these diligent creatures hence concluded to live in lawless anarchie, or that commended, but are set the examples to imprudent and ungovernd men, of a frugal and self-governing democratie or Commonwealth; safer and more thriving in the joint providence and counsel of many industrous equals, then under the single domination of one imperious Lord. It may be well wonderd that any Nation styling themselves free, can suffer any man to pretend hereditarie right over them as thir lord; when as by acknowledging that right, they conclude themselves his servants and his vassals, and so renounce thir own freedom. Which how a people and thir leaders especially can do, who have fought so gloriously for liberty, how they can change thir noble words and actions, heretofore so becoming the majesty of a free people, into the base necessitie of court flatteries and prostrations, is not only strange and admirable, but lamentable to think on. That a nation should be so valorous and courageous to winn thir liberty in the field, and when they have wonn it, should be so heartless[22] and

21. Prov. 6:6.
22. Cowardly.

unwise in thir counsels, as not to know how to use it, value it, what to do with it or with themselves; but after ten or twelve years prosperous warr and contestation with tyrannie, basely and besottedly to run their necks again into the yoke which they have broken, and prostrate all the fruits of thir victorie for naught at the feet of the vanquishd, besides our loss of glorie, and such an example as kings or tyrants never yet had the like to boast of, will be an ignominie if it befall us, that never yet befell any nation possessd of thir libertie; worthie indeed themselves, whatsoever they be, to be for ever slaves: but that part of the nation which consents not with them, as I perswade me of a great number, far worthier then by their means to be brought into the same bondage. Considering these things so plane, so rational, I cannot but yet furder admire on the other side, how any man who hath the true principles of justice and religion in him, can presume or take upon him to be a king and lord over his brethren, whom he cannot but know whether as men or Christians, to be for the most part every way equal or superior to himself: how he can display with such vanitie and ostentation his regal splendor so supereminently above other mortal men; or being a Christian, can assume such extraordinarie honour and worship to himself, while the kingdom of Christ our common King and Lord, is hid to this world, and such *gentilish*[23] imitation forbid in express words by himself to all his disciples. All Protestants hold that Christ in his church hath left no vicegerent of his power, but himself without deputie, is the only head therof, governing it from heaven: how then can any Christian-man derive his kingship from Christ, but with wors usurpation then the Pope his headship over the church, since Christ not only hath not left the least shaddow of a command for any such vicegerence from him in the State, as the Pope pretends for his in the Church, but hath expressly declar'd, that such regal dominion is from the gentiles, not from him, and hath strictly charg'd us, not to imitate them therin.

I doubt not but all ingenuous and knowing men will easily agree

23. Pertaining to Gentiles (i.e., heathenish).

with me, that a free Commonwealth without single person or house of lords, is by far the best government, if it can be had; but we have all this while say they bin expecting it, and cannot yet attain it. Tis true indeed, when monarchie was dissolvd, the form of a Commonwealth should have forthwith bin fram'd; and the practice therof immediatly begun; that the people might have soon bin satisfi'd and delighted with the decent order, ease and benefit therof: we had bin then by this time firmly rooted past fear of commotions or mutations, & now flourishing: this care of timely setling a new government instead of ye old, too much neglected, hath bin our mischief. Yet the cause therof may be ascrib'd with most reason to the frequent disturbances, interruptions and dissolutions which the Parlament hath had partly from the impatient or disaffected people, partly from som ambitious leaders in the Armie; much contrarie, I beleeve, to the mind and approbation of the Armie it self and thir other Commanders, once undeceivd, or in thir own power. Now is the opportunitie, now the very season wherein we may obtain a free Commonwealth and establish it for ever in the land, without difficulty or much delay. Writs are sent out for elections, and which is worth observing in the name, not of any king, but of the keepers of our libertie, to summon a free Parlament:[24] which then only will indeed be free, and deserve the true honor of that supreme title, if they preserve us a free people. Which never Parlament was more free to do; being now call'd, not as heretofore, by the summons of a king, but by the voice of libertie: and if the people, laying aside prejudice and impatience, will seriously and calmly now consider thir own good both religious and civil, thir own libertie and the only means thereof, as shall be heer laid before them, and will elect thir Knights and Burgesses[25] able men, and according to the just and necessarie qualifications (which for aught I hear, remain yet in force unrepeald, as they were formerly decreed in

24. The Long Parliament dissolved itself on March 16, 1660, after issuing writs for a free election.

25. Members from the counties were called *Knights,* those from the towns *Burgesses.*

Parlament)[26] men not addicted to a single person or house of lords, the work is don; at least the foundation firmly laid of a free Commonwealth, and good part also erected of the main structure. For the ground and basis of every just and free government (since men have smarted so oft for commiting all to one person) is a general councel of ablest men, chosen by the people to consult of public affairs from time to time for the common good. In this Grand Councel must the sovrantie, not transferrd, but delegated only, and at it were deposited, reside; with this caution they must have the forces by sea and land committed to them for preservation of the common peace and libertie; must raise and manage the public revenue, at least with som inspectors deputed for satisfaction of the people, how it is imploid; must make or propose, as more expressly shall be said anon, civil laws; treat of commerce, peace, or warr with forein nations, and for the carrying on som particular affairs with more secrecie and expedition, must elect, as they have alreadie out of thir own number and others, a Councel of State.

And although it may seem strange at first hearing, by reason that mens mindes are prepossessd with the notion of successive Parlaments, I affirme that the Grand or General Councel being well chosen, should be perpetual: for so thir business is or may be, and oft times urgent; the opportunitie of affairs gaind or lost in a moment. The day of counsel cannot be set as the day of a festival; but must be readie alwaies to prevent or answer[27] all occasions. By this continuance they will become everie way skilfullest, best provided of intelligence from abroad, best acquainted with the people at home, and the people with them. The ship of the Commonwealth is alwaies under sail; they sit at the stern; and if they stear well, what need is ther to change them; it being rather dangerous? Add to this, that the Grand Councel is both foundation and main pillar of the whole State; and to move pil-

26. In January and February the Rump had passed disabling acts against Royalists hampering their election to the next Parliament.

27. *Prevent or answer:* anticipate or control.

lars and foundations, not faultie, cannot be safe for the building. I see not therefor, how we can be advantag'd by successive and transitorie Parlaments; but that they are much likelier continually to unsettle rather then to settle a free government; to breed commotions, changes, novelties and uncertainties; to bring neglect upon present affairs and opportunities, while all mindes are suspense with expectation of a new assemblie, and the assemblie for a good space taken up with the new setling of it self. After which, if they finde no great work to do, they will make it, by altering or repealing former acts, or making and multiplying new; that they may seem to see what thir predecessors saw not, and not to have assembld for nothing: till all law be lost in the multitude of clashing statutes. But if the ambition of such as think themselves injur'd that they also partake not of the government, and are impatient till they be chosen, cannot brook the perpetuitie of others chosen before them, or if it be feard that long continuance of power may corrupt sincerest men, the known expedient is, and by som lately propounded, that annually (or if the space be longer, so much perhaps the better) the third part of Senators may go out according to the precedence of thir election, and the like number be chosen in thir places, to prevent the setling of too absolute a power, if it should be perpetual: and this they call *partial rotation*. But I could wish that this wheel or partial wheel in State, if it be possible, might be avoided; as having too much affinitie with the wheel of fortune. For it appeers not how this can be don, without danger and mischance of putting out a great number of the best and ablest: in whose stead new elections may bring in as many raw, unexperienc'd and otherwise affected, to the weakning and much altering for the wors of public transactions. Neither do I think a perpetual Senat, especially chosen and entrusted by the people, much in this land to be feard, where the well-affected[28] either in a standing armie, or in a setled militia have thir arms in thir own hands. Safest therefor to me it seems and of least hazard or interruption to affairs, that none of the Grand Councel be mov'd, unless by death or just conviction of som crime:

28. The loyal.

for what can be expected firm or stedfast from a floating foundation? however, I forejudge not any probable expedient, any temperament that can be found in things of this nature so disputable on either side. Yet least this which I affirme, be thought my single opinion, I shall add sufficient testimonie. Kingship it self is therefor counted the more safe and durable, because the king and, for the most part, his councel, is not chang'd during life: but a Commonwealth is held immortal; and therin firmest, safest and most above fortune: for the death of a king, causeth ofttimes many dangerous alterations; but the death now and then of a Senator is not felt; the main bodie of them still continuing permanent in greatest and noblest Commonwealths, and as it were eternal. Therefor among the *Jews,* the supreme councel of seaventie, call'd the *Sanhedrim,* founded by *Moses,* in *Athens,* that of *Areopagus,* in *Sparta,* that of the Ancients, in *Rome,* the Senat, consisted of members chosen for term of life; and by that means remain as it were still the same to generations. In *Venice* they change indeed ofter then every year som particular councels of State, as that of six, or such other; but the true Senat, which upholds and sustains the government, is the whole aristocracie immovable. So in the United Provinces, the States General, which are indeed but a councel of state deputed by the whole union, are not usually the same persons for above three or six years; but the States of every citie, in whom the sovrantie hath bin plac'd time out of minde, are a standing Senat, without succession, and accounted chiefly in that regard the main prop of thir liberty. And why they should be so in every well orderd Commonwealth, they who write of policie, give these reasons; "That to make the Senat successive, not only impairs the dignitie and lustre of the Senat, but weakens the whole Commonwealth, and brings it into manifest danger; while by this means the secrets of State are frequently divulgd, and matters of greatest consequence committed to inexpert and novice counselors, utterly to seek in the full and intimate knowledge of affairs past."[29] I know not therefor what should be peculiar in

29. This quoted passage may be an adaptation from Jean Bodin's *Six Books of the Republic* (1576), bk. 3, 1.

*England* to make successive Parlaments thought safest, or convenient here more then in other nations, unless it be the fickl'ness which is attributed to us as we are Ilanders: but good education and acquisit[30] wisdom ought to correct the fluxible fault, if any such be, of our watry situation. It will be objected, that in those places where they had perpetual Senats, they had also popular remedies against thir growing too imperious: as in *Athens,* besides *Areopagus,* another Senat of four or five hundred; in *Sparta,* the *Ephori;* in *Rome,* the Tribunes of the people. But the event tels us, that these remedies either little availd the people, or brought them to such a licentious and unbridl'd democratie, as in fine ruind themselves with thir own excessive power. So that the main reason urg'd why popular assemblies are to be trusted with the peoples libertie, rather then a Senat of principal men, because great men will be still endeavoring to inlarge thir power, but the common sort will be contented to maintain thir own libertie, is by experience found false; none being more immoderat and ambitious to amplifie thir power, then such popularities; which was seen in the people of *Rome;* who at first contented to have thir Tribunes, at length contended with the Senat that one Consul, then both; soon after, that the Censors and Praeters also should be created Plebeian, and the whole empire put into their hands; adoring lastly those, who most were advers to the Senat, till *Marius*[31] by fulfilling thir inordinat desires, quite lost them all the power for which they had so long bin striving, and left them under the tyrannie of *Sylla:*[32] the ballance therefor must be exactly so set, as to preserve and keep up due autoritie on either side, as well in the Senat as in the people. And this annual rotation of a Senat to consist of three hundred, as is lately propounded, requires also another popular assembly upward of a thousand, with an answerable rotation. Which besides that it will be liable

30. Acquired.

31. The plebian general responsible for the massacre of many aristocrats in his machinations with demagogues.

32. Sulla served under Marius, then seized power in 86 B.C. and ruled as a dictator until his death in 82 B.C.

to all those inconveniencies found in the foresaid remedies, cannot but be troublesom and chargeable, both in thir motion and thir session, to the whole land; unweildie with thir own bulk, unable in so great a number to mature thir consultations as they ought, if any be allotted them, and that they meet not from so many parts remote to sit a whole year lieger in one place, only now and then to hold up a forrest of fingers, or to convey each man his bean or ballot into the box, without reason shewn or common deliberation; incontinent of secrets, if any be imparted to them, emulous and always jarring with the other Senat. The much better way doubtless will be in this wavering condition of our affairs, to deferr the changing or circumscribing of our Senat, more then may be done with ease, till the Commonwealth be throughly setl'd in peace and safetie, and they themselves give us the occasion. Militarie men hold it dangerous to change the form of battel in view of an enemie: neither did the people of *Rome* bandie with thir Senat while any of the *Tarquins* livd, the enemies of thir libertie, nor sought by creating Tribunes to defend themselves against the fear of thir Patricians, till sixteen years after the expulsion of thir kings, and in full securitie of thir state, they had or thought they had just cause given them by the Senat. Another way will be, to wel-qualifie and refine elections: not committing all to the noise and shouting of a rude multitude, but permitting only those of them who are rightly qualifi'd, to nominat as many as they will; and out of that number others of a better breeding, to chuse a less number more judiciously, till after a third or fourth sifting and refining of exactest choice, they only be left chosen who are the due number, and seem by most voices the worthiest. To make the people fittest to chuse, and the chosen fittest to govern, will be to mend our corrupt and faulty education, to teach the people faith not without vertue, temperance, modestie, sobrietie, parsimonie, justice; not to admire wealth or honour; to hate turbulence and ambition; to place every one his privat welfare and happiness in the public peace, libertie and safetie. They shall not then need to be much mistrustfull of thir chosen Patriots in the Grand Councel; who will be then rightly call'd the true keepers of our libertie, though the most of thir business will be in forein affairs. But to prevent all mistrust, the people then will have thir several ordinarie assemblies (which will henceforth quite annihilate the odious power and name of Committies[33]) in the chief towns of every countie, without the trouble, charge, or time lost of summoning and assembling from far in so great a number, and so long residing from thir own houses, or removing of thir families, to do as much at home in thir several shires, entire or subdivided, toward the securing of thir libertie, as a numerous assembly of them all formd and conven'd on purpose with the wariest rotation. Wherof I shall speak more ere the end of this discourse: for it may be referrd to time, so we be still going on by degrees to perfection. The people well weighing and performing these things, I suppose would have no cause to fear, though the *Parlament,* abolishing that name, as originally signifying but the *parlie* of our Lords and Commons with thir *Norman* king[34] when he pleasd to call them, should, with certain limitations of thir power, sit perpetual, if thir ends be faithfull and for a free Commonwealth, under the name of a Grand or General Councel. Till this be don, I am in doubt whether our State will be ever certainly and throughly setl'd; never likely till then to see an end of our troubles and continual changes or at least never the true settlement and assurance of our libertie. The Grand Councel being thus firmly constituted to perpetuitie, and still, upon the death or default of any member, suppli'd and kept in full number, ther can be no cause alleag'd why peace, justice, plentifull trade and all prosperitie should not thereupon ensue throughout the whole land; with as much assurance as can be of human things, that they shall so continue (if God favour us, and our wilfull sins provoke him not) even to the coming of our true and rightfull and only to be expected King, only worthie as he is our only Saviour, the Messiah, the Christ, the only heir of his eternal father, the

33. Milton refers to the resentment felt toward local committees established by Parliament to consolidate its hold on the populace. These committees became especially odious under the Protectorate when they were under the leadership of eleven major generals.

34. Apparently Alfred, according to a popular Commonwealth supposition.

only by him anointed and ordaind since the work of our redemption finishd, Universal Lord of all mankinde. The way propounded is plane, easie and open before us; without intricacies, without the introducement of new or obsolete forms, or terms, or exotic models; idea's that would effect nothing, but with a number of new injunctions to manacle the native liberty of mankinde; turning all vertue into prescription, servitude, and necessitie, to the great impairing and frustrating of Christian libertie: I say again, this way lies free and smooth before us; is not tangl'd with inconveniencies; invents no new incumbrances; requires no perilous, no injurious alteration or circumscription of mens lands and proprieties; secure, that in this Commonwealth, temporal and spiritual lords remov'd, no man or number of men can attain to such wealth or vast possession, as will need the hedge of an Agrarian law (never succesful, but the cause rather of sedition, save only where it began seasonably with first possession) to confine them from endangering our public libertie; to conclude, it can have no considerable objection made against it, that it is not practicable: least it be said hereafter, that we gave up our libertie for want of a readie way or distinct form propos'd of a free Commonwealth. And this facilitie we shall have above our next neighbouring Commonwealth (if we can keep us from the fond conceit of somthing like a duke of *Venice,* put lately into many mens heads, by som one or other sutly driving on under that notion his own ambitious ends to lurch a crown) that our liberty shall not be hamperd or hoverd over by any ingagement to such a potent familie as the house of *Nassaw*[35] of whom to stand in perpetual doubt and suspicion, but we shall live the cleerest and absolutest free nation in the world. On the contrarie, if ther be a king, which the inconsiderate multitude are now so madd upon, mark how far short we are like to com of all those happinesses, which in a free state we shall immediatly be possessd of. First, the Grand Councel, which, as I shewd before, should sit perpetually (unless thir leisure give them now and then som intermissions or vacations, eas-

---

35. *The house of Nassaw:* the heirs of William of Orange who dominated the Dutch republic after 1579.

---

ilie manageable by the Councel of State left sitting) shall be call'd, by the kings good will and utmost endeavor as seldom as may be. For it is only the kings right, he will say, to call a parlament; and this he will do most commonly about his own affairs rather then the kingdom's, as will appeer planely so soon as they are call'd. For what will thir business then be and the chief expence of thir time, but an endless tugging between petition of right and royal prerogative, especially about the negative voice,[36] militia, or subsidies, demanded and oft times extorted without reasonable cause appeering to the Commons, who are the only true representatives of the people, and thir libertie, but will be then mingl'd with a court-faction; besides which within thir own walls, the sincere part of them who stand faithfull to the people, will again have to deal with two troublesom counterworking adversaries from without, meer creatures of the king, spiritual, and the greater part, as is likeliest, of temporal lords, nothing concernd with the peoples libertie. If these prevail not in what they please, though never so much against the peoples interest, the Parlament shall be soon dissolvd, or sit and do nothing; not sufferd to remedie the least greevance, or enact aught advantageous to the people. Next, the Councel of State shall not be chosen by the Parlament, but by the king, still his own creatures, courtiers and favorites; who will be sure in all thir counsels to set thir maister's grandure and absolute power, in what they are able, far above the peoples libertie. I denie not but that ther may be such a king, who may regard the common good before his own, may have no vitious favorite, may hearken only to the wisest and incorruptest of his Parlament: but this rarely happens in a monarchie not elective; and it behoves not a wise nation to committ the summ of thir welbeing, the whole state of thir safetie to fortune. What need they; and how absurd would it be, when as they themselves to whom his chief vertue will be but to hearken, may with much better management and dispatch, with much more commendation of thir own worth and magnanimitie govern without a maister. Can the

36. Milton refers to the Petition of Right forced on Charles in 1628 and the struggle over the king's claim to veto over all acts of Parliament.

folly be paralleld, to adore and be the slaves of a single person for doing that which it is ten thousand to one whether he can or will do, and we without him might do more easily, more effectually, more laudably our selves? Shall we never grow old anough to be wise to make seasonable use of gravest autorities, experiences, examples? Is it such an unspeakable joy to serve, such felicitie to wear a yoke? to clink our shackles, lockt on by pretended law of subjection more intolerable and hopeless to be ever shaken off, then those which are knockt on by illegal injurie and violence? *Aristotle,* our chief instructer in the Universities, least this doctrine be thought *Sectarian,* as the royalist would have it thought, tels us in the third of his Politics, that certain men at first, for the matchless excellence of thir vertue above others, or som great public benifit, were created kings by the people; in small cities and territories, and in the scarcitie of others to be found like them: but when they abus'd thir power and governments grew larger, and the number of prudent men increasd, that then the people soon deposing thir tyrants, betook them, in all civilest places, to the form of a free Commonwealth. And why should we thus disparage and prejudicate our own nation, as to fear a scarcitie of able and worthie men united in counsel to govern us, if we will but use diligence and impartiality to finde them out and chuse them, rather yoking our selves to a single person, the natural adversarie and oppressor of libertie, though good, yet far easier corruptible by the excess of his singular power and exaltation, or at best, not comparably sufficient to bear the weight of government, nor equally dispos'd to make us happie in the enjoyment of our libertie under him.

But admitt, that monarchie of it self may be convenient to som nations; yet to us who have thrown it out, receivd back again, it cannot but prove pernicious. For kings to com, never forgetting thir former ejection, will be sure to fortifie and arm themselves sufficiently for the future against all such attempts hereafter from the people: who shall be then so narrowly watchd and kept so low, that though they would never so fain and at the same rate of thir blood and treasure, they never shall be able to regain what they now have purchasd and may enjoy, or to free themselves from any yoke impos'd upon them: nor will they dare to go about it; utterly disheartn'd for the future, if these thir highest attempts prove unsuccesfull; which will be the triumph of all tyrants heerafter over any people that shall resist oppression; and thir song will then be, to others, how sped the rebellious *English?* to our posteritie, how sped the rebells your fathers? This is not my conjecture, but drawn from God's known denouncement against the gentilizing *Israelites;* who though they were governd in a Commonwealth of God's own ordaining, he only thir king, they his peculiar people, yet affecting rather to resemble heathen, but pretending the misgovernment of *Samuel's* sons, no more a reason to dislike thir Commonwealth, then the violence of *Eli's* sons [37] was imputable to that priesthood or religion, clamourd for a king. They had thir longing; but with this testimonie of God's wrath; *ye shall cry out in that day because of your king whom ye shall have chosen, and the Lord will not hear you in that day.* [38] Us if he shall hear now, how much less will he hear when we cry heerafter, who once deliverd by him from a king, and not without wondrous acts of his providence, insensible and unworthie of those high mercies, are returning precipitantly, if he withhold us not, back to the captivitie from whence he freed us. Yet neither shall we obtain or buy at an easie rate this new guilded yoke which thus transports us: a new royal-revenue must be found, a new episcopal; for those are individual: [39] both which being wholly dissipated or bought by privat persons or assign'd for service don, and especially to the Armie, cannot be recoverd without a general detriment and confusion to mens estates, or a heavie imposition on all mens purses; benifit to none, but to the worst and ignoblest sort of men, whose hope is to be either the ministers of court riot and excess, or the gainers by it: But not to speak more of losses and extraordinarie levies on our estates, what will then be the revenges and offences rememberd and returnd, not only by the chief person, but by all his adherents;

---

37. 1 Sam. 2:12–17.
38. 1 Sam. 8:18.
39. Privately owned.

accounts and reparations that will be requir'd, suites, inditements, inquiries, discoveries, complaints, informations, who knows against whom or how many, though perhaps neuters,[40] if not to utmost infliction, yet to imprisonment, fines, banishment, or molestation; if not these, yet disfavor, discountnance, disregard and contempt on all but the known royalist or whom he favors, will be plenteous: nor let the new royaliz'd presbyterians perswade themselves that thir old doings, though now recanted, will be forgotten; what ever conditions be contriv'd or trusted on. Will they not beleeve this; nor remember the pacification,[41] how it was kept to the *Scots;* how other solemn promises many a time to us? Let them but now read the diabolical forerunning libells, the faces, the gestures that now appeer foremost and briskest in all public places; as the harbingers of those that are in expectation to raign over us; let them but hear the insolencies, the menaces, the insultings of our newly animated common enemies crept lately out of thir holes, thir hell, I might say, by the language of thir infernal pamphlets, the spue of every drunkard, every ribald; nameless, yet not for want of licence, but for very shame of thir own vile persons, not daring to name themselves, while they traduce others by name; and give us to foresee that they intend to second thir wicked words, if ever they have power, with more wicked deeds. Let our zealous backsliders forethink now with themselves, how thir necks yok'd with these tigers of Bacchus,[42] these new fanatics of not the preaching but the sweating-tub,[43] inspir'd with nothing holier then the Venereal pox, can draw one way under monarchie to the establishing of church discipline with these new-disgorg'd atheismes: yet shall they not have the honor to yoke with these, but shall be yok'd under them; these shall plow on their backs. And do they among them who are so forward to bring in the single person, think to be by him trusted or long

40. Neutrals in the Civil War.

41. Milton probably has in mind the Treaty of Berwick between Charles and the Scots, upon which the king reneged within months (1639).

42. Bacchus, or Dionysus, the god of wine, was sometimes depicted riding in a chariot drawn by tigers.

43. Sweating tubs were used in treating venereal disease.

regarded? So trusted they shall be and so regarded, as by kings are wont reconcil'd enemies; neglected and soon after discarded, if not prosecuted for old traytors; the first inciters, beginners, and more then to the third part actors of all that followd; it will be found also, that there must be then as necessarily as now (for the contrarie part will be still feard) a standing armie; which for certain shall not be this, but of the fiercest Cavaliers, of no less expence, and perhaps again under *Rupert;*[44] but let this armie[45] be sure they shall be soon disbanded, and likeliest without arrear or pay; and being disbanded, not be sure but they may as soon be questiond for being in arms against thir king: the same let them fear, who have contributed monie; which will amount to no small number that must then take thir turn to be made delinquents[46] and compounders. They who past reason and recoverie are devoted to kingship, perhaps will answer, that a greater part by far of the Nation will have it so; the rest therefor must yield. Not so much to convince these, which I little hope, as to confirm them who yield not, I reply; that this greatest part have both in reason and the trial of just battel, lost the right of their election what the government shall be: of them who have not lost that right, whether they for kingship be the greater number, who can certainly determin? Suppose they be; yet of freedom they partake all alike, one main end of government: which if the greater part value not, but will degeneratly forgoe, is it just or reasonable, that most voices against the main end of government should enslave the less number that would be free? More just it is doubtless, if it com to force, that a less number compell a greater to retain, which can be no wrong to them, thir libertie, then that a greater number for the pleasure of thir baseness, compell a less most injuriously to be thir fellow slaves. They who seek nothing but thir own just libertie, have alwaies right to winn it and to keep

---

44. Charles's nephew Prince Rupert (1619–82) led the Royalist cavalry and subsequently was commander in chief.

45. Cromwell's veterans.

46. Royalist landowners whose estates were seized by Parliament.

it, when ever they have power, be the voices never so numerous that oppose it. And how much we above others are concernd to defend it from kingship, and from them who in pursuance therof so perniciously would betray us and themselves to most certain miserie and thraldom, will be needless to repeat.

Having thus far shewn with what ease we may now obtain a free Commonwealth, and by it with as much ease all the freedom, peace, justice, plentie that we can desire, on the other side the difficulties, troubles, uncertainties, nay rather impossibilities to enjoy these things constantly under a monarch, I will now proceed to shew more particularly wherin our freedom and flourishing condition will be more ample and secure to us under a free Commonwealth then under kingship.

The whole freedom of man consists either in spiritual or civil libertie. As for spiritual, who can be at rest, who can enjoy any thing in this world with contentment, who hath not libertie to serve God and to save his own soul, according to the best light which God hath planted in him to that purpose, by the reading of his reveal'd will and the guidance of his holy spirit? That this is best pleasing to God, and that the whole Protestant Church allows no supream judge or rule in matters of religion, but the scriptures, and these to be interpreted by the scriptures themselves, which necessarily inferrs liberty of conscience, I have heretofore prov'd at large in another treatise,[47] and might yet furder by the public declarations, confessions and admonitions of whole churches and states, obvious in all historie since the Reformation.

This liberty of conscience which above all other things ought to be to all men dearest and most precious, no government more inclinable not to favor only but to protect, then a free Commonwealth; as being most magnanimous, most fearless and confident of its own fair proceedings. Wheras kingship, though looking big, yet indeed most pusillanimous, full of fears, full of jealousies, startl'd at every om-

47. John Milton, *Treatise of Civil Power in Ecclesiastical Causes* (1659).

brage,[48] as it hath bin observd of old to have ever suspected most and mistrusted them who were in most esteem for vertue and generositie of minde, so it is now known to have most in doubt and suspicion them who are most reputed to be religious. Queen *Elizabeth* though her self accounted so good a Protestant, so moderate, so confident of her Subjects love would never give way so much as to Presbyterian reformation in this land, though once and again besought, as *Camden* relates,[49] but imprisond and persecuted the very proposers therof; alleaging it as her minde & maxim unalterable, that such reformation would diminish regal autoritie. What liberty of conscience can we then expect of others, far wors principl'd from the cradle, traind up and governd by *Popish* and *Spanish* counsels, and on such depending hitherto for subsistence? Especially what can this last Parlament expect, who having reviv'd lately and publishd the covnant, have re-ingag'd themselves, never to readmitt Episcopacie: which no son of *Charles* returning, but will most certainly bring back with him, if he regard the last and strictest charge of his father, *to persevere in not the doctrin only, but government of the church of* England; *not to neglect the speedie and effectual suppressing of errors and schisms;*[50] among which he accounted Presbyterie one of the chief: or if notwithstanding that charge of his father, he submitt to the covnant, how will he keep faith to us with disobedience to him; or regard that faith given, which must be founded on the breach of that last and solemnest paternal charge, and the reluctance, I may say the antipathie which is in all kings against Presbyterian and Independent discipline? for they hear the gospel speaking much of libertie; a word which monarchie and her bishops both fear and hate, but a free Commonwealth both favors and promotes; and not the word only, but the thing it self. But let our governors beware in time, least thir hard measure to libertie

48. Shadow.

49. Milton refers to William Camden's *Annals of the Reign of Elizabeth to 1588* (1615).

50. Milton here cites from a 1649 work probably authored by John Gardner, the *Eikon Basilike,* a panegyric to the slain king.

of conscience be found the rock wheron they shipwrack themselves as others have now don before them in the cours wherin God was directing thir stearage to a free Commonwealth, and the abandoning of all those whom they call *sectaries,* for the detected falshood and ambition of som, be a wilfull rejection of thir own chief strength and interest in the freedom of all Protestant religion, under what abusive name soever calumniated.

The other part of our freedom consists in the civil rights and advancements of every person according to his merit: the enjoyment of those never more certain, and the access to these never more open, then in a free Commonwealth. Both which in my opinion may be best and soonest obtain, if every countie in the land were made a kinde of subordinate Commonaltie or Commonwealth, and one chief town or more, according as the shire is in circuit, made cities, if they be not so call'd alreadie; where the nobilitie and chief gentry from a proportionable compas of territorie annexd to each citie, may build, houses or palaces, befitting thir qualitie, may bear part in the government, make thir own judicial laws, or use these that are, and execute them by thir own elected judicatures and judges without appeal, in all things of civil government between man and man. So they shall have justice in thir own hands, law executed fully and finally in thir own counties and precincts, long wishd, and spoken of, but never yet obtaind; they shall have none then to blame but themselves, if it be not well administerd; and fewer laws to expect or fear from the supreme autoritie; or to those that shall be made, of any great concernment to public libertie, they may without much trouble in these commonalties or in more general assemblies call'd to thir cities from the whole territorie on such occasion, declare and publish thir assent or dissent by deputies within a time limited sent to the Grand Councel: yet so as this thir judgment declar'd shal submitt to the greater number of other counties or commonalties, and not avail them to any exemption of themselves, or refusal of agreement with the rest, as it may in any of the United Provinces, being sovran within it self, oft times to the great disadvantage of that union. In these imploiments they may much better then they do now, exercise and fit themselves, till thir lot fall to be chosen into the Grand Councel, according as thir worth and merit shall be taken notice of by the people. As for controversies that shall happen between men of several counties, they may repair, as they do now, to the capital citie, or any other more commodious, indifferent place and equal judges. And this I finde to have bin practisd in the old *Athenian* Commonwealth, reputed the first and ancientest place of civilitie in all *Greece;* that they had in thir several cities, a peculiar; in *Athens,* a common government; and thir right, as it befell them, to the administration of both. They should have heer also schools and academies at thir own choice, wherin thir children may be bred up in thir own sight to all learning and noble education not in grammar only, but in all liberal arts and exercises. This would soon spread much more knowledge and civilitie, yea religion through all parts of the land, by communicating the natural heat of government and culture more distributively to all extreme parts, which now lie numm and neglected, would soon make the whole nation more industrious, more ingenuous at home, more potent, more honorable abroad. To this a free Commonwealth will easily assent; (nay the Parlament hath had alreadie som such thing in designe) for of all governments a Commonwealth aims most to make the people flourishing, vertuous, noble and high spirited. Monarchs will never permitt: whose aim is to make the people, wealthie indeed perhaps and well fleec't, for thir own shearing and the supplie of regal prodigalitie; but otherwise softest, basest, vitiousest, servilest, easiest to be kept under; and not only in fleece, but in minde also sheepishest; and will have all the benches of judicature annexd to the throne, as a gift of royal grace that we have justice don us; whenas nothing can be more essential to the freedom of a people, then to have the administration of justice and all public ornaments in thir own election and within thir own bounds, without long travelling or depending on remote places to obtain thir right or any civil accomplishment; so it be not supreme, but subordinate to the general power and union of the whole Republic. In which happy firmness as in the particular above mentiond, we shall also far exceed the United Provinces, by having, not as they (to the retarding and distracting oft times of thir counsels or urgentest occasions) many Sovranties united in one Commonwealth, but many Commonwealths under one united and entrusted Sovrantie. And when we have our forces by sea and land, either of a faithful Armie or a setl'd Militia, in our own hands to the firm establishing of a free Commonwealth, publick accounts under our own inspection, general laws and taxes with thir causes in our own domestic suffrages, judicial laws, offices and ornaments at home in our own ordering and administration, all distinction of lords and commoners, that may any way divide or sever the publick interest, remov'd, what can a perpetual senat have then wherin to grow corrupt, wherin to encroach upon us or usurp; or if they do, wherin to be formidable? Yet if all this avail not to remove the fear or envie of a perpetual sitting, it may be easilie provided, to change a third part of them yearly or every two or three years, as was above mentiond; or that it be at those times in the peoples choice, whether they will change them, or renew thir power, as they shall finde cause.

I have no more to say at present: few words will save us, well considered; few and easie things, now seasonably don. But if the people be so affected, as to prostitute religion and libertie to the vain and groundless apprehension, that nothing but kingship can restore trade, not remembring the frequent plagues and pestilences that then wasted this citie, such as through God's mercie we never have felt since, and that trade flourishes no where more then in the free Commonwealths of *Italie, Germanie,* and the Low-Countries before thir eyes at this day, yet if trade be grown so craving and importunate through the profuse living of tradesmen, that nothing can support it, but the luxurious expences of a nation upon trifles or superfluities, so as if the people generally should betake themselves to frugalitie, it might prove a dangerous matter, least tradesmen should mutinie for want of trading, and that therefor we must forgoe & set to sale religion, libertie, honor, safetie, all concernments Divine or human to keep up trading, if lastly, after all this light among us, the same reason shall pass for current to put our necks again under kingship, as was made use of by the *Jews* to returne back to *Egypt*[51] and to the worship of thir idol queen, because they falsly imagind that they then livd in more plentie and prosperitie, our condition is not sound but rotten, both in religion and all civil prudence; and will bring us soon, the way we are marching, to those calamities which attend alwaies and unavoidably on luxurie, all national judgments under forein or domestic slaverie: so far we shall be from mending our condition by monarchizing our government, whatever new conceit now possesses us. However with all hazard I have ventur'd what I thought my duty to speak in season, and to forewarne my countrey in time: wherin I doubt not but ther be many wise men in all places and degrees, but am sorrie the effects of wisdom are so little seen among us. Many circumstances and particulars I could have added in those things wherof I have spoken; but a few main matters now put speedily in execution, will suffice to recover us, and set all right: and ther will want at no time who are good at circumstances; but men who set thir mindes on main matters and sufficiently urge them, in these most difficult times I finde not many. What I have spoken, is the language of that which is not call'd amiss *the good Old Cause:* if it seem strange to any, it will not seem more strange, I hope, then convincing to backsliders. Thus much I should perhaps have said though I were sure I should have spoken only to trees and stones; and had none to cry to, but with the Prophet, *O earth, earth, earth!*[52] to tell the very soil it self, what her perverse inhabitants are deaf to. Nay though what I have spoke, should happ'n (which Thou suffer not, who didst create mankinde free; nor Thou next, who didst redeem us from being servants of men!) to be the last words of our expiring libertie. But I trust I shall have spoken perswasion to abundance of sensible and ingenuous men: to som perhaps whom God may raise of these stones to become children of reviving libertie; and may reclaim, though they seem now chusing them a captain back for

51. Num. 11:5.
52. Jer. 22:29.

*Egypt,* to bethink themselves a little and consider whether they are rushing; to exhort this torrent also of the people, not to be so impetuos, but to keep thir due channell; and at length recovering and uniting thir better resolutions, now that they see alreadie how open and un-bounded the insolence and rage is of our common enemies, to stay these ruinous proceedings; justly and timely fearing to what a precipice of destruction the deluge of this epidemic madness would hurrie us through the general defection of a misguided and abus'd multitude.

*The End.*

# MR. JOHN MILTON'S CHARACTER OF THE LONG PARLIAMENT

*Replying to Salmasius in the* First Defence *Milton had said the government obtained under the Commonwealth was not the best conceivable but the best that could be had under the circumstances. How severe was the qualification Milton had in mind may perhaps be gathered from what he admits in the following selection from his* History of Britain. *This description of the failings of officers in Cromwell's party was written probably in 1648 as a digression from Milton's account of similar failings among the British in the era soon after the Roman removal. From the parallels he draws between the squandering of two opportunities for establishing a broad liberty one can gather the difficulty Milton perceived a brave people confronted in wielding the weapon he here refers to as the two-edged sword of freedom.*

# MR. JOHN MILTON'S CHARACTER OF THE LONG PARLIAMENT

---

## and Assembly of Divines

*The Digression in Miltons History of England.*
*To come in Lib. 3. page 114.[1] after these words.*
*[from one misery to another.]*

### THE DIGRESSION

But because the gaining or loosing of libertie is the greatest
change to better or to worse that may befall a nation under
civil government, and so discovers, as nothing more, what degree of understanding, or capacitie, what disposition to justice and civilitie there is among them, I suppose it will bee many wayes profitable to resume[2] a while the whole discourse of what happn'd in this
Iland soone after the Romans goeing out: and to consider what might
bee the reason, why, seeing other nations both antient and modern
with extreame hazard & danger have strove for libertie as a thing in-
valuable, & by the purchase thereof have soo enobl'd thir spirits, as
from obscure and small to grow eminent and glorious commonwealths, why the Britans having such a smooth occasion giv'n them
to free themselves as ages have not afforded, such a manumission as
never subjects had a fairer, should let it pass through them as a cor-

---

1. The page numbers here refer to the first edition of Milton's *History of England* (1670–71).

2. To take up again.

---

dial medcin through a dying man without the least effect of sence or natural vigor. And no less to purpose if not more usefully to us it may withal bee enquir'd, since god after 12 ages and more[3] had drawne so neare a parallel betweene their state and ours in the late commotions, why they who had the chiefe mannagement ther-in having attain'd, though not so easilie, to a condition which had set before them civil goverment in all her formes, and giv'n them to bee masters of thir own choise, were not found able after so many years doeing and un-doeing to hitt so much as into any good and laudable way that might show us hopes of a just and well amended common-wealth to come. For those our ancestors it is alledg'd, that thir youth and chiefe strength was carried over sea to serve the Empire, that the Scots and Picts and Saxons lay sore upon them without respit. And yet wee heare the Romans telling them that thir enimies were not stronger then they: when as one legion drove them twice out of the Ile at first encounter. Nor could the Brittans be so ignorant of warr whome the Romans had then newly instructed; or if they were to seeke, alike were thir enimies, rude and naked barbarians. But that they were so timorous and without heart, as Gildas reportes them,[4] is no way credible; for the same hee reportes of those whom the Romans testifie to have found valiant. Wherof those alsoe gave not the least prooff, when a few of them, and these in thir greatest weakness takeing courage, not de-fended themselves onely against the Scots and Picts, but repuls'd them well beaten home. Of these who sway'd most in the late troubles, few words as to this point may suffice. They had armies, leaders and successes to thir wish; but to make use of so great advantages was not thir skill. To other causes therefore and not to want of force, or war-like manhood in the Brittans, both those and these lately, wee must impute the ill husbanding of those faire opportunities, which might

3. Here Milton means twelve centuries from the liberation from Roman rule to the revolution of the 1640s.

4. *De excidio et conquestu Britanniae* (London, 1525) by Gildas (c. 493–570) is the only contemporary British version of the history of the island dating back to Ro-man times.

seeme to have put libertie, so long desir'd, like a bird into thir hands. Of which other causes equally belonging both to ruler, priest, and people above hath bin related: which as they brought those antient natives to miserie and ruin by libertie which rightly us'd might have made them happie, so brought they these of late after many labours, much blood-shed, & vast expence, to ridiculous frustration, in whom the like deffects, the like miscarriages notoriouslie appear'd, with vices not less hatefull or inexcusable; nor less inforcing, whosoever shall write thir storie, to revive those antient complaints of Gildas as deservedly on these lately as on those his times. For a parlament being call'd,[5] and as was thought many things to redress, the people with great courage & expectation to be now eas'd of what discontented them chose to thir behoof in parlament such as they thought best affected to the public good, & some indeed men of wisdome and integritie. The rest, and to be sure the greatest part, whom wealth and ample possessions or bold and active ambition rather then merit had commended to the same place, when once the superficial zeale and popular fumes that acted thir new magistracie were cool'd and spent in them, straite every one betooke himself, setting the commonwealth behinde and his private ends before, to doe as his owne profit or ambition led him. Then was justice delai'd & soone after deny'd, spite and favour determin'd all: hence faction, then treacherie both at home & in the field, ev'ry where wrong & oppression, foule and dishonest things commited daylie, or maintain'd in secret or in op'n. Some who had bin call'd from shops & warehouses without other merit to sit in supreme councels & committies, as thir breeding was, fell to hucster the common-wealth; others did thereafter as men could sooth and humour them best: so that hee onely who could give most, or under covert of hypocritical zeal insinuate basest enjoy'd unworthylie the rewards of learning & fidelitie, or escap'd the punishment of his crimes and misdeeds. Thir votes and ordinances which men look'd should have contain'd the repealing of bad laws & the immediate constitu-

5. The Long Parliament dates from the royal order of summons issued September 24, 1640. This Parliament met for the first time on November 3.

tion of better, resounded with nothing els but new impositions, taxes, excises, yearlie, monthlie, weeklie, not to reck'n the offices, gifts, and preferments bestow'd and shar'd among themselves. They in the meane while who were ever faithfullest to thir cause, and freely aided them in person, or with thir substance when they durst not compel either, slighted soone after and quite bereav'd of thir just debts by greedy sequestration, were toss'd up and downe after miserable attendance from one committie to another with petitions in thir hands, yet either miss'd the obtaining of thir suit, or if it were at length granted by thir orders, meere shame & reason oft times extorting from them at least a show of justice, yet by thir sequestrators & subcommitties abroad, men for the most part of insatiable hands, & noted disloyaltie, those orders were commonlie disobey'd; which for certaine durst not have bin, without secret complyance if not compact with some superiours able to beare them out. Thus were thir friends confiscate in thir enimies, while they forfeted thir debtors to the state as they call'd it, but indeed to the ravening seisure of innumerable theeves in office, yet were withall no less burden'd in all extraordinarie assessments and oppressions then whom they tooke to be disaffected. Nor were wee happier creditours to the state then to them who were sequester'd as the states enimies; for that faith which ought to bee kept as sacred and inviolable as any thing holy, the public faith,[6] after infinite summs receiv'd & all the wealth of the church, not better imploy'd, but swallow'd up into a private gulfe, was not ere long asham'd to confess bankrupt. And now besides the sweetness of briberie and other gaine with the love of rule, thir owne guiltiness and the dreaded name of just account, which the people had long call'd for, discover'd plainelie that there were of thir owne number who secretly contriv'd and fomented those troubles and combustions in the land which openly they sate to remedy, & would continually finde such worke, as should keepe them

6.   In 1642 Parliament began soliciting public loans of money as well as personal property; these loans were secured at 8 percent on the "public faith" of the government.

from ever being brought to the terrible stand of laying downe thir authoritie for lack of new business, or not drawing it out to any length of time though upon the nesessarie ruin of a whole nation. And if the state were in this plight, religion was not in much better: to reforme which a certaine number of divines were call'd,[7] neither chosen by any rule or custome ecclesiastical, nor eminent for either piety or knowledge above others left out; onelie as each member of parlament in his private fancie thought fit, so elected one by one. The most of them were such as had preach'd and cry'd downe with great show of zeal the avarice & pluralities of bishops and prelates; that one cure of soules was a full imployment for one spiritual pastor how able so ever, if not a charge rather above humane strength. Yet these conscientious men, ere any part of the worke for which they came together, and that on the public salarie, wanted not impudence to the ignominie and scandal of thir pastor-like proffession & especially of thir boasted reformation, to seise into thir hands or not unwillinglie to accept (besides one sometimes two or more of the best Livings) collegiat master-ships in the universitie, rich lectures in the cittie, setting saile to all windes that might blow gaine into thir covetous bosomes. By which meanes those great rebukers of nonresidence among so many distant cures were not asham'd to be seen so quicklie pluralists and nonresidents themselves, to a fearful condemnation doubtless by thir owne mouthes. And yet the main doctrin for which they tooke such pay, and insisted upon with more vehemence then gospel, was but to tell us in effect that thir doctrin was worth nothing and the spiritual power of thir ministrie less availeable then bodilie compulsion; perswading the magistrate to use it as a stronger means to subdue & bring in conscience then evan-

---

7.    Milton is referring to the Westminster Assembly, a group of ministers nominated from the counties and approved by Parliament. Their charge was ecclesiastical and liturgical reform, but in Milton's view the Assembly operated to enforce a new version of conformity in Presbyterianism and opened new opportunities for clerical avarice by giving scope to Presbyterian ministers seeking to claim for themselves the lucrative benefices and "pluralities"—multiple clerical offices held simultaneously—once in the possession of the Church of England.

---

gellic perswasion.[8] But while they taught compulsion without convincement (which not long before they so much complain'd of as
executed unchristianlie against themselves) thir intents were cleere to
be no other then to have set up a spiritual tyrannie by a secular power
to the advancing of thir owne authoritie above the magistrate; And
well did thir disciples manifest themselves to be no better principl'd
then thir teachers, trusted with committiships and other gainfull offices, upon their commendations for zealous &, as they stick'd not to
term them, godlie men, but executing thir places more like childern
of the devil, unfaithfully, unjustly, unmercifully, and where not cor-
ruptly, stupidly. So that between them the teachers and these the disciples, there hath not bin a more ignominious and mortal wound to
faith, to pietie, nor more cause of blaspheming giv'n to the enimies
of god and of truth since the first preaching of reformation; which
needed most to have begun in the forwardest reformers themselves.
The people therefore looking one while on the statists, whom they
beheld without constancie or firmness labouring doubtfully beneath
the weight of thir own too high undertakings, busiest in pettie things,
triffling in the maine, deluded & quite alienated, express'd divers
wayes thir disaffection; some despising whom before they honour'd;
some deserting, some inveighing, some conspireing against them.
Then looking on the Church-men, most of whom they saw now to
have preach't thir own bellies, rather then the gospel, many illiterate,
persecutors more then lovers of the truth, covetous, worldlie, to whom
not godliness with contentment seem'd great gaine, but godliness
with gaine seem'd great contentment, like in many things whereof
they had accus'd thir predecessors. Looking on all these the people,
who had bin kept warme a while by the affected zele of thir pulpits,
after a false heat became more cold & obdurate then before; som
turning to leudness, som to flat atheisme, put beside thir old religion,
& scandalis'd in what they expected should be new. Thus they who

8.  In 1644 and 1645 Presbyterians in the Westminster Assembly began to pres-
sure the government to enforce their decisions in regard to reforming the church
along Presbyterian lines.

but of late were extoll'd as great deliverers, and had a people wholy at thir devotion, by so discharging thir trust as wee see, did not onely weak'n and unfitt themselves to be dispencers of what libertie they pretended,* but unfitted also the people, now growne worse & more disordinate, to receave or to digest any libertie at all.[9] For stories teach us that libertie sought out of season in a corrupt and degenerate age brought Rome it self into further slaverie. For libertie hath a sharp and double edge fitt onelie to be handl'd by just and vertuous men, to bad and dissolute it becomes a mischief unwieldie in thir own hands. Neither is it compleatlie giv'n, but by them who have the happie skill to know what is greivance and unjust to a people; and how to remove it wiselie; that good men may enjoy the freedom which they merit and the bad the curb which they need. But to doe this and to know these exquisit proportions, the heroic wisdom which is re-quir'd surmounted far the principles of narrow politicians: what wonder then if they sunke as those unfortunate Britans before them, entangl'd and oppress'd with things too hard and generous above thir straine and temper. For Britain (to speak a truth not oft spok'n) as it is a land fruitful enough of men stout and couragious in warr, so is it naturallie not over fertil of men able to govern justlie & prudently in peace; trusting onelie on thir Motherwitt, as most doo, & consider not that civilitie, prudence, love of the public more then of money or vaine honour are to this soile in a manner out-landish; grow not here but in minds well implanted with solid & elaborate breeding; too impolitic els and too crude, if not headstrong and intractable to the industrie and vertue either of executing or understanding true civil goverment. Valiant indeed and prosperous to winn a field but to know the end and reason of winning, unjudicious and unwise, in good or bad success alike unteachable. For the sunn, which wee want, ripens

---

* MS pretented.

9. Milton evidently looks now to the radical wing of his own party, the more extreme of the Independents and the socialist Levellers who were critical of the policies of the Westminster divines yet who carried their independence to a pitch Milton considers irresponsible.

---

witts as well as fruits; and as wine and oyle are imported to us from abroad, so must ripe understanding and many civil vertues bee imported into our minds from forren writings & examples of best ages: wee shall else miscarry still and com short in the attempt of any great enterprise. Hence did thir victories prove as fruitless as thir losses dangerous, and left them still conquering under the same grievances that men suffer conquer'd, which was indeed unlikely to goe otherwise, unless men more then vulgar, bred up, as few of them were, in the knowledge of Antient and illustrious deeds, invincible against money, and vaine titles, impartial to friendships and relations had conducted thir affaires. But then from the chapman to the retaler many, whose ignorance was more audacious then the rest, were admitted with all thir sordid rudiments to beare no mean sway among them both in church and state. From the confluence of all these errors, mischiefs, & misdemeanors, what in the eyes of man could be expected but what befel those antient inhabitants whom they so much resembl'd, confusion in the end. But on these things and this parallel having anough insisted, I returne back to the storie which gave matter to this digression.

# INDEX

# Index

# Index

# Index

# Index

# Index

This book is set in Bembo, a roman face originally cut by Francesco Griffo prior to 1495 for the Aldine Press of Aldus Manutius, with an accompanying italic cut by Giovantonio Tagliente in 1524. The modern versions of these typefaces were produced in 1929 by the design staff of the Lanston Monotype Corporation, under the direction of Stanley Morison, and were first introduced in the United States in 1938. The second book published by the Aldine Press was *De Ætna,* an account of a visit to Mt. Etna, by Pietro (later Cardinal) Bembo, in 1495.

This book is printed on paper that is acid-free and meets the requirements of the American National Standard for Permanence of Paper for Printed Library Materials, z39.48-1992. ⊗

Book design by Martin Lubin Graphic Design, New York
Typography by G&S Typesetters, Austin, Texas
Printed and bound by Edwards Brothers, Inc., Ann Arbor, Michigan